Witchfinders

Witchfinders

A Seventeenth-Century English Tragedy

MALCOLM GASKILL

Harvard University Press
Cambridge, Massachusetts
2005

© Malcolm Gaskill 2005

First United Kingdom publication in 2005 by John Murray (Publishers)
A division of Hodder Headline

The right of Malcolm Gaskill to be identified as the Author of the Work has been asserted by him
in accordance with the Copyright, Designs and Patents Act 1988.

Printed in the United States of America

Typeset in 11.5/14 Monotype Bembo by Servis Filmsetting Ltd, Manchester

Library of Congress Cataloging-in-Publication Data

Gaskill, Malcolm.
Witchfinders : a seventeenth-century English tragedy / Malcolm Gaskill.
p. cm.
ISBN 0-674-01976-8 (alk. paper)
1. Witchcraft—England—East Anglia—History—17th century. 2. Hopkins, Matthew, d. 1647.
3. Stearne, John, fl. 17th century. I. Title.

BF1581.G38 2005
133.4'.3'0942609032—dc22
2005046262

In memory of Stephen Williams

1967–1993

who understood well the strangeness of the past

Bear in mind that man is but a devil weakly fettered by some generous beliefs and impositions.

Robert Louis Stevenson

Every tragedy falls into two parts: complication and unravelling . . . By the complication I mean all that extends from the beginning of the action to the part which marks the turning-point to good or bad fortune. The unravelling is that which extends from the beginning of the change to the end.

Aristotle

Contents

CONTENTS

Illustrations

For full details of sources and permissions information, see p. 346

Preface

In seventeenth-century England people inhabited a magical universe, a cosmos full of spiritual and occult forces with the power to shape earthly events. Not everyone adhered to exactly the same beliefs, nor was there consensus about meaning. And yet a time-traveller would be astonished by the vigorous currents of supernatural thought common to men and women at every social level, from the hub of the metropolis to the darkest corners of the land. Barely fifteen generations ago, England was a God-fearing but by modern standards superstitious nation, where rivers of Christianity and pagan folklore flowed into one another. The past is always a foreign country, but at times it can feel like an alien world.

In this world, one of the strangest and most pervasive beliefs was that in witchcraft: unseen power, thought by many to be diabolical, harnessed for good and evil ends. Since this idea surely predates written records, and in New Age religion endures today, its historical significance mainly depends on the fact that between 1563 and 1736 witchcraft was a statutory offence punishable by death. Cases varied in character and cause; prosecution levels fluctuated over time and affected different regions in different ways. But England experienced only one witch-hunt worthy of the name – a sustained persecution over a wide area, orchestrated by people calling themselves witchfinders. It happened in the counties of East Anglia during the civil war of the mid 1640s.

At the centre of this tragedy stand a pair of minor gentlemen, Matthew Hopkins and John Stearne. How many suspects they interrogated is unknown; there were perhaps three hundred, of whom a third were hanged. Although much of Hopkins' life and the witch-hunt he

MATTHEW HOPKINS. *the famous* WITCH-FINDER *of* Maningtree *in* Essex, *who in only one year. during the reign of* James I. *hanged* 60. *reputed Witches. & was himself at last executed for a* Wizard.

Hopkins the witchfinder immortalized. He may have been responsible for the hanging of sixty witches in one year, as this eighteenth-century caption suggests, but it was not in the reign of James I, nor is there any evidence that he himself was hanged as a wizard inspired remain obscure, his notoriety has generated many myths. The orthodox version is a fable of wickedness, madness and perversion that banishes ambiguity and passes over unsightly gaps in the record. Yet however distorted this image, the fact remains that two men really did scour eastern England for witches – a story that deserves to be told without recourse to fantasy or fiction. Our seventeenth-century ancestors were mostly decent and intelligent people who could sink to the worst cruelty and credulity at times of intense anxiety. This is a book that reaches beyond monstrous stereotypes to a constituency of unremarkable people, who, through their eager cooperation with Hopkins and Stearne, themselves became witchfinders. In this they resemble the provincial nobodies of the twentieth century who engaged in genocide, demonstrating to the world the banality of evil.

This story had been in my mind for years, but it took film-maker Jonathan Hacker to make me see a book in it. I am grateful to him and to many besides. My agent Felicity Bryan has supported me throughout, and at John Murray Roland Philipps and Rowan Yapp have been enthusiastic and efficient. My diligent copy editor Liz Robinson made many valuable improvements to the text, as did Adam Lively, Ros Roughton and Sheena Peirse. Sheena arranged a stay in the haunted 'Witchfinder Suite' at the Thorn Hotel in Mistley – an unforgettable experience. Patrick Goodbody kindly invited me to his house at Great Wenham, once home to the Hopkins family. Acknowledgement is also due to the staff of the Public Record Office, House of Lords Record Office, British Library, Cambridge University Library, Bodleian Library, Dr Williams's Library, Thomas Plume's Library, the Pepysian Library at Magdalene College, Cambridge, and the county record offices at Bedford, Bury St Edmunds, Cambridge, Chelmsford, Colchester, Hertford, Huntingdon, Ipswich, King's Lynn, Northampton and Norwich. Harwich Town Council also generously granted me access to their archives.

Historians who have shared their time and research include Frank Bremer, Peter Elmer, Carolyn Fox, Ronald Hutton, Mark Lawrence, Diarmaid MacCulloch, John Morrill, Keith Parry, Jim Sharpe, Alex Shepard and Heide Towers. I am most indebted to Robin Briggs, Ivan Bunn and John Walter for commenting on an early draft. I would also like to thank the Arts and Humanities Research Board for funding sabbatical leave, likewise the Master and Fellows of Churchill College, Cambridge for their indulgence.

If Robert Louis Stevenson was right, and man really is but a devil weakly fettered, I can only say that the generous beliefs and impositions of all those mentioned here have mattered more.

Author's Note

Seventeenth-century England had yet to convert from the Julian to the Gregorian calendar. This meant that the New Year began on 25 March. To avoid confusion, I have rendered all Old Style dates as New Style, with the year starting on 1 January.

Original spelling has been kept for quotations, although punctuation has been modified to improve the sense of certain passages. As even within the same document the spelling of names tended to be erratic, these have been standardized for the sake of consistency.

Wisbech

Upwell

Outwell

ISLE of

N

R. Gt. Ouse

March

Wimblington

ELY

Chatteris

Littleport

HUNTINGDON

Sutton

Ely

SHIRE

Haddenham

Stretham

Keyston

Molesworth

Huntingdon

Aldreth

Bythorn

Great Catworth

Little Catworth

Over

Tilbrook

Fen Drayton

Kimbolton

Great

Staughton

CAMBRIDGE~

St Neots

SHIRE

Cambridge

Bedford

R. Cam

Newmarket

Haverhill

Keding

Ridgewell

LINCOLNSHIRE

The Wash

King's Lynn

NORFOLK

Norwich

Wisbech

ISLE OF ELY

NORTHAMPTONSHIRE

HUNTINGDON-SHIRE

Thrapston

Woodford

Olds

Denford

Ely

Burton Latimer

Raunds

Huntingdon

Bury St Edmunds

Rushden

CAMBRIDGE-

Northampton

SHIRE

Cambridge

SUFFOLK

BEDFORD-SHIRE

Ipswich

Elsenham

E

S

Colchester

HERTFORD-SHIRE

Chelmsford

ESSEX

Chelmsford

MIDDLESEX

Waltham Cross

Leigh

London

Maidstone

Faversham

Navestock

KENT

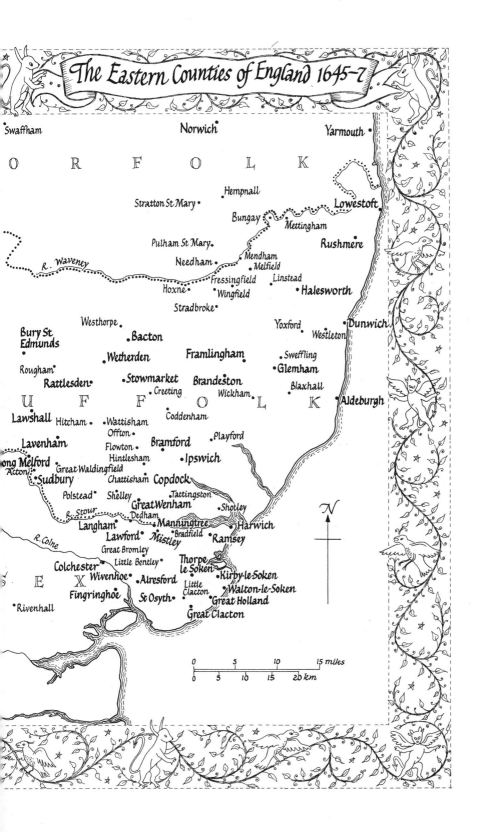

The Eastern Counties of England 1645–7

Swaffham

Norwich

Yarmouth

N O R F O L K

Hempnall

Stratton St Mary

Bungay

Lowestoft

Mettingham

Pulham St Mary

Rushmere

Needham

Mendham
Melfield

Hoxne

Fressingfield

Linstead

Halesworth

Wingfield

Stradbroke

Westhorpe

Yoxford

Dunwich

Westleton

Bury St Edmunds

Bacton

Wetherden

Framlingham

Swefling

Glemham

Rougham

Rattlesden

Stowmarket

Brandeston

Blaxhall

Creeting

Wickham

S U F F O L K

Aldeburgh

Lawshall

Hitcham

Wattisham

Coddenham

Offton

Flowton

Bramford

Playford

Lavenham

Hintlesham

Ipswich

ong Melford

Great Waldingfield

Acton

Sudbury

Chattisham

Copdock

Polstead

Shelley

Tattingston

Great Wenham

Shotley

R. Stour

Dedham

Manningtree

Harwich

Langham

Bradfield

Lawford

Mistley

Ramsey

R. Colne

Great Bromley

Little Bentley

Thorpe le Soken

Colchester

Wivenhoe

Alresford

Kirby-le-Soken

E S S E X

Fingringhoe

St Osyth

Little Clacton

Walton-le-Soken

Great Holland

Rivenhall

Great Clacton

R. Waveney

N

0   5   10   15 miles
0   5   10   15   20 km

Prologue

———•———

THE CHRISTMAS OF 1644 was a joyless time in the Essex town of Manningtree. Easterly gales funnelled down the Stour estuary, the river froze an iron grey, and snow drifted high against the warehouses. In the lanes leading up from the harbour the poor fretted over dwindling stocks of food and fuel, and at the waning of each pale sun huddled round fires, relishing their pottage and bread. At least in previous winters there had been festive cheer and revels. But now, throughout England, not only had the puritan authorities denounced celebrations as superstitious, but Christmas Day coincided with a compulsory public fast.[1] Unthanked in church for the Saviour's birth, God heard only the usual prayers that the old and frail, the young and the sick, and soldiers still fighting the war between king and Parliament, should be spared their lives until the blessed release of spring.

Least joyous of all, and most earnest in his prayers, was John Rivet, a tailor whose house stood on a hill off the high street. This winter he had little time for his patterns and fabrics, and customers wanting coats and capes could wait: his wife had been struck down by an all-consuming fever which now threatened her life. At first she had complained of dizziness and nausea but soon was confined to bed, her body flushing hot and cold, her senses dulled. As Rivet watched this suffering, his petitions to heaven unanswered, he wondered why God should treat his wife so cruelly, and so began to suspect that her condition was caused by 'something more then meerly naturall'.[2]

In the coming days, Goodwife Rivet's condition worsened. To lameness and delirium were added muscular tremors which increased in intensity until her body shook and contorted, finally convincing her husband that this affliction had no earthly cause. From the unnatural times in which they lived, such things might even have been expected. These were 'days of shaking' – of rebellion and fighting, of uncertainty, fear and grief; the orderly world created and governed by heaven was being turned upside-down. Fair was foul, and foul was fair. That year, brother had slain brother; Parliament had ruled without a king; harvests had spoiled in the fields while folk went hungry; and plagues and agues had touched high and low with a fickle hand. The devil reigned. 'If Witches and Wizards have any power in their black Art,' a preacher warned the House of Commons, 'now is a time for them to drive a full trade . . . either for love or money, for feare, hopes, or hatred.'[3]

Like Rivet's wife, the entire nation seemed to be in the grip of an incurable malady, leading people to believe that a wrathful God demanded repentence or retribution. In havens of piety like Manningtree and the adjacent port of Mistley, these were seen as the last days of man before Christ's final decisive battle with Satan, for behind the cannon-fire and cavalry charges raged an ideological war, as much spiritual as political in its passions. Calvinists at Westminster were busy sweeping away the religious innovations of the 1630s, which were seen as popish and idolatrous, and had confined their chief architect, Archbishop William Laud, to the Tower of London. The fever of change was infectious. Across Essex and eastern England puritans, supported by crowds drunk on chaos, unleashed righteous anger upon Catholics, Laudian ceremonies, and church decorations. To the reformers, Laudianism – much like the rituals of folk religion – was little better than diabolical magic.

But it was hard to shun superstition with Death peering through the window. A fortnight of prayer having brought neither reason nor remedy, John Rivet decided on an unlawful action to end his wife's torment. He set off for Hadleigh in Suffolk, a depressed cloth town across the river Stour, where he sought out Goodwife Hovey, a woman famed for her skill in healing and divination. Cunning folk such as she were popular but proscribed; the authorities taught that they were evil charlatans, deluded into believing they dispensed God's power. In fact, parish ministers and the ecclesiastical courts had long insisted that in theory they were witches. Yet to John Rivet's thinking, a witch was a hag who visited disaster upon her enemies, the sort of wretch who was trying to kill his wife.

There is no record of Hovey's methods; perhaps she boiled Goodwife Rivet's urine and hair in a stone bottle – a common diagnostic spell. By some magical means she confirmed Rivet's suspicion that his wife was bewitched, and suggested that a Manningtree woman up the hill from him was the cause of woe in his household. Without hesitation Rivet identified Elizabeth Clarke, an aged one-legged widow who lived alone, dependent on parish charity. It was common knowledge, he said, that 'Elizabeths mother and some other of her kinsfolke did suffer death for Witchcraft and murther'.[4] As a legacy of this shame it is likely she had been a marked figure all her life, reviled but perhaps also revered among her watchful neighbours.

The witchery in Widow Clarke's blood seemed plain enough, but usually it took many years for the pressure of suspicion to build before it exploded into an accusation. Even then a witch-trial was a risky undertaking: costly in time and money, and liable to backfire if the defendant was acquitted. For a prosecution to gain momentum, plaintiffs had to be unusually confident or foolhardy, or unusually afraid or angry.[5] John Rivet was certainly the latter, and did not hesitate to broadcast his convictions at his return. Word spread quickly through the gossip networks of Manningtree and Mistley, and so reached the ears of a callow, vainglorious gentleman named Matthew Hopkins.

For a younger son of a clergyman, whose life so far had held few ambitions or adventures, the news was electrifying. At last Hopkins sensed a mission, a chance to make his mark. According to a contemporary portrait he wore his beard short, but his hair long over a broad linen collar. The high-crowned hat, Geneva cape and bucket-top boots suggest that he affected the style of a country magistrate, his staff and spurs self-importance rather than real authority. He kept a greyhound that accompanied him around the town.[6] Although it is easy to imagine that Hopkins was sly and sarcastic, there is no reason to think him insincere in his convictions: a Calvinist belief in his own predestined salvation, and a loathing of witchcraft and idolatry as cancers at the heart of Christian society. And so, Rivet's accusation of old Bess Clarke focused his mind.

Not that Hopkins lacked first-hand experience of witches – or so he said. For some time now, once every six weeks or so and always on a Friday night, he had been disturbed by eerie voices drifting over the fields near his house. Standing at his bedchamber window, pressing an ear to the darkness and hardly daring to breathe, he had caught snatches of conversation between the witches of Manningtree and their accomplices from neighbouring villages. Gatherings known as

Hopkins' claim that a bear-like spirit had been sent to kill him may have been inspired by a number of stories in circulation, such as that recounted in this pamphlet of 1613

sabbats, where witches met to worship the devil and devise malevolent plots, had long been recorded by Continental inquisitors; but they were rarely heard of in England, where most people thought that communion with Satan was achieved through familiar spirits, or imps, disguised as animals. Convinced that the witches had detected his spying, Hopkins later claimed they had despatched a bear-like spirit to kill him, but that he had been protected by the carapace of his godliness. He added that the coven had commanded some imps to assist a particular witch living in Manningtree: the name he overheard was that of an old widow, Elizabeth Clarke.[7]

It is tempting to move to the bizarre climax of this episode, the catalytic moment in the tragic witch-hunt that was to follow. But, as if winter had frozen the matter of the witches pending the arrival of spring, this did not take place until March 1645. Only then did old hatreds thaw out, allowing a plan to germinate and grow. Suffice it to say that the suffering about to be inflicted upon Elizabeth Clarke would unite Matthew Hopkins and John Stearne, another Manningtree gentleman, and that together they would swear to have witnessed the ultimate display of a witch's depravity: a parade of offspring fathered by the devil himself. It was this shocking encounter which would set Hopkins and Stearne inexorably on the road to experience, and unrivalled expertise, as witchfinders.[8]

PART ONE

Complication

I

Origins

———•———

O NE DAY LATE in the reign of James I a crisis at the rectory of Great Wenham in Suffolk was reaching its peak. It was a trial endured by most women several times in their lives, but every occasion brought the same dread, pain and peril. The rector's wife was confined in an upstairs chamber, the bed surrounded by 'godsiblings' – her dearest female friends and relations. A drink of warm spiced ale, known as caudle, may have been held to her lips; a scented cloth mopped sweat from her brow. In this, Wenham's most godly household, prayers were said to keep Satan at bay, protecting the defenceless woman as her body and soul travelled between sacred states. Mary Hopkins was about to complete her labour, and would soon be delivered of a baby boy.

Like all puritans immersed in Holy Scripture, Mary Hopkins would have known of God's sentence upon Eve: 'I will greatly multiply thy sorrow . . . in sorrow thou shalt bring forth children.' Because of this, women endured the agonies of childbirth like a penance, and accepted heaven's judgement whenever offspring were taken from them. This was Mary's fourth baby to survive; she may have borne others less fortunate. But for the moment at least this boy, like his three brothers before him, grasped life, and God was content. The midwife severed the cord, and the child was washed and wrapped up warmly. The mother then rested while the women busied themselves in the chamber, stoking the fire and drying linen. The greatest danger had passed, a moment marked by prayers of gratitude. Mary's confinement probably continued for another month, during which time her godsiblings served her as lying-in maids.[1] Meanwhile her husband James was preparing to protect his son from the malign influence of the spiritual world.

In the previous century the English state had thrown off the authority of Rome to establish a Protestant national Church. Consensus had been elusive: reform went too far for some, for others not far enough. Catholics believed the Reformation should not have happened at all, and under Queen Mary they rejoiced as the clocks were turned back. Protestants refusing to recant were burned, then memorialized as martyrs in the reign of Elizabeth I, who restored the reformed faith. Yet the Elizabethan settlement was a fudged compromise, with many Catholic traditions preserved and codified in the Book of Common Prayer. Clergy continued to be ordained by bishops, themselves empowered by the monarch's divine right; images of saints still adorned parish churches; communicants swallowed bread and wine, even if officially it was no longer the actual body and blood of Christ. Outrage at what were seen as popish survivals stoked the fires of puritanism: a poorly defined Calvinist tendency towards dissatisfaction with the theology and liturgy of the Church of England, and a boundless appetite for the Bible and its moral lessons. Puritans – or 'the godly', as they called themselves – wanted a simplified religion based on Scripture and nothing else.[2]

It was not enough that the meanings of images and rituals had been changed – for example, that communion had been downgraded from a miracle to a mere remembrance. Puritans argued that the practices themselves originated with Antichrist, and that in any case the uneducated failed to distinguish between the symbolic and the real. Churching was a case in point. Once the ritual purification of a new mother, after the Reformation churching became a simple act of thanksgiving; but for the majority it remained a pagan defence against the dangers of life's transitions. Godly clergy tried to satisfy the law and their own consciences by performing these ceremonies in an understated way, consoled by the thought that God alone could determine the effects of their ministry on the congregation. In this way a puritan like James Hopkins might have churched his own wife with only mild discomfort, provided that she did not wear a veil or kneel at the altar.[3]

Where life and death were concerned, almost everyone was prone to superstition. It was said that a pregnant woman who gazed at the moon risked her child's sanity; a taste for red berries was thought to cause blemishes; and birth defects were linked to contact with animals. The herbs, charms and holy relics that before the Reformation had sanctified the birthing-chamber may have been easily banished, but the perception of proximate evil lingered on; even puritans succumbed to the temptation to protect themselves. Despite the abolition of saints, furtive supplications were made to St Margaret to alleviate birth pangs, and to St Felicitas to ensure the baby was a boy. Some went further: reassurance was sought from astrologers and cunning folk by people either unaware of the impiety of the act, or able to persuade themselves that it was permitted by God.[4]

Of all rituals surrounding childbirth, baptism stirred up most controversy. For radical Protestants, the christening of infants made a conjuror of the minister; and yet not only did the ceremony have by law to be performed but most parents demanded it, craving the peace of mind it brought. Again, whether the ritual constituted an actual spiritual transformation or just a public display depended on individual perception, though on this point, silent compromise between minister and congregation could not always be reached. Parents attached great importance to the minister making the sign of the cross on the child's head, and this was where puritan clergymen drew the line. Struggling to balance conviction with obligation, many refused to complete the sacrament as some parishioners desired. If they were lucky, they merely caused scandal; but they might also be summoned to an ecclesiastical court to explain themselves.

However James Hopkins coped with the dilemma, at some point between his wife's lying-in and her churching he baptized their son into the Christian Church at the ancient font of Great Wenham for all the parish to see. Hopkins (or the men he had chosen to be godfathers) had named his other sons James, Thomas and John after the Apostles, hopeful that God's power and determination to fight evil would be bestowed upon them, as recorded in the Gospels. Like his brothers, this boy was christened to symbolize a life-long devotion to Christ as mentor, guide, guardian and saviour: he was named Matthew.[5]

★

Until the age of about five, infants remained extremely vulnerable to illness and disease. Contrary to modern myth, mothers took great care to preserve their children's lives, and grieved bitterly if they failed. To extend the security of the womb and straighten a growing body, many babies were swaddled for the first weeks of life. Washing was a secondary priority, and cradle-cap was often left untreated until the bones of the skull had fused. Mothers trimmed a baby's nails with their teeth (it was believed that unmanicured children were more likely to become thieves) and the trimmings were burned or buried. Suspended between the animate and the inanimate, such human waste was ambiguous matter – raw material for witches, who were believed to turn traces of life back against the body of origin. Children, too young to protect themselves by faith, prayer or charm, were at greatest risk.

Breast-feeding was thought to encourage the child's development, especially when it was feared that cow's milk might infect the child with bestial qualities. In a well-to-do household like that of James and Mary Hopkins, it is possible that Matthew was breast-fed by a wet-nurse. Most children were weaned at about a year, and teething was seen as an unavoidable phase of illness. An infusion of poppies was a customary pacifier, and suffering children were given a piece of coral to suck – it was also a charm against witches.[6] The growing infant was now exposed to an environment where contact between humans and animals was commonplace, and the separation of sewage and water supply imperfect. Diarrhoea claimed many infant lives, and infestations of threadworm impeded weight-gain. Herbal remedies ranged in effectiveness from the benign and useless to the poisonous and fatal. Most feared were smallpox, diphtheria, scarlet fever, typhoid and, worst of all, bubonic plague, against which only prayer, fasting and public humiliation might prove effective.

Discipline was strict, but beatings rare. Ideally, order in the family was promoted through love of God and mutual respect, as defined by patriarchal convention. Experience of the holy household – a microcosm of the state – provided the basic influences Matthew Hopkins would have needed to meet the expectations of his elders. Play was important too, although some puritans preferred to use the time drilling their offspring in the habit of secret prayer.[7] At the fireside or in the company of friends, children soaked up stories, and not just improving fables but winter's tales about ghosts and witches, which invaded their dreams and shaped their perceptions. Where parents disapproved, a nurse was usually a reliable source of folklore. Children believed that backyards, gardens and the fields near their homes were infested with fairies and imps as real as mice and bugs; by searching for such creatures, and placating them with flowers and morsels, they developed a fear of the unseen world, and at the same time a fascination with its mysteries. By the time young Matthew came to hear his first sermon, his consciousness had already straddled the blurry borderland between natural and supernatural realms.

Another influence on his development was the mounting tension in public life which in 1642 resulted in England's worst political crisis since the Wars of the Roses. The attitudes of the juvenile Matthew Hopkins must have been deeply affected by the impact of Charles I's policies upon his own Suffolk community, especially in view of his father's pivotal role. Surely he overheard anguished voices at the rectory complaining no longer just that godly reformation had stalled, but that it was going backwards. It was a grievance to which James Hopkins was entirely sympathetic. Those men and women who believed themselves to be the elect – the saved already chosen by God – would have to fight to justify their special status. To walk the hard road ahead, it would be insufficient for Hopkins' sons merely to follow Christ in their hearts: they would have to demonstrate their devotion by public intervention and the setting of examples.[8]

James Hopkins hailed from Littleport in the Isle of Ely, the fenland north of Cambridgeshire. Situated on a hill by the river Great Ouse, the town was surrounded by water for much of the year, and even during the dry season was cut off by a broad mere, by tradition the colour of blood. Strong mint, used to pack smoked mutton in winter, grew around its banks where a monstrous wild dog was said to stalk the unwary.[9] As the name suggested the manor of Littleport had once sustained a busy port, and it had belonged to the Bishop of Ely until the Reformation, when it passed into the hands of yeoman farmers. Throughout England, such men then exploited soaring food prices by

13

An impoverished witch surrounded by a menagerie of animal familiars.
By 1621, when this drawing was made, the stereotype was fixed in most
people's minds

enclosing common land – land on which the poor depended – to
make it more profitable, and so recast themselves as gentlemen.

James Hopkins' father William was one of these. He married in
about 1560 and raised two sons, Robert and William. Robert, the
eldest, was sent to Cambridge in the mid 1570s, around which time

his mother died and his father married Martha Saunders; she gave birth to James and to two daughters, Martha and Anne. By now William Hopkins was a landowner of substance who had built a house and owned several others, as well as fields, crofts and fishing waters. He was one of twelve worthies chosen to administer property belonging to the royal manor of East Greenwich, the rents from which were put to charitable ends. In his will Hopkins pledged a cow to the parish poor, perhaps to expiate a feeling of guilt for having taken their land.[10]

When William Hopkins died in 1583 his widow Martha was named as his executrix, and the recipient of his main residence and lands. His eldest son Robert received most of the estate, plus his father's gold ring and an annuity of £5. The second largest share went to William, and the daughters were well cared for too. Of the sons, James, who can have been little more than a baby, received least, but even so was bequeathed three houses, a parcel of copyhold land, a croft, two feather-beds, a chestful of linen, three fine silver Apostle spoons, and £20, all to be held in trust until his twenty-second birthday. Moreover, he was named principal heir should his half-brother Robert die without issue. Robert Hopkins, who after leaving Cambridge instructed godless inmates in a house of correction, died four years later; but whether he married and had children is unknown. It is possible that the infant James became wealthy before the age of seven.

In 1597, when he was about fifteen, James Hopkins was awarded a Perne scholarship at Peterhouse, Cambridge University's oldest college.[11] By that time, he probably knew he was destined to enter the Church. His inheritance would make even the meanest stipend bearable, and his finances were about to improve yet further. His widowed mother had moved from Littleport to the city of Ely, to be closer to her daughters. She died in December 1600, leaving most of her estate not to her stepson William but to James, her own flesh and blood, who in addition to £25, a great deal of furniture and another three Apostle spoons was invested with what she termed 'all my right and title in that p[ar]te of the Manor of Littleport w[hi]ch I now injoye'. She favoured James, she explained, 'because I repose an extraordinarie trust & creadite in hym above others that he wilbe readie as nede shalbe to releave the great wantes w[hi]ch I heare will fall upon his

Sister Martha'. The younger Martha Hopkins had married, but why she should have needed protection remains obscure. What is striking is the evidence that James Hopkins was already displaying the sort of personal qualities that later enabled him to lead a Suffolk congregation during its most testing times, and to impart a sense of Christian duty to his children.[12]

James Hopkins was admitted as Bachelor of Arts in the year after his mother died and elected into a Fellowship around the time of his twenty-second birthday, when he also received his inheritance. He was still at Peterhouse in 1608, and the following year was ordained at Ely Cathedral; his marriage took place soon afterwards. In 1612 he was presented to the living of Great Wenham, a secluded parish of 1,000 acres and perhaps a hundred souls, and took his wife Mary to live there in the timber-framed rectory opposite the church.[13] It seems they also took with them a servant, possibly a sister-in-law of James's sister Martha. Within four years James and Mary had been blessed with three sons: James, the first-born, followed by Thomas and John.[14] James Hopkins must have sold off his land in Littleport, as he was not mentioned in a lawsuit at the Court of Chancery in 1613 by which poor tenants fought to defend their rights of common against the Peyton family, now sole lords of the manor of Littleport.[15] From the sale of this land or by some other means James acquired land thirty miles from Littleport, at Framlingham Castle – a location that later had a sinister significance for his son Matthew.[16]

The faith that Matthew Hopkins acquired in childhood provided his moral, emotional and intellectual compass later on. The phrasing of his grandparents' wills suggests Protestant conformity, if not enthusiastic godliness, and the fact that his father and uncle had entered the Church is significant. Puritan dissenters were strong in Cambridgeshire from the reign of Elizabeth, ranging from moderate Calvinists to Anabaptists with heretical opinions about souls and sacraments.[17] As compared with the beliefs of the majority, however, the similarities between these sects surpassed the differences. In the 1580s Richard Greenham, rector of Dry Drayton near Cambridge, had toiled to build a godly community, but found the people ignorant and refractory. The Reformation had turned clergymen from miracle-workers into mere spiritual counsellors, and among husbandmen faced with crop failure and disease there was no question which sort of ministry was most valuable. In the end Greenham admitted defeat, blaming rampant superstition and his parishioners' tendency to hold witches responsible for their misfortunes rather than searching their own sinful hearts and praying for guidance.[18]

Eventually many ministers confined their preaching to the converted, and ignored the rest. Not that this attitude entirely conflicted with God's plan, at least in the view of strict Calvinists, who believed that the division of the world into the damned and the saved was predetermined. For them, godliness and good works were neither an effort of will nor a means of salvation, but a natural extension of their innate being. In the first decade of the seventeenth century, when James Hopkins was teaching at Cambridge, he was surrounded by men who passionately avowed this doctrine; and there is every reason to believe that he was one of them. It was at this time that the king, James I, entrusted the learned doctors of the University with the translation of a new English Bible. When he arrived in Great Wenham in 1612 James Hopkins doubtless carried with him a copy of the new Authorized Version. In print for just a year at that time, in his lifetime it became the foundation of Protestant teaching and thinking, and remained so forever after.

James Hopkins' experience at Great Wenham probably did not differ greatly from that of Richard Greenham at Dry Drayton thirty years earlier. There were those who could not or would not hear the word of God, plus the usual scattering of tipplers and profaners, rogues and bastard-bearers, cunning folk and their clients. The devil was in every place. In his quest for order it was helpful to Hopkins that the lord of the manor was a devout puritan, unlike other Suffolk parishes where the gentry were lacklustre Protestants or even Catholic recusants. Great Wenham also benefited from its proximity to Dedham Vale, a region distinguished by energetic godliness, and early in his ministry James Hopkins became well acquainted with preachers and pious laymen from here and throughout the Stour valley. Powerful dynasties such as the Bacons and the Barnardistons offered patronage and hospitality to men like Hopkins as they journeyed from place to place, sharing their learning and stiffening people's resolve. In a sea of hostility and indifference, these communities were islands of piety, amity and hope.[19]

James Hopkins' first line of defence was his own household. On top of the sermons they heard and the catechisms they were set, Matthew and his brothers were directed by their father in study, contemplation and prayer, and had drummed into them an understanding of their election. They would have learnt their letters locally before progressing to grammar school, possibly in the nearby towns of Ipswich or Colchester, where the Latin and Greek necessary to enter a university were taught.

By this time King James had been succeeded by his son Charles, a man more refined than his father but less politically astute. Charles exalted God, but scarcely less did he exalt his own high office, thereby blinding himself to his responsibility to Parliament. In 1629, to satisfy his financial and religious ambitions, he had declared himself an absolute monarch. Among his aims was the introduction of a less austere form of Protestantism that would restore the ornament and ceremony of pre-Reformation days. To this end, he promoted to the episcopal bench clerics who favoured the anti-Calvinist teachings of the Dutch theologian Arminius, emphasizing free grace for all and opposing the idea of predestination. This was a serious affront to the puritan communities of the Stour valley and beyond: all that they held pure would be desecrated, their work undone. As a young man, Matthew Hopkins no doubt remembered his father's outrage at these innovations, a sentiment shared by all their godly friends. To them, it was as if idolatry and sorcery were being reinstalled at the heart of English life. If there was one aspect of his childhood more likely than any other to have initiated and inspired Matthew's career as a witchfinder, this was it.

In 1633, by which time Matthew Hopkins had reached adolescence, William Laud, Bishop of London, was appointed to the See of Canterbury. A committed advocate of 'the beauty of holiness' in worship and a stickler for Anglican uniformity, he became the focus of godly resentment and disgust. Although neither the Arminian nor the closet Catholic his enemies painted him, he refused to tolerate disobedience on the part of puritan clergy. Unsurprisingly Matthew Wren, the Bishop of Norwich, in whose diocese most Suffolk puritans lived, shared his new archbishop's views. It was not long before the Church's courts were routinely censuring ministers for refusing to make the sign of the cross during baptism, and numerous other abuses of the liturgy. Mere admonition was soon deemed inadequate, and the punishment was increased to dismissal.[20]

Archbishop Laud depicted as the Antichrist, accepting tithes from one man and popish trinkets from another. He has the Number of the Beast inscribed on his forehead

James Hopkins must have experienced despair and anger, feelings which may have contributed to the decline of his health by 1634. It is easy to imagine the pessimism he would have felt for his eldest son as he took his bachelor's degree at Cambridge that year and prepared to enter the ministry. The younger James Hopkins had been sent not to his father's Peterhouse but to Emmanuel College, the puritan nursery which had so far produced the finest foot-soldiers of godly reform.[21] But now the Church was in turmoil, and hopes began to fade. So far had matters deteriorated that even conformist clergy opposed the Arminian bishops, not least because of the draconian judgments handed down by the ecclesiastical courts. Puritans experienced Laud's reforms as nothing less than orchestrated persecution, and although the more stoical may have been energized by oppression, for the rest the dream of building Jerusalem in the land of their birth was over. The only option was emigration to New England.[22]

Those who had done so wrote to their Suffolk friends, firing their imaginations, filling them with longing for a promised land. In 1630 John Winthrop, a Suffolk clothier destined to be the first governor of Massachusetts, left the village of Groton, twelve miles from Great Wenham; his intention was 'to avoid the burthens and snares which were here laid upon their consciences'.[23] Among the friends he left behind was James Hopkins, from whom a letter of praise and encouragement survives. Sent to Winthrop in February 1633, this torn page speaks volumes about Hopkins' character, and the combative stance he passed on to his famous son. In language steeped in biblical allusion and a sense of divine providence, James Hopkins admires the challenges presented by New England, and even expresses satisfaction that Winthrop should have enemies, as this only proved his worthiness. 'The magistrate beinge the minister of god for the upholdinge of the good, and punishinge and suppression of the badd,' he commented, 'must needes have wicked mens mouthes open against him, as good ones will speak for him.'[24]

To James Hopkins, the opposition of virtue and evil was visible in all things. Winthrop's honour he contrasted with the actions of 'heathens [and p]apists whoe have taken great paines to fill the [nation?] with sup[erstiti]on and wickednes'. Hopkins had grown weak, he admitted, and drifted in thought from his Suffolk rectory to the shores of Massachusetts Bay. Praying for guidance, he told Winthrop: 'I have a purpose to make my selfe a member of your plantation, and when I come, I hope I shall not come alone.' But by the winter of 1634 Hopkins was confined to bed, and there his dreams evaporated. He dictated his will, made his peace with God, and in January 1635 he died. Matthew Hopkins was probably no more than fourteen, and had no special place in his father's plans. His eldest brother James, still at Cambridge studying to become Master of Arts, received all his father's books, to assist him in his career as a minister; the second son, Thomas, was to be sent away 'ov[er] the seaes to such our frinds in Newe England'. What had eluded the father, it seemed, the sons were exhorted to achieve, and although Matthew received no formal instructions, when the time came he knew what he had to do.[25]

Between 1638 and 1642 England slid into chaos. Attempts to impose the Arminian Prayer Book in Scotland precipitated a Calvinist rebellion, forcing King Charles to call the first Parliament for eleven years in order to raise money for the defence of his crown. He met stiff opposition from lawyers guarding the constitution, and from English Presbyterians sympathetic to the Scots. The next two years saw the king driven into a corner, his allies impeached, his authority restricted, and his subjects across the three kingdoms thrown into rebellious turmoil. After many years of fretfulness, at last godly activists caught the scent of victory. In 1641 a puritan zealot named Lewis Hughes published a tract attacking the 'blasphemies and lying fables' of the Book of Common Prayer, including the superstitious churching of women: this, he asserted, transformed the officiating minister into a kind of witch.[26] In an age when politics and religion were two sides of the same coin this was fighting talk, and there was plenty more besides. In the spring of 1642 Charles fled London, his Catholic wife Henrietta Maria sailed for the Continent, and Parliament passed the Militia Ordinance passing military power to the lords lieutenant in the shires. By the summer, both sides were recruiting and equipping armies.

In August Charles raised his standard at Nottingham, branding his opponents 'rebels' in response to Parliament's declaration that royalists were 'traitors'. The battle-lines were ideological, even metaphysical, the fighting thought to mirror the conflicts of the celestial sphere, where Christ would vanquish the forces of evil. It was easy for one side to accuse the other of diabolical inspiration; but whereas the language of most royalist propaganda was figurative, that of their enemies was more literal. For puritans these really *were* the last days of mankind, the war was an *actual* prologue to Armageddon, and the king was a *real* agent of Antichrist. Among the men who had resisted the king most aggressively in Parliament – and who now were most active in organizing troops – were the strictest Calvinists, who had been fighting for further reformation of religion long before the first musket was fired in 1642.[27]

In the streets, terrifying stories of judgements and omens were on everyone's lips. A cavalier in Cornwall drank a health to Satan and was driven insane. In London, the devil appeared at a secret meeting of Jesuits, 'all as black as pitch, as bigge as a great Dogge'. On the banks of the Thames the cry went up that a witch had been seen walking on the water, and tidal waves were interpreted by the watermen as 'Newes from Heaven' – a warning to the nation. The truth of ancient prophecies seemed confirmed. In 1642 a sea-monster, described as 'the devill in the shape of a great fish', was put on display in Woolwich, an example of 'the fore-runners and sad harbingers of great commotions and tumults in States and Kingdomes, if not mournfull Heraulds of utter desolation'.[28] Royalist propagandists exploited the story of a puritan woman in Northamptonshire who announced that she would prefer her child to be born headless than to have it baptized with the sign of the cross, only for her terrible wish to be granted.[29] Visions of armies were seen in the skies, and the phantom sounds of battle were heard around Edgehill and elsewhere.[30]

To the godly, these omens meant one thing: they were about to live through the Second Coming, prior to being invested as Christ's saints. Meanwhile, opportunities for them to justify their election were legion, from extemporary preaching on street corners to training with a company of pikemen. If indeed Matthew Hopkins had planned to go to New England and these plans had been scuppered by the outbreak of war, surely these were the compensations. His father's dying wish had been only that Matthew and his siblings should be educated to the highest standard possible, 'and that they may be brought up in the feare of God & in such honest callings as shall best suite w[i]th there disposicions & eastates'. Why Matthew did not follow his father, uncle and brother to Cambridge and into the Church will never be known. The family could have afforded it. As well as the estate left to Matthew's mother, the six children each received a legacy of a hundred marks (equivalent to perhaps £70,000 today), to be held in trust until they reached the age of twenty-two, not to mention various properties.[31] But in an age of religious uncertainty, a commercial apprenticeship perhaps held more appeal than a clerical career. Legend has it that while still an adolescent Matthew Hopkins found an opening as some kind of lawyer's clerk based in Ipswich, but the evidence is flimsy in the extreme.[32]

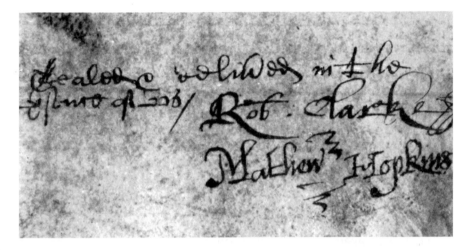

Only one of Matthew Hopkins' signatures is known to survive, here on a conveyance document from 1641 – virtually all there is to substantiate the claim that he was a lawyer

The civil war brought chaos, but to someone like Hopkins it offered exhilaration, and vindication too. Bishop Wren had persecuted preachers of 'new and strange' doctrine but now the positions were reversed and so-called 'scandalous' clergymen, like the Essex minister who had denigrated 'Spirit-mongers, Puritans, & People of phanatical Spirits', were ejected from their livings.[33] Among other grievances against the Laudian clergy were excessive drinking, profaning the Sabbath, molesting female parishioners, and persuading men not to fight for Parliament.[34] But what the godly most appreciated was not having to watch a minister bow to the altar or make the sign of the cross.

To most people, church decorations were fragments of heaven on earth. To reformers they were false idols, inventions of Antichrist that contravened the second commandment and imperilled the soul, and as such had been under attack even before war broke out. 'Idolatry is the principall crime of mankinde,' a polemicist wrote in 1641, 'the greatest guilt of the world, the totall cause of judgement'; stained-glass windows he lumped in with astrology, magic and witchcraft.[35] In that year, Parliament had ordered the destruction of altar rails, candlesticks and crucifixes; spontaneous outbursts of iconoclasm followed. Catholics were attacked and their property destroyed, according to one observer, 'as if there had been a dissolution of all government'.[36] Naturally the authorities preferred a more orderly purge. By 1643 the puritan Earl of Manchester – Captain-General of the army in East Anglia – was using money sequestered from royalists to fund the religious revolution; agents working for Parliament's Committee for Scandalous Ministers each received five shillings a day.[37] Manchester also commissioned William Dowsing, a farmer from Stratford St Mary in Dedham Vale, to tour the churches of the eastern counties smashing whatever 'monuments of idolatry and superstition' he could find. Meticulous and uncompromising, Dowsing was one of the new breed: a yeoman recently self-styled as a gentleman, backed by a puritan community and parliamentarian leaders, well-versed in the Gospels but not a university graduate, and fiercely ready for action – a man rather like Matthew Hopkins, in fact.[38]

Institutions were collapsing, authority was dispersed, old certainties had been dashed. The Militia Ordinance arrogated to Parliament the right to legislate without royal assent; and the exclusion of bishops, impeachment of the Archbishop of Canterbury and dismantling of the church courts secularized ecclesiastical government. Hierarchy and obedience by no means disappeared, but initiative and imagination gained importance, especially at regional and local level. By commissioning Dowsing, the Earl of Manchester had customized an official order (aimed solely at magistrates and churchwardens) into his own personal edict, thus allowing this obscure yeoman to become

'Iconoclast General'.[39] In these strange, turbulent days such things had become possible, even necessary if the holy war was to be won and a new order imposed. Besides, if the executive failed them, the Bible offered amateur reformers like Dowsing all the independent justification they needed.

William Dowsing, the 'Iconoclast General', whose tour of Suffolk in 1643–4 resembled the route taken by the witchfinders a couple of years later

A budding witchfinder could trace his call to arms to the same source. Many biblical texts condemning religious images also contained injunctions against witchcraft; like idols, witches dishonoured God and disobeyed the cardinal command that He alone be worshipped. It had long been conventional for sermons and treatises against witchcraft to cite Exodus 22:18, 'Thou shalt not suffer a witch to live'; but less well known was the prohibition of sacrificial offerings which followed that text. Similar rules were set down in Deuteronomy; and in Chronicles could be found the story of Manesseh, ruler of Jerusalem, who not only 'set a carved image, the idol which he had made, in the house of God', but 'used witchcraft, and dealt with a familiar spirit'.[40] Then there was Micah 5:12–13: 'And I will cut off witchcrafts out of thine hand; and thou shalt have no more soothsayers. Thy graven images also will I cut off, and thy standing images out of the midst of thee.' And finally, the Book of Revelation predicted that into the fiery lake would go not just murderers, whoremongers and liars, but 'sorcerers and idolators'. No surprise, then, that many East Anglian activists came to regard witches as they did devotional art: as yet another symbol of idolatry and evil to be rooted out and destroyed.[41]

2

Strange Effects

———————•—————

A s LAWYER'S CLERK, entrepreneur or man of leisure, in the early
1640s Matthew Hopkins moved to Manningtree, nine miles
across the Stour from Great Wenham. Now in his early twenties, he
had come into his inheritance, enough to enable him to take a house
and establish himself as a gentleman. According to later tradition, he
lived on South Street and bought the Thorn Inn at Mistley. Before
long he had begun to worry about witches. He may already have been
acquainted with the theory from works like James I's *Daemonologie*,
and *A Guide to Grand-Jury Men* by clergyman Richard Bernard; but
real events put flesh on the bones. Newcomers to any town became
familiar with the memories and myths that rooted the community in
space and time. Sad and mysterious incidents were linked to landscape
and landmarks: barren ground where a murdered corpse was found, a
creaking tree from which a man had hanged himself, a stone scarred
with the claw-marks of the devil. People recalled storms and floods,
eclipses and meteors, plagues and monstrous births, visions and visi-
tations. And they remembered witches, a legacy the families of the
accused were never allowed to forget. Memory, like witchery, ran in
the blood.[1]

In 1644 the crime of witchcraft was a century old in England, and
during that century the county of Essex had staged more trials than
any other. Henry VIII's original Act of Parliament had barely been
used before its repeal in a legislative overhaul, then Edward VI died
before it could be replaced.[2] His Roman Catholic successor Mary
showed little interest in witches, but when Elizabeth became queen in
1558, senior Protestant clerics came back from their Continental exile
concerned about the dangers of sorcery.[3] The threat of Elizabeth I's

Catholic enemies was often conflated with the witch-menace, while word from the provinces indicated that fear of witches (defined as apostates as well as murderers) was escalating. In the early 1560s ecclesiastical courts in the diocese of Canterbury, not far from Essex, were no longer hearing just minor accusations of incantation and magical healing, but cases of full-blown *maleficium* – that is, those in which livestock and other property were alleged to have been destroyed, or people killed and injured. Since it was inappropriate for the Church to be trying capital crimes, a new statute was passed in 1563.[4]

In the implementation of the Witchcraft Act, Essex led the way. The first execution occurred there in 1564, followed two years later by a multiple trial reported in a cheap pamphlet; by 1581 there had been another eight significant outbreaks. In that year, anxiety at Westminster led to the passing of a statute forbidding magical forecasts of the queen's death.[5] A few months later at least ten women from St Osyth, a town with strong Catholic traditions, were tried as witches, and an account also went into print. Indictments for witchcraft were filed at the Essex assizes throughout the last two decades of the sixteenth century, amounting to more than two hundred in all. Although as few as one in six of those indicted were executed, no Elizabethan man, woman or child a day's ride from Chelmsford need have missed the excitement of a witch-hanging at some point in their lives. Executions were popular with all social ranks and degrees, and for those unable to travel to the assizes, eyewitness accounts were spread by word of mouth and the broadsides and books sold by itinerant pedlars. With every year the black inventory of witches grew longer in folklore.[6]

By the time the crown passed to James VI of Scotland, Essex was the English shire that had best squared up to the devil, having tried 180 suspects. Almost all had been charged with attacking persons and property, however, rather than compacting with evil spirits. Just as it had been thought inappropriate for *maleficium* to be tried by the ecclesiastical authorities, so the invocation of demons had been considered an unfit matter for secular law, but by 1600 attitudes were changing.[7] Elizabethan thinking on the subject, mostly among Protestant clerics, had raised the status of witchcraft from a part of the squabbles and suspicions of rural society into the ultimate spiritual crime. The effect of this was felt in everyday life, notably in a proliferation of cases of alleged diabolic possession. And yet the twist given to witchcraft accusations by an increasing number of adolescent girls blaming old women for their frenzies was less significant than the ensuing propaganda war between evangelical puritans and their Catholic opponents. Each side laid claim to a unique efficacy in dispossession, identifying

Witches hanged at Chelmsford in 1589. A toad copulates with a ferret, a sign that they are diabolic spirits; another comes to suckle the witch, who cups her breast in anticipation

this gift as a divine imprimatur. For a monarch and episcopate trying to steer a middle way for the Church, these claims were tiresome and dangerous. It was necessary for the state to punish witches; it was vital that it should restrain wanton exorcists.

In 1604, the year after James succeeded Elizabeth, new Church canons forbade unlicensed exorcism, and a revised Witchcraft Act made the conjuration of spirits a capital crime.[8] At a stroke, genuine cases of possession – those that were not palpably fraudulent – were taken away from the firebrand exorcists and placed under the jurisdiction of the courts. The enduring image of the king as a slobbering bon viveur of dubious sexuality almost invariably embraces witch-hunting as well. As King of Scotland he had helped to interrogate

King James interrogates the North Berwick witches, c. 1591

witches in North Berwick, and in 1597 had written a learned tract, *Daemonologie*. Small wonder that when this was republished in London in 1603, it became required reading not just for clergymen but for anyone interested in the mind of England's new monarch; naturally this included the gentry from whom the magistracy was drawn. According to James, the devil was a tangible force of evil, waging war on mankind in its last age. Although simple folk exaggerated the effectiveness of diabolic power, he argued, witches were none the less vermin to be exterminated, because they had switched their allegiance from God to Satan. For all its philosophical subtlety, *Daemonologie* was both an academic manifesto in favour of witch-hunting, and a practical manual for the job.[9]

Yet no sooner had the king thrown down the gauntlet than his policy of restraining religious extremists necessitated a change of tack. The Archbishop of Canterbury Richard Bancroft, appointed in 1604, had declared war on militant Calvinists (for whom a belief in possession was a shibboleth), and James backed him; Jesuit exorcists would also be made to conform. In private the king adhered to his ideas about witches; in public he was now far more sceptical. Not only did he order investigations – in 1611, for instance, one 'to search out the truth of a supposed witchcrafte Comitted upon six young maydes' – but he delighted in exposing fraud at first hand.[10] By the time *Daemonologie* was republished in 1616, James was more passionate about deer-hunting than ever he had been about witch-hunting. In that year he castigated a pair of judges for executing nine witches at Leicester, an intervention with profound consequences in an age when ambitious men kept an ear cocked to catch every royal hint. Only a judge without a care for his future career would have ignored this one; executions abated.[11]

More cases of imposture came to light in the early 1620s, such as that of Katherine Malpas, who claimed to have seen shape-shifting witches in her bedchamber. Drawing on countless stories in circulation, Malpas knew how to fake an accusation and attracted good audiences with her insane fits and Bible-hurling.[12] Not all prosecutions failed because fraud was detected. Edward Jorden's *Briefe Discourse of a Disease called the Suffocation of the Mother* (1603), which attributed the hysteria of bewitchment to an affliction of the womb (or 'mother'), promoted natural explanations for apparently supernatural illnesses. Jorden may have been the mouthpiece of the anti-puritan, anti-exorcist Archbishop Bancroft, but it was his effect upon the thinking of physicians that mattered.[13] In 1622 Richard Napier, a Buckinghamshire rector moonlighting as a healer, diagnosed 'Epilepsie of the Mother' in a girl locals believed to have a witchfinding spirit working through her. Using her voice, the spirit was alleged to have said 'I have sent this Child to speake to shew all these wiches.' Napier did not hesitate with his diagnosis: she was branded a hysteric.[14] By the time Charles became king in 1625 witch-trials were highly likely to fail, for one or more of three reasons: exposure of the accuser as a fraud; insufficient evidence; or a natural medical explanation that chased witchcraft from the courtroom.

The witch-hunt that flared up in 1645 was therefore partly a reaction against the decline of prosecutions under Charles I, and partly a sign that witchfinding and the persecution of Catholics were linked in people's minds. Under Elizabeth anxiety about popish traitors had coincided with a high tide of witch-trials, so it was logical that the arrival of an anti-Calvinist king should have marked the ebb. Between 1625 and the start of the civil war, there were just twenty-seven trials at the Home Circuit assizes (covering Essex, Kent, Surrey, Sussex and Hertfordshire), and of the convictions that resulted only two were upheld.[15] This was not to say that the population at large had forgotten about witchcraft; on the contrary, anxiety may have been increasing precisely because the law no longer seemed to offer protection. For all James's exposures of fraudulence, most witchcraft accusations were not cynical plots cooked up to further private vendettas, but resulted from a sincere perception of danger.[16]

No words from on high could make people less scared of witches. Everyone knew that accusations might be malicious and that symptoms were easily faked; yet personal experiences of bewitchment were quite different. Fear of specific individuals was palpable, stemming from a widespread belief in the reality of witchcraft. Village life was full of ambiguity and aggression, suspicion and superstition. Most disputes were easily resolved, but if one party had a bad reputation, an unexplained misfortune occurring to another might be interpreted as the first blow of the second round. Magical or violent counter-measures might follow, failing those an arrest warrant from a magistrate. Such feelings were not confined to the lower orders. In the 1620s the children of the Yorkshire poet Edward Fairfax were troubled by visions, leading to a series of arrests. The suspected women were initially discharged, then retried at Fairfax's insistence. This time the cautious judge advised the jury that the case had 'reached not to the point of the statute', and so despite the plaintiff's status the suspects were acquitted.[17] Like many who had been poorly served by the law, Fairfax was bemused, observing that many people doubted his judgement 'for they thincke th[a]t there be noe Witches at all'. He disagreed, warning that 'I hear & fear there be many'.[18]

The pattern was fixed for a decade: Crown and Church opposing puritans and their demonology; anxiety about witches unchecked by the courts; and widening divisions over religion, taxation, land and authority. By 1640, as Charles I fought Calvinists in Scotland and tussled with a reconvened Parliament at Westminster, the tide was turning again. As the political crisis deepened, so popular fears resurfaced.[19] Clients of England's most famous astrologer William Lilly – inveterate worriers about illnesses, journeys, lawsuits, missing persons and lost property – now seemed more anxiety-ridden than ever.[20] In 1642 every English person was thrown into times which, in Lilly's own words, were 'very troublesome and expensive, when warr and the souldier comand, and faction and division both in Church & Comonwealth, do aboundantly afflict us'.[21] Once again, the dangers of witchcraft were voiced with confidence in public. In March 1645 nowhere was this more true than at Manningtree, where the tailor John Rivet's wife lay sick.

The Manningtree known to Matthew Hopkins was a small but prosperous market town on the northern edge of the Tendring Hundred, a dense maze of marsh, wood and farmland. A riverside path led to the port of Mistley, by tradition a place where mistletoe grew, and where the eldest residents remembered waving ships off to fight the Spanish Armada. The harbour with its warehouses and jetties overlooked the mile-wide estuary of the Stour where at high tide ships would dock and depart, taking grain to London and returning with manure. When the tide went out activity subsided and sea birds picked over the mudflats. Across the water, mists permitting, Hopkins could have seen the Suffolk villages of Brantham and Stutton: chimney smoke by day, and at twilight candles in the windows. Manningtree itself occupied just twenty-two acres, its narrow lanes packed with the homes of weavers, brewers, artisans and tradesmen. At the central crossroads, where the high street met the road to the south, stood the market-place with its assembly room and clock tower. At Whitsun a fair attracted many visitors who drank Manningtree ale and feasted on the roast ox to which Shakespeare had referred. At the fringes, where the bounds of the township gave way to fields, were scattered the shacks and tumbledown cottages of the poor: the labourers, dockers and beggars, the decrepit and the dispossessed.[22]

At the Reformation the ecclesiastical manors of Manningtree and Mistley had passed to Sir John Rainsforth, but by the time Matthew Hopkins arrived several families had come to dominate as landowners, magistrates, manufacturers and merchants. Dynasties old and new left monuments in the churches of St Mary at Mistley Heath and St Michael at Manningtree. A generation earlier Manningtree folk had been forced to walk the mile to St Mary's, their own church having burnt down; but complaints about the town's vulnerability to pirates while its people were at prayer led to the building of a chapel of ease in 1616. The roof timbers came from old ships, a mixture of the spiritual and the mercantile representative of its congregation. Traditions were solidly Protestant and, by the 1640s, Presbyterian. In the reign of Queen Mary townsmen had tried to stop a man being burned for refusing to attend Mass, but had been restrained by Bishop Bonner's guards. The martyr's memory never faded. Reactions to a visit in 1633 by another hated prelate, Bishop William Laud, were not recorded, but it is easy to imagine what local people muttered under their breath. Laud generously gave St Michael's four pieces of communion plate bearing his coat of arms, but from the time he was made Archbishop of Canterbury that year, in the eyes of the godly his influence was entirely negative.[23]

To a Manningtree puritan of the 1640s Laud's legacy may not have been actually evil, but it was certainly scandalous – a word used throughout Essex whenever criticism of the clergy was voiced. From the parish of Stisted, for example, came news that the minister, Christopher Newsted, was a base Arminian who incited opposition to Parliament and denied the Solemn League and Covenant. Introduced in 1643, this was a popular pledge to replace episcopal

34

hierarchy with local Presbyterian church government; but, like the Protestation Oath, from 1641 sworn by thousands of men and women 'against all popery and popish innovation', it became an oath of allegiance to Parliament – a semi-sacred ritual to distinguish friend from foe, Christ from Antichrist.[24] By the outbreak of war, the godly camp saw its enemy as a many-headed monster breaching every political, religious and moral code. At Stisted, not only did the parishioners have Christopher Newsted removed by the Committee for

A godly minister and his parishioners take the Protestation Oath against popery

Scandalous Ministers but rumours spread that the local gentry hosted orgies at which spirits were invoked by a black-suited sorcerer. Scandal first flirted with evil, then went the whole way with accusations of demon worship. In this climate, the number of witches presented for trial in Essex began to creep upwards.[25]

In 1638 four women were sent to Colchester prison by a magistrate named Sir Harbottle Grimston, a gentleman who lived at Bradfield Hall, just outside Manningtree. All were from the Tendring Hundred, where Grimston held manors in Mistley, Ramsey, Kirby, Lawford, and Tendring itself.[26] Despite being in his mid seventies Grimston still toured his estates, although at that time almost certainly in a carriage. Knighted early in the reign of James I and made a baronet in 1611, he had married into a respectable family from Lavenham in Suffolk and in 1614 was elected sheriff of Essex and MP for Harwich. In the 1620s he represented his county in Parliament and resisted Charles I's forced loan, for which he was imprisoned. Grimston's dissent in the matter of royal finance was reinforced by his puritanism. He sent his three sons to the godly seminary, Emmanuel College, Cambridge, from which his middle son and namesake emerged as a committed Presbyterian with his sights set on the law and government; in Parliament in 1640 he denounced Archbishop Laud as 'the sty of all pestilential filth that hath infested the state and government of this commonwealth'. Alongside his religious values, Sir Harbottle Grimston taught his sons not to flinch from using the law to suppress evil. Without him, Matthew Hopkins' mission might never have got off the ground.[27]

Almost all the suspicions that lay behind the witchcraft accusations of March 1645 originated in Sir Harbottle Grimston's jurisdiction, mostly on his estates. In 1640 a woman named Sarah Hatyn was said to have threatened the constable of Ramsey, Francis Stock, after he pressed her husband to serve as a soldier. Soon afterwards Stock's wife reported having seen a snake in the house; she believed it to be a diabolical imp, and when she tried to kill it with a spade, it vanished. Within a few days, Goodwife Stock and two of her children were dead. In the following year Stock's servant fell sick after striking Sarah Hatyn's son, and swore on his death-bed that she had bewitched him. In 1642 Hatyn found herself in the frame for yet another mysterious murder.[28]

Since then, two widows named Elizabeth Harvey and Marian Hocket had also fallen under suspicion, but the people of Ramsey lacked the will or the courage to initiate a prosecution, doubtless aware of how few had been successful in recent years. Meanwhile, at Thorpe-le-Soken, a few miles to the south, Margaret Moone was accused of bewitching the Rawbood family, occupants of a house from which she had been evicted. In 1640 Moone was thought to have murdered the baby daughter of an influential farmer, and three years later to have destroyed another man's cow. For all four women, time was short.[29]

In Manningtree the evil spread to Richard Edwards, a figure well connected to Sir Harbottle Grimston in religion and administration. One of the largest landowners in Mistley and Lawford, Edwards was easily the richest man in the town, and had been made chief constable of the Tendring Hundred in 1642. He was thus a formidable enemy. In the summer of 1644 two of his cattle died as they were being driven past a witch's house in Mistley; the insides of the carcasses bore no signs of disease. Worse followed. Edwards' newborn son was placed in the charge of a Manningtree wet-nurse who lived close to the prime suspect, Elizabeth Clarke. Before long the baby fell into 'very strange fits, extending the limbs, and rowling the eyes', and within a few days had died.[30]

Edwards knew he was not the only one under attack. Sarah Bright stood accused of having killed the child of a prosperous stonemason, and Robert Tayler, another well-heeled citizen and leading Presbyterian, suspected a 'lewd woman' named Elizabeth Gooding of having bewitched his horse.[31] Some trials had already taken place at Chelmsford by then, including those of two of the women committed by Sir Harbottle Grimston in 1638; the case of a labourer's wife from Hatfield Broad Oak had also been heard. Another woman was imprisoned at Colchester and charged. Like Grimston, Edwards owned an estate in Ramsey, where whispering about witchcraft was rife. At a time when prominent gentry were warning magistrates that the county was being flooded with Catholics and other enemies of the state, it began to seem as though a conspiratorial network of popish and diabolical traitors spread across the Tendring Hundred.[32]

Concern also focused on the parish of Lawford. Anne West and her daughter Rebecca had migrated from Rivenhall in 1638, and were said to have adopted pious manners to conceal a reputation for witchcraft.[33] But word had spread. In their second year at Lawford John Cutler, a prominent yeoman, blamed Anne West for his son's death, and although he did not prosecute her, in 1641 his neighbour Thomas Hart did, for causing the death of a sow. Anne West was tried that spring and acquitted; but at the following assizes a petition branding her 'a very dangerous p[er]son amongest her neighbours' was presented to the judges, who instructed local magistrate Sir Thomas Bowes to arrange for her to be prosecuted. She was unable to raise the bail money, so Bowes had her arrested and carted the eight miles back to Colchester, and from there, in March 1642, to the assizes at Chelmsford. Again she escaped punishment. But the magistrate, who lived at Great Bromley Hall, seven miles south of Manningtree, was, like Robert Tayler, a man in his prime and an enthusiastic Presbyterian, and now his interest was aroused. Another leading Presbyterian in the region was George Francis of Rivenhall, a principal inhabitant of his parish whose child had died mysteriously when the Wests lived there.[34] Hostility was growing, to witches in general and to Anne West in particular.

Matthew Hopkins' claim to have been menaced by witches in 1644 was just one strand in a web of conflict, suspicion and godly conviction. The beliefs of John Stearne were another. Older than Hopkins, in his mid thirties, Stearne had like him grown up in rural Suffolk, and may also have shared his Cambridgeshire ancestry.[35] At Long Melford, possibly his birthplace, he met and married Agnes Cawston, and together they set up home in Lawshall near Bury St Edmunds, where Agnes's mother had moved after her own remarriage.[36] John and Agnes's first child, a girl, was baptized there early in 1644.[37] The pride of the parish was the church of All Saints, rebuilt in the fifteenth century with profits from the cloth industry and now a powerhouse of Protestant preaching. Reform had spread quickly in Lawshall, and by 1600 the Catholic community had been driven to practise their religion in secret, at Coldham Hall. Stearne himself was a staunch puritan, with a censorious manner and a mind steeped in Scripture. What he was doing in Manningtree in 1645 is not known, but since he maintained a house there he was presumably engaged in business of some sort.

Stearne was a man after Matthew Hopkins' heart, and each saw a future in collaboration with the other. As well as similar geographical origins, the two men shared a gentility that originated more in self-assertion than in wealth, estate, breeding, or title. Like many puritans of their age they chose to define themselves according to the present, not the past, not only in the matter of their gentility but specifically with regard to their predestined election to the sainthood, an unswerving duty to God, and a heartfelt calling to serve the commonwealth. Above all, they were men of action.

The first weeks of 1645 offered little hope of peace. Division, it seemed, bred only more division. The Earl of Manchester had parted company with Oliver Cromwell, second-in-command of the Eastern Association Army, after a disagreement about the conduct of the war; and in Parliament Cromwell's Independents, who opposed a national Church on the old model, were a thorn in the side of the Presbyterian majority. The last major battle had been indecisive, and in February peace talks ended in disarray. In frosty streets and markets people talked of stalemate and despair, as if both war and winter would last forever. Public anxiety reached new heights. The astrologer William Lilly was inundated with clients, and recorded their special concerns in his notebooks: which side to support; whether particular soldiers were alive; and, if so, the date when they would come home.[38]

Early in January Lilly was asked to predict how and when Archbishop Laud would die. He deliberated over his answer and was overtaken by events: Laud was beheaded on the 10th. Though he had been despised by many in life, his violent death on Tower Hill was nevertheless seen as another sign that the ordered world was coming apart at the seams. Some of Lilly's clients, both rich and poor, reflected this public alarm in a private belief that they were possessed or bewitched.[39] Rumours circulated that Major-General Cromwell looked to Satan for military power, when what he really needed was better leadership and organization.[40] To this end, Parliament replaced the Earl of Essex as commander-in-chief with the youthful, dashing Sir Thomas Fairfax, and plans were approved to recruit and train a New Model Army: a tough, ruthless killing machine run on discipline and godliness. Some of the worst fighting lay ahead. Early in March 1645 Lilly calculated what he called 'An Astrologicall judgment upon the Sunn', a horoscope for the year to come, which, he said, would be thick with 'many hott skirmishes [and] much bloodshead in those unseasonable tymes of the yeare'. Men's minds, he warned grimly, would be corrupted by the planets, causing their conduct to be 'rapacious, cruell, treacherous'.[41]

At Lawford, Thomas Hart and his wife Prudence were preoccupied with the punishment of Anne West. In 1641 their pursuit of West in the courts had ended in acquittal, which meant that she had returned home bearing an extra grudge against them. They waited nervously, not knowing where or when the next blow would fall. Meanwhile Anne West's daughter Rebecca had started giving Prudence Hart that familiar spiteful look: a wounding power believed to flow from the eyes of envious women. In the summer of 1644 Goodwife Hart became pregnant, and fared well through the autumn and winter. But one Sunday towards the end of February 1645, a severe abdominal pain forced her to leave the church. Before she could get home, she collapsed in the street and gave birth prematurely to a stillborn child.[42]

Again and again the memory of her dead child and a craving for vengeance against the Wests coursed round Prudence Hart's brain until a terrifying experience overwhelmed her:

> . . . being in her bed, in the night, something fell down upon her right side, but being dark, she cannot tell in what shape it was: And that presently shee was taken lame on that side, with extraordinary pains and burning, but recovered again within a few dayes after. And . . . she verily believeth, that Rebecca West, and Anne West her mother, were the cause of her pains . . . because the said Rebecca West ever thought this Informant to be her greatest enemy.

The rector of Lawford, John Edes, was a Presbyterian respected in the community for thirty years, and well connected to ministers throughout the Tendring Hundred and Dedham Vale. He had seen Prudence Hart stagger from the church that day, and he knew what she had suffered at the hands of Anne and Rebecca West. He vowed to help if he could. At the beginning of March 1645 the collective will to punish the Wests was given an additional boost when yeoman John Cutler, who believed Anne West had killed his son five years earlier, pledged to back both Thomas Hart and John Edes if they took legal action.[43]

Events a mile away at Manningtree provided the final encouragement. By now the town was a tinder-box of grief, wrath and excitement, just waiting for a spark. Gossip about witchcraft was rife, including the allegations made by John Rivet against Elizabeth Clarke, and people looked to their leaders for deliverance. Unable to contain their frustration, some townsmen confronted Widow Clarke, and were shocked and gratified to hear her admit an association with several witches, although she declined to name them. Her faltering confession was compressed into coherent prose and entrusted to John Stearne, who was known to have the ear of Sir Harbottle Grimston and Sir Thomas Bowes. The lord of the manor had died in 1638, and the town's rector Thomas Witham had left for London in 1643 and since died himself. In the absence of any powerful seigneurial or clerical influence in Manningtree and Mistley, personal connections of the sort Stearne had nurtured with the magistrates had come to acquire great political significance.[44]

It was Friday 21 March 1645, a day when the magistrates made themselves available to hear complaints about sin, crime and disorder, probably at the assembly room in the market-place. The elderly Grimston and his younger colleague – Bowes was around forty – settled themselves, and the necessary papers and reference works were arranged on the table.[45] A clerk sat in attendance, inkpot filled, quills cut to his liking. John Stearne was announced, and was shown into the room. At the request of the townsmen, he told the magistrates, he had brought a transcript of Clarke's confession for their consideration. Grimston and Bowes discussed it a while, then, at the stroke of a pen, unwittingly initiated the most savage witch-hunt in English history: Stearne departed holding what he later described as a 'warrant . . . for the searching of such persons as I should nominate'.[46] It had been agreed that before going any further, Stearne was to discover from Elizabeth Clarke the names of the other witches. Matthew Hopkins volunteered to assist him, and together they discussed how best to proceed. Stearne, particularly, was all for seeing whether the old woman would float in water – the swimming test once favoured by James I – but it is likely that the magistrates forbade this as a dubious and sinful ordeal.[47]

Grimston and Bowes were not completely above making concessions to superstition, however. Eager to testify against Elizabeth Clarke, John Rivet presented himself to them that same Friday. The fact that he had incited a cunning woman to commit an illegal act of sorcery the magistrates overlooked, in view of the gravity of the situation. Grimston was the kind of godly man who counselled a patient acceptance of the workings of providence, advising with regard to diseases that, 'be they never so grievous and continuall, thou oughtest to kisse these rods as love tokens received from the Almightie'.[48] But he and Bowes were also instruments of God's law, and justice had to be done. They ordered that Elizabeth Clarke be arrested and her body searched by four honest and experienced women for signs that she had suckled evil spirits. After this, she was to be watched for three nights to see whether her imps came for sustenance.

The main source of information about the investigation that now unfolded is a printed account which omits some testimonies and muddles the dates of the rest. It is fair to assume that when news of events at Manningtree reached Lawford, Anne and Rebecca West were arrested and questioned there and then. There is nothing to suggest that the old woman admitted anything, but this did not matter: the accusations of others were incriminating enough. If by this stage Elizabeth Clarke had not already pointed the finger at 'that old beldame West', she certainly had within a day or so. Then there was West's daughter Rebecca. In her, John Edes seems to have identified a key to unlock the enigma. Before mother and daughter were sent to the magistrates to be examined he managed to coax the girl into revealing her innermost secrets, probably with promises of lenience if she cooperated.

Back in Manningtree, no such gentle treatment awaited Elizabeth Clarke, who despite her earlier confession was to prove a far tougher nut to crack. From his window John Rivet may have observed the searchers and watchers pass by as they made for Clarke's house – a sight sure to raise hopes for his wife's recovery. Before the weekend was out two godly gentlemen of the town were also to be seen heading in the same direction. They were John Stearne and Matthew Hopkins.

★

Hopkins and Stearne had grown up in the shadow of the devil, a dark, peripheral presence tempting them, deceiving them, stirring others against them. He was the quintessential opposite of all that was holy; a warped reflection of Christ; an object lesson in what not to do or to become. The preachers of their youth had walked a fine line between making Satan raw and real and attributing to him more power than might be pleasing to God. Some thought of him as God's hangman, an instrument to make the weak succumb to sin, the sooner

A woodcut from 1642 in which demons pay homage to their master, Satan

to bring their souls before a heavenly tribunal. It was believed that when 'ignorant, wicked people, filled with envie and malice' secretly wished harm upon others, God might permit Satan to grant their wish so that they would be convicted of witchcraft, 'thus justly punishing their envie and malice'.[49] Another popular image of the devil was of a creature sitting idle while Antichrist, in the guise of the Pope, deluded Christendom. The Protestant Reformation, it was said, had sent the fallen angel back into the fray, his mission to lead as many souls as he could astray before Armageddon and the start of Christ's reign on earth.

Unsurprisingly, as far as the common people were concerned the devil had never really gone away. Throughout the Middle Ages he was thought of as a black humanoid beast with horns, hooves and a tail, and was thus depicted in the doom paintings adorning parish churches up and down the country. In morality plays and folk stories (and the nightmares they inspired) he represented night against day, famine against plenty, fornication against chastity, despair against hope, and enmity against charity. Satan lurked round every corner. When it came to witchcraft accusations, however, he had at best a walk-on part. Instead, familiars — or imps — in the shape of animals, birds and insects took centre-stage.[50]

At the first significant trial in Essex, in 1566, the accused confessed to a pact with 'Sathan' — a white cat she kept in a basket and fed on bread and milk.[51] More commonly familiars were believed to suck blood from teats on a witch's body, a notion too deeply engrained in homespun demonology to be eradicated by Protestant reformers. Preachers did their best, insisting that this distorted the truth of man's relationship with the spiritual realm. People no more needed an imp in order to commune with the devil, it was argued, than they needed priests to feed them Christ's remains. There were attempts at compromise. One suggestion was that familiars suckled the witch to remind her of her fealty to the devil: a black parallel to holy communion, now repackaged as a commemorative act.[52] But for all their neat symmetry, abstract arguments were either incomprehensible or irrelevant to men and women whose intelligence was shaped by the solid things of daily life. So long as evil remained a tangible destructive force it could be challenged and defeated. *Maleficium* was the real crime of witchcraft for the majority; the rest was book-talk and eyewash.

Although witch-trials had dwindled after 1600, those that did occur increasingly featured graphic accounts of dealings with the devil. The Lancashire trials of 1612 exemplifed a new type of real-life story presented as legal evidence, namely that witches congregated at secret locations to hold their sabbats.[53] By the 1630s a number of activities about which people had been made to feel guilty since the Reformation were being actively inverted and perverted in testimonies. Traditional merry-making had involved feasting, drinking, dancing and courtship (including pre-marital sex) – community events that kept the very poorest going. Then they began to be frowned upon by the godly, and the piety and restraint these men attempted to enforce explain why tales of public devil-worship included harmless recreations made heinous, and why so many

The witches' sabbat, depicted here as a licentious country dance led by devils

private encounters with Satan were said to involve sexual intercourse. The active suppression of both Catholicism and puritanism strengthened this dark inversion of the Christian ideal. Bishop Wren's visitation articles for the diocese of Ely in 1638 set out to expose 'any unlawfull assemblies, conventicles, or meetings, under colour or pretence of any exercise of Religion'. Refracted as a nightmarish version of such gatherings, the witch's sabbat shimmers into life.[54]

The Lancashire trials were briefly reprised in 1634, at a time when witchcraft prosecutions had become very rare indeed. Margaret Johnson confessed that the devil had visited her as a man in a black suit offering food and revenge in exchange for her soul; it was a time of her life, she explained, when she was 'in greate passion & anger & discontented & w[i]thall oppressed w[i]th some want'. She admitted having attended a meeting in Pendle Forest where witches arranged the deaths of people and their livestock.[55] The leading witness against her was a boy who claimed to have been abducted to a sabbat; as part of the investigation, he was paid to travel around pointing at women whose faces he remembered. Despite a subsequent admission that he had made it all up, followed by the acquittal of four suspects, the story of the Lancashire witches remained popular and influential, spawning pamphlets, ballads and plays. Sir William Pelham gossiped about 'a huge pack of witches' that had sent a tempest to sink Charles I's ship, much as the North Berwick witches had pursued his royal father. In Holland Charles's sister Elizabeth, the exiled Queen of Bohemia, relished the news she heard from Lancashire.[56]

The most significant aspect of the case was that the king had ordered the suspects to be brought to London for examination by his own physician, William Harvey; it was felt that the genius who had discovered the circulation of the blood would uncover the truth. Indeed, the search for evidence of witchcraft had never been more clinical. Assisted by a team of seven surgeons and ten midwives, Harvey found nothing on the bodies of the first three women, but the case of Margaret Johnson furrowed some brows. The official report concluded that

> . . . wee fynd two things [which] maye bee called Teats the one betweene her Secretts & the Fundament on the Edge thereof, the other on the middle of her left buttock, the first in a Shape lyke to the teate of a Bitche, but in our Judgementes nothinge but the Skin of the Fundament drawen out as yt wilbe after the pyles or applicac[i]on of leeches: The Seacond is lyke the nipple or Teate of a womans bodye but of the same Colour with the Rest of the Skin, without any hollownes or yssue for any bloode or Juyce to come from thence.

46

All in all, Harvey judged the marks to be natural. And so the women were exonerated and the sceptics vindicated. Science, it seemed, had triumphed over superstition.[57]

Yet there was an unexpected outcome of this and other medical studies. English criminal law was becoming more inquisitorial, in the Continental style, meaning that the authorities were increasingly demanding and discerning in the matter of evidence. Proving witchcraft at law came to require something more substantial than rumour, hearsay and personal conviction – the voice of the country on which three generations of judges had relied. Rather than discouraging accusations, however, the call for material proof actually encouraged humiliating ordeals, tests and examinations: in 1645 the job of the searchers at Manningtree was not to prove that Elizabeth Clarke had committed acts of *maleficium*, but to lay bare her demonic pact.[58] By this time many magistrates thought of the pact itself as the real crime; one, writing in his commonplace book, defined witchcraft simply as 'Conjuration of evill spirits. Covenanting w[i]the th[e]m. Taking up any dead body to use it about witchery.'[59] This interpretation ran counter to judicial opinion of the previous decade, which held that only murderous witches should be executed. The godly clerics of the Westminster Assembly of Divines officially shifted the emphasis to the compact with Satan, a more heinous crime but one harder to prove unless witchfinders could extract confessions or search-women discover signs.[60] Some puritan clerics scorned the notion of physical intimacy between humans and demons; others acceded to it because it demonstrated graphically the existence of the spirit world, in an age when doubts were increasing about such things.[61]

Concentration on the pact itself also intensified as the significance of spiritual and political covenants grew increasingly sacred in character. It was perhaps inevitable that the puritan covenant of grace, coupled with the public ritual of swearing oaths of allegiance (principally the Protestation Oath and the Solemn League and Covenant), would be thought of and spoken of in a reversed form to describe the witch's pact, or 'covenant' as it became known.[62] As early as 1640, in a sermon to the House of Commons, Dr Cornelius Burges illustrated the Calvinist union between God and man with a visceral description of its evil opposite: 'There is not a Witch that hath the Devil at her beck', he feared, 'but she must seale a Covenant to him, sometimes with her blood, sometimes by other rites and devices, and perhaps he must suck her too.'[63] By 1645 witches were commonly said to have entered into 'a solemn league' with the devil – the dramatic terminology favoured by the witchfinders.

The women who came knocking on Elizabeth Clarke's door on Friday 21 March 1645 were Mary Phillips, Grace Norman, Frances Mills and Mary Parsley. Goodwife Parsley was expecially eager, her daughter having died in circumstances suggestive of witchcraft.[64] Searching bodies was women's work: as well as witches, they investigated suspected plague deaths, murder victims, infanticidal mothers, and felons pleading pregnancy. 'Juries of matrons', which usually included a midwife, had both special experience and a privileged access that enabled them to search out medical proof in delicate cases.[65] Witchcraft was female power, and belonged to the female sphere of running a household: the image of a witch tended to be that of a supremely disobedient and destructive mother or wife, and other women were thought to be the best detectors of such failings.[66] It is not recorded whether Clarke protested, but there were many hands to restrain her if she did. Nor is it said whether her bodily hair was shaved off – a clinical preparation to be sure, but also a spell to make a witch confess.[67] It is known that the search-women found three teats, probably in the genital region, which they certified to be unnatural.

Next came the task of waiting for the familiars, and in this the searchers were assisted by two men, John Bankes and Mary Parsley's husband Edward, a bricklayer committed to the godly cause who once had rioted at Ipswich against Archbishop Laud.[68] Widow Clarke was kept under house arrest, seated in the middle of the room. The watchers gathered round, drawing closer as the sun went down and the shadows cast by rushlight, candle and hearth loomed like ghostly spectators. They yawned and nudged each other awake, but by dawn had nothing to show for their vigil. The procedure was repeated that Saturday night, again without success. On Sunday they probably took a break, for a few weeks earlier the new Directory for the Public

Worship of God had been introduced; a replacement for the detested Prayer Book, it stipulated that the Sabbath was to be spent in piety, charity and mercy, which presumably did not include subjecting witches to ordeals.[69] On Monday the watchers went back to work; but the results were the same.

Tuesday 24 March was the last day of the year according to the old Roman calendar. At Bess Clarke's house the patience of the six watchers – John Bankes, Edward and Mary Parsley and the other three search-women – was wearing thin: it was the third and final day of watching, and still no imps had appeared. Yet the proverb 'Say no ill of the year till it be past' was to prove apt.[70] After dark that evening they were waiting and watching as they had on previous evenings, the atmosphere still crackling with anticipation, when the cottage door opened. Outlined in the gloom was a cloaked figure which might have been the devil himself, but for his familiar voice. In walked John Stearne and behind him Matthew Hopkins, accompanied by his greyhound.

Neither intended to stay in this frowzy room any longer than it took to get what they wanted. As their eyes adjusted to Clarke's faintly illuminated figure – an old beldame in rags balanced on a stool, crutch in hand – Stearne and Hopkins began their menacing demands that she divulge the names of her accomplices.[71] Despite their persistence Widow Clarke remained impassive, and it seemed they had no choice but to leave and perhaps try again in the morning. But just as Matthew Hopkins reached the door the widow spoke up, her voice faint with fear but hopeful. Asking only that they should not hurt her, Clarke begged them to stay, adding: 'I will shew you my Impes, for they bee ready to come.' Hopkins forcefully declined her offer, despite her assurance that the creatures posed no threat to his welfare. At this point someone interrupted to ask why she had no fear of such things, to which she replied: 'What, doe yee thinke I am afraide of my children?'

Pointing to a spot close to her, Widow Clarke instructed Hopkins and Stearne to sit. This they did. One of the other men, probably Edward Parsley, then ventured a question that on a previous occasion had gone unanswered; it was, in fact, *the* question, the point at which disgust at sexual perversion and guilt over sexual fantasy converged.

This time, she was implored to tell the truth. 'Bess,' she was asked, 'hath the Devill had the use of your body?' She wondered why her examiner wanted to know such a thing, to which he replied chastely on behalf of all present: 'I desire to know the truth and no otherwise.' Elizabeth Clarke sighed, then said: 'It is true.' The impact of these three words was dramatic. Matthew Hopkins asked her in what form the devil had come to her. No longer as meek as she had been earlier, Clarke looked hard at this presumptuous young man and retorted: 'A tall, proper, black haired gentleman, a properer man than your selfe.' Asked by Stearne with whom she would rather share a bed, she had no doubt: the devil.

Clarke related fondly how she had first enjoyed 'carnall copulation' with Satan six or seven years earlier. From that time he had been a regular visitor to her bedchamber, always presentable in his lace collar, and ready with his breathy plea, 'Besse I must lye with you.' She had never refused, and their love-making usually lasted half the night. As if the shock of this were not enough, the watchers were warned of the imminent arrival of her imps. Smacking her lips with a kissing sound, Clarke called out the name 'Holt' in a sing-song voice, as one might call a cat for its supper. Nothing happened and nobody moved. For the next half-hour an air of tense expectation hung in the room, but it seemed that whatever display the old widow had planned was just a figment of her imagination.

Then Hopkins, Stearne and the other watchers became aware of another presence. Before their eyes crept a white creature, like a cat but smaller, which silently greeted its mistress before retreating into the shadows. Next she called 'Jermarah!' According to Hopkins, 'there appeared an Impe like to a Dog, which was white, with some sandy spots, and seemed to be very fat and plumpe, with very short legges, who forthwith vanished away.' The one after that, 'Vinegar Tom', Stearne described as 'like a Greyhound, with legs as long as a Stagge'. There followed an imp resembling a polecat or ferret, and one like a toad. Were there more? asked Hopkins. The same ones would return in different shapes, Clarke replied, but there was another who had not yet appeared: a black beast called 'Sack & Sugar', still out at work. It would be home soon, she promised, and would tear Master Stearne into pieces for trying to have her swum in the river. But when 'Sack & Sugar' finally arrived, it seemed to be no more than a harmless rabbit. None the less, Clarke assured Stearne he was lucky it had not leapt onto his face, squeezed itself down his throat, and deposited 'a feast of Toades' in his belly.

With so many witnesses present, Hopkins and Stearne can hardly have lied about events that night. But what were those events? A

Matthew Hopkins interrogates Elizabeth Clarke and Rebecca West. He was known as 'Witchfinder General' by the time this woodcut was printed in 1647, though he may not have used the title himself. This particular copy was once owned by Samuel Pepys

deluded woman, long suspected of witchcraft and now confessed, introduced two believers and the watchers to a menagerie of pets in her dark home, an enclosed space bristling with fear and expectation: in the circumstances a sinister interpretation was more likely than an innocuous one, not least because Elizabeth Clarke actually *told* those present that they were seeing the devil's imps. She explained that five of the creatures were her own (including a pair given to her by her mother), and that two were on loan from Anne West of Lawford; the imps were not fussy about whom they suckled. Anyone found with marks like hers was a witch, she declared, although the absence of marks was not necessarily proof of innocence. She went on to describe meetings with Satan, the ways in which he was worshipped there, and how he had pestered her until she gave him permission to kill a selection of livestock, specifically Robert Tayler's horse and Richard Edwards' pigs.

On hearing this, Hopkins set off into the night, his greyhound at his heels. He went straight to the house of Richard Edwards, whom he informed that Widow Clarke had confessed to bewitching his property. Hopkins left there between nine and ten o'clock, and made for home. On the way, his greyhound spied a small white creature the size of a kitten and gave chase. Hopkins watched as the creature ran circles round his dog, but was unable to see clearly what happened. The next he knew the dog had returned to his side, whimpering, its shoulder bleeding from what Hopkins assumed to be the bite of an imp. Arriving at his house, Hopkins saw what appeared to be a huge black cat-like creature squatting on a strawberry bed in the yard. The beast fixed his gaze for a moment, then darted towards the gate. The greyhound raced after it, but with less enthusiasm this time, and soon gave up the pursuit. It skulked back to its master, 'shaking and trembling exceedingly'.

The next morning, Lady Day – start of the new year – Hopkins and Stearne gave Grimston and Bowes a full account, requesting that Elizabeth Clarke be formally questioned. The magistrates insisted that she be allowed to rest, so that she would be clear-headed. The female watchers had held to their posts until midnight at least, at which point more imps had appeared and Clarke had alleged that Anne West was responsible for various deaths: a woman at Lawford, a clothier's child at Dedham, and the wife of William Cole of Manningtree. The jaded search-women gave evidence now, as did their male companions, who confirmed what Hopkins and Stearne had said. A man named George Turner also came forward, to say that after Elizabeth Clarke was apprehended he had asked her whether two and a half years earlier she had caused his brother's death by casting his ship out to sea. She had informed him that Anne West had raised the fatal storm.

Thomas Turner of Manningtree is swept away by a storm raised by Anne West

Once the witness statements had been taken, Clarke was roused and taken before the magistrates. They encouraged her to start at the beginning, and a woeful tale unfolded. About six months earlier she had been gathering kindling near her house when Anne West passed by. West had expressed pity for Clarke's disability and poverty, telling her 'there was always wayes and meanes for her to live much better then shee did', and promising to lend her a kitten that would bring her food. Several nights later, two furry creatures had visited and promised to 'helpe her to an Husband, who should maintaine her ever after'. Overjoyed at the prospect, Bess Clarke had let the creatures suckle her.

There was pity in this, but horror was the emotion that drove events forward. Elizabeth Clarke had revealed herself to be Satan's servant and had implicated others. The detail in which Stearne later remembered such experiences suggests that he started to keep a notebook, as William Dowsing had to record the destruction of religious images. In Stearne's record of his destruction of witches, the name of Elizabeth Clarke would have been entered on the first page. He and Hopkins understood that the path ahead would be rocky and their work difficult and dangerous; what Christian mission could be otherwise? Yet their goal was clear. The past few days had begun the fulfilment of their avocation, and by producing what Stearne called 'true and strange effects', searching and watching had proved an effective means of aiding God's providence to break a witch's resistance and so penetrate her mysteries. Unwittingly, Elizabeth Clarke had set Matthew Hopkins and John Stearne on a journey, for as Stearne later recalled, she 'was the first accused, and her markes and confession the beginning of our knowledge'.[72]

3

The Initiation

——•——

AROUND MID APRIL 1645 Matthew Hopkins had business in
Colchester, once the Roman capital of Britain, now a bustling
godly town of poor weavers and rich Dutch merchants. Before
returning to Manningtree he rode up to the old Norman castle. For
three centuries it had steadily decayed until it was fit only to be used
as a gaol; in the 1630s parts of the roof had collapsed, leading to complaints that the wretched prisoners were exposed to the elements.[1] No
such protest came from the gaoler: it was an office with the worst
reputation for cruelty and corruption. Gaolers beat prisoners, locked
them up for weeks in darkness and without sanitation, then charged
them for their stay. At Colchester, felons were kept shackled; the most
notorious double-shackled, hand and foot. As a special punishment
inmates were shut in 'Little Ease', a high alcove reached only by
ladder, or 'the Oven', a cramped windowless hole in the ground. All
prisoners slept on bare stones and filthy straw, and during the wet
season the walls of the prison ran with water. Fatal illness was so
common it had a name: gaol fever. Long before they could be tried,
convicted or hanged, many prisoners perished from a combination of
cold, malnutrition and disease.[2]

Even without a pass, Hopkins could have relied on his appearance
and bearing to gain him entry. Witches were supposed to be 'close'
prisoners – that is, denied visitors – but Hopkins persuaded the gaoler,
Stephen Hoy, that he had good reason to see the women held there.
Through the great arch in the gatehouse, and beyond the rampart and
ditch, lay the inner bailey and the keep: a maze of ante-chambers and
narrow staircases. As Hopkins followed Hoy into the crumbling heart
of the fortress, he would have caught the stench of the prisoners before

he saw them. This work was dangerous to the health as well as depressing; but these were dangerous and depressing times, and Hopkins was galvanized by his sense of duty. The gaoler unlocked an oak door studded with nails, and showed his guest through into a small room where the smell of human waste intensified and sounds of movement and murmuring could be heard. There was no natural light here. Leading off this space were two cells, one for men, the other for women. Opening the door to the women's cell, Hoy held his lantern high to illuminate a tableau of despair. There among the shadows were the huddled shapes of Elizabeth Clarke, Elizabeth Gooding, Anne West and her daughter Rebecca, and Anne Leech and her daughter Helen Clarke.

After the testimonies against Elizabeth Clarke made on 25 March there had been a lull until the second week of April. Anne and Rebecca West had been taken from Lawford to Manningtree, and from there to Colchester; for the time being, Thomas and Prudence Hart would see no more of them. Anne Leech, widow of Mistley, was found to have suspicious marks 'around the privie parts of her body', prompting her to admit a catalogue of offences, including the murder of Richard Edwards' son. She implicated Elizabeth Gooding, and mentioned a meeting at Elizabeth Clarke's house attended by Gooding and Anne West. Someone had read aloud from a book, she had recalled, 'wherein shee thinks there was no goodnesse'. From here the accusations had extended to Leech's daughter Helen Clarke of Mistley Street, the wife of a stonemason and prime suspect in the murder of Anne Parsley, both whose parents had served as Elizabeth Clarke's watchers.

A great store of fear, hatred and resentment had been released by these revelations, as if a community holding its breath had been allowed to exhale. News of the confessions of Clarke and Leech now moved Richard Edwards, Manningtree's richest man, to air his grievances and formalize them at law. Presbyterian victualler Robert Tayler did the same; he blamed Elizabeth Gooding for having infected his horse with an illness that had mystified four skilled farriers. Tayler confirmed that Gooding had a poor reputation in the community, adding that she was often seen in the company of the three malevolent widows suspected as witches, Elizabeth Clarke, Anne Leech and Anne West.[3]

Elizabeth Gooding was questioned, but insisted she had done nothing wrong. Her husband had been a shoemaker, and in 1640 their household was doing well enough to be rated for tax: in this prosperity she was unlike any of the other accused witches. But few people bought shoes when times were hard, and by 1645 Edward Gooding was scratching a living as a labourer while his wife was reduced to begging and borrowing. She went to Robert Tayler's shop for half a pound of cheese, but was refused credit and, according to Tayler, 'went away, muttering and mumbling to her self'. That very night his horse had fallen sick, thrashing around in the stable, its belly rumbling like a fire in a blocked chimney.

Trivial disputes led to threats, encouraging the interpretation of misfortune as revenge. A quarrel between Mary Parsley and Helen Clarke had ended with Clarke shouting into Parsley's house that her baby girl 'should rue for all': the child sickened, and within six weeks was dead. Anne Leech was a poor widow, an outsider from Suffolk, who confessed that she had attacked the horses of a prosperous neighbour because his wife had called her 'a naughty woman'. A cycle of suspicion and exclusion was set in motion. Evicted from her farmstead, Leech was alleged to have killed the new occupant's daughter; another woman had died after refusing to give her a linen bonnet. Tension led to anger, anger to paranoia. According to Richard Edwards, even going near the suspects' houses incurred risk. They were beacons of evil, radiating malign power.

Despite the weight of this evidence Hopkins saw the need for more, and that was why he had gone to Colchester gaol: to make a deal with Rebecca West. Having isolated her from the rest, Hopkins invited her to repeat what she had confessed at Lawford, gently manipulating her into becoming an informer for the Crown. By this means the girl would save her neck, and he would uncover the full extent of the witches' conspiracy. Hopkins realized that they might sweat blood to get these women into court, only to see them walk free because the proofs were too weak. The most recent trials – of two women in 1638, and Anne West in 1641 – had ended this way. In fact, as the witch-trials of the last thirty years had demonstrated, it might not even be enough that Elizabeth Clarke and Anne Leech had made full confessions, or that Helen Clarke now admitted to having fed milk-pottage to a dog-like spirit called 'Elimauzer' which had persuaded her to deny Christ.[4] Hopkins decided they would need a first-hand account of a sabbat, from a witness whose innocence and penitence would win over a jury and satisfy a judge that the case fell within the compass of the law.

In her interview with John Edes at Lawford Rebecca West had described how she first gave her heart to the devil as a child, some seven years earlier. He had appeared to her and her mother in various shapes, including that of 'a proper young man' who asked Rebecca to turn from God. Subsequently the devil became her deity, providing for her and protecting her; he was, it seemed, an idealized man in a household where men were missed.[5] To Rebecca he was father, master, brother and, in due course, lover. Even as she grew into adolescence she made no distinction between these roles: they added up to love. While she and her mother were living at Rivenhall the patriarchal values of George Francis, one of the chief inhabitants, were such as to cast a long shadow over a disreputable widow and her daughter. But witchcraft reversed the flow of power, as when Francis's only son was cut down – like reaped barley, Anne West had said – leaving the parents to suppose that he had fallen victim to a witch. Rebecca West remembered her mother slyly remarking that if Master Francis thought the boy bewitched, then surely he was right.

That Rebecca West had damned herself and her mother was transparent; but Hopkins was aiming higher. He had flexed his muscles at Manningtree, and Elizabeth Clarke had given him the names he and Stearne required; now he needed to know more about the rendezvous with Satan mentioned by Anne Leech. Spurred on by the promise of liberty, that day in Colchester Castle Rebecca West described the daemonologists' darkest fantasy: the story of the sabbat, and of her initiation into the cult of witches.

Some details differed from what she had told John Edes: seven years became one, bringing events forward to early 1644. One afternoon Rebecca was at work when her mother encouraged her to be finished by sunset. When Rebecca asked why, Anne West whispered that she had an appointment in Manningtree and would like Rebecca to accompany her. Tasks completed with half an hour of daylight to spare, Rebecca and her mother started out on the road to Manningtree, and as they walked Anne West made her daughter promise that whatever she saw at their destination she would keep the closest of secrets. Rebecca promised. They arrived at a house where they met Elizabeth Clarke, Anne Leech, Elizabeth Gooding and Helen Clarke, who asked mysteriously whether the girl was prepared. Anne West replied that she was, so the women sat on chairs arranged in a circle, and the proceedings began.

Demons shaped like dogs and kittens appeared, jumping into the laps of everyone except Rebecca. Asked if she wanted to join the witches' society, Rebecca said yes, whereupon she was made to swear on a book that she would keep their secret even if 'the Rope were about her necke, and shee ready to be hanged'. If she betrayed them, 'shee should endure more torments on earth then could be in hell'. As soon as Rebecca had given her word a demon leapt up, kissed her, and 'promised to doe for her what shee could desire'. Then it suckled her at the teats found by the search-women, a ritual John Stearne called 'the sealing of the Covenant with her blood'. But this proved to be a mere token of the devil's love. One evening in the autumn Rebecca was going to bed when he appeared, this time as an irresistible young suitor. He kissed her on the mouth with lips as cold as clay, and they were married there and then – 'a fearful thing to declare', remarked Stearne later on. In his own account Hopkins described the wedding vows thus: 'He tooke her by the hand and lead her about the Chamber, and promised to be her loving husband till death, and to avenge her of her enemies.' At this point in the ceremony, her heart melting, 'shee promised him to be his obedient wife till death, and to deny God and Jesus Christ'. After that, Rebecca confessed, the devil became her instrument of revenge upon Thomas and Prudence Hart, and 'shee tooke him for her God and thought he could doe as God'.[6]

Her story told, Rebecca West was returned to her fellow prisoners, and Hopkins rode back to Manningtree. The next day, Friday 18

April, Hopkins appeared before Sir Harbottle Grimston and Sir
Thomas Bowes. As he relayed the girl's confession to them it was
recorded by the clerk as evidence. Once everything had been signed
and sealed, it was ordered that Rebecca West should be taken back to
Manningtree.[7] The magistrates retired to their country homes for the
weekend, and returned to Manningtree on Monday. Rebecca West's
story, recounted a third time, was subtly different again. The seven
years that had become a year now shrank to a month, moving her initiation to a time just before Elizabeth Clarke's arrest. The confession
also specified *maleficia* against named individuals:

> . . . forthwith their Familiars appeared, and every one of them made
> their severall Propositions to those Familiars, what every one of them
> desired to have effected: And this Examinant saith, that first of all the
> said Elizabeth Clark desired of her Spirit, that Mr Edwards might be
> met withall about the middle bridge, as hee should come riding from
> Eastberghoult in Suffolk; that his Horse might be scared, and he
> thrown down, and never rise again.

Elizabeth Gooding wished harm upon Robert Tayler's horse; Anne
Leech asked for a cow to be lamed; her daughter Helen wanted a
neighbour's pig to die and another to be lamed; which left Anne and
Rebecca West. The mother asked 'that shee might be freed from all
her enemies, and have no trouble'; the daughter that her imp might
paralyse Prudence Hart down one side of her body. The witches
agreed to meet again, Rebecca West told the magistrates, and so went
their separate ways.[8]

In the coming days, three more witnesses came forward. Apprised
of Rebecca West's confession, Richard Edwards confirmed that as he
was returning from East Bergholt one evening, near Manningtree's
middle bridge his horse had indeed reared up. As he was struggling to
regain control of the reins, he had heard a sound 'much like the
shrieke of a Polcat'. Fortunate to avoid a fall, he had arrived home in
a state of shock, and told his wife and neighbours what had happened.
His statement was added to the growing pile. Next, Prudence Hart
was summoned from Lawford: she described her painful miscarriage
and paralysis, attributing all her misfortunes to the Wests, Rebecca in

particular. Finally, the minister John Edes gave his account of the girl's confession.[9] It seemed that the witnesses, witchfinders and committing justices had the case covered now; whether the trial focused on conspiracy, conjuration, apostasy or *maleficium*, they would be ready.

The women in Colchester Castle might have comforted themselves with the thought that convictions would be difficult to secure – especially might Anne West, who had already been cleared twice. With the exception of her daughter Rebecca, none of them could have imagined how hard Matthew Hopkins was working to ensure a successful outcome.

Listening to Rebecca West describe her initiation had been an initiation of a sort for Hopkins too. In the Stygian depths of Colchester Castle he had glimpsed a diabolical nether-world beyond even what Elizabeth Clarke had confessed, and in it he saw an opportunity to overcome the problem of proof in the courts. In time he and Stearne built on this information, but for the moment both men receded from the picture as the magistrates Grimston and Bowes went about their duties with renewed purpose. Grimston was a philosophical and peaceable man but also highly principled, with half a century's experience of defending truth in religion and politics. Any doubt he may have had about the Tendring Hundred accusations was offset by his intolerance of evil and his sense of his own responsibility for justice. Not all justices and judges believed that witches copulated with the devil or transformed themselves into animals; but the social and spiritual danger of witchcraft was real enough. Concern was intensified by war and rebellion, a time when the old superstitions would crumble, clearing a plot on which to raise a new moral nation.

Around the same time that Hopkins gave them his evidence, 18 April 1645, the magistrates received a worried delegation from Thorpe-le-Soken. Thorpe was a crowded and divided agricultural community south-west of Manningtree, enclosed by cliffs and marshland and overshadowed in trade by Harwich to the north. There was a high street, a market-place and, backing onto the churchyard, an inn where the vestrymen met to discuss parish matters. In 1643 these men and their supporters had prompted the ejection of their vicar, a

Laudian ceremonialist who believed that religious dissenters should be burned at the stake; he had started slander proceedings to clear his name, but soon gave up. His godly replacement also faced rowdy opposition, however, as an 'intruder' to the vicarage. Like the vestrymen, the overseers of the poor also gathered at the inn, to distribute charitable relief. Inflation and consequent impoverishment had blighted the lives of English working people for at least two generations, but since the start of the civil war the cost of livestock and grain had risen even more dramatically – 12 and 15 per cent respectively – while wages and parish handouts had stayed the same.[10] Men and women who had once just about been able to make ends meet were dragged into the depths of poverty without hope of rising again.

Margaret Moone, widow, of Thorpe-le-Soken, was one of these.[11] While rising prices hit buyers hard, sellers were in clover, and she had been a victim of greed, evicted from her cottage in the 1620s when a man named Rawbood offered an extra ten shillings a year in rent. Capitalism beat custom every time. On this occasion, however, Widow Moone hit back, or so it was claimed. The Easter after she was evicted, Goodwife Rawbood, 'a very tydy and cleanly woman', was chatting to a neighbour, waiting to go to church, when she was engulfed by an army of lice, so dense 'they might have been swept off her cloaths with a stick'. The evicting landlord's brother, Richard Caley, was present, and swore that these long, thin creatures formed no part of God's creation.

Margaret Moone was blamed for much else besides, mostly deaths of livestock, and spoilt food and beer. One crime stood out, however: the murder of a child. In 1640 Moone had asked Henry Cornwall, a yeoman farmer, if he would swap his bill-hook for a basket of apples. He agreed. At home, Cornwall ate an apple and was taken sick 'with an extreme shaking and pain in all parts of his body'. Knowing Moone to be a suspect woman who had already been questioned about witchcraft, Cornwall's wife threw the rest of the poisoned fruit away. But Goodwife Cornwall fell sick anyway, as did their baby daughter Joan. The whole family languished for weeks, and finally the child died.

Now, at last, the Cornwalls saw an opportunity for justice. Supported by two of his neighbours, Henry Cornwall took the initiative against Margaret Moone. No doubt it was they who went to Manningtree for a warrant, and there hired two of Manningtree's search-women, Frances Mills and Mary Phillips. Widow Phillips nearly did not make it to Thorpe: crossing a footbridge, she received a savage blow to the head that knocked her from the bridge into several feet of water. Struggling to the bank, she caught her breath and looked up to see whether her assailant was still in the vicinity. There was no one there, nor, she imagined, had there been anyone there: it was the forces of darkness that were against her. Soaking and in shock, she pressed on towards Thorpe, where she met Frances Mills and the three local women appointed to help them. When they were taken to where Margaret Moone was being held, the suspected woman snarled: 'Manningtree Rogues . . . Who [the] Devill sent for you?'

Widow Moone did not undress willingly for the searchers, but she had little choice. Frances Mills took the lead in examining her, and quickly found what she described as 'three long teats or bigges in her secret parts, which seemed to have been lately sucked'. These were not haemorrhoids, Mills insisted: she knew, because she suffered from those herself. Moone was asked to surrender her familiars, to which she replied that she would if the women gave her some bread and beer. This they did. Moone dipped the bread in the pot of beer, placed it next to a hole in the wall, and marked a circle around the pot. The searchers watched in silence as Moone called out 'Come Christ, come Christ, come Mounsier, come Mounsier.' When nothing happened Moone flew into a rage, railing against her 'Devillish Daughters', who she said must have stolen her imps. She recommended that they be searched too, for they were 'naught'; the two sisters were duly examined, and the same bodily marks discovered. Judith Moone confessed only that her mother had recently threatened her for refusing to fetch a bundle of wood, and that the same night 'she felt something come into the bed, about her legges, being at that time broad awake'.

After the searching came the watching, which took place over the weekend of 19–20 April. Henry Cornwall did the first stint with another man. As Moone paced up and down something dropped from her skirts, filling the room with an unbearable smell. When they asked her what the thing was – it had looked like a rat – she challenged them to try and catch it. They demurred. Nothing much happened until Monday 21 April, when news spread that Moone was about to confess. Neighbours rushed to the scene, and heard from the witch's own lips that she had twelve imp-disciples, among them 'Jesus', 'Jockey', 'Sandy', 'Collyn', and 'Mistress Elizabeth'. All her sins spilled out: she had spoiled a batch of Philip Berriman's bread; made Philip Daniel's horse break its neck as it pulled his cart downhill; destroyed a pig and a cow belonging to Henry Robinson; and killed Thomas Cooker's cow. Worst of all, she had murdered Henry Cornwall's daughter Joan. All this was written down, ready to deliver to the magistrates.

Magistrates hear evidence from two witnesses in deferential pose.
A scribe makes a record of their depositions to be forwarded to an
assize court

Grimston and Bowes were busy dealing with the Manningtree witches, and did not make it to Thorpe for another week. On Friday 25 April they travelled to Little Bentley, accompanied by searchers Elizabeth Hunt and Priscilla Briggs. There, Susan Sparrow testified that thirty years earlier she had lived with Mary Greenliefe of

Alresford, who had a bad name even then. The two women were so poor that they shared not only a house but a bed, in which their daughters – both then around the age of fourteen – also slept. One night they were all asleep when Susan Sparrow was roused by Mary Greenliefe's daughter crying 'Oh Mother, now it comes, it comes, oh helpe mother, it hurts me, it hurts me.' Sparrow told the girl's mother to wake her in case anyone thought it was the sound of imps being suckled; but Greenliefe was impassive, remarking that she did indeed suckle imps and promising they would come to both girls in due course. The next night, Sparrow's daughter screamed. Flinging her arms round her mother's neck, her face wet with tears, she sobbed that something had bitten her leg. In the morning, Susan Sparrow found above the girl's right knee a bruise the size of her hand; it lasted a month. Sparrow suspected that one of Greenliefe's imps was the hare she sometimes saw sitting outside their house – a peculiar tameness in a wild animal. Once a dog ran at it, then froze as if held by the hare's gaze. The dog died soon afterwards.

That same day, 25 April, Grimston and Bowes were taken to Alresford to find Mary Greenliefe, now a widow in her eighties. The searchers set to work, and discovered genital excrescences that to them appeared unnatural in size and shape. Greenliefe said she had never noticed them, and could only think she had been born like that. She admitted having seen the strange hare, but denied it was her imp.[12]

Rumour or the latest intelligence directed the justices next to Wivenhoe, a port three miles south-east of Colchester divided into factions by the war and recently deserted by its royalist minister. They were approached by Elizabeth and Daniel Otley, who accused Mary Johnson, a sailor's wife, of having bewitched their child the previous autumn. Johnson had given the Otleys' small child an apple and a kiss, whereafter the child perished. Alice Dixon, a neighbour now on remand for witchcraft herself, had accused Johnson of slipping a rat-like imp through a hole in the Otleys' front door, 'bidding it go rock the Cradle'. Dixon and Johnson had blamed one another, but only Johnson had made the mistake of protesting her innocence over and over – a strategy bound to arouse suspicion. Next, Elizabeth Otley herself had fallen dangerously ill, and scuffled with Mary Johnson, trying to scratch her face to break the spell. Sure enough, as soon as Otley saw a trickle of blood between the witch's teeth, she felt her health returning; her appetite came back and she was able to sleep. Taken before the magistrates now, Mary Johnson vehemently denied the charges against her. Grimston and Bowes ordered that she be watched, and promised to return within a few days.[13]

After the weekend, the magistrates arrived in Thorpe-le-Soken to see Margaret Moone. She denied everything, including her previous confession, but Henry Cornwall and others deposed at length about what she had said. Grimston asked Richard Caley, the witness to Goodwife Rawbood's lice, whether Moone had been in command of her senses when she confessed, to which he answered that she had spoken 'very plainly and very intelligently, discoursing of some things done long before, her memory serving her very exactly'. On the subject of his daughter's murder, Cornwall was emphatic: Moone had owned up to this 'freely and voluntarily . . . without any question being asked'. But what interested the magistrates most was Margaret Moone's admission that she had been a 'partner' to Elizabeth Clarke in the murder of Richard Edwards' son at Manningtree, and that she had also helped sabotage Edwards' brewing enterprises.[14] The news from Thorpe, spreading to Manningtree, seemed to supply further proof that a secret association of witches was plotting to tear down Christian society in the Tendring Hundred.

In late April and early May Sir Harbottle Grimston and Sir Thomas Bowes, following the twisting lanes through the hills and hollows of their dispersed estates, discovered witches in an ever-widening area. Around every corner they encountered people who now felt it both safe and worthwhile to voice their suspicions, and with rising clamour. Their charges dated back anything between a few days and a few decades.

Several women from the coastal town of Great Clacton were suspected, at least three of whom had already confessed. The vicar, Joseph Long, had arranged for them to be questioned and prosecuted, an act of leadership that won him much-needed approval. Known as a cruel exacter of tithes, a foul-mouthed drunk and a pluralist, the previous year Long had been censured by a court and deprived of his second living at Fingringhoe. He had also displayed Laudian tendencies, which was not surprising since his patron was the Catholic recusant Lord Rivers of St Osyth. Long's fervent pursuit of witches – specifically, three generations of the Cooper family – was a bid to reintegrate himself in the moral life of his community. As at Thorpe, feelings ran sufficiently high for the Manningtree searchers to be paid from the parish chest.[15] This was not a decision Long could make alone: the parish had decided it was time to be rid of the witches in their midst.

Joan Cooper, an eighty-year-old widow, confessed to having become a witch in the 1620s, and to having entertained three familiars, two mice and a frog – 'Jack', 'Prickears' and 'Frog' – which she sent on a killing spree in the neighbouring parish of Great Holland. Labourer's wife Anne Cooper (possibly Joan Cooper's daughter-in-law) also confessed to keeping imps; hers were called 'Wynowe', 'Jeso' and 'Panu' and suckled 'on the lower parts of her body'. She had corrupted her own daughter with another two. Neighbours blamed Anne Cooper for deaths going back several years, and implicated a widow named Mary Wiles as well, accusing her of also suckling Anne Cooper's imps. Body-searches conducted by Priscilla Briggs and two women from Wivenhoe, Helen Mayor and Elizabeth Hunt, provided confirmation. Prior to her examination by the magistrates, Wiles had confessed to having obtained two of her familiars from a yeoman's wife named Elizabeth Hare. Challenged with this accusation, Hare had raised her hands towards heaven, imploring God for a providential sign if she were guilty. The result was sudden and remarkable. According to Roger Hempson, another leading figure in the Clacton witch-hunt, 'she shaked and quivered, and fell down to the ground backward, and tumbled up and down upon the ground'. Since then, it was noted, Hare had been incapacitated.[16]

The magistrates also took evidence at Kirby-le-Soken and Walton-le-Soken, where Elizabeth Hunt and Helen Mayor searched a pair of women accused of killing children and feeding imps.[17] In Wivenhoe, meanwhile, Annabel Durrant, from nearby Fingringhoe, threw herself frantically behind the prosecution of Mary Johnson, claiming she had poisoned her two-year-old son. Goodwife Durrant had first met the witch when they passed each other on a road. Johnson had stroked her child's face and given him some bread and butter. It took the boy eight days to die. Annabel Durrant's grief had been manifested as a physical pain lasting several months – like childbirth, she told the magistrates. One day, startled by an apparition of Mary Johnson, she was struck dumb and lost the use of her arms, until the constable came to her bedside to show her a warrant from Manningtree. She felt better immediately and agreed to testify. But on the morning that the coach carrying Grimston and Bowes arrived in Wivenhoe, George Durrant went upstairs to help his wife get ready and was himself struck down with chest pains. Collapsing onto the bed, he lay wheezing and sweating, denouncing Mary Johnson and pointing at a buzzing hornet that had entered the room. 'It comes, it comes,' he cried. 'Now goodwife Johnsons Impe is come. Now she hath my life.' It was at this moment that part of the wall in the room fell down, raising the Durrants' torment and terror to near-hysteria.

After the searchers Briggs, Mayor and Hunt had examined Johnson, Annabel Durrant agreed to endorse their written accusation that Mary Johnson had allowed familiars to suckle between her legs.[18] Grimston and Bowes bound the witnesses to appear at the next assizes, committed Mary Johnson to gaol, then headed back to Manningtree.

But there was little time for rest. On Saturday 3 May Grimston set off to deal with the accusations flying about his estate at Ramsey, a hamlet near the port of Harwich for which he was MP. He may already have ordered the searching and watching of Sarah Hatyn and the widows Elizabeth Harvey and Marian Hocket mentioned earlier. Francis Stock, the former constable whose family had suffered at Hatyn's hands, linked Hatyn to Hocket and her sister Sarah Barton, a resident of Harwich. Barton was duly arrested. Accompanied by John Felgate, Stock hurried the four miles through the wastes and marshes to the tiny grid of streets that made up Harwich Town. The borough court here tried a witch every few years, often at the instigation of sailors – sailors were notoriously afraid of witchcraft, and suspicious-looking women were apt to beg from laden vessels in dock.[19] At the gaol, a one-roomed lock-up close to the harbour, Felgate and Stock began their interrogation of Sarah Barton. If violence was used, it was seen only by the gaoler and the other prisoners. The petrified woman confessed that her sister had given her three imps named 'Littleman', 'Prettyman' and 'Dainty', and that she had cut off the teats on which she suckled them and covered the wounds with plasters. Stock and Felgate returned to Ramsey to meet the magistrates and two other Manningtree witchfinders, Mary Phillips and John Stearne.[20]

On the bodies of Sarah Hatyn and Elizabeth Harvey a local midwife, Bridget Reynolds, showed Widow Phillips several teats, each the length of her little finger. Although no marks were found on Marian Hocket's body, Widow Harvey tearfully accused her of having sent three reddish mouse-like creatures that had nibbled between her legs at night until she permitted them to harm Francis Stock.[21] Sarah Hatyn and Marian Hocket, cowering before the magistrates and praying that Harvey would hold her tongue, refuted all the charges against them. But John Stearne, who was bound as a witness against Hocket, was quite convinced by the evidence of diabolical familiarity put before him.

In the summer of 1668, more than twenty years after the East Anglian witch-craze, a clergyman in Ipswich sent the Secretary of the Royal Society a story concerning a peculiar occurrence at Great Bromley Hall, home of Sir Thomas Bowes.[22] A man had turned up at the Hall, begging for help. Not only was he 'Emaciated & look[e]d like a Skeleton', but a cacophony of sounds was heard coming from his stomach: the raised voices of scolding women, confused, discordant singing, and clashing musical instruments. The man blamed three witches in his parish, who were duly arrested and taken before the magistrate for examination. Bowes ordered them to lift their curses, but, knowing the secretive ways of such women, sent them into a walled courtyard so they could confer. After some discussion, they began to quarrel: two of the suspects had agreed to release the man from their magic, but the third refused. Sure enough, only one noise remained audible. The afflicted man died anyway; but so did the three women – executed for the crime of witchcraft. Over the years, some of the details had changed – originally there was a fourth suspect, and the odd sounds were different – but there is no doubt that the story described events which had taken place in the first week of May 1645.

The accused were Rose Hallybread, a pauper in her mid sixties, Joyce Boanes, the wife of a yeoman, and Margaret Landish and Susan Cocke, both of whom were married to husbandmen. They came from Chiche St Osyth, known to locals as 'Oosy Island', a decaying port tucked away behind salt marshes and joined to the sea by a maze of creeks. Most of the men living there were labourers, sailors and dockers whose families eked out a living harvesting oysters and by begging and pilfering. St Osyth was also a place of powerful Catholic traditions, having been a destination for pilgrims before the Reformation. According to legend, Osytha, an Anglo-Saxon queen who founded a priory at Chiche, was beheaded by the Danes and the village renamed in her honour. The priory had been dissolved by Henry VIII and became a country house, and was sacked by a mob early in the civil war.[23] By 1645 St Osyth was a community worn down by commercial decline, raw with religious emotion, and about to rekindle memories of ten witches from sixty years earlier.

Towards the end of April 1645 old Rose Hallybread and her friends were walking together when they reached the house of a carpenter. Hallybread asked an apprentice there if she could take some wood-chips for kindling, but he refused. It was a decision he would regret: a short while afterwards the boy's master was standing at his bedside, watching him convulsing and screaming that Hallybread had bewitched him. On Tuesday 6 May, in Sir Thomas Bowes' parlour at Great Bromley, the carpenter described how his apprentice

> . . . hath crowed perfectly as a Cock; sometimes barked like a Dog; sometimes violently groaned beyond the ordinary course of nature; and struggling with such strength (being but a youth) that four or five strong men were not able to hold him down in his bed; and sometimes sung divers and sundry perfect tunes: And that this Informant could not perceive his mouth to open, or so much as his lips to stir all the time of his singing.

Next, the suspects had their say. Hallybread confessed that fifteen or sixteen years previously a neighbour had given her an imp, which she had nourished on oatmeal and the suck of her own body until it disappeared. Then, late in 1644, Joyce Boanes had given her a new imp, like a small grey bird, which she had squeezed into a cranny of a neighbour's door to murder his young son. Most recently her imp had joined forces with those of Boanes, Margaret Landish and Susan Cocke to invade the body of a youth with strange noises and sickness. This Joyce Boanes confirmed, saying that her imp, 'Rug', made the youth bark, Hallybread's made him sing, Landish's made him groan, and Cocke's, perhaps predictably, was responsible for his impression of a cockerel. Boanes had also sent her familiars to slaughter newborn lambs and cause devastation throughout St Osyth. In her confession, Susan Cocke extended the litany of crime; but Margaret Landish admitted only to having suckled imps, and that against her will.

Resentment between neighbours was endemic at St Osyth. According to Susan Cocke, once when she was pregnant she had been denied a bowl of curds by John Spall's wife; and she had been enraged when Thomas Mannock's wife had refused her alms on the grounds 'that shee was a young woman, and able to worke for her living' – a sarcastic jest, since by then she was in her mid forties. So when Spall's sheep and Mannock's pigs died, she was glad.[24] Another yeoman farmer estranged from his poor neighbours was Thomas Bumstead. He beat a boy he caught with his fingers in his honey, incurring the wrath of the boy's mother Rebecca Jones. Jones, who had been born outside St Osyth, was a widow of little credit, struggling to feed her children, for whom begging had become a way of life. When Bumstead and his wife died, Rebecca Jones, like Susan Cocke, believed the devil had made her vengeful dreams come true.

The pattern emerging from the accusations seemed to indicate a cycle of malice and misfortune that extended out of St Osyth and into the villages of Great Holland, Great Clacton and Little Clacton.[25] As a young woman Rebecca Jones had been maidservant to a farmer at Clacton, and confessed to having caused harm there. Joan Cooper – the witch whose imps were 'Jack', 'Prickears' and 'Frog' – was also from Clacton, and now confessed to having murdered a woman there. Pent-up ill-feelings about food, money and charity, long harboured as much by those who gave as those who received, were pouring into the open. Anne Cade, one of the women Sir Harbottle Grimston had sent for trial in 1638, now admitted that she had murdered the child of the woman later killed by Cooper, because the woman had refused her a pint of milk.

While the St Osyth suspects were being transported to Colchester gaol, Rebecca Jones was searched by experts Helen Mayor and Priscilla Briggs, assisted by two local women who had already proved their worth. A clergyman, George Eatoney, also took a leading role. It is likely that Jones was watched afterwards, and that the confession heard by Grimston and Bowes on Friday 9 May was the fruit of that labour. One morning, she said, while in service at Clacton, she had answered the door to 'a very handsome young man', who had greeted her and asked to see her left wrist. Pulling a pin from her sleeve, he had pricked her and taken a bead of blood onto the tip of his finger. Then he left. Some weeks later she had been on her way to St Osyth to sell her master's butter when a ragged man with bulging eyes jumped out at her. He produced three mole-like creatures and invited her to care for them, feed them milk and, with discretion, make use of their powers. Jones had accepted, and had named the imps 'Margaret', 'Amie' and 'Susan'. Before long she was experiencing the unprecedented satisfaction of watching her enemies suffer.

On the same day Joan Cooper confessed to the magistrates that she had killed several children at Great Holland. Anne Cade was similarly forthcoming. In June 1638 she had been acquitted of murdering a butcher's wife, but now confessed to having killed the woman's daughter. She also admitted to having used a deadly sparrow-like imp called 'Sparrow' to fatally torture Grace Wray, a woman of yeoman stock who had refused to give her tuppence. Goodwife Wray's child had also died. Two other women were accused at Great Holland, Anne Thurston and Bridget Mayers, wives of a husbandman and a seaman respectively, but neither seems to have confessed. Like Joan Cooper, Mayers was accused of having cared for a secret mouse-imp called 'Prickears', an offence for which Dorothy Walters had sworn as a witness, perhaps even as a searcher. But Walters was under suspicion herself, and within a month she too had been committed for trial. Seven witnesses from Great Holland and Little Clacton were formally bound to give evidence against Anne Cade, including two members of the Freeman family. They did not bring an indictment of their own, but were enraged by Cade's confession that one of her three mouse-like imps had been sent after Robert Freeman, and had inflicted a small but lethal bite to his knee.

Grimston and Bowes had heard enough for one Friday afternoon. The paperwork was set in order, the magistrates' coachmen were summoned, and Rebecca Jones, Anne Cooper and Anne Cade were despatched to Colchester Castle to join the other witches.

On 30 May 1645 Leicester was taken for the king by Prince Rupert of the Rhine, but whether this was due to his diabolical power or the weakness of the garrison was debatable. The war was not going well for Parliament. In Scotland the Marquis of Montrose – himself linked to witches through his mother – had the Covenanters on the back foot, and the way was open for the king to advance through the Midlands into East Anglia.[26] County towns like Cambridge, Chelmsford and Bury St Edmunds were on high alert, expecting the onslaught at any time. The townsfolk were fearful and fractious, over-stretched and overtaxed. Maintaining a garrison was expensive, and unpaid defenders were almost as dangerous as the enemy. The principal concerns of the county committees were money and order, resources and obedience. Civil discipline was tightened and parish constables became powerful enforcers; unwilling men were pressed into service and deserters hanged.[27] It is surprising that communities fighting for their lives should have been so bothered with witches; but it was precisely because they seemed to threaten from within an existence already threatened from without that sensitivity was so great. Witches pillaged the neighbourhood, invaded the body, and besieged the soul; and the sense that victory in the field depended on godliness at home made hunting them feel like part of the war effort.

Elsewhere, Fairfax was preparing the New Model Army for a counter-attack, with Oliver Cromwell as his General of Horse. What the troops of the New Model lacked in experience they made up for in self-belief and integrity. They were Cromwell's 'russet-coated captains': men of all social ranks who prayed as hard as they trained, many of them radicals as contemptuous of presbyteries as they were of bishops. By the start of the summer their crusading spirit was already an inspiration to two obscure provincial gentlemen preparing to unleash their own counter-attack against the forces of Antichrist. Matthew Hopkins and John Stearne had learnt a great deal about the discovery of witches since the end of March. So far the magistrates Grimston and Bowes had been foremost in taking the initiative; but by June Hopkins and Stearne were gaining confidence. Accompanied by the Manningtree search-women Frances Mills and Grace Norman, the novice witchfinders examined three suspects at Langham, a depressed cloth town near the godly community of Dedham. Both men swore to appear as witnesses against Mary Starling, the wife of a yeoman farmer, accused of murder and familiarity with evil spirits; Hopkins also endorsed the prosecution of a widow named Susan Wente, again for feeding imps.[28]

The witch-hunt had spread east from Manningtree to Harwich, and south towards the mouth of the river Colne, but without straying far beyond the territory controlled by Grimston and Bowes. Of the twelve communities that comprised the Tendring Hundred, not one had escaped involvement. By contrast, very few prosecutions originated in any other place at the time – a remarkable fact, considering that Tendring was just one of several hundreds in its division, and that there were six divisions in Essex as a whole.[29] No suspect living west of Colchester was prosecuted, and there was but a single case south of Chelmsford, on the coast at Leigh.[30] In other words, the greater part of the county was completely untouched, despite suffering stresses and suspicions similar to those prevalent in Manningtree. Public life at this time was conducted within intersecting spheres of alliance, acquaintance and affinity, a geography of power that determined the success or failure of individual ambitions. Chance associations in this place at this time through kinship, office-holding, shared political loyalties and religious persuasion had made an intensive witch-hunt possible, but not an extensive one.

Where favour opened doors, disdain might equally keep them closed, of course, and many puritan gentry had mixed feelings about self-motivated enthusiasts like Hopkins and the iconoclast

William Dowsing.[31] The fact that the witchfinders ceased to operate in Essex in the summer of 1645 was almost certainly the result of opposition raised against them at Colchester. Like other East Anglian towns during the civil war, Colchester was preoccupied with urgent matters of assessment, sequestration, requisition, recruitment and desertion. But here, fears for civic order created no consensus about the need to purge witches, and criticism of the witch-hunt was pointed and voluble. The political divisions that had polarized opinions in the town on a range of issues by 1642 make this criticism more understandable.[32] Chamberlains' accounts for 1645–6 record no payments to the witchfinders, suggesting that they were not authorized to be there, although an invitation to Colchester from the mayor, Robert Buxton, to Sir Harbottle Grimston, Sir Thomas Bowes and 'the Rest of the Gentlemen' is intriguing.[33]

One source of opposition among the townsmen may have been concern for the welfare of prisoners in the gaol. The six women visited by Hopkins in April had grown in number to at least thirty by June, and conditions were unspeakable. Overcrowding and poor sanitation doubtless explain why in the space of a fortnight between May and June four of the women died: Joan Cooper, the old widow from Great Clacton; Rose Hallybread, one of the four from St Osyth; Elizabeth Gibson, a middle-aged housewife from Thorpe-le-Soken; and sixty-year-old Mary Cooke, recently interrogated by Hopkins and Stearne at Langham. At hastily-convened inquests the coroner recorded verdicts of 'visitation by God', but without specifying the cause of death; it was almost certainly bubonic plague, carried by fleas, or typhus, passed on by the lice with which every prisoner was infested – typhus could kill within forty-eight hours of infection. That year, it was said, the air was 'so infectious that dogs, cats, mice, and rats died', and birds dropped from the sky.[34] At the least, those who objected may simply have feared that packing the gaol so full would breed a pestilence likely to spread throughout the town. And of course the risk of revolt made it undesirable to hold so many prisoners in time of war.

At least part of the controversy that beset the witchfinders in Colchester was factional. During the summer of 1645 they became involved in the prosecution of a townswoman named Alice Stansby, a poor widow from the parish of St Giles. The itinerant Wivenhoe searchers Helen Mayor and Elizabeth Hunt examined her body, observed by four women from neighbouring parishes. Widow Stansby insisted that she was entirely innocent, but the body-search suggested otherwise. A weaver's wife from Holy Trinity deposed that

> Alice Stansby had in her secrette p[ar]tes two bigges the one about the bignes of a strawe and about halfe an inche long: And after that the said Hellen Mayor had taken that bigge & laid it upon her finger it blead: And the other bigge was about a quarter of an Inche longe & a great deale bigger then the other, & blood did appeare at that short bigge.

A midwife from St Botolph's testified that she had 'seene maney women, but never did see any women in such a condic[i]on as shee the said Alice Stansby was'.[35]

Although neither Hopkins or Stearne gave evidence in this case, the presence of the Wivenhoe search-women surely implicates them. Widow Stansby was to spend many months in gaol, and was probably convicted at the borough sessions, but was finally exonerated. The proceedings racked up a bill of at least £1 13s. 4d., thirty-three shillings of which went to the borough attorney. Such expense lavished on a single prisoner – equivalent to more than £1,000 today – may well have raised eyebrows among Colchester's well-connected ratepayers, especially opponents of the mayor, Robert Buxton, who had authorized the payment.[36] John Stearne later referred to action taken by two of the most powerful townsmen to have a condemned witch reprieved, and it is reasonable to suppose this was Alice Stansby. These same men also prevented several other suspects even being questioned, and caused Stearne and his fellow witnesses to be summoned before a court. When Stearne failed to appear, a writ outlawing him was issued. This sounds worse than it was, and would have been reversible had he pleaded innocence or petitioned for a pardon.[37] But the witchfinders had been called into disrepute in Essex, and it was time for them to sound the retreat.

On 14 June 1645 the victory of the New Model Army at Naseby drove the king's army westwards, making it safer for Hopkins and

Stearne to head north into Suffolk. Here, among old friends and kin, they were received with greater enthusiasm than at Colchester. But possibly Naseby had a deeper significance. Letters captured after the battle revealed Charles's intention to make concessions to Catholics, a plan which to radical minds proved him a traitor prepared to entertain idolators, as witches entertained Satan's imps. Among the puritans in government, the Independents led by Cromwell – hawks who desired the royalists' absolute defeat – now had a weapon wherewith to silence the doves, mostly moderate Presbyterians like the Earl of Manchester. After Naseby, England moved closer to godly revolution and the fulfilment of the New Model's vow to tear down Babylon. It was with the same fire in their bellies and bellicose joy in their hearts that the witchfinders rode out of Manningtree that summer, heading for horizons both dark and new.

4

Dark Horizons

———•———

THE WITCHFINDERS CROSSED the river Stour into Suffolk in June or July 1645, arriving first in the godly enclave of Dedham Vale.[1] This was the heartland of further reformation, a network of parishes where enforcement of the Solemn League and Covenant was as strict and the will to suppress idolatry as strong as anywhere in England. Heading north over the rolling landscape, lined with hedgerow and wild honeysuckle, punctuated by farmstead and copse, Matthew Hopkins could have spied the tower of St John's at Great Wenham, the parish where his father had laboured to build a new Jerusalem. James Hopkins' ministry had not been in vain: visiting St John's the previous year, the iconoclast William Dowsing had noted that 'there was nothing to reform'.[2] For the son, it was time to summon the strength that had sustained the father. Political and military zeal surged through public life, encouraging decisiveness in the war against Satan. Without an appreciation of that inner commitment – that Christian passion – it is impossible to understand what happened over the course of the next few weeks, when as many as 150 Suffolk men and women, from some fifty towns and villages, were identified as witches.

But reformers who acted on the authority of God alone easily fell foul of the law. There is no doubt that John Stearne heard the clarion call of heaven, yet he had not involved himself in investigations at Manningtree without a magistrate's warrant. Since this would have been invalid outside the Tendring Hundred, it is tempting to think that the witchfinders had obtained a more comprehensive commission from higher up the chain of command, such as that procured by Dowsing from the Earl of Manchester. Contemporaries certainly came to believe that Parliament, or a representative thereof, had appointed Hopkins an agent with 'a Commission to discover Witches'.[3] At the very least, he and Stearne would have required letters of safe-conduct to avoid apprehension as spies: strangers who came from the direction of the enemy camp without a written pass, or unannounced by trumpet or drum, were liable to be strung up, according to the custom of war.[4]

Even if they carried the right papers, the witchfinders still needed to choose their destinations carefully. A written invitation was to be preferred, but local knowledge alone did much to ensure a warm reception. Communities already noted for their godly enthusiasm were most likely to find their way onto the itinerary, especially those

Iconoclasts burn religious art perceived to be idolatrous

where destructive outbursts against Catholic gentry and Laudian clergy had erupted in 1642. Dowsing's iconoclasm of 1643–4 had also paved the way for the witchfinders, mapping areas of receptivity and resistance. More than a simple assessment of popular fervour was required: it was necessary to hook up with networks of patronage and favour – the means by which success had been achieved in the Tendring Hundred. Hopkins and Stearne had learnt this lesson the hard way at Colchester. More than any other single factor, the fate of a witch-suspect was determined by the politics and religion of the prevailing local authority, usually the lord of the manor. In Suffolk, however, the salient characteristic of the places targeted by the witchfinders was not parliamentarian dominance but local conflict with royalist, and in many cases Catholic, traditionalists. Rural puritanism was not nearly such a cohesive force here as in Essex; instead, the godly kept their edge by detesting recusants in their midst.[5]

Armed with authority and intelligence, what the witchfinders needed was a plan. It was decided that Stearne should take the western side of the county while Hopkins set off to the east. The line between them was roughly the old Ipswich-to-Norwich road. West of this lay twenty-three places where accusations are known to have been made; it is possible to place John Stearne in sixteen of them, Hopkins in just one. Of twenty-six locations east of this line, Stearne appears only once (and that barely a mile from the main road), whereas there is substantial evidence of Hopkins' presence on that side. Perhaps this seemed the most efficient means of cleansing the county, and a fair division of the work. They may have visited a similar number of places, but Stearne was never more than a few hours' ride from his family at Lawshall; Hopkins, the younger, unattached man, embarked on a trek of perhaps three hundred miles, venturing as far east as Dunwich and as far north as the river Waveney. Whereas Stearne's destinations suggest several short sorties, Hopkins' were so far-flung that it seems likely he made a single circuit. Perhaps it suited his image of himself as a lonely but valiant Christian crusader. Thus it was that at a point near Great Wenham – if not at Wenham itself – the witchfinders went their separate ways.

Allowing for rest and refreshment, a horseman might cover fifty miles in a day, more if he took advantage of the ferries on East Anglia's many navigable rivers.[6] Roads varied in quality from mere tracks flattened by cattle to maintained carriage roads. The passability of many routes depended on the weather, for in rain horses got stuck in mud or slipped on hillsides. To navigate, travellers used the sun and church spires; maps had become plentiful during the war, and officers kept great tubes of them strapped to their saddles; very likely the witchfinders did the same.[7] Hopkins at least stayed at inns, although he probably accepted private hospitality whenever it was offered. Later he was to complain about his expenses, describing how 'his Companie' would travel twenty miles to investigate a case and might have to stay a week: for this, he said, he would be paid just twenty shillings (but that was a month's wages for a labourer or foot soldier). Exactly what 'his Companie' comprised is hard to say. He also mentioned that he needed to maintain three horses: perhaps one carried a servant, the other luggage; or perhaps they were for search-women. At this time, a mounted trooper spent a shilling a day feeding his horse. It cost sixpence to replace a horseshoe, and on long journeys saddle-cloths wore out quickly; these cost a shilling. There were inns where a man could find a bed of sorts for sixpence, but a gentleman's quarters – the kind of private rooms Hopkins expected – were not to be had for less than a shilling, a tariff that usually included a simple supper. One typical hostelry of the mid 1640s served bread, chicken, cheese, neatsfoot, rabbit, tripe, beer and wine, and charged an additional two shillings for a fire to be laid in the grate.[8]

The search-women certainly inflated the cost of the operation. Though they were usually paid directly by the parishes that hired them, they still needed bed and board on long journeys. Yet the witchfinders simply could not do without them. When John Stearne began work in the village of Shelley, three miles west of Great Wenham, Manningtree veteran Priscilla Briggs was at his side. Also present was Abigail Briggs, either a local or a relative along for the ride, who was put in charge of watching.

Situated some distance from the highway and flanked by low hills, Shelley was a remote agrarian community comprising 1,000 acres, a church, and a scatter of houses and huts along a river-bank. Here, as elsewhere, the balance between survival and disaster was sensitive to ripples in the moral order: sin attracted the devil, enraged God and broke the equilibrium. In the summer of 1645 paranoia engendered by this atmosphere was directed at the calloused soul of Thomasine Ratcliffe. A downtrodden widow, she found herself in situations

where her begging both embarrassed and frightened the neighbourhood. A man cutting down a tree who refused her woodchips became
smothered in lice; a farmer who crossed her lost cattle and pigs. When
a child drowned in the river, the grieving mother accused Ratcliffe,
who warned her to take care of her other children; a short while
later she was bereaved a second time, as doubtless she had feared
she would be.

Overseen by Abigail Briggs, Widow Ratcliffe was held in custody
for six days. Though she was not deprived of food or sleep, the pressure on the old woman was extreme, and in the end she confessed to
having an unnatural power over her enemies. She explained that
twenty years earlier, she had been lying in bed when an apparition
resembling her husband, who had died the previous month, emerged
from the shadows and began drifting towards her. At first she felt sure
her husband had returned, but when the apparition spoke – 'with a
hollow, shrill voyce' – she realized it could not be him, and became
afraid. The next she knew, the thing was lying heavily on top of her.
In a terrified gasp she asked whether it was going to kill her; the spirit
said no and then, switching to her husband's voice, added soothingly,
'I will be a loveing husband to you.' Stearne asked whether she had
consented to share her bed with this fiend; she admitted she had.
Thomasine Ratcliffe was handed over to Priscilla Briggs for physical
examination: two incriminating teats were discovered. Their work
done, Stearne and the two Briggs women accompanied the widow to
a magistrate, and with mixed disgust and satisfaction heard her admit
that Satan, the creature who had promised to be her husband, was
nothing but a liar.[9]

Eleven miles to the west lay Polstead. The passing traveller saw a
serene cluster of hamlets surrounded by ponds and cherry orchards,
but beneath the surface lay simmering discord. There was no single
large estate in the area, therefore no one manorial lord to exert leadership; nor was there spiritual unity in the parish. Traditionalists had
learnt to hide their reverence for the Gospel Oak of St Cedd, and had
been further subdued by William Dowsing's visit the previous April:
forty-five precious images in painted glass had been sized up by the
iconoclast, then smashed with a hammer. Doubtless this would have

gladdened the hearts of those puritans who in 1630 had left Polstead to join the great migration to New England; here, as throughout Suffolk, reform came too late for many. Those left behind had coped as best they could, never losing sight of their day of liberation.

The predictions of the Book of Revelation were coming true in the fields and pastures of Dedham Vale. As the idolators had been cast out and their monuments of superstition toppled, so too would witches and sorcerers be held to account. At Polstead this meant Joan Ruce. Modestly well-off until 1640, she had lost her husband and fallen on hard times, reduced to a state of dependence and desperation that bred suspicion among her neighbours. For these people, the arrival of John Stearne brought relief. His interrogation of Widow Ruce revealed a weighty conscience, knotted with anxiety and guilt. She confessed she had caught three chickens that transformed themselves into mice called 'Touch', 'Pluck' and 'Take', and in a strange hollow voice had tempted her with the food, clothes and money she needed so badly. Ruce described how she had wavered as good and evil fought for possession of her soul, before finally surrendering. With her permission the mouse-spirits had suckled her greedily, and thus the pact was sealed. From time to time the imps came home with a few shillings, and in return she was obliged to let them perform baneful deeds that filled her with remorse. At least now, she sighed, her conscience 'had ease'. This sense of relief was not shared by John Stearne, to whom each confession was a reminder of the work still to be done.[10]

Everywhere he went the witchfinder heard variations on the same story. In the town of Sudbury another poor widow, Anne Boreham, confessed that 'as she awoke out of a dreame' she saw two ugly men fighting in front of her. The victor climbed into her bed, and exhibited the usual heaviness and coldness — the opposite of the choleric humour associated with masculinity. Her unnatural lover promised her immunity from hell's torments, which struck Stearne as a particularly 'fearefull and subtill delusion'.[11]

Up to this point all the discovered witches had been female, but extending the search into Suffolk confirmed what Protestant clergy had warned of for many years: although men were more morally robust than women, even they remained vulnerable to the devil. Having lived at Long Melford in his youth John Stearne would have known the house where briefly he lodged that summer, and must have been acquainted with Alexander Sussums, a man of modest means oppressed by conscience who came to the door asking to be searched. Stearne undertook the examination in person, and since by convention female suspects were searched exclusively by women, this was possibly a new experience for him.[12] Sussums, anxious to disclose his secret, directed the witchfinder to the place where his marks were, explaining that diabolical imps had suckled him there for more than sixteen years. He could not help this, he told Stearne, 'for all his kindred were naught', including a mother and an aunt hanged for witchcraft and a grandmother burned at the stake. That was enough for Stearne, who saw to it that Sussums was committed for trial.[13]

Sudbury and Long Melford had seen significant anti-Catholic riots in 1642, as had the next two parishes to which Stearne travelled, Great Waldingfield and Acton, where male witchcraft suspects were also examined.[14] At Waldingfield John Bysack confessed to having made a pact with the devil in the shape of a rough-coated dog, which had climbed in through a window and pierced his leather doublet with a razor-sharp claw. In exchange for blood drawn from his heart Bysack received six imps, all in the form of snails, five of which specialized in the killing of particular types of livestock, the sixth in the murder of 'Christians'. He placed the snails on his body to feed, pretending to his wife that they helped to relieve his aches and pains. Goodwife Bysack herself now fell under suspicion, so Stearne had her searched too. She was cleared. Acton had already got rid of its anti-parliamentarian vicar, and was also ready to stamp out ungodliness. Here, a poor man confessed to having bewitched a woman he hated, but protested feebly that he was helpless to reverse the spell – only a white witch could do that.[15]

Each day taught John Stearne a new lesson, and fresh horrors added definition to his nebulous impression of the witches' world. Even so, as he headed north to Bury St Edmunds, he could not have realized how much there was to do.

★

After several miles of indifferent, undulating farmland, travellers on the road from Acton were rewarded by the sight of Lavenham church reaching to heaven as its founders had intended. Its grandeur – in Suffolk, matched only at Long Melford – contrasted sharply with the diminished congregation of ragged fullers, spinners and weavers encountered by John Stearne as he rode into the heart of this angry, impoverished community. A century earlier Lavenham had been one of the richest cloth towns in England; but Continental competition had taken its toll, and most recently an influx of Dutch clothworkers into Essex had established the pre-eminence of Colchester over its rivals.

One of the few families to have preserved their power and prosperity was the Copingers, lords of the manor and long incumbents of the rectory. But even their authority was not unassailable in these days of doubt and upheaval. Dr Ambrose Copinger died late in 1644, and was succeeded by William Gurnall, a committed puritan who as an undergraduate would have known Matthew Hopkins' brother at Emmanuel College. Knowledgeable about witches and fearful of their power, Gurnall had been rector of Lavenham for just a few months when John Stearne arrived in 1645, but already his apocalyptic style of preaching had fired up the idealists to whom Stearne now addressed himself. The signs were encouraging. In 1642, as Stearne was probably aware, more than three thousand people had gathered in the town centre to sack the houses of Catholics and Laudians; now they could turn on their witches.[16] Gurnall encouraged his parishioners to see the passions of their lives in the broad setting of war and transformation. The bloodiest battle that had ever been fought, the rector inveighed from the pulpit, would be 'but sport and childes play' compared to the furious end-game in prospect between the elected saints and their arch-enemy, Satan.[17] It was a future both terrifying and uplifting.

It was evident that William Gurnall had first-hand experience of witchcraft. He refuted the idea that witches needed to receive alms to cause harm, and described how, like Aaron in the land of Egypt, they sent plagues of lice to their enemies 'to make them loathsome to themselves'. He was also well-versed in the ways that witches were enslaved to the devil, and related how some had confessed to being tormented by imps begging destructive missions.[18] No doubt he heard

Anne Randall's confession in 1645. With Stearne leading the questioning, she admitted having made a pact and having entertained two kitten-imps called 'Jacob' and 'Hangman' for more than thirty years. Marks were found on her body. Among various *maleficia*, she admitted having raised a storm to kill William Baldwin's horses after he refused her some wood, and added that she had sent her imp 'Hangman' to destroy Stephen Humphrey's pig: Humphrey had come home one day to find Randall begging at his door, and 'chid her, or gave her such words as she liked not of'.[19]

The most serious confession involved Henry Copinger, lord of the manor, into whose family Sir Harbottle Grimston had married. Like the possible acquaintance between the rector William Gurnall and Matthew Hopkins' brother, this connection suggests that Stearne may have had a personal introduction to Copinger.[20] Whether Copinger would have needed a witchfinder to give him the confidence to pursue Anne Randall at law is another matter. Randall may already have confessed to having sent an imp to remove bushes belonging to him, laid out ready for planting, in retaliation for Mr Copinger having angered her. Perhaps the intention to enclose part of his estate with a hedge, thereby undermining her livelihood, was what had made her so furious. Mysteriously, the bushes all turned up on another man's land, which would have been incriminating for him had a witch not owned up to the crime. Randall was not the only woman to express hostility towards Henry Copinger. After she had been searched by some townswomen, Susan Scot confessed to Stearne that 'the Devill us'd to have the use of her body, and spoke to her with a great easie voyce, and that she had two Impes like Cats and Dogs, which sucked on those markes found upon her'. She admitted a list of sadistic and subversive acts, the most heinous being the murder of Copinger's beloved daughter, Thomasine.[21]

For his part William Gurnall, though appalled by such confessions, remained circumspect in his thinking. Like many puritan clergy he was at pains to keep the malevolence of the devil before the eyes of his parishioners, without himself losing sight of the fact that there were those who would blame misfortune on witches without searching their own consciences. 'Never let us spit at the witch for suffering the devil's imps to suck on her body', he advised, 'while we can prostitute our souls to any of his lusts.'[22] The line to be drawn was a fine one.

John Stearne spent the next fortnight travelling what appear to have been two connected circuits, examining suspects in at least twenty villages. There is no need to recount the whole story. No doubt Stearne kept notes of his visits, but even he was selective when he came to write them up, observing that 'if I should goe to pen all of these sorts [of witches], then I should have no end, or at least too big a volume'.[23] Most important to him was not the piling of horror upon horror, but the way his travels provided a practical education, broadening his experience and deepening his understanding of the relationship between man, morality and the spirit-world. Wildly fanatical he may have been, but he was also meticulous, and relished the opportunity to advance a godly cause through learning. His investigations reveal much about order and disorder too, and about the extent to which a century of ideology had permeated the mentality of ordinary people. The chaos he exposed was in part a measure of the self-discipline which English communities had come to expect by the 1640s. In contrast to the humanist's model of an organic commonwealth, or a divine hierarchy of the great chain of being, or the Reformation ideal of the holy household, witches reflected the reality of the impact of political crisis on the life and mood of the nation.

By now Stearne knew broadly what to look for in a suspect, but still the people he examined presented fresh signs of turmoil, secret doubts and desires surfacing from the depths of consciousness. Time and again, simple men and women who had probably never much thought about such things, still less spoken about them, turned to ponder the dividing line between body and soul in order to describe how they understood their existence.

The prevailing emotion was guilt. In Bramford, a village of about three hundred people some three miles outside Ipswich, five women and two men faced censure. Alice Marsh insisted that although she had given her body to the devil she had denied him her soul, despite having signed a contract in blood. With no prospect of mercy in this life, she pinned her hopes of resurrection on that distinction, however futile it must have seemed to Stearne. The sexual shame hidden in the recesses of Goodwife Smith's mind was revealed when she confessed that 'her imps hange in her secret parts in a bag', producing sensations both stimulating and tormenting. Another feature of the Bramford confessions was their revelation of the traditional fantasy of the poor that against the odds they might improve their lot, amounting to a magical magnification of their own sense of themselves in an oppressive society. This would explain why so many servile familiars shared the names of their masters and mistresses, like 'John', the toad-imp that John Chambers said he had used to murder his own child.[24] After all, in God's great chain, what but animals was left for paupers to command?

These people's lives, like the households they inhabited, were upside-down and out of control. Elizabeth Richmond of Bramford no longer trusted her husband or any other natural patriarch, but turned instead to a man calling himself 'Daniel the Prophet', thereby placing herself at the centre of her own warped biblical story. John Stearne recorded how 'Daniel' – an illusion he knew to be demonic in origin – 'bad her not be afraid of him, for he was so [i.e., a prophet], and tooke her by the hand, and bad her trust in him and he would avenge her of all her enemies'. This reassuring spiritual presence had embraced her, asked for her love, and required her to renounce God, Christ and their ministers.[25]

A desire for the alleviation of suffering lay behind all the Bramford confessions. After an interrogation lasting eight days a man named Payne confessed to Stearne that many times in his hard life the devil had encouraged him to hang himself; in the end, his route to spiritual oblivion had been witchcraft. In wet conditions, to push a plough through clay and chalk was a grinding labour, and Payne, despairing as he sweated and cursed, had been approached by the devil, who asked for his soul. Craving relief, he had agreed. The same mental anguish was conveyed by Alice Wright of Hitcham. As a child sixty years earlier she had met a strange youth who enticed her and her brother into a field with the promise of money. Who can say what dangerous game they were playing, or into what abusive trap they had stumbled? Whatever happened, that day was seared into Goodwife Wright's memory. Forever after, she admitted, she was 'much troubled and tormented, and in extreame paine' as her imps nipped and sucked at her, incessantly demanding evil tasks. Her neighbour Anne Cricke confessed to Stearne that she had sent a familiar to bewitch a pig belonging to a farmer who had denied her eggs. The farmer had cut off the pig's ears and burnt them, a remedy that forced the witch to break cover. Stearne asked Cricke why she had gone to the farmer's house to own up, to which she replied: 'she could not keepe from going . . . they must needs goe [when] the Devill drives.'[26]

The interrogation of Anne Cricke reveals that more than a hunger for practical education lay behind Stearne's *modus operandi*. Clearly fascinated, he enquired about her satanic pact and whether 'she did grieve for it after she had done it', to which she replied with characteristic fatalism that 'when it was done it was too late to repent'. His questions kept coming. She said 'she was left weak, and the Devill got the upper hand of her for want of faith, through want and otherwise', indicating that her soul was as malnourished as her body. She declined to go into detail about the consummation of her marriage, and when the witchfinder asked whether the devil had 'performed nature or not' – that is, achieved an erection and ejaculated – she feigned ignorance. Unquestionably prurience drove the interrogation forward; but at the same time, in the interests of observation, experiment and the extraction of legal evidence, Stearne was committed to getting under every witch's skin. He approved of the fact that Alice Marsh of Bramford was searched several times, until it became apparent that her requests to change her clothes gave her an opportunity to disguise her teats. At Coddenham, Stearne himself noticed that an obstinate woman on whom marks had been found was carrying herself strangely. He ordered a second search, which revealed that the teats had changed in size and shape, after which the suspect made 'a large confession'.[27]

The search for truth – which was the impetus behind reformed religion and natural philosophy alike – could be as incisive as the surgeon's blade or as blunt and crushing as a Juggernaut. The confessions noted by Stearne and recorded by the Suffolk magistrates indicate that suspects had been starved of sleep and that confinement, intimidation and physical violence had caused the mental health of all but the most resilient to deteriorate. Arrest itself was 'an instantaneous, shattering thrust, expulsion, somersault from one state to another . . . a blow that shifts the present into the past'.[28] But that was only the beginning. Isolation and surveillance led to confusion and self-doubt, compounded by the disintegrative effects of the *tormentum insomniae*. After several nights awake suspects entered a void between waking and sleep, their eyes open but their brains dreaming. Neither they nor their examiners considered the possibility of any natural explanations for the phenomena they described in such detail and with such conviction. The experience of chronic sleeplessness was like moving through a borderland between the body's existence in life and that of the soul after death.[29] Fact fused with fantasy: nothing was too mundane to be elevated to supernatural significance, no suggestion from the witchfinder too outlandish to harden into truth. Some suspects even started to hallucinate – which for even the soundest and most learned minds of the seventeenth century was a sensation inseparable from genuine supernatural manifestations.

Sometimes people's perceptions were so distorted that to seek the objective reality contained in their statements is all but futile. A woman from the village of Wattisham explained to a magistrate that injuries to her forehead had been caused when one of her imps hurled her from her chair while she was being watched by neighbours; they, meanwhile, claimed not to have seen this happen because they were too busy trying to stop another imp escaping from the fire into which they had flung it. Exactly what was going on remains a mystery.[30]

John Stearne took it all at face value; to equivocate was to prevaricate, and that was hazardous. At Creeting St Mary, a parish outside Stowmarket, Anne Hammer confessed to him that shortly after her mother's death she had been visited by two imps, which she duly sent to kill a child. Soon afterwards, a calf had asked her to serve him as her lord in return for earthly dominion and an escape from the fires of hell. But as all witches soon discovered, the real prizes of satanism were less glittering. As Stearne later recalled,

> . . . she said the Devill never performed any thing but revenge, and that the Devill in the likenesse of a black man us'd to come in at the key hole, and to bed with her, and have the use of her body, but was heavier and colder, and lay all over her as [a] man, and us'd not to speake but onely to aske to lie with her, and as she thought performed nature.[31]

Here, as so often, Stearne's questions can be read between the lines of the confessions. Another Creeting witch, Nicholas Hempstead, was browbeaten by him. Like a godly minister battling to save a sinner, the witchfinder lambasted Hempstead with 'the hainousnesse of the sinne, and Gods Judgements, and Gods mercie', exhorting him to repent. As in the tales of religious conversion of which puritans were so fond, at first Stearne's efforts earned him only abuse, so he abandoned his subject as lost. But a little while later – because of exhaustion, a troubled conscience, or God's grace – Hempstead asked for Stearne to come back, whereupon he begged forgiveness and confessed to a diabolical pact. With a sorrow Stearne found remarkable, Hempstead admitted having killed the horse of a constable who had pressed him to be a soldier, and to having further undermined the war effort by setting his imps on the best horses in Colonel Rossiter's regiment.[32] Such confessions vindicated the ambitions of Parliament and of militant puritans like John Stearne. They were rousing providential signs to men who, contrary to Catholic belief, held that the age of miracles had passed. But in Stearne's book, they were also a means of obtaining what he and Matthew Hopkins needed above all: proof that would stick in a court of law.

In 1645 England's godly reformers were active and passive at the same time, impatient and impetuous yet content to allow providence to shape their decisions. This accurately reflects John Stearne's mentality and movements in Suffolk that summer as he passed from village to village, making enquiries, setting searchers to work, and pocketing his fees – a few pence or shillings in each place – before moving on. Without fail he saw the hand of God in the circumstances of his departures and destinations: a chance invitation; a premonition that he was needed; the clemency of the weather; and the soundness of roads and bridges. Guided by such contingent factors as these Stearne followed a north-easterly course across the county, through the neighbouring villages of Rattlesden, Wetherden and Bacton. Here his conviction that the canker of evil had eaten deep into the heart of the nation hardened, and he redoubled his efforts to have it excised.

Rattlesden, low in a valley between Sudbury and Stowmarket, made a profound impression. No doubt Stearne paid his respects at Clopton Hall, the hilltop residence of Lieutenant Colonel John Fiske, lord of the manor; Fiske's wife was certainly at home, for she was expecting her first child.[33] Rattlesden was not a happy place into which to be born, for it was strained by poverty and social dislocation – numerous families had left for New England – and literally haunted by the past. Local legend told of the shuck of Clopton Hall,

A stereotypical devil hands out familiar spirits (or possibly wax images of potential victims) to a group of witches, watched from above by monstrous demons

a black devil-dog with the head of a monk; in fact, demons and witches abounded at Rattlesden. As always, Stearne listened to the principal inhabitants, probably at the Moot Hall in the shadow of the church where he received the approval of the elderly rector, William Bedell. Old Mother Orvis, Stearne learnt, was the infernal matriarch, matching initiates with imps from her collection. Presumably she had supplied Meribell Bedford – one of those wretches, Stearne observed, 'who with greediness gape after worldly wealth, or feare poverty'. In around 1639, Bedford confessed, a black thing called 'Meribell' had been sent to her, which had promised her power and prosperity. She had then received four new imps – a spider, a beetle, a wasp and a moth – which crawled towards her. As they sucked her blood, so she felt her veins infused with the vitality to unleash violence upon her neighbours.[34]

Elizabeth Deekes – a 'silly ignorant young woman', according to Stearne – said that her mother, executed as a witch, had bullied her to renounce God. Deekes had resisted; but the sins of the mother were visited upon the daughter and she, feeling her resolve melt, 'did make a League and Covenant with the Devill, and sealed it with her bloud'. Stearne gave instructions to the search-women before turning his attention to two male suspects. The first, John Scarfe, was related by marriage to both Deekes and Mother Orvis, and was known to godly neighbours as 'a heathenish man'. He confessed that at the outbreak of war he had made pets of three grey rats – 'Tom', 'Will' and 'Harry' – which he kept in a box and fed from the two swollen marks Stearne had located on his body.[35]

The other man, Henry Carre, Stearne described as a 'Scholler fit for Cambridge (if not a Cambridge scholler)', but this may have been a sarcastic comment on his pretensions to learning, possibly even on his membership of a radical sect.[36] When Stearne asked him about some strange contusions on his body, Carre confessed that his 'hairy and heavie' mouse-familiars had suckled him for two years. In a state of emotional dissolution, Carre admitted that want had driven him to the devil, and said that he now accepted his fate. Stearne unleashed a broadside of questions and entreaties, but was denied the *coup de théâtre* he had pulled off at Creeting St Mary:

> . . . seeming to bewaile his condition, [Carre] said, that he had forsaken God, and God him, and therefore would confesse no more, he said, untill he came on the Gallowes to be hanged, for he had confessed enough for that, and then he would confesse all, and make all other[s] knowne he knew of, but in the meane time, he would confesse no more, nor did, yet he was much importuned to it, but that was always his answer . . .

93

Henry Carre and the other Rattlesden suspects were taken before a magistrate. Stearne washed his hands of them, and climbed back into the saddle.[37]

This work of Stearne's was not concerned just with destroying evil by the application of righteousness, but extended to banishing the malign influence of the past. Since the reign of Elizabeth, the Clopton family, one of the most powerful dynasties in East Anglia, had spawned Catholic recusants, and something of that legacy hung over Rattlesden – explanation enough of the monk-headed shuck, which was said to guard a secret store of gold. Similar ghost stories had abounded in many places since the dissolution of the monasteries, fixing the memory of desecration and confiscation in the oral tradition.[38] At a time of acute religious sensitivity, airing suspicions of witchcraft was an exorcism of sorts, a chance for honest folk to make a stand against the powers of Antichrist and corrupt tradition.

Half an hour's ride away, at Wetherden, the situation was more stark. There the Sulyards, another recusant family, lived in the manor house in Haughley Park, where they employed many local people as servants. A woman recorded as 'Elizabeth Fillet' was brought to John Stearne's attention; this was a slip of the pen for 'Tillott' – a family connected with the Sulyards, possibly even sharing their religion.[39] More people craved godly reformation, however, and now they got their way. First offensive images were removed, then offensive people. In February 1644 William Dowsing had chiselled superstitious brass inscriptions from the Sulyard tomb and elsewhere in St Mary's church, to the weight of sixty-five pounds; as usual, the metal was sold and the money returned to the parish to be spent on further godly improvements – like hunting witches.[40]

A cobbler named John Spink recalled how in about 1638 Elizabeth Tillott had been angry with his manservant because her shoes had not been mended. From this time, the shop was haunted by a strange rat that was impossible to catch. It disappeared only once Spink decided to shoot it, but was replaced by a mole that also darted across the floor like quicksilver. On another occasion Spink's wife had refused to visit Tillott when she lay sick, saying 'she shold lie and rot before she wold come at her'. Consequently, the Spinks' child had suffered spasms and an infestation of lice. The Spinks' suspicions of Tillott lay dormant for the next seven years, until the arrival of John Stearne. Hearing that a witchfinder had come to Wetherden, Thomas Jennings rushed to inform Elizabeth Tillott, and to ask her if she would agree to be searched. 'Let the honest wemen come and she wold be content', was her defiant reply; the devil had forewarned her, she said, and had recommended that she kill herself. Tillott was watched and searched, as was another woman, whose imps resembled a beetle and a fly. Both women were committed for trial. Within a year or so the Sulyards also suffered in Suffolk's godly purge. At the start of the civil war they had been menaced by a mob, and eventually they were forced off the manor.[41]

From Wetherden John Stearne passed through Haughley as he climbed the hill and followed the rising and falling contours towards the north-east, the horizon by turns the nearby brow of a corn-field or a hazy band of treetops in the distance. Where open fields met woodland, the broad plains dipped and narrowed into winding tunnels of dappled light and shade as branches reached to interlace overhead; in such places, even leisurely travellers would break into a canter in case of thieves and vagabonds. Barking dogs and the whiff of woodsmoke heralded the end of every journey, and now meant that Stearne had reached Bacton, a community in the grip of social and spiritual peril. Here, corrupted by sin and inflamed by desire, a group of women had traded their souls to reverse the natural flow of power in the parish. Perhaps only an unshakeable conviction of his election preserved the witchfinder's nerve and prevented him giving up his lonely heroic fight and returning to the safe mundanity of his earlier life. He was a new Daniel, Bacton the lion's den – an English Babylon. Such thoughts brought him refreshment at each polluted place where he dismounted as the darkness closed in.[42]

The principal Bacton inhabitants from whom Stearne heard their suspicions and sought a mandate for his actions were Henry Prettyman, lord of the manor and owner of 450 acres; John Marleton, the moderate puritan rector of St Mary's, presented to the living by the Prettymans; a substantial yeoman farmer named Garnham, whose family owned more than two hundred acres; and Mr Lockwood, whose estate was comparable to Garnham's. Another well-established landowner brought to Stearne's attention was Widow Hoggard, who farmed cattle on forty acres. Once, people like these had lived in peace with the poor, observing such charitable customs as providing bread and beer for those who came to their doors. But a century of rising prices and the conversion of commons and arable land to pasture had upset the balance. Hard times for the majority meant profits for dairy farmers like the Garnhams and the Hoggards, whose rising prosperity pulled down the shutters between them and the rest. In Bacton, as throughout England, by 1600 the scale of poverty had required that poor relief be organized, with a mandatory collection to support those unable to support themselves. Thus did the difference between rich and poor acquire a legal definition.[43]

Events at Bacton reflected how the poor law had served to heighten sensitivities by 1645. As the prospect of increased revenue tempted landlords to consolidate their estates, tenants defended their right to stay put according to custom. At the same time, everyone from comfortable husbandman to wealthy gentry was obliged to subsidize what many saw as plebeian fecklessness; to make matters worse, many poor people expected alms as well. The newly-prosperous shut the door against beggars, choosing to live with the guilt rather than give away even small quantities of food and money. 'Charity seldom goes to the gate', they told each other, 'but it meets with ingratitude.'[44] As trust faded, this became increasingly true. Even when alms were given, recipients suspected that the donors could spare more; no longer an expression of love, charity had become a medium of exchange, to be weighed in the mind. Puritan moral discipline, which equated idleness with sinfulness, helped to harden the divide. One Laudian minister, ejected from his living in 1643, linked declining neighbourliness to the spread of the new godly order, saying that 'it was never [a] merry World since there was so much preaching; for now all Hospitality & good-fellowship was laid a Bed'. By this time, ballad-sellers on the streets of London were singing the same nostalgic lament.[45]

Donors had their suspicions too, chiefly that the impotent poor might use magic to wreak revenge. To their neighbours, the poverty of these dangerous people was not just material but spiritual and biological, further inflaming their resentments and jealousies. In rural economies fertility was a commodity for a woman, the journey from puberty to menopause an arc of inflation and deflation, of appreciation and debasement. Sexual vitality was female capital: infinitely precious yet impossible to hoard. With age came social ambiguity (especially for widows, spinsters and paupers), and ambiguity brought anxiety to youthful, productive households. In the confines of a moral world now made strange by time, the unspoken fears and transgressive fantasies of an entire parish might converge on a single individual: her life-force became a death-force, her emblems in nature no longer the sunrise and the harvest, but the chill of winter and the midnight moon. Thus Hopkins' and Stearne's conception of the witch – her seduction by the devil, her illusory enrichment at others' expense – was rooted in East Anglian life, part of an ancient urge to survive and reproduce against the odds. So, however hard the witchfinders laboured to cut uniform confessions around their template, in the end the damnable stories that piled up owed as much to the lives of the agrarian poor as to anything to be found in the pages of the learned demonologies published on the Continent. The witch was plebeian fear made flesh.[46]

After one of Widow Hoggard's cows died, another sickened and a mare fell lame, her thoughts turned not to nature or providence but to the grudges of certain women. Her neighbours had also suffered: Prettyman and Garnham livestock ailed, and Garnham's wife believed herself to be under some malign influence after refusing a beggar a pint of butter. The suspect was Margaret Bennett, an unmarried woman in her early twenties, who probably came from outside Bacton.[47]

Goodman Garnham and Mr Prettyman had reason also to fear Mary Bush. Born a Hoggard and now in her sixties, over the years Widow Bush's line had fared less well than that of her kinswoman. Her husband of eighteen years had died in 1630 leaving her childless and penniless. In 1645 she was begging door-to-door to eke out the pittance she received from the overseers of the poor. This had antagonized ratepayers like Mr Prettyman and Goodman Garnham, who saw to it that her regular dole from parish funds was stopped. The rage she expressed at their action may have surprised them; it certainly made them afraid. Elizabeth Heath, a maidservant in the village,

already knew what Widow Bush was capable of, having been trau-
matized by a demonic spirit in the shape of a mouse after she denied
the old woman an alms. She described how, in a panic to save her own
life, she had fought back, scratching Bush's face in an attempt to break
her power.[48]

In league with Bennett and Bush were two other women. Middle-
aged Elizabeth Watcham had probably come to Bacton as a child, and
had not married. Perhaps her parents never fitted in, not least because
as paupers they were regarded as parasites.[49] This was how the
Greenliefes were perceived. Like the Watchams and the Bushes,
Nicholas Greenliefe's family had probably arrived in Bacton during
the harsh years of the 1590s. Apprenticed as a cooper, in 1624 he had
married Ellen Barnard, almost certainly from another migrant family.
The following year she had given birth to a stillborn son, a loss for
which the couple were compensated by the eight babies baptized
between 1627 and 1641. By the time she came face to face with John
Stearne she was in her mid forties, with children aged between four
and eighteen. She often contemplated suicide. Matters of charity
probably led to a falling-out with the Hoggards, leading them to
suspect her of witchcraft, and the hostility was intensified when
elderly Ralph Hoggard threatened to have her searched for the devil's
mark and his horse went lame in consequence.[50] The beleaguered
landowners of Bacton were bristling to see justice done.

One Monday evening shortly after John Stearne's arrival the four
women were arrested, and the rector Mr Marleton heard the confessions of Margaret Bennett and Mary Bush. Bennett told him that the
devil had come to her as a man with cloven feet, and that she had
renounced Christ in exchange for revenge upon her enemies. Their
union had been consummated in a bush and sealed with blood. An
imp named 'Kit', nourished from her own body, had been sent to
infect Widow Hoggard's cows and to kill Goody Garnham for refusing to give her some butter. Cows belonging to others had also sickened and died. Mary Bush talked throughout the night. Three weeks
after her husband died, she explained, a black man had come to her
bedside, speaking in a hollow voice. Creeping beneath the covers, he
had tried to make love to her but 'could not performe nature as man'.

She made a blood pact instead and received two mouse-like familiars, one of which she sent after the maidservant, Elizabeth Heath. Confident of her powers, Widow Bush picked off twenty-three turkeys and several cows, including some belonging to Mr Prettyman and Goodman Garnham who, she recalled bitterly, 'took her collection from her'.[51]

The tale told by Ellen Greenliefe completed the pattern. In the version heard by the magistrates, in 1626, shortly after her stillbirth, her mother-in-law had presented her with three imps like a rat, a mouse and a mole. From that moment, said Greenliefe, she was 'spoiled'. In 'a great hollow voyce' the mole had demanded her body and soul so that he might save her and bestow special powers upon her. Getting ahead of her betters for the first time – or so it seemed to her – she had lamed Goodman Garnham's cow and sent a swarm of lice to torment Master Lockwood. The rat-imp, she recalled, had lamed Ralph Hoggard's horse in return for his threat to have her searched. After nineteen years of suckling her spirits, the noose was tightening around Ellen Greenliefe's neck. The mole, who often scratched her, had issued a warning about the water ordeal, and threatened to drown her and steal her soul if she confessed.[52]

The account recorded by Stearne differed from this. He remembered Ellen Greenliefe saying that the devil *had* penetrated her, and that his body had been soft, cold, and 'so heavie as she could not speake'. That this was not recorded by the magistrates suggests either that Greenliefe was less open with them than with Stearne, or perhaps that the witchfinder's imagination was getting the better of him and his clinical procedures. For all his cold-eyed detachment, Stearne betrayed a weakness for a good story – something he shared with Matthew Hopkins, who that summer had been hard at work elsewhere in Suffolk. He, too, had some fabulous tales to tell.

After the witchfinders' parting in Dedham Vale, Matthew Hopkins' initial destination was probably Chattisham, a village five miles west of Ipswich. There he heard about Anne Alderman, who claimed to have had a finger twisted off by the devil 'for refuseinge to seale the covenant' by which she would forfeit her soul; her body, however, was apparently not so precious to her. On the day of her apprehension she confessed that she had invited the devil into her bed and that his body felt cold. Thereafter she had regularly suckled an imp that she had used to kill her daughter before unleashing it on her grandchild: 'She wished her sons child cold in the mouth', she admitted to her watchers, '& it died likewise.'[53]

The other suspects Hopkins met at Chattisham were Mary Bacon and her husband Nathaniel. Bacon confessed to a watcher, Moses Rayner, that he had made a blood pact with a dog-like devil that promised him an annual income of £14. Mother Skipper in the neighbouring village of Copdock had supplied him with two imps, which he fed from his nipples. One he sent to fetch oatmeal, the other salt. His wife Mary told Rayner and a man named Edward Smith that she had been a witch for eight years, and had received her imps from a witch called Mother Cortnell. The Bacons, together with Anne Alderman, were committed by a magistrate, and Hopkins undertook to back the case against Mary Bacon personally. Within a few months, another Nathaniel Bacon – an adolescent from nearby Bramford and possibly the Bacons' son – fled England for Connecticut, never to return.[54]

The methods used to extract these confessions are as shrouded in darkness as the deeds the confessions described. Those of the Chattisham watchers Rayner and Smith may have been over-enthusiastic, their insistence that the confession of Rebecca Morris was made without 'any violence, watchinge, or other threts' dubious. Hopkins was probably no more scrupulous than John Stearne, and just as averse to handling witches with kid gloves. After all, if they were innocent, they had nothing to fear; but if guilty, then potential harm had been averted. The witchfinders were now used to seeing how isolated cases might be related, like a web of evil unpicked thread by thread. The conspiracy could be traced from Chattisham and Copdock to Hintlesham, one of many outposts of aristocratic Catholicism visited by the witchfinders; Stearne's own town of Long Melford was also thus tainted. The Rivers family, for instance, had recusant branches in the Stour valley, but was based mainly in the witch-hunting centre of St Osyth. At Copdock the infamy belonged to the Forsters, an ancestor of whom had persecuted Protestants there in the reign of Queen Mary; at his instigation a minister had been burned at Ipswich, and the memory lingered.[55]

The offenders at Hintlesham were the Timperleys, whose patronage of local Catholics was no better than entertaining Antichrist – or that at least was what their obstinate recusancy meant to Hopkins and Stearne, as it had to William Dowsing, who had stripped St Nicholas's church of its inscribed pleas to pray for the souls of dead Timperleys. The four women interrogated at Hintlesham may have belonged to this island of spiritual resistance. Bridget Bigsby's husband had died in the winter of 1644–5, whereupon the magistrates ordered that she be returned to her birth-place in Norfolk, to prevent her becoming a burden on the parish. In June 1645 the order was rescinded, but when Matthew Hopkins arrived soon afterwards she possibly wished she had gone after all. In her confession, ostensibly made without duress, Widow Bigsby described how two mice had scratched her foot as she lay by the fire; her grandmother had seen this and 'bad her not be affraid but ent[er]teine the[m] and she shold be avenged of all her enemies'. Within a short time, a voice had commanded her 'to denie god & Ch[rist] and he wold be a husband to her'. She had refused, but still the imps came to feed, and threatened to torment her for as long as she refused to make a covenant with Satan. Marks found on her body seemed to bear the story out.[56]

Another widow, Susan Marchant, was arrested at Hintlesham late one Sunday and confessed the following night that the devil had come to her as she sat milking, singing a psalm. He had asked what good a psalm might do when she was 'a damned creature' – that is, not one of the elect. She had received three imps – two rabbits and a crow – which she had nursed for twenty-eight years; the crow she had sent to lame her brother's cow. Conflict within families reflected the unnatural oppositions of the war, and was also apparent in the other Hintlesham cases. Susan Stegold had found that 'what so euer she wished came to pas', including that her pig should lose its appetite and her husband should leave her. The pig stopped eating; her husband went mad; both died. She said she knew the devil had entered her soul. She had remarried, but was soon wishing ill on her second husband. Joan Potter confessed to having sent imps to kill her own grandchild. After being watched, she confessed she had signed a covenant with the devil using blood from her nose. One of the watchers, Richard Glamfield, reported that the imps had suckled her as she spoke to him. Susan Stegold tried to retaliate by sending a beetle-imp to attack another of the watchers, but it did him no harm.[57]

At Copdock at least four women were interrogated, one of whom, Susan Manners, like Bridget Bigsby at Hintlesham, blamed her grandmother 'for destr[o]yinge her selfe & all her kindered'. Another Copdock suspect, Mary Skipper, implicated by Nathaniel Bacon of Chattisham, was watched for three days before she confessed

> . . . that [the] devill appeared unto her in the shape of a man after her
> husbands death and told [her] if she wold enter a covenant w[i]th him
> he wold pay her debts and he wold carrie her to heaven and that she
> shold never want, w[hi]ch she did & and sined it w[i]th her blod . . .
> & that the devill bad her goe [to] church and make a greate show but
> if she attended diligently he wold nip her . . .[58]

She described having entertained three imps, whose suckling marks were discovered on her body. A note on the legal records to the case of Alice Muntford of Copdock reveals that Mary Phillips and Frances Mills, the Manningtree search-women, were present.

It was not just the efforts of Matthew Hopkins and his searchers that brought the investigations at Copdock, Chattisham and Hintlesham together: Hopkins was supported by the enthusiasm of volunteers wherever he went. Richard Glamfield testified against all the Hintlesham witches and participated in the interrogations at Chattisham; here, Moses Rayner testified against every suspect in the parish. Suspects were also willingly examined by locals at the neighbouring village of Belstead. At Copdock a man named Robert Hitchcock led the way, and ensured that the accused were committed for trial. Instead of being taken straight to Bury St Edmunds, the Copdock suspects were sent first to the gaol at Ipswich – a source of regret for Hitchcock and his neighbours when the keeper sent them a bill.[59]

Like the fees charged by Hopkins, Phillips and Mills, the keeper's bill served as a reminder that witchfinding cost more than just time and toil. The civil war was accustoming people to paying for reformation in blood and tears; but when real wages were falling and taxation to pay for everything from poor relief to arming a regiment was increasing, silver was cherished and its expenditure – even, in due course, on witchfinding – was resented.

5

First Blood

———•———

IPSWICH WAS ONE of the largest towns in Suffolk, a magnet for the entrepreneurs and consumers, labourers and paupers who every day passed through its gates. On high were the recent fortifications, the grand steeples, and the façades of merchants' houses; below, the traders selling the fish that gave the market its pungent aroma. Elizabeth I, visiting, had castigated the townsfolk for the filthiness of their streets. They were no better now; and the moral contamination was intolerable. A decade earlier the bailiffs had petitioned the king, 'grievously complaining against their diocesan', and Bishop Wren had reacted by painting them as models of disobedience and disorder.[1] In the countryside the puritan movement may have been dispersed, but in densely populated places like Ipswich it dominated political life. Observance of the Sabbath was strenuously enforced, and inhabitants of several town parishes were unsparing with their enemies: the fornicators, gossip-mongers, alehouse-haunters, bastard-bearers – and witches.[2]

The extent of Matthew Hopkins' involvement in investigations at Ipswich is obscure; but the evidence – not least recorded expressions of concern about the mounting costs of witchfinding – points to his influence. In the summer of 1645 a town sergeant was sent by the borough authorities to Colchester 'to invite the men of that Towne to come to Ipsw[i]ch by a warrant'; it is tempting to think these anonymous guests were the witchfinders. They dined richly on venison at The Lion in Ipswich on 20 August, less than two weeks before the town staged its first significant witch-trial.[3] The benefits a godly community might derive from his services, Hopkins later stressed proudly, were considerable. At least seven suspected witches were questioned around this time, four of whom were believed to have committed murders. Most notorious was Mary Lakeland, whose terrible fate will be described later. Hopkins made such wretches as these disappear; he uprooted them as if they were so many parasitic weeds sapping the strength of the people. Yet parish income had to go a long way, especially while a war was being fought. Significant costs at St Peter's parish in Ipswich in the mid 1640s included setting the poor to work, mending the church clock, gravelling the path, and copying the Solemn League and Covenant. Money spent on witchfinding would have to be justified against the demands of routine expenditure.[4]

Predictably, there were all sorts of well-known ways to deter, identify and fight witches. One might boil the victim's urine and hair in a bottle, or stick a hot poker in the suspect's faeces. Pricking a drawing of the witch with a pin was believed to bring her running 'speedelye in all hast possible in payne or under payne of eternall damnation'; burning thatch from her house had a similar effect. Cunning folk were also employed to diagnose and reverse witchcraft: suspects might be paraded before a wise woman who would watch for changes in a pail of water. Another custom was that of weighing a witch against the Bible, an ordeal for which suspects readily volunteered. Priests and Protestant ministers alike used counter-magic: some called witches to the font during divine service, and made them repeat tracts of Scripture.[5] Most clergymen, however, respected Church canons. The Jacobean minister and healer Richard Napier asked God to devolve to him 'that gift & power of casting out evill & uncleane spirites', or at least to help him 'discerne betwixt the workes of darknes & the workes of light'. Yet even Napier knew that the most popular methods would always be ones that could be seen and felt: drawing blood, searching for teats, and ordeal by water.[6]

The swimming test – the guilty were believed to float and the innocent to sink – was certainly cheap, and persuasive too; it may even have seemed like a pious ritual, a providential miracle in which the pure element of water rejected those who had renounced their baptism. James I had thought of it in this way – and who was Hopkins to argue with the royal author of *Daemonologie*? The problem was that the test was regarded as a superstition, and it was illegal: by law, to swim a witch was to assault her; if she died, it was murder. God expressed his will in the courtroom, insisted the authorities, without need for judicial ordeals. Effusive proscription was not the same as effective prevention, however. Not only had a king approved swimming, but during his reign pamphlets had helped to popularize it. A printed account of 1613, of a family of Bedfordshire witches – billed as a 'Tragicke Comedie' – described how a suspect's opposing thumbs

The swimming test or water ordeal. The outcome could be determined by the degree of tension applied to the rope, as is clear in this illustration from 1613

and big toes were tied together, and a rope attached to her waist, before she was thrown into a mill pond. Men on either side, holding the rope to stop the woman being carried away, were unable to make her sink however hard they shook. Richard Napier read this little book with interest.[7]

Yet King James's perspective on witches did alter, and by the 1620s he was urging judges to copy his scepticism, not of witchcraft *per se* but of most evidence at law. One immediate effect was a decline in trials; but in time the other consequence, as mentioned earlier, was to force accusers to provide tangible proof that a suspect had entered into a diabolic pact. The adoption of new empirical standards of proof may actually have encouraged the use of brutal and superstitious methods by the people – methods which tested God, and also infringed a suspect's rights as these were enshrined in common law. Even Michael Dalton's *Countrey Justice*, a best-selling legal handbook first published in 1618, advised magistrates 'not alwaies to expect direct evidence [from witches], seeing all their works are the works of darknesse'.[8] Thus did ordeals, experiments and examinations seem all the more necessary. By the 1640s the swimming test, as it was described in the 1613 pamphlet, was widely known, and must have been employed more often than it was recorded.

North-east of Ipswich lay Playford – a few houses, a church, a moated manor house and a water-mill on the river Deben. Evidently Hopkins passed through, mobilizing people to act against Margaret Legat, long suspected as a witch. Seven years earlier the miller William Wells had attributed what looked like wasp-stings on his son's body to the boy having quarrelled with Legat's son. A physician in Ipswich was at a loss for a diagnosis. When Legat went to Wells's house soon afterwards he banished her, swearing to take her to his mill and swim her if she ever returned. She did return, and even sat on his bed, but whether Wells carried out his threat is unknown. He certainly dragged her outside, probably still threatening her, whereupon she begged forgiveness. In 1645 several villagers chosen to watch Legat saw a mole creep under her skirts and suckle her 'in the secret p[ar]ts'. After three days, they said, Legat finally admitted that 'a thing lyved by her like a child but she never saw it nor heard it speake', adding that she was a 'damned creature and if she had not beene taken she shold have done much harme'.[9]

All this was consistent with the expectations of juries and judges. From first-hand experience and works like Dalton's *Countrey Justice* a new generation of magistrates had learnt the evidential value of deponents who could swear to have witnessed – in ascending order of significance – confessions, familiars, and witches' marks. Matthew

Hopkins had made obtaining such proof his business, a fact he demonstrated repeatedly in the remainder of his journey through Suffolk.[10] After leaving Ipswich and its outlying villages behind his next destination was probably Brandeston, sixteen miles to the north-east. Extraordinary events there will be recounted later; for now Framlingham, a few miles down the road, provides the focus of the story. Here the witchfinder was to orchestrate one of his most devastating witch-hunts.

Framlingham swarmed with the ghosts of Protestants and Catholics who had battled for England's soul. For generations the village had been dominated by the Howards, dukes of Norfolk faithful to Rome, who lived in the magnificent moated castle and interred their dead in the chancel of St Michael's. It was here that in 1553 Princess Mary had declared herself queen, making it a rallying point for aristocratic Catholics. Elizabeth I had turned Framlingham Castle into a prison for priests and recusants, but her successor James I returned it to the Howards. In 1635 it was sold to the puritan philanthropist Sir Robert Hitcham, who in turn bequeathed it to Pembroke College, Cambridge with instructions for its future use. When Matthew Hopkins arrived a decade later, the keep was already in ruins, and the site was used as a source of stone and of water, drawn from the medieval well.[11] But Framlingham Castle held an additional meaning for Matthew Hopkins: his family had owned land and tenements there, an estate possibly acquired by his father shortly before his death in the mid 1630s – about the time the Howards sold up. The revenues from this property, it would seem, were a principal source of the witchfinder's inheritance.[12]

Had the Howards remained in Framlingham instead of retreating to Sussex their home would doubtless have been ransacked like so many others, yet even in 1645 there were still Catholics in the parish, thorns in puritan flesh. Local landowner John Waldegrave lived at Borley near Long Melford; a tenant of James Howard, 3rd Earl of Suffolk, he was a prominent Catholic related by marriage to the Rivers family of St Osyth. At the time Hopkins rode into the village, Waldegrave was on the point of being sued for non-payment of tithes by the rector, Richard Golty, himself a Laudian royalist appointed by the earl in 1630. Golty was also under pressure, but for the time being had managed to retain his living. The battlefield was complex. Many more of Golty's defaulters were parliamentarians, puritans and sectaries (especially Baptists) who objected to his very presence in the parish, quite apart from his tithes. The conflict was neither narrowly religious nor narrowly economic; rather, it was broadly cultural. Ordinary people in Framlingham turned against 'known papists' – neighbours with whom they had lived in peace for years – with the intention of seeing their property sequestered and their lives ruined. The innocent families of men who had left to fight for the king suffered a similar fate.[13] Now, at Framlingham in the summer of 1645 a coven of witches was exposed, at least twelve women from the parish and three others from there or the surrounding countryside.

Land, houses and work were in short supply at Framlingham, breeding bitterness between neighbours. After 1642 Irish refugees began to arrive in significant numbers, and by 1645 bitter discontent about the rates levied on the town had resulted in legal action. The prosperous were overstretched by a Parliament at war and their dependants at home. Recognizing the problem of poverty a decade earlier, Sir Robert Hitcham had stipulated in his will that Pembroke College should build a new workhouse within the castle walls where paupers could be employed. This was small comfort to the poor in 1645, for it was twenty years before Hitcham's wish was carried out. In the mean time, disputes multiplied and resentments festered. Infringements of custom were flashpoints: unfairness in trade, parsimony in almsgiving, a tenant's inability to pay rents and tithes, a landlord's reluctance to wait. Elizabeth Warne, an old widow reliant on the parish for money and firewood, quarrelled with her landlord about her rent, then was accused of exacting retribution on his sick child. She and the other suspected women all lived 'outside the borough' – that is, beyond the ancient Saxon ditch of old Framlingham, the heart of wealth and authority. They were too poor to pay taxes.[14]

Domestic servants, themselves marginal figures, were caught in the crossfire. Mary Gunnell, a maid to the prosperous Waites household, reported that after she had refused Mother Palmer a drink at the door, the old woman stormed off 'thret[en]inge she might want a cup of beare her selfe eare longe'; thereafter, the servants could not keep the beer from going bad. Doorstep confrontations could have dire consequences. Marianne May, servant to the Pallant family, deposed that Mary Edwards had mumbled a malediction after receiving from her an alms of milk that she considered inadequate. Before long the Pallants' baby son had started shaking and screaming, and died the following day. Edwards was also blamed for the deaths of two other children, one of whom she allegedly despatched with a poisoned apple. Both Robert Waites and Robert Pallant gave evidence, as did several of their well-to-do neighbours, the most enthusiastic being Edward Weeting, an active figure in the correction of all sorts of anti-social behaviour. The fact that he testified to the confessions of at least six women suggests that he was a watcher.[15]

Whether these women were tried by ordeal in the castle moat was not recorded, but it is possible, since a suspect from Brandeston was swum here. Certainly the usual routines of searching and watching were implemented, with the addition of a new technique: suspects were not only kept awake, but marched up and down until they were exhausted; a disoriented state, it was thought, would break a witch's silence. After being watched for three nights, Elizabeth Warne confessed 'that pride and lustfullnes had brought her to this, and desired she might be walked apace for she had the devill w[i]thin'. As Hopkins had seen in Manningtree and John Stearne at Rattlesden, the outline of a secret confederation of witches was emerging. Hopkins was especially interested in Margery Chinery. A witch called Mother Man told a search-woman that Chinery had commanded the devil to murder John Sheldrake's son – information that Man had received from the devil. Mother Chinery confessed to Hopkins that Satan had provoked her to destroy the corn of one of the wealthiest farmers in Framlingham; she was also suspected of having bewitched a baby that had died covered in blue eruptions. Even after eighteen hours, *rigor mortis* had not set in.[16]

This Mother Man was probably Elizabeth Man from Wickham Market, five miles to the south. There, Goodwife Stannar was facing a dilemma. She had fallen out with Man, and her child had been sick ever since; but should she just accept the witch's revenge, or risk making things worse by retaliating? Clearly Man was dangerous: her own mother, it was said, had been hanged as a witch, and bad blood flowed in the daughter's veins. The Stannar child lay 'shreekeinge and crieinge' for two days, and was menaced by a buzzing insect until the moment it died. Feeling the death as if it were her own, the child's mother threw caution to the wind and accused Elizabeth Man to her face. Then, overcome with grief, she collapsed and had to be carried home. Hearing that Man was to be taken to 'the searchers' – probably Hopkins and his helpers in Framlingham – Goodwife Stannar summoned the energy to accompany them, and was relieved to hear that 'teats and the marks of a witch' had been found on the suspect's body. Her relief was short-lived. When she arrived back in Wickham after dark, her husband had bad news: 'one of her childerin was taken w[i]th a strainge fit of shrekeinge and clawinge at theyre faces when they wold hold it in theyr armes, and so held in this fit untill midnight'. These convulsions went on for days.[17]

In Framlingham, word of Margery Chinery's wickedness spread. She had revealed to Hopkins that a Mother Nevill had been her accomplice in destroying the corn-crop, and so the web of complicity grew more intricate. Hopkins, the bit between his teeth, connected Mother Nevill with another suspect, Margaret Wyard, who after three nights of watching confessed that Mary Edwards had murdered the Pallants' baby. Both Nevill and Wyard were widows surviving on parish handouts. Wyard had also been asked by the devil to blast the cornfield, she said, but had disobeyed him, likewise his order to kill John Sheldrake's son. Subsequently the devil had told her, as he had told Elizabeth Man, that Mother Chinery had carried out the deed.

Yet Margaret Wyard had not always been so strong-willed. Seven years earlier, she told her interrogators, 'the devill appeard to her in the likenes of a calfe',

> . . . and told her he was her husband and asked her to have the use of her body w[hi]ch then she did denie, after this he came to her in the shape of a handsome yonge gentleman w[i]th yelloow hayre and black cloaths & often times lay w[i]th her . . . & she observed he had a cloven foote, & he made her denie god and [the] Ch[urch] and came and

brought wrightings in[to] her hand and fetcht blood of her thygh and
Catched it in a thinge & writt in the paper . . .

If this was little more than a sensuous romance imagined by a woman
with her courting days behind her, the mere fact that she could shock
her auditors by recounting it must have filled her with a sense of fresh
vitality. But the devil's hint that he had a gold ring for her had come
to nothing – a glimpse of the reality behind the dream of love – and
soon she was struggling to feed seven hungry imps. These creatures –
flies, beetles, spiders and mice – clamoured for space at her body, she
lamented, but since she had only five teats, 'when they came to suck
they fight like pigs with a sow'. She had become a drudge again, her
prince charming nothing but the prince of darkness. The devil gave
notice that strangers were coming to Framlingham, a man and a
woman who would search her, and that she should keep her mouth
shut. As she started to confess, Wyard said, the devil had loomed like
a dark shadow, and had tried to beat her into submission.[18]

Ellen Driver, yet another old widow living off the parish, also confessed to having married the devil, back in the reign of Elizabeth I,
though her neighbours, she said, would never have seen him. She
knew he was the devil, she explained, by his cloven feet, which she
had felt in bed.[19] Confessions like this bothered the many English
clergymen who understood the devil to be an intangible spirit, not an
articulate bed-hopping goat, but such academic objections were
difficult to sustain in a charged atmosphere of suspicion, especially
among people not used to making sharp distinctions between the
world around them and the spiritual world in their heads. The poor
knew little privacy, and it was a struggle even to isolate their thoughts
from exterior influences. Every week in church they were reminded
that God looked into their souls and judged them against the commandments painted on the walls of the nave. Dreams could be
demonic invasions, evil thoughts projected to cause harm. The result
was guilt, especially in women: a burden of fear, failed responsibility,
and spiritual vulnerability.

And no guilt was more acutely felt than sexual guilt, in the chasm
between the ideals of chastity, modesty and love on one side, and the

reckless insistence of desire on the other. Sometimes there was a sexual edge to the questions posed by the witchfinders, but the stories they took away amounted to more than the fulfilment of their own repressed fantasies. In the confessions of these women could be heard the lament of age for vanished youth, yearning for intimacy and kindness, indulgence in heart-fluttering seduction and abandon. Margaret Bayts had two secret nipples suckled by unseen imps which scuttled beneath her skirts pleasuring her while she worked. One of her neighbours described nothing less than an orgasm: 'she felt 2 things like butterflies in her secret p[ar]ts w[i]th w[a]tchings dansings and suckinge & she felt them w[i]th her hands and rubbed the[m] and killed them'. Mary Scrutton sheepishly told her husband that suckling noises beneath the bed-clothes must be mice; and another woman, persuaded by Satan that she was too sinful to be saved, allowed herself to be ravished by two great flying beetles which came in the night. She felt she had nothing to lose.[20]

Matthew Hopkins had come to see himself as a warrior of reformation bearing the sword of the law in one hand, the shield of his election in the other. It is ironic, then, that some would consider him an English Torquemada, the model of a Dominican inquisitor, as bigoted and sadistic as any in the ecclesiastical dungeons of Spain or Rome. The comparison might have amused him, or it might have offended him; but there was truth in it. He *had* become a fearsome confessor, and he *did* force the most egregrious sinners to, as he saw it, break ranks with the devil. From the spiritual limbo of their last days on earth, furthermore, these apostates did implicate others, and so saved Christians from harm.

It is hard to imagine the mood of the people Hopkins left behind at Framlingham: were they were elated or troubled, or an uneasy mixture of the two? Surely they realized that some of the women sent for trial would be discharged or acquitted, which meant they would have to face them again. The consequence of a witch's vindication, everyone knew, would be at best humiliation and at worst lethal vengeance. And what of those who at their neighbours' behest were to be hanged? How steadfast were the convictions of Edward Weeting and his co-accusers as they lay awake those warm nights, scratching at lice and listening to mice in the rafters? Once passions had cooled and the witches had gone, righteous anger could subside into guilt, gnawing at the conscience. As the rot of doubt set in, the sensation of being guided by God might come to seem more like a satanic illusion.

Had Hopkins felt such qualms he would surely have gone home to Manningtree. Instead, he pressed on to the north and east, across the sandy heathland and through conifer woods, at his side a Manningtree searcher, silver coins in the pocket of her apron. The greater the discovery, the greater the service to God and man – and the greater the remuneration. In Essex the witchfinders had learnt about small gatherings of witches, and had seen how the sin passed from mother to daughter; but in Suffolk, great nests were uncovered – men, married couples, even whole families. Outside Framlingham Hopkins passed through Sweffling, where Ellen Crispe, her husband and parents were all suspected; a farmer claimed that after he had refused Goodman Crispe some hay, his cow gave 'nauglty milke' before drying up.[21] In the next village, Great Glemham, eleven or twelve stood accused, including one man, and a relative of the Framlingham witches.[22] Nine were watched, of whom two-thirds resisted – resistance that must have occurred before in other places but until now had not entered the formal record. Three of the women did make confessions, all described as 'free', which suggests that brutality was employed on other occasions. At the same time, the unabashed attitude to torture makes the 'free' confessions all the more remarkable.

Anne Barker's statement was such a one. Two years earlier, she said, a small brown dog had promised her that 'if you will cleave to me thou shalt want nothinge', but its early ventures to provide for her had failed. The spirit had commanded her allegiance anyway, and wrote her name on a paper using blood from her toe – a parody of a minister making parishioners sign the parliamentary Covenant. After a neighbour refused her some rye, the dog-imp had ensured that he 'died very strangely'. The grudges of women throughout Glemham were laid bare. Mary and Rachel Sexton freely confessed that they had been visited by spirits as they lay sick; one had suckled Mary's tongue and offered revenge against the constables who once had charged her with a misdemeanour. The Sextons were taken to Ipswich to be examined by Nathaniel Bacon, the town's chief magistrate – and a close friend of Matthew Hopkins' father in the 1620s. Their neighbours Anne and Mary Smith also confessed, but only after two nights of sleeplessness. They too were taken before Bacon, who allowed them to rest for twenty-four hours; even so, he heard from their own mouths how they had received imps, which they sold to other women up to twelve miles away. Those they kept for themselves were used to sow discord and kill cattle. One imp Anne Smith had given to her son as he went off to war; now, she said, he was 'resolved to goe to the king's p[ar]ty w[i]th it' – perhaps as an assassin, perhaps as a turncoat.[23]

Like the Copdock accused, those from Great Glemham – and, indeed, those from Hintlesham, Belstead, Chattisham, Tattingstone and Shotley – were being concentrated at Ipswich, perhaps because the gaol at Bury St Edmunds was already full. So many witches had been committed for trial that most of the smaller gaols must have contained at least one, and those in the towns were overstretched. Respite was close, however. The Bury assizes were just weeks away, and before then the witchfinders were expected back at Chelmsford to give evidence at the assizes there.

Matthew Hopkins continued his journey in what seems to have been a wide northerly arc taking him back towards Stowmarket. In the secluded and swampy parish of Rushmere, five miles from the port of Lowestoft, sisters Sarah and Alice Warner, women of some substance, confessed to having sent lice-carrying imps to their neighbours.[24] This may have been mere mischief, but the case of Susanna Smith was more worrying. The day after her arrest she confessed that eighteen years earlier the devil had appeared to her as 'a red shaged dog' and had tempted her to murder her children. For a day and a night, she said, she had wrestled with the temptation, until finally the devil left her. Unconvinced by this story, one of the watchers encouraged Goodwife Smith to say more, at which point her throat began to swell so that she could no longer speak. The next night the watcher came back to find her quivering with fear and her food untouched. She said the devil had returned to her as a black bee, entering her body and threatening death if she succumbed to interrogation. She was brought fresh food, of which she ate a little, her body still trembling. Sensing the devil had gone, Smith managed to explain how she had signed a covenant with a cross, and how the devil-bee had advised her to kill herself using a rusty knife hidden in the house. The watchers confiscated the knife in case Smith decided to cheat the hangman.[25]

From Rushmere, Hopkins rode twenty miles to the south and west across a green expanse of farmland scattered with oak woods and clay pits, looking for the ancient market town of Halesworth. Hidden from distant view by an enclosure of hills, approached by road it suddenly appeared; from the river, the first signs of its existence were the barges carrying cloth and grain to the mouth of the Blyth at Southwold. Its best days were in the past, but Halesworth remained fiercely godly. The school and almshouses Hopkins passed reflected a tradition of Protestant piety and philanthropy; at St Mary's church the image of the patron saint had been destroyed long before Dowsing came to finish the job.[26]

Moral discipline was vigorously enforced at Halesworth, and malefactors were either reformed or removed. In the summer of 1645 godly anxiety was channelled towards one family in particular.[27] A number of years earlier, a cooper's apprentice named Thomas Everard had been sent on an errand and took a dog with him for company. On the way a black water-hound appeared, jumping over a hedgerow with unnatural ease and without a sound. Everard's dog refused to go further, twisting round his legs, whining, and making him more afraid. Reaching his destination, the lad was informed that the beast had been seen several times, and he was directed back by a longer route where he would feel safer. That night, Everard fell into a troubled sleep,

> . . . and drempt that somethinge crep[t] upo[n] his legs and go to his shin, and then he waked and felt it and it was like a rabbet and this asked him if he wold love it and if he wold denie god [and the] Ch[urch] &c. but he refused then, but consented to it after ward, when he met it in the field, and y[a]t it scratcht him under his ear and got blood of him & syd now it had what it wold have . . .

A change had come over Everard: teats appeared on his body, and imps came to feed there.

After qualifying as a cooper Thomas Everard had married Mary More, another witch, and together they had worked in the brewhouse at Halesworth. They had raised children, at least one of whom, Marian, had also become a witch; on becoming grandparents, they had murdered the baby. Everard, who had also killed other children, and livestock, had tried to foist an imp on his brother-in-law, James More, who lived seven miles away at Metfield. More resisted, until he received an imp sent by his niece Marian, after which he was visited by a boyish devil. Thus initiated, James More accepted another imp from Marian's father, which he ordered to attack his brother for cheating him out of a legacy. The orgy of destruction was endless: soon More was collaborating with his sister's family, reuniting his imp with one of theirs to flatten a corn-field. At the start of the war they had all pitched in to help the royalist cause, and Mary Everard had asked her brother to donate an imp to send to Prince Rupert. All three Everards confessed to these crimes, and at Metfield James More confirmed their stories 'freely w[i]thout watchinge'. Thomas and Mary also admitted to having bewitched beer in the brewhouse. 'The odiousnesse of the infectious stinke of it', it was said, 'was such & so intollerable that by the noysomnesse of the stinck or tast[e] many people dyed.'

A sequence of confessions was made a few miles apart beyond Halesworth. Hopkins' name was hardly ever recorded, but his prime intention was to set others to work before moving on; that way, the fruits of his labours were great, the risk of censure slight. Besides, for one man to be bound as a witness against so many was not practical; that was a job for neighbours who knew the suspects well and were best able to inform a jury as to their character and intent. At Linstead, three men were encouraged to give evidence. The daughter of one had fallen sick after a disagreement with a reputed witch, who had then visited their house to reverse her magic; she was unsuccessful. After his girl died the man was enraged, but unwilling or unable to seek redress until Hopkins' arrival.[28] This changed the atmosphere, and women long suspected saw new confidence in their neighbours. Even a rumour of the witchfinder's coming might be enough, while gossip and rumour also explain why suspects so openly believed the devil, acting as their protector and provider, had tipped them off about Hopkins; the fact that during the war male protectors and providers were so thin on the ground makes such fantasies easier to understand.

Although Suffolk saw little actual fighting in the civil war, it was Parliament's main recruiting ground. At a time when mortality was high in the ordinary course of events, this imposed a particularly heavy burden. At Mendham, all Margery Sparham's men had disappeared from her life. Known as 'a lewd woma[n] sildome come to Church', she confessed freely that when she was an unmarried maid-servant, an imp in the shape of a white mole had attached himself to her, but claimed she had sent him to sea to 'git his liveinge' – just like an idle son in a folktale. She had married but her husband had gone to the war, leaving her alone with her elderly father. Following his death she had been visited by two blackbirds, 'Will' and 'Tom', which she sent to protect her husband in battle. Then, alone again, while walking in the woods she had come face to face with the devil who had assumed the form of a black man. He had warned her 'that there wold come a man to her to search her for her imps', and that if she had any left she should get rid of them at once.[29]

Discoveries at Fressingfield, Wingfield, Stradbroke, Westhorpe and Wickham revealed the same dearth of men. One outcome of a world without men was that women were freer to take charge of their lives – a symptom of chaos in the eyes of England's governors. By this time the Presbyterian majority in Parliament was less threatened by Roman Catholics than by radical sects and their political champions, the Independent party that also dominated the army. Women were prominent in the sects, whose proliferation parish clergy viewed with dismay and alarm. At Wickham Skeith, the minister Edward Willan was actively opposed to the communities of Shakers, Familists, Baptists and Anabaptists that threatened to bring down the walls of Jerusalem before the stones had even been laid. And witches were another sign of this degeneracy. Willan heard the confession of a woman who 'p[ro]fessed anabaptisme' and admitted to being a 'runner after the new sects'.[30] Perhaps the other four women arrested at Wickham – one of whom was her daughter – shared her faith.

The guilt of a number of witches at Horham and Athelington, also

along this stretch of road, was confirmed by Hopkins. Their neighbours soon began to bridle at the cost of their prosecution, however,
and disquiet on moral grounds was also becoming apparent. At
Hoxne, close to the Norfolk border, 'a Gentlewoman of very great
Piety and Virtue' later recalled her outrage at what seemed to be going
on in her own parish:

> She said, when the Witchfinders came into that Neighbourhood, they
> had one woman under Tryal who, she verily believed was innocent;
> but being kept long fasting and without Sleep, she confess'd and called
> her Imp Nan. This good Gentlewoman told me, that her Husband,
> (a very learned ingenious Gentleman) having Indignation at the Thing,
> he and she went to the House, and put the People out of Doors, and
> gave the poor Woman some Meat, and let her go to Bed . . .

As had happened at Colchester, this intervention showed what could
be achieved when people in authority stood up to Hopkins. It also
indicated the savage effectiveness of his torture. The suspected woman
had woken up unaware of what she had confessed and, when quizzed
about 'Nan' the imp, explained that she had a chicken she sometimes
called by that name, but that was all.[31] Whether or not the gentlewoman believed in witches was irrelevant: it was important only that
she chose to fight the witchfinders' methods by expressing her revulsion in public. Nor was she the last to do so.

In the third week of July 1645 Arthur Wilson, 49-year-old steward to
the Earl of Warwick, rode into the county town of Chelmsford as part
of his master's retinue. Warwick, a swashbuckling privateer, had long
been a staunch defender of the rights of Parliament and the gentlemen of Essex, where he was Lord Lieutenant. An opponent of
Arminianism and of Archbishop Laud, he had offered his patronage
to puritan clergy and in 1642, assisted by his Presbyterian protégé
Harbottle Grimston, son of the magistrate, had implemented the
Militia Ordinance in the county. Wilson − dramatist, historian, and
sometime court clerk − had entered Warwick's service in 1633, and at
the start of the war was sent to Long Melford to rescue Countess
Rivers from an anti-Catholic mob. Warwick had been Lord High

*Robert Rich, 2nd Earl of Warwick, portrayed as Lord High Admiral of
the Fleet*

Admiral of the Fleet until April 1645, when he resigned to comply
with the Self-Denying Ordinance, a measure designed to separate military and political power.[32] Victory at Naseby in June had proved the
worth of the New Model Army, confirmed by another royalist defeat
in Somerset on 10 July. Prince Rupert advised the king to sue for
peace but Charles moved east, threatening East Anglia again. Such
alarms had disrupted the assize circuits on which judges rode from
London to dispense justice in the regions.[33] Thus it was that in July

1645 the Earl of Warwick was commissioned to preside at the Essex summer assizes to be held in Chelmsford.

Neither Warwick nor his steward possessed much legal expertise. Warwick had been at Cambridge – another scion of Emmanuel College – but was no scholar. A competent colonial administrator and shrewd in politics, he was happier directing a sea-battle than he was debating theory. As a young man Arthur Wilson had been similarly restless and at Oxford had dabbled in the study of physic and politics, without mastering either. As the most powerful man in Essex, what Warwick brought to the Chelmsford assizes was authority. Until 1642, when he was ejected from the commission of the peace by the king, Warwick had been *custos rotulorum*, the principal county magistrate – but that was an honorific rather than a qualification.[34] Assize judges, by contrast, were talented professionals immersed in the law by both training and experience, and for Warwick to perform their role required him to work closely with the county magistrates on the bench: Sir John Barrington, Sir Martin Lumley, Sir Henry Holcroft, Sir Henry Mildmay and William Conyers, Esquire. As a good Presbyterian, Warwick shared with his steward a faith in providence and perhaps also his habit of morbid introspection. Whether he was given to the same soul-searching about the reality of witchcraft is another matter.[35]

Chelmsford lay on the old Roman road to London, at the confluence of the Can and the Chelmer. Like Colchester and Ipswich it was self-governing, and provided a market for its hinterland and a seat for the assizes. The town had impressive godly credentials. Sir Walter Mildmay, founder of Emmanuel College, had lived there, and his descendants remained lords of the manor. The esteemed divine Thomas Hooker had been a town lecturer in the 1620s, but like so many had emigrated to New England – in his case, to found the community of Hartford, Connecticut. Mildmay's grandson, Sir Humphrey, belonged to the faction that had made the lives of the godly unbearable. A Laudian supporter of Charles's personal rule, he natur- ally took the royalist side, and criticized Warwick for his popular following in Chelmsford: while Mildmay had been exacting unconsti- tutional taxes, Warwick had been listening to the weavers' complaints,

and now it paid off. A clothworking depression and religious innovation bred plebeian anger, and by 1641 it was fit to explode. When it
did, church collections were seized and given to the poor, Catholics
were harassed, and devotional images were smashed. A mutinous
assault on a deputy lord-lieutenant sounded the death-knell of social
deference.[36] And now, to add to the iconoclastic mayhem, Chelmsford's hotheaded crowds were about to be treated to the largest witch-
trial ever staged in England.

Raised on four pillars at one end of the market square, near to St
Mary's church, stood a courthouse known as the Market Cross. The
town had no purpose-built gaol, but a chamber beneath the courthouse held prisoners awaiting trial. Barely fit for the quarter sessions,
the Market Cross was wholly inadequate for the assizes, so the Shire
House was used instead, but even this was unsuitable. Dilapidated in
parts, with an insanitary cell, it was cramped, and too close to the
streets, the noise from which – not least from three unruly inns – often
interrupted proceedings.[37] And the inns were never more unruly than
during the assizes. Even before the judges had arrived there was a
mounting air of carnival, a mood reminiscent of pre-Reformation
festivals. Out in the countryside, people downed tools and saddled
horses to begin the journey into town. Chelmsford's victuallers
stocked up on pies and puddings, and barrels and bottles were hauled
from the cellars, ready for an onslaught of hungry and thirsty people.
Ballad-sellers set up stalls at which to sing samples of their wares
(sometimes bogus 'last dying speeches'), and enterprising joiners
constructed platforms from which paying customers might have an
unimpeded view of the gallows. Upstairs rooms overlooking this
theatre of blood were rented out at a premium.

The date was set for Thursday 17 July 1645. Upon receipt of his
commission from Westminster Warwick sent a summons to the
sheriff, who instructed the bailiffs to notify witnesses and jurors; the
sheriff then prepared a list of law officers required to be present, and
a schedule of prisoners was compiled from the returns supplied by
magistrates. Warwick may not have checked this before passing it to
the clerk of assize, but must surely have noticed the unusually large
number of witches to be tried. The clerk, too, was surely surprised by

how often he had to copy the same Latin formula onto the feint-lined rectangles of parchment that would become bills of indictment once the specific details had been added. These forms invoked the terror of God, and the certainty of detection and punishment of 'malas et diabolicas artes . . . witchcrafts, incantac[i]ones'. Meanwhile Stephen Hoy, the gaoler at Colchester, made his own inventory of prisoners, which was literally as long as his arm. At the top were twenty-nine names bracketed together and annotated 'These are accused for Sorcery & Witchcrafte', followed by another twelve, mostly common thieves.[38] The last task was to check Hoy's list against the assize clerk's to see whether the prisoners who left the gaol for trial matched those who had gone in. A discrepancy might reveal an escapee, but more often it was due to death. Hoy noted that a total of six prisoners had perished due to 'visitation by God', four of them the suspected witches for whom inquests had been held some weeks earlier.[39]

As the 17th drew near the surviving prisoners were unshackled and led out of Colchester Castle, squinting at the daylight some had not seen for nearly four months. The old widow Anne West was among them, but her adolescent daughter Rebecca was not: she had accepted Matthew Hopkins' offer to act as a witness in return for immunity from prosecution, and had already been moved. The women were herded onto carts bound for Chelmsford, accompanied by Hoy the gaoler and an escort, and after twenty-four spine-jolting miles arrived in the town where their fates would be decided. They were probably all taken to the hellish Shire House prison, where two witchcraft suspects were already held.[40] They passed the time in conversation or prayer, patiently measuring out what they imagined would be the remains of their lives. On the morning of the assizes, they might have heard the peals of bells and trumpet blasts as the Earl of Warwick's cavalcade entered the town, flanked by pikemen liveried for the occasion. By now, Arthur Wilson must have been aware of the Solomonic task ahead.

With his flowing locks and moustaches, Robert Rich, 2nd Earl of Warwick, looked more like a cavalier than a russet-coated roundhead. But the people lining the streets of Chelmsford saw him as a champion of custom and a defender of their faith; now he would be their judge as well. Donning robes, he proceeded to St Mary's to hear a sermon, typically a weary peroration about the sword of the magistrate tempered with Christ's merciful blood. Magistrates, jurors and witnesses were still arriving, among them the witchfinders, their six searchwomen, and as many as ninety others bound to give evidence. The recognizance slips recording their obligations had been passed to the assize clerk, who had added names, places, dates and offences to his bills of indictment. Finally, he sorted the prisoners – all but a few of them were charged with witchcraft – into batches on a series of trial calendars. The completed file was wrapped in a sheet of parchment ready for the grand jury, whose job it was to screen cases to see if any could be dismissed before trial.[41] For now, the hopes of every woman in gaol were pinned on this possibility.

By mid morning the square in front of the Shire House was thronged with people clamouring for a space inside. Most were disappointed, and would have to content themselves with word passed back from those with an ear to the chamber. The lucky few who had found places in the gallery unwrapped bundles of bread and cheese and passed bottles, speculating about the witches to be paraded before them.[42] The Earl of Warwick's steward Arthur Wilson was among them, but his mood was more sombre.

At last the town cryer called the court to order. The sheriff and clerks took their places in front of the prisoners' dock; the grand jurors, respectable county men, were seated nearby; and at the front of the courtroom were the justices of the peace, including Sir Harbottle Grimston and Sir Thomas Bowes. Finally, the six justices named on the commission from Westminster entered the chamber and positioned themselves on the bench, with Warwick in the middle. Beneath their feet lay a scattering of petals and herbs as a prophylactic against gaol fever, and in among the books, papers and inkpots were nosegays of fresh flowers. Next the clerk of assize read the commission by which the court was convened, a register of magistrates was taken, and the grand jury was sworn in. Warwick issued a formal charge reminding the jurors of their duty and outlining the offences they were about to try – including nearly fifty charges of witchcraft.

The court then adjourned to let them digest the thick file containing the bills of indictment, witness statements and confessions.

In the afternoon the court reconvened, and the clerk sorted the bills returned by the grand jurors. Upon those where there was a case to answer had been written '*billa vera*' ('a true bill'), on the rest '*ignoramus*' ('we know not'); but it seems that every accused witch had at least one bill against her found true. Dorothy Brooke and Mary Greenliefe had their cases postponed, so they were left in gaol when the rest were ordered to their feet to be taken to the courtroom.[43]

At last the clerk gave the order to bring up the prisoners – twenty-nine women suspected of witchcraft, plus various other malefactors: an arsonist, a man who had tried to kill his wife, a mother who had thrown her baby down a well, and a motley collection of thieves. The first batch shuffled into the dock: Elizabeth Clarke of Manningtree, Anne Leech of Mistley, Rebecca Jones of St Osyth, Margery Grew of Walton-le-Soken, and Helen Bretton of Kirby-le-Soken.[44] To many spectators they must have seemed models of witchery: dirty, ragged and hunched, their faces ravaged by age, hunger and fear. Yet to Arthur Wilson their appearance suggested rather the poor and unfortunate, the decrepit and diseased – mere victims of imagination, hardly the handmaidens of Satan. The grand jury had thought otherwise that morning; now it was time for the trial jury to decide.

Rebecca Jones, a widow, was the first to be called to the bar, and was asked by the clerk to hold up her right hand. Translating from the Latin, the clerk told her she was charged with bewitching Thomas and Katherine Bumstead to death, and asked how she pleaded. She answered 'not guilty', thus putting herself on God and the country, as the contemporary legal formula phrased it. This process was repeated until all five women had pleaded (all 'not guilty', any earlier confessions notwithstanding), at which point the trial jury – twelve just and sufficient freeholders – was sworn in. The arraignment was complete. Trials were usually short and raucous, with the defendant interrupting the plaintiff, and witnesses on both sides protesting; the judge also interjected whenever he saw fit. To add to the cacophony, the spectators heckled and hissed like gamblers at a cock-fight, and the crowd at the windows was even less restrained. By the time the minister

George Eatoney had denounced Widow Jones as a witch, backed by the search-women and two local witnesses, and the suspect's own confession had been read out, her chances of acquittal had all but vanished.[45] Her place at the bar was taken by one-legged Elizabeth Clarke, who steadied herself as the first witness was called. Arthur Wilson watched from the gallery as a self-assured gentleman – Matthew Hopkins – took the stand.

For the court Hopkins recalled the night in March when he had witnessed Widow Clarke's terrifying display of familiarity with the devil. Some spectators, like Arthur Wilson, thought his tale too fantastic to be true; others found it equally impossible that such a story could have been invented. The names of the imps in the indictment were surely the inventions of Satan: 'Holt' the cat; a 'Sandee Span[i]ell' called 'Jeremarye'; 'Vineger Tome', a greyhound; a black rabbit called 'Sacke and Sugar'. Once John Stearne had confirmed this testimony and the Manningtree gentleman Richard Edwards had described the death of his son and other misfortunes, the jury's minds were made up.[46] Hopkins, Stearne and Edwards also testified against Anne Leech but not against the last two defendants, although for them the evidence of the searchers was damning enough. After what had been alleged against Jones, Clarke and Leech, it seemed certain that Margery Grew had *indeed* entertained a spirit shaped like a jay, and *must* have murdered Samuel Munt's son.[47]

After the witnesses had been heard and the confessions read out, the Earl of Warwick asked the jury for their verdicts; the quantity of business they had to get through may have meant they were not allowed to retire. All five women were found guilty, and the clerk duly marked each indictment '*cul*' – short for '*culpabilis*'. It was normal practice for sentencing to come at the end of such proceedings; but with so many accused, and in conditions so cramped, it is more likely that judgment was passed there and then, so that the guilty prisoners could be taken down and the next batch ushered forward. There was only one sentence that could be passed, recorded by the clerk as '*susp*': the five women, tried according to statute and proven to be witches, were to be suspended by their necks until dead. With what resignation or shock the women received this pronouncement as they returned to the gaol cannot be known. Arthur Wilson was appalled, the accusers and witnesses relieved, the witchfinders satisfied. And the trial had barely begun. To recount every indictment, verdict and sentence here would have the numbing effect it probably had on the court, whose initial fascination with the testimonies must surely have waned somewhat by the time the twenty-ninth witchcraft suspect was brought to the bar. But there were still a few surprises to come.

A mid seventeenth-century witch conjures up evil spirits using a spell from a book of magic

First, one of the prosecuting magistrates, Sir Thomas Bowes, appeared as a witness against Anne West – a highly unusual occurrence in a criminal trial, especially considering that he had not actually seen the event he described, and that his informant was not present; the latter, moreover, who claimed to have seen West's familiars cavorting, was not a fellow gentleman but a humble glove-maker.[48] Even more startling was the way Rebecca West had been persuaded to turn witness for the Crown against her own mother and assorted cronies, an achievement for which the prosecution had Matthew Hopkins to thank. An indictment against her for entertaining evil spirits had been drawn up – perhaps to wave in front of her terrified face – but she was never required to plead.[49]

For a woman to lose the loyalty of her daughter was as diabolical a sign of the times as it was for a nation to make war on its father the king. What was perceived as an unprecedented need to fight the devil's influence perhaps explains why the jury reacted so harshly when confronted by the arraigned witches. At the final tally, only one, Joan Rowle of Leigh, was fully acquitted.[50] Anyone with previous experience of witch-trials would also have found extraordinary the extent to which the jury was prepared to find defendants guilty of witchcraft based solely on their conjuration of evil spirits, proof of how far this aspect of the crime (as distinct from *maleficium*) had since the start of the war established itself as a principal definition of witchcraft. At the same time, the fact that the jurors were not persuaded with regard to certain indictments – ten in all – does demonstrate some discernment on their part.

What was discernment in some was in others rank scepticism. Having listened to the witnesses striving to hang the accused women, Arthur Wilson still

> . . . could find nothing in the Evidence that did sway me to thinke them other then poore, mallenchollie Envious, mischevous, ill disposed, ill dieted, atrabil[io]us Constitutions, whose fancies working by grosse fumes & vapors might make the imagination readie to take any impression whereby their anger and envie might vente it selfe into such expressions as the hearers of their Confessions, that gave Evidence, might find cause to beleeve, that they were such people as they blazon[e]d themselves to bee . . .

After the proceedings were declared closed, six concerned magistrates and a clergyman approached Warwick and the bench to beg reprieves for a number of the condemned, nine of them witches. Others were concerned too, among them one of the commissioners, William Conyers. To some extent the Earl of Warwick must have shared his steward's feelings, for their request was granted: application was made to Parliament on behalf of the convicts, stating that 'the Court was not fully satisfied w[i]th the Evidence given ag[ains]t them', and that they were deemed 'fit for mercy & pardon'.[51] The subtlety of discussions such as these about proof can be seen in the case of the three Ramsey witches, all of whom were found guilty. Whereas Elizabeth Harvey had confessed, Marian Hocket and Sarah Hatyn had consistently denied their involvement. It might have been expected that Hocket and Hatyn would be reprieved; in fact, it was the untrustworthiness of Harvey as a witness against herself that made her alone worthy of clemency.[52]

Two things stand out from this. First, all but one of the nine witches reprieved had been convicted solely for conjuring spirits, indicating that whatever the jurors might think about witchcraft, the county magistracy was not unanimously persuaded by the women's confessions. The magistrates' objection, upheld by the commissioners, must have entailed some criticism of Hopkins and Stearne, as it was they who had extracted the confessions. Many present must have been aware of their involvement, especially as the witchfinders and searchers had testified several times. The second observation, however, is an indication of just how effective Hopkins could be with the right backing: none of the reprieved women came from the witch-hunting epicentre of Manningtree and Mistley, where Sir Harbottle Grimston and Sir Thomas Bowes had expended most energy. Perhaps in recognition of this, it was ordered that four of the condemned – Helen Clarke of Manningtree, Anne West of Lawford, Anne Cooper of Great Clacton and Marian Hocket of Ramsey – should be hanged not at Chelmsford but at Manningtree.[53] The two last villages marked the extent of the witch-hunt far to the south and east of where it had begun.

The next day was Friday 18 July, the day set aside for the executions at Chelmsford. The fifteen condemned women were separated from those with whom they had shared the last weeks of their lives, and taken to the market square to face a tumultuous crowd. On the way to the gallows Margaret Moone of Thorpe collapsed and died from the strain, having protested her innocence to the last. According to one report, she cried out that the 'Devil had often told her she should never be hanged' – an indication that he was 'truer to some of his servants then some wicked men are to their neighbours'. The others, one by one, climbed the ladder, to be turned off by the hangman and dangled between heaven and earth, as if unworthy of either. Her disability meant that Elizabeth Clarke had to be helped up to a height where the noose could be put around her neck. The Manningtree executions took place a fortnight later, on 1 August. Meanwhile, the nine reprieved women remained in gaol at Chelmsford, and there they would stay without hope of release until their pardon application was sent to Parliament – a procedure that in this case took nearly five months. Of the two women whose trials had been postponed, Dorothy Brooke had not months but years in prison ahead of her as she waited for the wheels of justice to turn. For the 84-year-old widow Mary Greenliefe relief came sooner: a month after her trial she died, probably from plague. Two weeks later Elizabeth Harvey, the Ramsey widow reprieved by reason of her dubious confession, also left the gaol in a winding-sheet.[54]

By that time the judicial circus had gone from Chelmsford and life had returned to normal. The gallows had been dismantled, the Shire House had been dusted and swept, and the ballad-sellers had moved on. The magistrates went back to their county seats, the witnesses to their neighbourhoods; and Hopkins and Stearne, having tasted blood, were preparing for another trial, this time at Bury St Edmunds. The Earl of Warwick returned to his affairs in London, his steward Arthur Wilson to his master's Essex estate.[55]

Wilson was disgusted by what he had seen and heard. 'There is nothing upon the Stage of the World acted by publique Justice comes so crosse to my Temper', he wrote, 'as putting so many Witches to death.' But his conscience collided with his intellect, and he wrestled with the fact that wise rulers had punished witches since time immemorial. Even harder to ignore was the knowledge that the Bible commanded that witches be executed. At first Wilson prayed, begging for a sign if he was wrong to think the Chelmsford witches innocent;

but immediately he regretted testing God in this way, and began to quiver at his presumption. No sign appeared, but Wilson was so relieved to be spared that he abandoned the contemplation of witches.[56] Others – magistrates and ministers, pamphleteers and politicians – did not give up their close scrutiny of the witch-hunt so easily. And so the complication of this tragedy was soon to be followed by the unravelling of the witchfinders' deeds and lives.

PART TWO

Unravelling

6

Malignants

———•———

A FORTNIGHT AFTER the executions at Manningtree, Henry
Overton, a bookseller in the City of London, was entrusted with
a curious manuscript. A gentleman known only as 'H. F.', who had
been present at the Essex trials, had managed to get hold of the witness
statements and confessions, which he had then edited, annotated, and
prefaced. 'Ingenuous Reader', he began, 'Thou hast here presented to
thee a sad Emblem of the strange sleights and cunning subtilties,
whereby Satan labours daily to insnare soules, and at last to bring them
to utter ruine.' The author, whose censorious bluster resembled that
of Matthew Hopkins, warned against attributing to witches power
which was God's alone, but condemned them anyway for foolish
pride in believing in Satan's delusions. From the dawn of time, he
observed, the Old Serpent had tempted women, and in the present
age at Chelmsford had 'drawn these poore silly creatures into these
horrid and detestable practises, of renouncing God and Christ, and
entring into a solemne league and contract with the Devil, the
thought whereof is sufficient to cause a man to be filled with horror
and astonishment'.[1]

Horror and astonishment were the stock-in-trade of Henry
Overton and his fellow booksellers who plied their trade all the way
up Cheapside to the churchyard at St Paul's, heart of the printing
industry. Even by metropolitan standards this warren of streets, alleys
and entries was home to a remarkable amount of free expression and
fast exchange – a maelstrom of energy and excess. A stone's throw
from Overton's shop, at the junction of several busy streets, stood
Stock's Market, and just off there was Coleman Street, where female
preachers lectured to crowds, fomenting 'confusion and disorder' in

the eyes of their critics.[2] Street conversation was dominated by politics and religion, and the desire for new information was intense. The collapse of censorship in 1641 had resulted in a deluge of printed works, especially hitherto illegal news-sheets, encouraging the growth of literacy among even the humblest men and women. Across England the outbreak of war had raised the obsession with cheap print to fever-pitch, and nowhere was the demand greater or more energetically supplied than in London.[3] 'For a peny', marvelled the scholar Henry Peacham, 'you may have all the Newes in England, of Murders, Flouds, Witches, Fires, Tempests, and what not.'[4]

Henry Overton, a specialist in religious texts, recognized the commercial potential of H.F's manuscript and invited a neighbour, Benjamin Allen, to join him in the enterprise. They composed an attention-grabbing title-page – *A true and exact Relation Of the severall Informations, Examinations, and Confessions of the late Witches* – and hired a printer to do the work. The forty-four-page pamphlet was on sale in their shops in Pope's Head Alley by 19 August, barely a month after the first executions.[5]

It must have sold well. Paramount in a kaleidoscope of reactions was fascination, combined with a desire to be first in spreading the news. It is possible that the gossips around Pope's Head Alley heard of events at Chelmsford faster than did most people in Essex. The legal and theological implications of the story were less appealing than its sensational content: the curses, deaths, infestations, satanic pacts – all further proof that the times were out of joint. People were enthralled by witches, prodigies and omens because, in an age of catastrophe, they feared for their futures. An eclipse of the sun on 11 August, watched by thousands, was interpreted as a sign that there would be barrenness after a plentiful harvest. According to the astrologer William Lilly, well known to Londoners for his almanacs, it presaged an 'insorrection of the Comunalty against the nobility and gentry, horrible warrs, many slaine, Counties depopulated, plagues, famine, &c.' The impact, predicted Lilly, would be felt throughout England for more than two years.[6] Anxiety about the Apocalypse seeped into the grain of daily life. That summer, the capital was also gripped by the fear of 'spirits', abductors who under false authority sold children into slavery on the American plantations – another sign of unnatural disturbance and grief.[7]

Rumour passed in both directions between the alehouses and the parliamentary chambers. Never before had so many ordinary people been engaged in politics, never had their attitudes mattered so much to those in power. The growing fear of child-abduction found its way into the House of Commons, where it was debated, and magistrates instructed to be diligent. Public order, especially in moral and religious life, had become a priority for England's governors in 1645, and parliamentiary business was peppered with reformist proposals. The year had begun with the replacement of the Book of Common Prayer by the Directory for Public Worship, followed by a ban on anyone without proper religious understanding receiving the Lord's Supper; adulterers, fornicators, drunkards and profane swearers were to be permanently excluded. A day of public humiliation was to be observed by all, as were fast-days; idolatrous images were to be pulled down, and blasphemous books burnt by the hangman.[8] Sermons attended by MPs during official fasts spelled out the dangers of failure, but promised glory for the elect when Christ came to destroy the sinful.[9] Until then, however, Parliament would continue to resemble a body wasted by illness, an 'occult evill humour [which now] is broken out with botches and boyles' – thus was the unnatural bloodshed committed by brother against brother characterized.[10]

The bizarre news stories that proliferated during the first half of 1645 were also symptoms of this strange malady threatening the life of the nation. A royalist woman from Lancashire – 'No part of England hath so many Witches, none fuller of Papists' – gave birth to a headless baby; the body of a profane-speaking man was dug up and eaten by dogs; and in Leicestershire people dipped handkerchiefs in a pond where the water had turned to blood – the last just one of many 'prodigious and wonderfull things [which] have appeared as no age before have ever seene or heard of'.[11] In London, not only had religious sects and schismatics multiplied in type and number (all of them captained by the devil, according to one preacher) but 'Shee Cavaliers' had appeared – women who, unguided by absent husbands, 'drinke, roare, and sweare, as lustily as any in the Campe'.[12]

News of the Essex witches, which seemed to confirm this sense of chaos, quickly reached Parliament. The Earl of Warwick returned to the House of Lords on Monday 21 July, and in subsequent days may have communicated to his fellow peers his misgivings and those of his fellow magistrates.[13] Then Henry Overton's pamphlet went on sale as well, and it must have come to the attention of at least a few MPs. In time Parliament would hear the petition from Chelmsford on behalf of the reprieved women; but before it did so news arrived of a witch-craze that had broken out in Suffolk. The Westminster Assembly of Divines (learned authors of the new Directory) had agreed that 'the Witch deserves present and certain death', and that the real crime was not causing harm but compacting with the devil – that was high treason against God, the devil's chiefest enemy – yet neither the Westminster Assembly nor Parliament was prepared to countenance extra-legal counter-measures.[14] After all, the war was being fought so that the rule of law might triumph. A decision was taken to intervene in subsequent Suffolk trials to ensure that proper procedures were observed and proper evidential standards upheld. The matter became especially pressing once it was known that among those awaiting trial at Bury St Edmunds was an ordained clergyman.

On the banks of the river Deben, four miles south-west of Framlingham, lay the parish of Brandeston, where about a hundred people subsisted on 1,000 acres of land. At the centre of their lives were the parish church of All Saints and next to it Brandeston Hall, home to the Revett family, lords of the manor and justices of the peace. John Revett had inherited the estate in 1643 but as a royalist was forced to leave the village, and the following year attended the king's Court at Oxford. The other pillar of local authority, the vicar, was an equally dubious figure, and at a time when leadership had never mattered more. John Lowes had been the incumbent for as long as most could remember. Now nearly eighty, he had been presented to the living in 1595 after graduating from Cambridge. During a brief spell as a preacher in Bury St Edmunds he had been reprimanded by a synod at Ipswich for not conforming to the rites of the established Church; almost certainly he had been leaning towards popery rather than puritanism. In 1599 he had married at Brandeston and settled into a life of distasteful preaching and the unstinting exaction of tithes. Perturbed that the chancel and pulpit of his church were falling into ruin, Lowes arranged for them to be rebuilt according to his own tastes – at the expense of the parish, naturally.[15]

In the words of one contemporary, tithes provided 'a never-failing Fund of Contention', making most villagers 'a secret Enemy to the Parson of the Parish'.[16] That had been the experience of Richard Golty at Framlingham, and it was shared by John Lowes at Brandeston. Lowes' parishioners knew him as a 'turbelent sperite being possessed w[i]th an humor of multitude of vexac[i]ons' who had 'most inviously plaged and molested his neighbours'. When he failed to get his way by confrontation he took out lawsuits, earning himself a reputation for barratry, or malicious litigation. The year 1615 was the turning-point. A delegation led by a yeoman, Jonas Cooke, testified at a quarter sessions court at Woodbridge that John Lowes was a common barrator and disturber of the peace. Protesting that any jury would be biased against him, Lowes appealed for the case to be removed to the Court of King's Bench in London. His request was granted.[17]

In such cases as this, resentment over customs and rights on the land was generally bound up with religious grievances. The godly faction at Brandeston found John Lowes' anti-Calvinist attitudes offensive, and alleged that it was his habit frequently to 'checke div[er]se of his poore and honest neighbours w[i]th manye reproches and most com-monlie inveyinge against the Scotishe nation'. Even more damaging was their claim that 'in catteckisinge of the youth he doth teach strange points of doctrine'. In his own defence, Lowes declared that his preaching merely exposed the guilty consciences of men 'hating to be reformed from div[er]se inherent and enormous vices and deeds by them comitted'.

Soon after the Woodbridge trial had been brought to a halt, Lowes was again impugned, this time with more sinister overtones. Jonas Cooke and others had accused a woman named Ann Annson of being 'a most vilde & wicked wiche', whereupon the vicar had declared her to be no more a witch than he. This was interpreted as a confession, an interpretation confirmed by the way he gave Annson refuge in his house while the men waited outside, shouting insults and threats. When the constable came to arrest her Lowes denied she was there, but later she was snatched from his house and committed. Furious, Lowes threatened the persecutors with violence (he had brawled with them before), and had his brother Nicholas stand bail for Annson. In February 1615 Cooke's men testified against Ann Annson for the murder of John May by witchcraft: she was convicted and hanged. Soon afterwards, livestock belonging to the witnesses 'did most stranglie perishe and decay', and suspicion fell upon John Lowes. Jonas Cooke also claimed that his sick son had been treated by Lowes with a golden chain used as a charm. The boy recovered slightly, and was diagnosed as having been bewitched by Lowes. In May his daughter died, and Cooke was heard to say: 'Mr Lowes ys a Wytche and I will p[ro]ve him so and I have sene him and his impes or evell sprites appeare to me in the night time in my chamber and he did bewitche a childe of myne.'[18]

Lowes filed a suit for slander which was heard at the Bury St Edmunds assizes in July 1615. Jonas Cooke was found guilty, and ordered to pay damages and costs of more than £28. At the same sessions, however, Cooke prosecuted Lowes for witchcraft, having already arranged for him to be arrested after divine service. Lowes was presented for trial on four charges, including having caused the death of Mary Cooke and abetted Ann Annson in her destruction of cattle; for good measure, he was also accused of having poisoned the son of a gentleman at Framlingham. The grand jury threw out all the charges, but one was found 'billa vera' on appeal. Lowes was tried on that indictment but acquitted, and so was discharged.

Lowes now sought to clear his name and returned to the Woodbridge quarter sessions where he filed a suit to be heard at Star Chamber at Westminster – one of the most feared courts in the land. Jonas Cooke and his co-conspirators were summoned to answer the charge, but whether the case reached a conclusion is unclear. More certain is it that Cooke attempted to launch yet another counterattack, this time at the Court of King's Bench, but was forced to drop the case, probably because of the cost.[19] The feud continued in and out of the courtroom. Lowes' enemies laid siege to his house, forcing the vicar to have Nathaniel Man, one of the ringleaders, bound over by a magistrate to keep the peace. In the mid 1630s Lowes was summoned to the assizes again, and convicted of barratry. Ecclesiastical justice proved more elusive: repeated petitions to the Archbishop of Canterbury pleading for Lowes to be removed were ignored.[20]

It was not unusual for a minister to be at war with his congregation; nor was Lowes the only minister ever to be prosecuted for witchcraft.[21] But in 1641 – after the impeachment of Archbishop Laud, Parliament's condemnation of images, and the introduction of the Protestation Oath against popery – many more communities felt justified in visiting retribution upon their enemies. 'Scandalous' and 'malignant' aspects of clerical lives were emphasized, specifically enthusiasm for Laudian ceremonialism and the liturgy of the Book of Common Prayer. John Lowes was reviled as a 'painful preacher' and a 'reading parson' – a slave to Anglican orthodoxy. In August a gentleman from Woodbridge (where Lowes also had enemies) swore an affidavit before the Court of Chancery that Lowes had been tried for witchcraft and convicted of barratry.[22] No action appears to have been taken against him, nor could Jonas Cooke and his followers appeal to the courts of High Commission or Star Chamber, for both had been abolished the previous month. There was only one option open to them: publication of a pamphlet.[23]

The scabrous tract that resulted was entitled *A Magazine of Scandall*. As a young man with interests in Framlingham, Matthew Hopkins must have heard the rumours about Lowes, and may have read the pamphlet. The seeds of Lowes' destruction had now been widely scattered. By 1645 not only was the scale of his wickedness akin to the scandalous lives of other clergymen – not least his friend Thomas Fowkes at Earl Soham, a Laudian minister convicted of manslaughter – but it formed patterns with known witches in and around Framlingham.[24] In Essex, outward shows of godliness had not served to deflect accusations of witchcraft. Anne and Rebecca West had behaved 'as if they had been Saints on earth', and Mistress Waite, a minister's wife 'of a very godly and religious life', also seems to have been sucked into the vortex and charges against her publicized in print.[25] Hopkins knew from the Bible that holy men might be diabolical impostors, 'for Satan himself is transformed into an angel of light'. After all, had Lowes not been protected by that acolyte of Antichrist, William Laud? Had he not consorted with papists, cunning folk and witches? His parishioners certainly thought so. And when Hopkins rode into Brandeston that summer, he too was quite convinced that they had unmasked this monster thirty years before.[26]

Nathaniel Man came forward to testify that after procuring a warrant against him, Lowes had given his wife two shillings and sixpence to feed their child. 'After this mony [was] received', recalled Man, 'the child fell sick, languished, and though it eate the meate yet it gathered no strength but so continued untill it died.' Alongside this, definite links with suspicions at Framlingham were beginning to emerge. Margery Chinery told her captors that 'Mr Lowis did come to her and bad her never to confes any thinge about witchcraft', which seemed to suggest that the vicar of Brandeston was a leader of their sect.[27] Hopkins promised that the old man would confess. For the second time in his life Lowes was arrested for witchcraft. This time he had no means of retaliation or escape: the mood of the people was brutally unforgiving; the old institutions had been transformed or abolished; and the men who might have protected him were gone – men like John Revett of Brandeston Hall. Later his son recalled that 'my Father was always of ye opinion that Mr Lowes suffered wrongfully, and have often said that he did beleave he was no more a wizard then he was', adding carefully that 'my Father was not concerned with the matter, and would willingly have prevented it, if he could'.[28] Lowes was stripped and his body searched for the marks where he suckled his imps. Then Hopkins put the watchers to work.

In the 1660s John Revett, returning to Brandeston as manorial lord and magistrate, enquired about the fate of John Lowes and jotted down the following record:

I have heard it from th[e]m th[a]t watched with him th[a]t they kept him awake several Nights together, & ran him backwards, and forwards ab[ou]t ye Room, until he [was] out of Breath. Then they rested him a little, & then ran him again; & thus they did for several Days & Nights together, till he was weary of his life, & was scarce sensible of what he said, or did . . .

Yet still Lowes had not confessed. Hopkins ordered that he be carried the six miles to Framlingham Castle, site of the witchfinder's family estate, and thrown into the stagnant waters of the castle ditch. For all his floundering and gasping, it was plain to spectators that the vicar was floating, thereby proving his guilt. To underline the fact, blameless volunteers leapt into the ditch as a control experiment; but, as John Revett later observed, 'th[a]t was no true Rule to try him by: for . . . they swam as well as he'.[29] Nevertheless, exhaustion prevailed, and little by little Lowes confessed to the searchers.

John Lowes was broken in body and spirit. The Brandeston parish register records that 'Hopkins his cheif Accusor . . . kept ye poor Old Man waking several Nights till he was delirious & then confest such Familiarity with ye Devil as had such Weight with the Jury & his Judges.' Lowes showed Charles Knowles marks on his head and beneath his tongue where he had fed his imps for the past five years. He denied having made a contract with the devil even though his largest familiar, 'Thomas', had tried to persuade him to do so 'in a hollow voyce'. Thomas, he said, also suckled from Anne Sherwood of Framlingham, but came to Lowes whenever she grew weary. Lowes also admitted to Daniel Rayner that his imps would make him send them on destructive errands, including killing cattle, and sinking boats between Yarmouth and Winterton on the Norfolk coast.[30]

Maritime atrocities loomed large in the confession Lowes now made to Matthew Hopkins. On one occasion, he revealed, he had gone to preach at Landguard Fort, a defensive position at the mouth of the Stour that royalists at Bury were plotting to seize in 1645; the resident chaplain was also said to have royalist sympathies. From the ramparts Lowes had seen a fleet approaching, and at that instant one of his imps had appeared. He had commanded the beast to swim to a new vessel sailing out of Ipswich, then watched as the ship 'began tumbling up and downe with waves, as if [the] water had been boyled in a pot'. As the rest of the fleet moved on, so it sank, making 'fourteen widdowes in one quarter of an houre'. Hopkins asked Lowes if he did not grieve to see so many die; the old parson was reported to have replied 'no, he was joyfull to see what power his Impes had'.[31] The witchfinder and the watchers dragged Lowes to a magistrate, who recorded the essential evidence before committing him to Ipswich gaol pending the next assizes at Bury St Edmunds.

At some point during this summer of discovery the witchfinding campaign spread into Norfolk, a vast expanse of countryside bounded by river, sea, breckland and fen. As in Essex and Suffolk, by 1645 puritan and parliamentarian confidence had already inspired several purges of Catholics.[32] Now perhaps forty witches were apprehended, of whom just a few details survive: a widow hanged for attacking livestock early in June; another accused of bewitching a man at Needham a few days later; a Hempnall woman condemned for the murder of a girl in July; and two cases from August – a widow from Stratton St Mary who was acquitted, and a stonemason from Pulham St Mary, sentenced to death for using witchcraft to kill his neighbour's wife. Most striking is that the accused all came from an area of fifty square miles in England's fourth largest county; all locations were south of Norwich and none further than ten miles from the Suffolk border.[33] Southern parts of Norfolk had experienced dramatic economic change after 1600, with reclamation schemes and forced enclosure bringing landowners and magistrates into conflict with the common people whose 'tumults' were suppressed.[34]

In view of the propinquity of these cases, and their proximity to Suffolk, it is likely that Matthew Hopkins had a hand in them (the first three, at least), and that he gave evidence at the Norwich assizes towards the end of July. In response *A Perfect Diurnall*, a parliamentarian newspaper printed in London, ended ten pages of war reports with this brief curiosity:

> But that I want room I should have told you of the late tryall of the Norfolke Witches about 40 of them, and 20 of them already executed, and what strange Prophesies some of them had before their death of the downfall of the Kings Army, and that Prince Rupert should not now longer be shot free, and much more but of this I conceive I have already said more than most will have faith to believe, though it be never so true, however by the next, if I be not prevented by others, I will give you all at large, and from unquestionable Authority.[35]

As the report seems never to have been followed up, this was as much as many ever got to hear. Whether the gallows predictions were really made or whether they were propagandist embellishment remains obscure. News about witches certainly made the war between Christ and Satan seem closer to that between Crown and Parliament. A pamphlet printed some days later asserted that the civil war was punishment for the nation's sins, and that abundant wonders signified worse to come. 'Have there not beene strange Comets seen in the ayre, prodigies, sights on the seas, marvellous tempests and storms on the land?' asked the author. 'Have not nature altered her course so much, that women framed of pure flesh and blood, bringeth forth ugly and deformed Monsters?' These horrors led into a discussion of the witches in Essex, Suffolk and Norfolk, fourteen of whom had been hanged at Chelmsford, and most recently twenty at Norwich, and the pamphlet ended with a lurid account of the births of a limbless hermaphrodite and a one-eyed, eight-footed kitten with the hands of a child.[36]

English gaols were crammed with prisoners just when the authorities wanted them empty for reasons of security, sanitation and expense – which was possibly why the witchfinders had been challenged at Colchester. Special pardons were granted to alleviate the problem: in January forty prisoners, twenty-two of them women, had been freed from Newgate Prison by this means.[37] Predictions of royalist defeat, like those of the Norfolk witches, may have comforted some; but Parliament still had to deal with the fact that the king was once again threatening the eastern counties – the buffer protecting London and the south-east – and that prisoners were a liability. Intelligence of a plot to seize Norwich Castle prompted an order from Westminster that no one else was to be incarcerated there, and that existing inmates should be moved so that the castle could be fortified.[38]

Meanwhile, at Ipswich, John Lowes was suffering humiliation, hardship and dread. *The True Informer* for 23 July reported

That there are at least 38 Witches imprisoned in that Town: all of which (except one) by the testimony of the town-Searchers, confesse that they have one or two paps on which the Devill sucks: divers of them voluntarily, and without any forcing or compulsion, freely declare, That they have made a Covenant with the Devill, to forsake

Signes and wonders from Heaven.

With a true Relation of a Monster borne in *Ratcliffe High-way*, at the signe of the three Arrows, Mistris *Bullock* the Midwife delivering her thereof.

Also shewing how a Cat kitned a Monster in *Lombard street* in *London*.

Likewise a new discovery of Witches in *Stepney* Parish.

And how 20. Witches more were executed in *Suffolke* this last Assise, Also how the Divell came to Softam to a Farmers house in the habit of a Gentlewoman on horse backe.

With divers other strange remarkable passages.

Printed at *London* by *I. H.*

A pamphlet from 1645 reports the birth of a monstrous child, accompanied by the latest news about witches — more gossip for the alehouses depicted in the background

God and Christ, and to take him to be their Master: and like wise do acknowledge, that divers Cattell and some Christians have beene killed by their means . . . It is further certified thence; that there are divers women apprehended upon suspition from day to day, which if they should all be found guilty, there is scarce a village in those parts free.[39]

One rumoured explanation for the discovery of so many witches was that the devil's book containing all their names had been seized by a witchfinder – a popular tale which later returned to haunt Matthew Hopkins.[40] Chatter was rife in Ipswich, four convicted witches having already been hanged there, and excitement about the remaining prisoners was intense. Every morning the gaoler James Rigges admitted a stream of thrill-seekers in return for an entry fee. It was said that the most voluble and intransigent of sceptics had changed their minds after speaking to the witches: to the deluded who believed their own confessions, the demoralized who delighted in outraging others, and the desperate who sought mercy in self-abasement – those who, John Stearne said, 'by bitter curses upon themselves, think thereby to clear themselves'. Clergymen also visited the prisoners, some content to let divine justice take its course, others believing it to be 'a matter of doubt and trouble . . . to discerne and find them [real witches] out, so that none may be put to death unjustly'.[41]

In London the news from Suffolk triggered a sarcastic war of words between royalist and parliamentarian propagandists. Responding to the apparent irony that so many witches should have been found in the godly heartland of East Anglia, one newspaper made a valiant effort to turn the tables:

> It is the ordinary mirth of the Malignants in this City to discourse of the Association of Witches in the Associated Counties, but by this they shall understand the truth of the old Proverbe which is, that where God hath his Church the Devill have his Chappell. To labour in to the depth of this Mistery of Iniquity, we must dive as low as Hell.[42]

Some went further, insisting that witches were recruited by the devil to assist the king's forces – even to protect Prince Rupert from enemy guns, as the Norfolk witches were said to have predicted. Many remembered the story of the royalist woman executed as a spy after the battle of Newbury in 1643, rapidly recast as an indestructable witch who sailed on a plank and chewed any bullets fired at her, until a roundhead trooper broke her power with a sword-cut to the face. She died, it was said, with a magnanimous prophecy on her lips: 'And

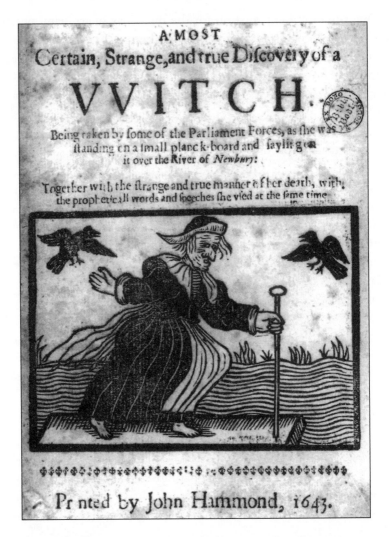

The Witch of Newbury — a stereotypical crone — sailing down a river on a plank

is it come to passe, that I must dye indeed? why then his Excellency the Earle of Essex shall be fortunate and win the field.' Witches like her were allegories expressing deep-rooted subconscious fears about patriarchy and the state, and their deaths fulfilled fantasies about restoring male authority and order.[43]

The idea that the devil recruited witches in the king's interest went beyond mere propaganda, enjoying serious popular currency. After all, the Everard family of Halesworth in Suffolk had confessed to having sent familiars to help Prince Rupert; and rumours that the prince's pet dog 'Boy' was a diabolical imp were repeated so often that many must have concluded they were true. Boy was called 'a counterfeit Lapland Lady', 'a witch in the shape of a white Dogge' who like the strange woman at Newbury was 'weapon-proof' and able to catch bullets in its teeth.[44] As such, the dog was denounced as 'an Enemy to Parliament', and great significance was attached to its death at Marston Moor in July 1644 – killed by 'a Valiant Souldier, who had skill in Necromancy'.[45] One newspaper, however, dismissed the idea that Prince Rupert had any involvement with witchcraft as 'a meere fable'.[46]

'Boy', a dog belonging to Prince Rupert of the Rhine, was widely believed to be a diabolical familiar. Here, a witch laments its death at the battle of Marston Moor

The number of witches apparent by the end of July 1645 suggested entire maleficent regiments, rather than just the odd diabolical spy or sniper. Hearing of events in Norfolk and Suffolk, one parliamentarian writer observed: 'It seemes our adversaries have had all the assistance that the Devill could helpe them to.' 'There is an infection in wickednesse', remarked another, 'And the spirit of the Caviliers, because it could not prevaile with our men, hath met with some of our women, and it hath turned them into Witches.' Royalist newspapers pointed to the biblical text 'rebellion is as the sin of witchcraft', one revelling in the fact that the army of two hundred witches in Suffolk and Essex – 'which Counties from the beginning have beene onely the Rebels Quarters' – was no longer simply trying to bewitch Prince Rupert but was attacking friend and foe alike.[47] A rival newspaper made a rebuttal, denouncing the royal Court at Oxford as a place where the cavaliers raved like men possessed, covenants were signed with England's blood, and 'the Court-Sorcerers had like to have bewitch't the whole Kingdom'. That much of this was satirical and metaphorical did not necessarily blind either side to the fact that for every witch executed in Essex and Norfolk there were forty more in Suffolk who might yet benefit from a fair trial. Furthermore, countless others might be spared the tortures which, it was said, were being applied by unauthorized witchfinders prowling around the countryside.[48]

A routine assize commission for Suffolk was drawn up at Westminster on 24 July 1645 and recorded at the Crown Office of the Court of Chancery. Twenty-seven men were named as commissioners, including three barons, four knights and various prominent county magistrates, among them Nathaniel Bacon, Brampton Gurdon (senior and junior), and Sir Thomas Barnardiston. The judge was to be Serjeant-at-Law John Godbold, who had served at the Suffolk assizes for several years.[49] But within a few days the situation had changed. A report was delivered to Parliament which, while it did not name the witchfinders, raised concerns about the number of confessed witches in Suffolk, 'as if some busie men had made use of some ill Arts, to extort such confession from them'.[50] As a result, Parliament decided to grant a Special Commission of Oyer and Terminer (to hear and determine) – an emergency power issued by the Lord Chancellor under the Great Seal and normally used to deal with dangerous cases requiring speed and discretion: ringleaders of riots and seditious plots, for example, were despatched by this means.[51] As a respected jurist of thirty years' experience, and a Suffolk man to boot, Serjeant John

Godbold was an ideal man to lead the commission – though judges were normally appointed to circuits distant from their principal place of residence, to ensure objectivity.[52] Apart from the county magistrates, the other commissioners were, unusually, not lawyers but eminent clergy, Edmund Calamy and Samuel Fairclough. Both were godly men of age and wisdom, well-regarded in London but also sensitive to the politics and beliefs of the environment into which they would be sent.

Edmund Calamy, a tradesman's son who rose to prominence as a puritan minister under the patronage of the Earl of Warwick

In his youth Edmund Calamy, like John Lowes, had been a lecturer at Bury St Edmunds, but had resigned in opposition to the Arminian bishop, Matthew Wren. Around 1640 he was one of the puritan ministers who secured the patronage of the Earl of Warwick, and was presented to the rectory of Rochford in Essex. At the outbreak of war he regularly delivered sermons at St Mary Aldermanbury – though never from the pulpit, for an ague had left him intolerant of heights. He was appointed to the Westminster

Assembly, where he was outspoken on constitutional and doctrinal issues, and committed to fighting the diabolical influences that were causing the divisions of the war. 'Wee by the fall of Adam are stung by that old serpent ye devill,' he thundered in one sermon, 'wee are all by nature under the slavery of ye devill, led captive by him at his will.' A well-received address to the House of Lords on 25 December 1644 argued that God would make peace for men who learnt to make peace with God; that meant renouncing Satan, suppressing sectarianism, and banishing evil.[53]

For all his hellfire Calamy was a Presbyterian moderate like his fellow commissioner Samuel Fairclough, who also detested the war. Fairclough was born in Suffolk in 1594, and formulated his austere code of ethics early in life. As a student at Cambridge he had refused to dress as a woman in a play performed for James I, choosing the approval of God over that of his sovereign; and after his appointment to a lectureship at King's Lynn was reprimanded for refusing to make the sign of the cross at baptisms. In 1629 his patrons, the Barnardiston family, presented him to the living of Kedington, near where he had been born, and there he devoted himself to reading, catechizing his parishioners, and preaching from his imposing three-decker pulpit. Devoted to the peace of the parish above all else, at the outbreak of war he remained with his people, and the following year declined an invitation to join the Westminster Assembly.[54] To Parliament's request that he sit on the Special Commission of Oyer and Terminer, however, he was more favourably inclined. He believed in truth and fairness, but also in the need to fight sin and idolatry. It was the duty of God's servants, he said, to 'prescribe the cure of a disturbed State by a sentence of totall extirpation of the offenders'.[55]

Fairclough already had personal experience of the witch-hunt, and on one occasion had even met John Stearne. Most of the places visited by the witchfinder were tightly grouped, but a single destination lay well to the west: Haverhill, meeting-point of the borders of Cambridgeshire, Essex and Suffolk. There Stearne had ordered a suspected woman by the name of Binkes to be searched and watched, and had heard her confess. A horsefly buzzing round the room was her imp, she said – a claim confirmed when it landed on her skin and bit her. Normally that would have ended the investigation; but Binkes had the presence of mind to ask for the rector of Kedington.

Samuel Fairclough duly arrived at Haverhill, his birth-place and the parish where his father had been vicar. Stearne acquainted Fairclough with Binkes's confession, and the minister – 'an able Orthodox Divine' according to the witchfinder – was taken to her. Confounding everyone's expectations, in Fairclough's presence she denied being a witch, 'desiring withal, that if she were such a manner of person, that

Samuel Fairclough, puritan divine and rector of Kedington in Suffolk

the Lord would shew an example upon her; and that if she had any Imps, that they would come whilst he was there'. Just then, a horsefly was again seen, at which Binkes cried out 'A just judgement of God, they are come indeed!' The fly landed on her body and fastened itself near her existing bite, making her groan. Fairclough, Stearne and the watchers waited a quarter of an hour, the female spectators increasingly afraid. Meanwhile, a number of other women gathered to see what all the fuss was about, one of whom mustered the courage to wipe the fly away with a cloth. It, too, had left a bite-mark. Fairclough's reaction is unknown, but Binkes was sent for trial. Stearne at least was sure: 'Was this woman fitting to live', he asked rhetorically in his account of events, 'this evidence, with others, being against her, by credible witnesses?'[56]

The assizes were not scheduled to take place until late August, but the commissioners set off from London as much as three weeks in advance. The judge, John Godbold, accompanied by a Mr Woodward, visited Bury St Edmunds twice 'about the tryall of the witches and other malefactors', and stayed there for about a month in all. On 6 August in the Westminster Assembly, Edmund Calamy begged a fort-night's leave of absence, to begin that afternoon. It seems likely that Samuel Fairclough had to cut back on his customary four weekly sermons, including the lectures he gave on Thursdays, which were attended by clergy from as far away as Cambridge. He may have been among the worried ministers who visited the prisoners at Ipswich; perhaps his concerns had been the impetus behind the Special Commission in the first place. No doubt Godbold and Woodward travelled beyond their base at Bury, visiting prisoners 'in the severall Gaoles in this County'.[57] They already knew that John Lowes' name was linked to witchcraft in a libel action; now that he was on trial for his life, it was vital they should fully understand the case against him and his co-defendants.[58]

The revulsion the commissioners felt on entering these dank gaols was considerable. Edmund Calamy cherished the image of Christ the physician curing spiritual diseases, with the minister a conduit for that healing.[59] Yet his task now was not to reach out to the shackled dregs of humanity he encountered but to judge them; to determine not whether their spirits were diseased with witchcraft, but whether there was sufficient evidence to prove them guilty according to statute. Once the commissioners' demand for physical proof of a demonic pact would have disqualified many witchcraft prosecutions; now that there were men at large fanatical about discovering such proofs, the outcome of a trial would be different, however dubious the witchfinders' methods.[60]

★

By mid August John Lowes' misery was absolute. He had been man-handled, intimidated and half-drowned, and now he was compelled to endure conditions of extreme privation. Weather, season, time of day made no difference in gaol: here it was always twilight, always winter. And however bountiful the harvest outside, however sweet the air, inside the pickings were always slim and every breath sucked in pestilence. Bubonic plague, which around this time killed Mary Greenliefe in the gaol at Chelmsford, had spread to Suffolk, and every inmate knew the signs: the enervating fever, aching limbs and fearful black swellings.[61]

Meanwhile, another spectre of the Apocalypse appeared on the horizon. A rumour spread that the king was on his way to Huntingdon, having already plundered St Ives, Cromwell's home town. Like most rumours this was an exaggeration, though not without foundation or consequence. The king was indeed heading down the Great North Road, which worried the garrison at St Ives into destroying their main bridge. The prospect of royalist plunder also caused chaos further east, at Cambridge, where 'the scholars came running away 6 upon a horse in great confusion'. 'These allarms generated strange, wild, and indigested propositions,' noted one observer, 'such as were not to be hearkened unto by any person of Judgement and experience'; and yet even he could not deny the genuine panic.[62] On 24 August the king's army took Huntingdon, with considerable violence inflicted upon the civilian population. The hordes of prisoners in the gaol – murderers, thieves, and doubtless witches – were freed, and the men among them inducted into royalist regiments. Even the town's anti-puritan malignants changed their minds about the king after seeing the lawlessness he stirred up. The cavaliers who once had been thought of as saints, wrote one diarist, were now branded devils.[63]

Forty miles to the east, at Bury St Edmunds, the Special Commission was preparing for a witch-trial in an atmosphere of trepidation. In the small hours of 25 August the county committee at Bury wrote to its counterpart at Ipswich warning that 'the Alarum holds very strong' and urging them to send cavalry and foot-soldiers; the outside of the letter was inscribed 'hast[e], hast[e], hast[e]'. Men all over East Anglia were forced to abandon the harvest and rendezvous at Cambridge.[64] Tales of barbarity from Huntingdon had concentrated minds: houses ransacked, horses stolen (forcing country folk to carry grain-sacks on their backs), and great sums extorted. One impecunious man was said to have been strung upside-down and tortured with lighted tapers.[65]

A trial date was set for the following day, Tuesday 26 August. Prisoners detained at Ipswich were delivered by cart to Bury and detained. There may have been as many as 150 accused of witchcraft alone, and a barn had to be used to contain them all, probably the Almoners' Barn owned by the corporation and sometimes used as a pest-house.[66] Meanwhile, carpenters hammered together the gallows in the market square; the clerk of assize laboured to organize a gaol calendar and indictment file of great complexity; and Samuel Fairclough, whose heavy conscience made him fearful lest he fail in his duty, finished preparing not one but two assize sermons. The next morning Serjeant Godbold, Edmund Calamy, the justices named on the commission and the other county magistrates filed into St Mary's church and watched Fairclough ascend the pulpit. They were gratified to hear him affirm, without equivocation, that the sins of witchcraft and of entertaining familiar spirits were real, and that sceptical Sadducees and atheists were dangerously mistaken. The second sermon drew in the reins, however, pointing to 'the hainousness of the sin of those who would violently prosecute, or unduly endeavour to convict any person, except plain convincing evidence could be brought'.[67]

The commissioners and magistrates digested this on their journey to the courtroom. Serjeant Godbold – resplendent in violet robes – delivered a solemn charge to the grand jury, addressing a three-fold problem: witchcraft had become hard to prove unless the suspect confessed; yet it was essential that confessions should be 'purely voluntary and unconstrained'; however, reports indicated that recent confessions in Suffolk had been anything but voluntary and unconstrained. This address resembled the instruction issued to the Special Commission itself, namely 'that there might be a most special care taken, both of the execution of the Law, and that also all tenderness might be used, in a matter wherein the Lives and Immortal Souls of many were concerned'.[68] The grand jurors then retired with their bundles of presentments to sort the wheat from the chaff.

However many trials the assize clerk expected to get through that day, there could be no hope of processing them all; the proceedings would inevitably run over into Wednesday, and probably Thursday as well. On that first day the grand jury considered around ninety cases, devoting no more than a few minutes to each. At least sixteen of these were thrown out, and sixty or so approved for trial. Of the remainder, for which no return was made, a handful may have been carried over to the next assizes; probably the prisoners named in the rest had been found to have died in gaol.[69]

Once the trial had begun the accused were brought forward in small groups for arraignment, the trial jurors were sworn in, and a procession of witnesses took the stand. Among these were Matthew Hopkins and John Stearne, who if they had not been in St Mary's to hear it for themselves must by now have learnt the substance of Samuel Fairclough's second sermon. The charge Godbold delivered to the grand jury implied the same criticisms of the witchfinders' methods as Fairclough's sermon, and must have intensified their discomfort. Between them Hopkins and Stearne had been bound by recognizance to testify against at least seven of the suspects, from as far apart as Stowmarket and Framlingham, although it seems that two of Stearne's cases had been rejected by the grand jury; another three were destined to end in acquittal. One was the case of Binkes, the Haverhill woman who had called for Fairclough. 'She never confessed any more', Stearne noted with contempt, 'but denied what she had formerly confessed.'[70] The witchfinder's feelings were directed as much at a trial jury willing to excuse someone who in his opinion was so obviously guilty as at Binkes herself.

Another indicator of the mood in the courtroom was the trial of Alexander Sussums, Stearne's acquaintance from Long Melford: though Sussums appears to have repeated his confession before the jury, he was acquitted. Yet apparently the jurors had not set their faces indiscriminately against the witchfinders, but were prepared to consider cases individually. Mary Bacon of Chattisham, against whom Hopkins testified, was found guilty and sentenced to death by the commissioners. More arresting still was the case of John Lowes. The old vicar was convicted, despite a strident retraction of his confession before the court. At the same time, regardless of whether or not he believed Lowes to be guilty, Serjeant Godbold was clear on one point: no more suspected witches were to be subjected to the water ordeal. Calamy and Fairclough reinforced this warning by expounding its religious unlawfulness.[71]

This was perhaps the clearest public rebuke to the witchfinders so far. By the end of the day perhaps half the accused presented by the grand jury had been tried, of whom sixteen women and two men – one of them Lowes – had been sentenced to death. Samuel Fairclough was content that though some of the guilty might have escaped, at least none had been condemned unjustly. And he was satisfied with his own contribution. 'Both in the Pulpit, and on the Bench,' wrote an admirer, 'he did very much influence the whole Court by his judgment, viz. by his learned, pious and prudent management of the whole affair.' The grand jury had certainly been more discerning than its counterpart at Chelmsford, although the Bury trial jurors had proved themselves as willing to convict when the evidence seemed strong as they were to acquit when they smelt a rat. In the case of the Everards from Halesworth, Thomas and Mary were both convicted, while their daughter Marian appears to have been cleared. Mary Everard's brother, James More of Metfield – who had confessed to sending an imp to help Prince Rupert – had his case carried over to the next day, when the court was scheduled to reconvene.[72]

But it did not. Before the court adjourned, news had arrived of the latest alarm from Cambridge, where troops were mobilizing to defend the city and to march to Huntingdon to engage the king's forces. It was ruled that the assizes should be suspended, and that prisoners already condemned were to be executed the following morning. Henry Carre, the penitent scholar of Rattlesden, had even been arraigned at the bar, but was removed before judgment could be passed and returned to the dark confines of the gaol, where, according to one estimate, there remained well over a hundred prisoners yet to be tried or so much as properly arraigned.[73]

From a wish to keep the convicted separate from the accused or because of overcrowding in the gaol, John Lowes and the other seventeen condemned witches were not confined there but were taken instead to the edge of town and locked in the requisitioned barn. Guards were posted outside for the duration of the night. Whispering to one another in the darkness, the prisoners made a pact 'not to confesse a word next day at the gallowes, when they were to be hanged, notwithstanding they had formerly confessed' – even those who had confessed in gaol, or that very same day in the courtroom. All except 'one penitent woman' consented, and together they sang a psalm to fortify themselves against their plight.[74] Afterwards they slept fitfully on the floor of the barn, their thoughts heavy with the prospect of the hangman's noose. Too soon morning broke over another day, and they were led blinking into the sunlight, ready as they ever could be to meet the hour of their death.

Wednesday 27 August was an official day of public humiliation, a fast when no work was supposed to be done except duties performed in the service of God. Many people among the crowds in the market square must have persuaded themselves they were performing just such a duty, perched on walls and in the boughs of trees, standing tiptoe on buckets and barrels, craning their necks to catch a glimpse of the open-topped cart drawing near to the place of execution. Of the witchfinders, John Stearne at least was present, still sure in his heart of the virtue of the work that had helped bring about this spectacle.

All the condemned prisoners except one – the penitent woman who had refused the pact – remained silent as the cart pulled up and they were helped out of it. As voices from the crowd bellowed for their blood, they looked up at the gallows, an oak frame as high as nearby houses, a row of hemp nooses dangling from the cross-beam. A minister was present to exhort them to allow Christ into their hearts at this, the twilight of their lives, and to make their contrition plain to the town. For whatever good she thought it would do her, the penitent woman railed against the other prisoners, revealing to the world their secret pact and her decision to have no part in it. Stearne held out hope for a puritan conversion of the damned, even at this final, fatal stage, and like that miserably remorseful woman believed that

. . . if honest godly people discourse with them, laying the hainousness of their sins to them, and in what condition they are without Repentance, and telling them the subtilties of the Devill, and the mercies of God, these wayes will bring them to Confession without extremity, it will make them breake into Confession hoping for mercy.[75]

But these ideals were not to be realized: as the under-sheriff of Suffolk read out his charge with the executioner standing by, there was no time left for miracles.

The shackles around the prisoners' feet and ankles were struck off, creating a fleeting illusion of freedom. The first of them, perhaps the penitent woman, was pushed towards the ladder resting against the gallows and made to climb. Nearing the top – light-headed, her hands shaking and heart thumping – she turned to face the crowd, her heels hooked over a rung, a final prayer on her lips. Climbing up on to the cross-beam, the executioner lifted a noose and placed it over her neck like a halter, then pulled the knot tight beneath one ear. At a signal from the under-sheriff the ladder was twisted away and the woman fell a short distance, enough to jolt her neck but not to break it. The crowd groaned and cheered to see how she choked and thrashed, clenching and unclenching her bound hands as instinct fought to pre-serve her life against the odds. Before she was dead – the hanged sometimes took half an hour to expire – the next prisoner was turned off in the same manner. Then another, and another, all of them dying, as Stearne recalled, 'very desperately'. The hangman, meanwhile, tried to ensure that the suspended bodies were 'comfortable' – that is, not touching one another, as custom dictated.[76]

The spectators were particularly interested in the death of John Lowes: it was something to behold a man of God transformed into a thing of the devil. Word spread that he had boasted about a charm that would protect him from hanging, a rumour that may have arisen because of a final request Lowes had planned, and which he now announced at the foot of the ladder. He asked the under-sheriff whether he might be permitted to conduct his own funeral service according to the Book of Common Prayer – the ceremonial liturgy so derided by the godly, and for his devotion to which Lowes had earned himself the sneers of 'reading parson' from his hateful parish-ioners. This was duly granted, thus enabling him to commit his body to the ground in the traditional way, 'in sure and certain hope of the resurrection to eternal life'.[77] John Lowes was already sure that his soul would go directly to God, and so devoted every last terrible second to preparing for that glorious ascension.

7

Hellish Invention

———◆———

THE LOATHSOMENESS OF witches did not make heroes of their hangmen. Execution crowds were fickle, their mood a stew of levity, melancholy and rage. Hangings were what people made them: part stage play, part sporting contest – visceral dramas of moral and emotional ambivalence. In the common calculus of rank executioners were considered base, dishonourable, unclean; some were rogues or thieves working off a sentence. In contrast, even the worst of sinners might elicit sympathy and admiration from the mob if they showed penitence and courage. Occasionally one was found to be alive after being cut down, and had to be hanged again; crowds surged forward, incensed at the unfairness.[1] But the witches at Bury St Edmunds died as God's law intended, and their corpses were carted off before the summer heat and the souvenir hunters could get to them.

Witches were buried in pits beneath the gallows or behind the gaol, sometimes held down by a stake or rock to prevent them rising on Judgement Day. Otherwise there was the unconsecrated north side of the churchyard, a dump for the disreputable dead where the placards erected on posts were intended as warnings, not memorials.[2] Those who escaped the noose returned home, if friends or family paid their gaol fees. John Stearne was dismayed to hear, some time later, that Alexander Sussums was getting on with his life at Long Melford, likewise that Binkes from Haverhill had rejoined her community.[3] Branded as witches but exonerated by heaven, these people must have had a mixed reception. Neighbours who had been afraid enough to seek to hang them must now have been more afraid than ever.

The Bury assizes were not over, of course, merely suspended due to the alarm from Cambridge. Nothing happened for at least three weeks, possibly for more than a month. Meanwhile the remaining prisoners – some tried but not sentenced, others arraigned but not tried – were transferred from Bury to Ipswich, away from the royalist advance. This was an undertaking not without risk. James More of Metfield was one of those to be moved, and in the confusion managed to escape; his absence was not noticed until the beginning of October. Some accused witches were tried later that year, among them Sarah and Alice Warner of Rushmere, both of whom were executed, but more were abandoned to the squalor and despair of Ipswich gaol, where conditions were at least as bad as at Bury. Henry Carre, the scholar of Rattlesden, never did make his peace with God at the gallows: he died waiting for the assizes to resume, probably from some infectious disease.[4] The loss of possibly innocent life was just one regrettable cost of the witch-hunt, and to Suffolk ratepayers not necessarily the most important one.

Following his prohibition of the water ordeal, the judge Serjeant Godbold had ruled that the scale of arrests was such that the prosecution of suspected witches in the county should be a general charge upon the towns and villages presenting them. This was not well received by communities where half the adult males were away at war, the horses had been requisitioned, and levies to support soldiers, paupers and Irish refugees were already oppressive. Some places that still owed fees to witchfinders, searchers and watchers felt their enthusiasm for the witch-hunt subside; many such debts were never settled. One problem was simply how to feed so many prisoners, and it led to the appointment of an officer to collect bread-money for local people who, as the accounts recorded, had been 'committed for Witchcrafte to Bury gaole'.[5] The crowd that had enjoyed the executions of John Lowes and the others soon found themselves paying for the privilege, and forced to reconsider the wisdom of witch-hunting in that light.

The assizes were not cheap at the best of times. A sheriff had to find the funds to accommodate the various officers and administrators, with a house rented specially for the judges; then there were servants to be hired for everything from carrying luggage and tending horses to carrying water and polishing pewter; wood, coal and charcoal had to be provided for fuel, as well as a great deal of food. At one assizes the meat list included beef, veal, lamb, capons, chickens, duck, pike, tench, carp and a salmon, washed down with ale, beer and wine in dizzying quantities. Candles, rushes, quills, paper, ink, pipes and so on were other items entered on bills of cost; even drawing up a bill was charged at a shilling.[6] At Bury St Edmunds the cook was paid twelve shillings for meals prepared for Godbold and his fellow commissioners. Godbold himself sent an invoice for a staggering £130 to cover his and Mr Woodward's costs for the month they had spent in Suffolk; in October this sum – equivalent to well over £100,000 today – was paid by the county committee using the confiscated wealth of royalists and Catholics. The town of Sudbury spent £2 6s. on paperwork and the hire of horses to send witnesses to Bury.[7] On top of everything else for which he had to budget, the large number of executions had put the under-sheriff 'att extraordinary Charges', so a special disbursement of £3 was ordered by the magistrates. Ordinary accusers also petitioned the court for expenses. John Pope of Rushmere, for example, had transported the Warner sisters to Bury and had financed their trial. In due course he was reimbursed from the dead women's assets, money and property, which his neighbours had been quick to seize but were far slower to surrender to the Crown.[8]

In London, Godbold presumably reported to Parliament; no record survives of this (or of any official reaction), but he remained in favour as a judge. Edmund Calamy returned to the Westminster Assembly to catch up on business. Soon a sermon he had missed, preached at Westminster on the day of the executions, became available in print. John Lightfoot's comforting message had been that though the devil was raging as never before in the history of the world, inevitably Christ would prevail through the endeavours of his servants in Church and state: 'the ministery of the Gospel overthrews the Idolatry of the Heathen', Lightfoot had told Parliament, 'and the Magistracy can hang a Witch.'[9] As a special commissioner, Calamy had been in the uncommon position of doing both.

News of the witch-trial was eagerly consumed. As well as eyewitness accounts, retold hundreds of times at the fireside, copies of the Suffolk confessions also did the rounds. A full set of notes – made by a magistrate from Hoxne, where the witchfinders had been challenged

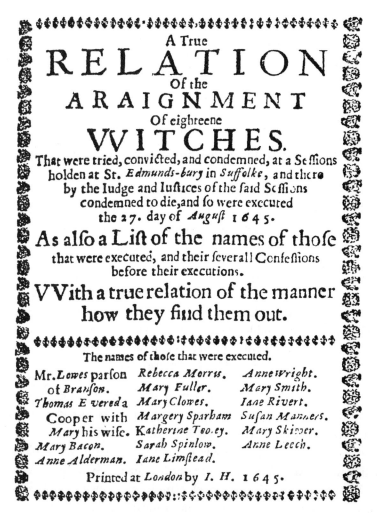

A True

RELATION

Of the

ARAIGNMENT

Of eighteene

WITCHES.

That were tried, convicted, and condemned, at a Seſſions
holden at St. *Edmunds-bury* in *Suffolke*, and there
by the Iudge and Iuſtices of the ſaid Seſſions
condemned to die, and ſo were executed
the 27. day of *Auguſt* 1645.

As alſo a Liſt of the names of thoſe
that were executed, and their ſeverall Confeſſions
before their executions.

VVith a true relation of the manner
how they find them out.

The names of thoſe that were executed.

Mr. *Lowes* parſon	Rebecca *Morris*.	*Anne Wright*.
of *Branſon*.	*Mary Fuller*.	*Mary Smith*.
Thomas Evered a	*Mary Clowes*.	*Iane Rivert*.
Cooper with	*Margery Sparham*	*Suſan Manners*.
Mary his wiſe.	*Katherine Tooley*.	*Mary Skinner*.
Mary Bacon.	*Sarah Spinlow*.	*Anne Leech*.
Anne Alderman.	*Iane Limſtead*.	

Printed at *London* by I. H. 1645.

Title-page to a pamphlet about the Bury St Edmunds trials, 1645.
The names of those executed are listed, starting with John Lowes and
followed by Thomas and Mary Everard

by the local gentry – was taken home and preserved as an heirloom.[10]
In London, several pamphlets and newspapers mentioned the Suffolk
executions. The best known was *A True Relation of the Araignment of eighteene Witches . . . at St Edmunds-bury*, rushed into print early in
September. The work was undertaken by John Hammond, a specialist

in religious and political tracts who had published a famous account of
the Witch of Newbury in 1643. The *True Relation* was thin stuff, men-
tioning only John Lowes and the Everards by name, padded out with
a Hopkins-style guide to watching a suspect and, incongruously, the
confession of one of the Essex witches. The exposition was not short
on horror, however: readers learnt all about the outrageous confessions, including that of a woman who had conceived after having sex
with the devil; the offspring had 'run away in most horrid long and
ugly shapes' as soon as they left her womb.[11]

The pamphlet caused quite a stir. The author of a contemporary
theological tract read it, and remarked 'what strange thinges have been
acted by Witches . . . and are known to be approved as truths'. *The
Scotish Dove* was equally trusting of its sources:

> It is certified, that at Bury in Suffolke, there were last weeke (besides
> those formerly) Executed more then 20 Witches, and above 100 more
> discovered in those parts. Some of them confessed they had beene in
> the Kings Armie, and have sent out their Hags to serve them . . . His
> Majesties Armie it seemes is beholding to the Devill; you may be sure
> it is a just cause where the Divell takes part . . .

The Parliaments Post reported a similar story, adding the usual explanation for why the eastern counties seemed so besotted with witchcraft: 'You must understand that although the Witches were taken in
the Association, yet their association with the Devill was to please the
Malignants, and indeed what greater Malignant than the Devill.'[12]

The Moderate Intelligencer struck a more cautious note: 'Life is precious, and there's need of great inquisition before it be taken away.'
The anonymous author was particularly suspicious of a reply made by
one woman during her interrogation. 'She said, the Devil told her, he
could not bewitch Mr such a one, because he was a Ministers sonne,
and well-affected to the Parliament' – this must have been Matthew
Hopkins. He went on to question why 'Devils should choose to be
conversant with silly Women that know not their right hands from
their left', and why killing hens and geese should better advance their
cause than helping royalist generals win the war. Cruel irony, too, that
whereas the devil was prince of the air, the Suffolk witches were two

feet underground. These were sound arguments; but overall the cheap press did more to promote fear of witches than it did to provoke debate about their existence. At this time rumours of witches at Stepney in the east end of London were widely reported, although as 'persons of eminence' their names were kept a secret. Some accounts made a direct connection with the Suffolk witches: 'they have had converse with many Witches about London', read one report; most of them were concentrated in St Katherine's parish, not far from Stepney. In West Ham, the house of a godly silk-weaver was said to be possessed by a tiresome poltergeist 'with a soft hollow voyce' who repeatedly lifted a heavy stone up the stairs.[13]

Printers and rumour-mongers heightened sensitivity to witches far beyond London and East Anglia. By mid September one pamphlet was calling to people throughout England to 'doe their utmost in discovering and finding out wicked persons which by confederacy with the Devill do not onely cast away their soules and bodies, but make spoyle and havock of their neighbours goods'. Apparently whole flocks of geese were reeling, screeching and dying; some had been found with their quills stuck up their backsides, an inconvenience 'thought apparently to exceed from witchcraft'.[14] In the Sussex Cinque Port of Rye the mayor, doubtless unaware of Godbold's ruling, ordered that a pair of suspected witches be put to the water ordeal. In Cornwall, a nineteen-year-old girl who claimed familiarity with fairies was interrogated by ministers and magistrates and confined without food; her fairies were thought to be imps in disguise.[15] The news was everywhere. It is hard to imagine that the witches used to represent the unnatural power of Parliament in an amateur drama – an anti-masque – written by the daughters of the exiled Duke of Newcastle in 1645 were not a tacit reference to recent events.[16] For some, witchcraft was an arresting metaphor; but for ordinary people it remained a crime, and word from eastern parts spread fear and further accusations.

One case in particular shows the infectious nature of the witchfinding campaign. It occurred at Faversham in Kent, like Rye a self-governing Cinque Port, which in common with towns in Suffolk and Essex had endured epidemics, riots, religious enmity and mass emigration to New England from the 1620s onwards. Barely a month after the executions at Bury St Edmunds, three women were hanged after confessing to having attended a sabbat where they had feasted with the devil and signed his covenant in blood. Their confessions were identical in style to those extracted by Hopkins and Stearne, suggesting that news of the witchfinders' work had reached Faversham – or even that they had visited in person.[17]

Independent by royal charter and governed by a godly oligarchy, Faversham was just the sort of place where Matthew Hopkins might have been welcomed. If the mayor and aldermen wanted a witchfinder, they had only to vote among themselves and authorize a disbursement from the town coffers. This was also how things worked in the urban corporations of Suffolk and Norfolk. On 15 August 1645 the town assembly of Yarmouth on the Norfolk coast discussed reports that there were witches at large, and minuted this:

> It is agreed that the gentleman Mr Hopkins imployed in the Countrie for discovering & finding out of witches shall be sent for hither to come to Towne; to make search for such wicked p[er]sons if any be here; and shall have his fee and such allowance for his paines & labour in that kinde as he hath in other places in the Countrey.[18]

By the time the invitation reached Hopkins the assizes at Bury St Edmunds were approaching, and he replied that he would not arrive until early the following month. From Bury he went first to the small port of Aldeburgh, where he was engaged in interrogations until Monday 8 September, the day he was paid by the town chamberlain. He received £2, probably a flat fee rather than a daily or *per capita* rate. Mary Phillips from Manningtree was paid £1 'for her paynes for searching out witches', and another thirteen shillings and tenpence was expended on 'sundry men for watching dayes and nightes w[i]th such as were apprehended as witches'. Widow Phillips's reward exceeded what most of her neighbours earned in a month.[19] Before the ink was dry on the accounts the restless Hopkins had bade her farewell and continued up the coast towards Yarmouth. It was a tortuous journey through forty miles of bleak marshland and heath, his only company the clanging geese in the high skies and the harriers swooping over the reed beds.

Yarmouth thrived on mercantile trade, notably with the Low Countries, and was well-connected to its hinterland by a network of waterways. Though not on the same scale as Norwich twenty miles to the west, it was also a centre of spinning and weaving, particularly the manufacture of hosiery. Tradesmen from artisans to attorneys flourished there too. But it was herring for which Yarmouth was best known, and in the autumn most men were employed as mariners, carpenters, coopers and net-makers. The coal trade ensured a steady influx of apprentices from as far away as Durham, most of whom entered maritime occupations and positions in the worsted industry. By day the long streets and connecting lanes criss-crossing the sandbank on which the town had grown, heavy with the smell of smoked herring, hummed with the sound of wheels and looms. In the 1630s the puritan townsmen had locked horns with the Dean and Chapter of Norwich; but whatever they thought of Charles I's spiritual headship, they had him to thank for keeping Dutch competition out of sovereign waters. Fortunes were made from textiles and fish, enabling local merchants to build grand houses on the South Quay.[20]

Prosperity did not always bring peace. Not only were there differences of doctrine and devotion but, as in the Cinque Ports of Faversham and Rye, the corporation of Yarmouth was frequently in conflict with its neighbours over fishing and trading rights. Its geographical advantage, moreover, was also its weakness. Strategically Yarmouth was a gateway to the heart of England for seaborne invaders – a fact that was a source of intense paranoia, especially during the civil war. In the spring of 1645 the bailiffs of Yarmouth went cap in hand to the mayor of Norwich about building coastal fortifications, pointing to the inland threat should they be overwhelmed.[21] As happened across East Anglia that year, fear of the enemy without was experienced and expressed as fear of an enemy within. In print and from pulpits, ministers no longer preached just about the dangers of royalist and papist malignants but warned of the 'wolves in sheeps' clothing', the spies (some dressed as women), charlatans, sorcerers, sectaries and false prophets – devils disguised as angels of light.[22]

Yarmouth's recorder – the chief magistrate, second only to the mayor – was Miles Corbett, chairman of the fearsome Committee of Examinations and every royalist's model of an uncompromising puritan. To one he was 'bull-headed, splay-footed, bacon-faced Corbett'; to another, England's 'Inquisitor General'.[23]

In his capacity as a magistrate Corbett had ordered the arrest of several witches that year, but it was two godly ministers, Mr Brinsley and Mr Whitfield, who were appointed to question them under the direction of Matthew Hopkins. John Brinsley, yet another Emmanuel graduate, believed passionately that magistrates and ministers should unite to eradicate wickedness – 'this bitter and deadly weed, which hath overrun and almost overspread the whole Garden of God'. Brinsley had suffered: the son of a puritan schoolmaster (who had taught the astrologer William Lilly), he had been dismissed from his living on the orders of Archbishop Laud, then banned from preaching by the king. Only the patronage of the puritan Sir John Wentworth and the abolition of ungodly offices and institutions had enabled him, the previous year, to claw his way back. He had waited for two decades: no deviants would now be permitted to stand in Brinsley's way, least of all witches.[24]

Hopkins advised that the suspects be watched, which was somewhat at odds with the vigorous interrogation John Brinsley had had in mind. Elizabeth Bradwell, an elderly woman, was known to Mr Whitfield, for twice a week she came begging at his door. She was the kind who scavenged on the beach, and would 'dine or suppe with a roasted crab squittering in the fire, or with a few boiled Onions, and a draught of Buttermilke which of her neighbours gave her for fear more then love'.[25] And Bradwell did make people afraid. She was suspected of conjuring spirits and of various *maleficia*, including having inflicted a lengthy, life-threatening sickness upon the infant son of Henry Moulton, a town alderman. After several periods of watching by Hopkins and others, Bradwell uttered her first self-incriminating words. She kept an evil spirit like a blackbird, and had dealt with the devil to seal her covenant; she pointed to a mark on her hand where he had drawn blood. Her motive in becoming a witch, she admitted, had been an insatiable lust for money and revenge.[26]

Henry Moulton owed his political position to his wealth. A hosiery merchant, he was prominent in Yarmouth as an employer of casual piece-workers. Early in 1644 Elizabeth Bradwell had presented herself at his house, and asked a manservant whether they needed a stocking-knitter. The servant replied that Moulton was away on business for a fortnight, and he could not give her work without his master's approval. The old woman took the news hard. In desperation she asked a maidservant for help, but received the same answer. Lying in bed that night, fuming at the servants' intransigence, she heard a knock at the door. Peering out of the window, she saw a tall black man in the moonlight, and felt afraid. When she plucked up courage to ask him what he wanted, he replied that he knew she was discontented and could arrange things so that she never had to work again. Her fear overtaken by curiosity she unlatched the door, and the strange man slipped inside. Cutting her hand with a small penknife, he dipped a quill in her blood and guided her hand across a page in his book until her name was inscribed in fresh crimson. Leaving behind money for food he departed, promising revenge on the Moulton household.

The following night, the black man brought bad news: Henry Moulton and his maid were invulnerable because of their faith and piety – but Moulton's eighteen-month-old son John was a softer target. The man handed Bradwell a wax effigy of the boy, and they stuck it with a pin before burying it in St Nicholas's churchyard. As the wax rotted, so John Moulton sickened – 'a hellish invention', according to John Stearne.

By the time Elizabeth Bradwell finished her story, darkness had fallen over Yarmouth. She was taken before the magistrates and they, mindful of the need for hard evidence, ordered that a search for the wax effigy should be made in the morning, and that in the mean time the abject woman should be taken to Henry Moulton's house. Moulton led the way straight through to the room where his son John, now three years of age, lay sick. As Bradwell repeated her confession the boy sat up and laughed, and looked better than he had at any time in the previous eighteen months. To the witchfinder this was a sign that confession had broken the witch's power, just as watching had

171

elicited the confession in the first place. They could all sleep now, Elizabeth Bradwell included.

Early the next morning the witchfinder and the ministers woke Bradwell, and took her to the graveyard. There she pointed with her foot to the spot where the wax charm was buried. They dug deep, but 'whether because it was so wasted that they lost the relicks of it in the digging, or removed by the Devil, or whatever else was the reason, it could not be found'.[27] Physical proof could still be provided by the searchers, however: following Hopkins' instructions Elizabeth Howard, a midwife, led a team of respectable women given a shilling a day to share; watchers were also paid at public expense, as at Aldeburgh.[28] By the evening of Tuesday 9 September, the investigation was complete.

The following day a general sessions of the peace was held in the great chamber of the ancient Tollhouse Hall, situated behind South Quay.[29] Miles Corbett took his seat as recorder and committing magistrate, and was joined by various justices, bailiffs and constables and by fifteen grand jurors, among them Henry Moulton. Gaolers described as 'keepers of various felons, transgressors and witches in this town' stood by with their shackled charges. The clerical investigators Brinsley and Whitfield were in attendance as witnesses, as was Matthew Hopkins. This was a committal hearing rather than a trial, where evidence was heard and indictments framed. First up was the case of a labourer accused of theft, followed by that of a gardener, Mark Pryme, charged with bewitching a goldsmith and his son, and with using 'charms & sorceries' to find lost property. These bills found true, the prisoners were taken back to the gaol. The same then happened with Barbara Wilkinson, a widow, and Nazareth Fassett, an unmarried woman from a family of coopers, both of whom were presented for having 'wickedly, diabolically and feloniously consulted and compacted with evil, wicked and diabolical spirits and did use these evil spirits with the intention to cause harm on the 12th of June 1645 and on various other days before and after'.[30]

Most of the charges related to suspicions that had arisen over the previous three years. In all, eight women, plus Pryme the gardener and a sailor who had employed him to find his hat, were presented for trial, scheduled for December. Mary Vervy, spinster, was arraigned on five separate indictments: for consorting with spirits, and for bewitching the wife of another prominent hosier and also three babies belonging to a sailor, a cordwainer and a merchant. Elizabeth Bradwell, the beggar who had confessed to bewitching Henry Moulton's son, was accused of conjuration and causing sickness. Together with Wilkinson and Fassett, four other women were charged solely with entertaining evil spirits. Hopkins was formally bound to appear as a witness. How long he stayed in Yarmouth it is difficult to say, but within a week he was probably back in Aldeburgh to endorse the committal of suspects there. The search-women and the watchers kept on working after he had left Yarmouth, and more witches were arrested. By early October at least one other suspect, Joan Lacey, a widow, had been charged with familiarity with imps and imprisoned. This made a total of ten accused witches in the Tollhouse gaol, plus Pryme's client, accused of seeking advice from a witch.[31] There for the next three months they languished, as autumn surrendered to winter.

On Tuesday 9 September, as Matthew Hopkins was getting down to work at Yarmouth, fifty miles to the south the people of Ipswich were preparing to witness a rare spectacle of execution. Mary Lakeland, a woman probably in her fifties convicted of witchcraft, was due to be burned at the stake, a unique instance of this punishment in the East Anglian witchfinding campaign. She and an accomplice, Alice Denham, had been sentenced to death at the Ipswich town sessions eight days earlier; four more suspects – three women and a man – remained in the gaol while witnesses came forward to give evidence.[32]

Indelible myth, as old as witch-trials themselves, holds that in England condemned witches were executed by burning. Stories of the more bloody and extensive witch-hunts in Scotland (where burning *was* the statutory punishment) have become muddled with the legacy of the Marian martyrs to create an enduring image of apostates on bonfires. By the mid seventeenth century this image was current among the common people even though the last heretic had been burned in 1612, and almost every witch convicted in England since 1563 had been hanged – the customary punishment for convicted felons. However, the law against treason did prescribe burning for a woman who murdered her husband – for in so doing she was held to have risen up treasonably against her natural lord and master.[33]

Mary Lakeland was the respectable wife of a barber, John Lakeland, and so pious in her manners that the parish of St Stephen's knew her as 'a professour of Religion, a constant hearer of the Word'. Perhaps she went too far with her godliness: for a woman to 'profess' religion did not seem natural to conventional Presbyterians, and the use of that word may suggest membership of one of the radical sects with congregations in Ipswich; it may be significant that a witness against her was a minister from Colchester. Earlier that year the county authorities had taken steps to restrain Baptists, so possibly she was one of their number.[34] Mother Lakeland, as she was known, certainly had enemies in the parish, and had developed a reputation for witchcraft – just as Quakers, Baptists and other sectaries were to in the next decade.[35] When the diarist John Evelyn visited a group of Quakers in gaol at Ipswich in 1656 he recorded his impression of them as 'a new Phanatic sect of dangerous Principles, the[y] shew no respect to any man, magistrate, or other & seeme a melancholy proud sort of people'.[36] Disobedience in one form could set off a chain-reaction of associations in people's minds, and just as a homicidal wife was a symbolic attack on the authority of the state, so the rebel against religious authority was painted as a rebel against God. And rebels against God were servants of the devil, and sworn opponents of their conformist neighbours.[37]

In Mother Lakeland's case, there is no way of knowing whether the belief that she was a servant of the devil and not simply irksome in her piety was malicious or sincere. The gossip in St Stephen's was that she had conspired with Alice Denham to send a pair of dog-like imps to harm William Lawrence after he called in a debt of twelve shillings; Lawrence's child had also been bewitched. Lakeland confessed to this, presumably under pressure from either Hopkins or the eager townsfolk he galvanized into action. As tiredness wore away her defences, opening her mind to fantastic suggestion, she began to piece together memories of how she had converted to satanism. Early one morning, she said, 'between sleeping and waking', the devil had crept into her bedchamber, murmuring his usual entreaties in a hollow voice, promising that if she served him she should want for nothing. She had resisted but he had persisted, and in the end she had consented. He pierced her hand with his claw, then wrote a solemn covenant in her blood. She was not asked to deny God and Christ, but did as much by her 'nourishinge of evil spirittes'. Then she embarked on a gleeful spree of vengeance. Mrs Jennings' maidservant had made the mistake of being 'earnest' with her about a small debt, then compounded the offence by refusing to lend her a needle. All three – Lawrence, his child, and the maid – were soon cold in their graves.[38]

Others had blundered into Mary Lakeland's line of fire. Her grand-daughter was to have married Henry Reade, master of an Ipswich ship, but early in 1644 he broke off the engagement. The furious grandmother admitted having ordered an imp to burn his ship, then turn on the faithless Reade himself. In September 1645 he was said to be 'in very great misery, and is verily conceived by the Doctors and Chirurgions that have him in hand, that he consumes and rots, and that halfe of his body is rotten upon him as he is living'. A tumour on his leg had grown into the shape of a dog and he was in such pain that he could only walk doubled up, with his head touching his knees. Among the nine indictments against Lakeland, the most shocking was that for the torture and murder of her husband, an atrocious sin that damned her as not only a murderous witch but a *traitorous* one. For this there was only one possible sentence open to the magistrates, and the clerk recorded it in his crabbed hand: '*Incendetur ad Cindres*' (to be burnt to ashes). As she sat in gaol awaiting execution Mother Lakeland did not apparently retract her confession, even after she had been allowed to sleep. Instead, she

> . . . seemeth to be very penitent for her former lewd and adominable indevours, and acts, and desires to have Petitions put up to divers godly Ministers that they would be pleased to pray in their severall Congregations that her said Impes may have no further power, to do any more such like hurt neither by Sea nor Land, as they have divers times formerly done, to the destruction, losse, or utter undoing of many sundry good and honest people.

Her body she surrendered to the law; but through Christ she might yet save her soul. Meanwhile Alice Denham, her alleged accomplice in the murder of William Lawrence, was paraded shamefaced around the centre of Ipswich, then hanged.

A woman is burned at the stake for murdering her husband – the crime of petty treason

By tradition the burning of heretics and traitors was performed in the south-east corner of Cornhill, where the balcony of the colonnaded shambles offered a commanding view. The ceremony was similar to a hanging, attended by a bellman to summon the townsfolk and a drummer to solemnize the proceedings. Weak in her limbs, and praying to stave off despair, Mother Lakeland was lowered into a barrel of pitch, then chained to a post set into the ground – ropes would have burned away, allowing her to leap from the flames half-consumed. At the signal, the executioner lit the stacked-up layers of straw, brushwood and faggots, and stood back to watch the filthiest day's work even a wretch such as he could perform. To pacify the crowd, whose appetite for suffering was not boundless, it is possible that he first garrotted Lakeland, or stopped her heart with a blow to the sternum. As the pitch oozed through the planks the pyre bellowed a black fog that hid the shrinking and stripping of flesh from eyes that had seen too much already. As the sun waned the fire blazed on, probably into the night, so that by the time the curious returned next morning all that remained was a scattered white heap. They would have raked over the greasy ashes just the same, mindful of the magical power even a small bone might have.[39]

At least one man was miraculously affected. By an invisible balance of fortunes, as Mary Lakeland's body withered in the flames, so Henry Reade was released from many months of misery. A weeping sore (or fistula) on his stomach that had resisted every remedy and procedure known to the surgeons began to heal, and even the dog-shaped tumour on his leg they had given up trying to lance started to crack.[40]

News of Reade's recovery helped suppress any doubts about Lakeland's guilt among the people of Ipswich. But the story did not stop there. By mid October it had found its way to a London printer's shop, where it was appended to an anonymous seven-page guide to the law against witches comprising a verbatim transcript of James I's statute of 1604, followed by 'Observations for the discovery of Witches' – a neat distillation of legal experience copied without attribution from Michael Dalton's *Countrey Justice*. John Stearne, who later proved himself something of a plagiarist, may have been behind this. The concluding section, on Mother Lakeland, is closer to the writing style of Stearne's partner, however. [41] An aside offered at one point on the subtlety of evil – a suggestion that the devil had not forced Lakeland to deny God lest it should drive her away from him – sounds very much like Matthew Hopkins, the wily opportunist, exploiting the commercial value of his trade to the full.

For others, the witch-hunt proved nothing but a drain on resources. Burning Mary Lakeland cost the town more than three times what it would have to hang her, a total of £3 3s. 6d. – pitch-barrels of the sort used by shipwrights and sailors were an expensive commodity.[42] It all added to the soaring cost of witchfinding in Ipswich, and the fact that the more the town spent the greater the problem seemed to be only made matters worse. A week before Mother Lakeland was put to death the borough authorities had passed a resolution based on Godbold's ruling at the Bury assizes:

> For as much as there hath been much monney laid out by severall p[er]sons w[i]thin this Towne by the Order & apointm[en]t of Mr Bayliffes in the searchinge watchinge & further p[ro]secutinge of diverse p[er]sons of this Towne suspected for Witches and in the bringinge of them to a legall triall at this Sessions . . . It is nowe therefore Ordered that the Chardge of searchinge watchinge and p[ro]secutinge of all such p[er]sons . . . shall bee borne by the Inh[ab]itants of this Towne as a general Chardge.[43]

Churchwardens and overseers of the poor throughout Ipswich were instructed to collect this levy whenever the bailiffs issued a warrant. An officer in the parish of St Mary Tower would administer the fund, making disbursements as necessary.

Imprisonment was a major expense. At three pence per prisoner per day, the witches at Ipswich may have cost as much as £50 a month to keep as they awaited the assizes.[44] The gaoler James Rigges petitioned the magistrates, asking that parishes be compelled to make a contribution because the prisoners themselves were usually too poor to pay their fees if and when they were acquitted – so they stayed put, and the debt increased. His request was granted and an order published recognizing that, as the court put it, 'very many p[er]sons of sev[er]all p[ar]ishes have bynn committed to his Ma[jes]ties goale att Ipswich for this County for witchcrafte which hath caused a very great & extraordinary Charge to the goaler'. From now on constables were to set a rate for witch-hunting at the discretion of the magistrates, but there is a sense that the revenue was never enough. It hardly helped that the municipal court sometimes handed down custodial sentences, as it did upon husband and wife James and Mary Emerson. Acquitted on two charges, they were found guilty of sending swarms of lice to torment their enemies and imprisoned for a year, during which they were to be pilloried four times.[45] If the Emersons were unable to pay the costs of their year's imprisonment, however, their neighbours would now be charged.

The astrological forecasts for 1645 had been far from auspicious. The predominance of Saturn and Mars, predicted one almanac, would bring 'horrible misrule and tragicall mischiefes', culminating in a melancholic autumn and a freezing winter. Hopes faded that the king would swap his sword for a sceptre, as the stars had suggested, and despite a string of parliamentarian victories in September, with the onset of the rains the war settled back into stalemate. Plague had been rife since the summer, affecting towns as far apart as Bristol, Newcastle and King's Lynn; every day in London another five victims were recorded. Ministers asked whether famine would follow war and pestilence – a question that seemed to be answered as farmers toiled first to gather a damp harvest and then in October to plough and sow in thick mud, all without enough horses or labourers. Fairfax's army, also beset by the freakishly wet weather, covered much shorter distances than it had during the summer.[46] As fear of the fighting receded, so economic unrest increased. People in Suffolk and Norfolk were reported to be 'very much given to dispute with their masters taxes, and speak high'.[47] In the self-governing towns of the Suffolk coast emotions were particularly turbulent. Patience with witches ran out: rotting crops, ailing livestock and ships lost at sea all now seemed more like mischiefs of the devil than acts of God.

Every storm to hit the town of Dunwich carried some of it back beneath the waves. Once it had been a shipyard and port to rival Yarmouth, sustaining a thriving trade with Iceland; in about 1640 its harbour finally silted up, but by then most of the grand merchants' houses and churches were already submerged. Mariners feared these ruins, and fancied they could hear ghostly bells ringing from the depths. Within living memory the high road had disappeared, and now even the market – the heart of economic life – was threatened. As one of the Cinque Ports Dunwich looked after its own political and legal affairs, and frequently quarrelled with its neighbours over fishing rights, repairs to sea-defences, and so on.[48] In many ways these disputes were sad echoes of past battles – there now was little left of the town to defend – yet decay only served to stiffen the determination to preserve godly virtues.

No wonder, then, that in the summer of 1645 suspicions about witches had intensified, and an invitation had been sent to Matthew Hopkins. On his way to Dunwich he stopped off at the villages of Yoxford and Westleton and scored successes there. At Westleton, Katherine Tooley's confession was a sign of the subversive times: she admitted having sent an imp to steal money from Sir Robert Brooks, lord of the manor, and she had also tried to harm her minister, Mr Driver, but failed 'because he served god'. Driver himself had heard her confession, prior to Hopkins' arrival.[49] At Dunwich the minister Mr Browne also helped bring witches to justice. Priscilla Collit told him that, surrendering to a demonic urge, she had tried to burn her child on the fire, and that she had bewitched a coastal barge. After the devil told her she could walk under water she had set off for Boston in Lincolnshire, but had had to be rescued by sailors. Another woman, Elizabeth Southern, confessed that Collit had sent her a crayfish-imp, and that she had slept with the devil, who was 'cold as a stone'. None of these women had received even the paltry sums of money they had been promised. A black hairy boy Southern met on the road to Westleton had offered her two shillings and sixpence, but later returned empty-handed complaining of 'the hardnes of the times'.[50]

The influence on its people exerted by the exposure of Dunwich to the elements was similar to that exerted by the threat of enemy invaders elsewhere. At Yarmouth, twenty miles up the coast, paranoia about deviant conduct was endemic, the desire to correct it desperate: the worldly works of man would crumble – and were crumbling – but a spiritual empire, pious townsmen reasoned, would last forever. Apostasy and witchcraft amounted to the murder of the soul, and called for punishment from magistrates and counselling by ministers. The discovery of witches in September had the same effect as in other places: a flush of triumph and relief, then a haunting sense that more lay undetected. John Brinsley, the minister who had participated in the interrogation of Elizabeth Bradwell, was an orthodox Presbyterian who believed that the world was divided into covenanters of Christ and covenanters of Satan. He feared separatism of any kind, and saw the witches he had helped send to the Tollhouse as extreme versions of the Independents and sectaries all around him, many of whom were women. In October 1645 he delivered a sermon on the perils of sects, describing how Satan seduced the weaker sex to deceive themselves and their husbands, as Eve had in Eden. Women should obey their masters to preserve their households – and by implication the state – and should be silent in congregations, as the Apostles had taught.[51] These were the principles guiding those who exercised power in Yarmouth and Dunwich.

On Wednesday 10 December the Tollhouse Hall at Yarmouth filled with spectators. The corporation officials entered, as did Matthew Hopkins and his fellow witnesses. At one o'clock the court was called to order, and Miles Corbett, the saturnine recorder, took up the presiding position; he was, some said, 'prologue to the hangman, that looks more like the hangman himself'.[52] There were twelve to be arraigned: the thief, Pryme the cunning man, his client, and nine women, two of whom – Elizabeth Bradwell and Mary Vervy – were charged with specific *maleficia*, the rest with having compacted with the devil with intent to cause to harm. The clerk of the court ordered the gaoler to release the prisoners, and they were called to the bar. The serjeant-at-mace ushered in a panel of twelve jurors and they, after hearing the evidence, returned their verdicts.

The thief was found guilty and sentenced to a whipping; Pryme and his client were acquitted. Barbara Wilkinson and Nazareth Fassett were also acquitted (possibly because they had resisted pressure to confess), and so was Mary Vervy, despite the five indictments against her. Elizabeth Bradwell, who had spoken freely about her liaisons with Satan and the bewitching of Henry Moulton's son, was found guilty, as were Joan Lacey and four other women. When it had been established that none of these six had any goods or chattels to forfeit, they were sentenced to be hanged. All must have hoped for a reprieve, but only Widow Lacey was spared. The rest died wretchedly beneath a wintry Norfolk sky.[53]

By this time, Matthew Hopkins was already heading south into Suffolk. His destination was the borough of Aldeburgh, where he had detected several witches in September but where, like the Hydra's heads, more had since appeared. The going was harder now: the firs hung heavy with jewels of ice and puddles cracked under hoof. Through gorse and heath Hopkins reached the bare fields north of the town, over which wind-driven sheets of snow shimmered like Lapland ghosts.[54] No doubt he was received at the half-timbered Moot Hall, built when Aldeburgh was still a flourishing port. No longer: Aldeburgh had shared the fate of Dunwich, its estuary blocked by a shingle bank, its quay flooded, never to resurface, its corporation status an anachronism. As fortune deserted the town, so had its people: even the few hundred left were rapidly dwindling. As elsewhere, the civil war had tightened the stranglehold: first, a poll tax to pay for the war in Ireland, then an influx of refugees, followed by a trade slump, meaning there was not enough work even for the indigenous population. On top of this, the shifts of war meant that Aldeburgh was now more vulnerable than ever. By early 1645 the corporation was begging the committee at Bury St Edmunds for money for cannon and fortifications, just as Yarmouth had begged Norwich. Recorded in the church accounts for that year were entries for repairing firearms, building gun-carriages, and nursing a man injured by exploding gunpowder.[55]

Aldeburgh had been a puritan town at heart since the 1560s, when parishioners had boycotted services and defaced church ornaments. Eighty years later formidable godly gentlemen like Captain Thomas Johnson were in the ascendant. An adherent of Fairfax, he was a town bailiff, led the militia, and chose the lecturers. He was sensitive to the imminent Apocalypse and the obligation to resist Satan. Returning home in a thunderstorm in 1642 he had watched a meteorite fall, and arriving at Aldeburgh had found the townsfolk in panic, fearing the end of the world. The lecturer Mr Swayne had preached that the meteorite was an omen of war, famine and pestilence to come, unless the town repented. Whatever effort was made in this direction, it was not enough: three weeks later hostilities commenced, the people grew poorer, and plague and smallpox struck: the afflicted were shut up in their homes. Two years later, at last, Aldeburgh had started to reform itself. Johnson and Swayne supervised the destruction of images ordered by William Dowsing, and the ejection of their Arminian vicar as a royalist and an 'enemye to preaching'. And where iconoclasts and sequestrators went, witchfinders were bound to follow.[56]

Matthew Hopkins had already received £2 in the summer for hunting witches at Aldeburgh; now the cash-strapped corporation dug deep and paid him the same again. When Hopkins informed them that Mary Phillips's services were also required, Captain Johnson gave two men twelve shillings and sixpence to ride the forty miles to Manningtree through snow and ice to fetch her.[57] By the time she arrived Hopkins had already settled himself at The Lion Inn, in the care of the landlady Mrs Howldine. After confirming her fee of £1 with the corporation Widow Phillips was also roomed there and, like the witchfinder, made the most of her stay. By the time they left Aldeburgh, having brought the number of witches in the gaol to seven, Hopkins and Phillips had run up a bill of over £4; Mrs Howldine was renowned as a dab hand at mixing drinks.[58]

As if this were not drain enough on Aldeburgh's finances, at the end of the first week of 1646 the witchfinders were back to give evidence – paid at the usual rate, plus another eight shillings for again fetching Mary Phillips from Manningtree. The trial was set for Wednesday 7 January. The recorder, Francis Bacon (half-brother of Nathaniel), arrived from Shrubland Hall and was greeted by bailiffs Thomas Johnson and William Thompson. Also in town was William Bloys, a magistrate who had been present at the Bury St Edmunds trial in August. Six men were hired as ceremonial guards at a shilling each a day, plus an allowance of sixpence for drink, provided as usual by Mrs Howldine, who also cooked for the recorder and the rest of the commission of peace.[59]

The prisoners were brought out and the trial began. After lying for three weeks in a freezing cell, fed only on bread and beer, finally to get into a warm courtroom was a blessing for Widows Wade and Gardner and the other five women, albeit a mixed one. The proceedings were straightforward. The women were indicted for entertaining evil spirits, Hopkins and Phillips impressed the court with their experience and confidence in the discovery of witches, and the

jury promptly found all seven guilty. Then the judge solemnly condemned them to death, sentence to be carried out on the Friday.[60]

On 23 February 1646 the corporation treasurer settled his
accounts. The fees and expenses of Matthew Hopkins and Mary
Phillips were recorded, as were payments to the watchers they had set
to work; the gaoler received just over £2 and the guards fifteen
shillings and sixpence. Mrs Howldine was paid £15 for supplying

*Women hanged, women grieving, and others looking on from the gaol. To
the left two sergeants and a bellman oversee proceedings, and to the right a
witchfinder is paid his fee*

food and drink during the trial. A carpenter received £1 for erecting
the gallows, a roper eight shillings for '7 halters & for making the
nogts', and the executioner a total of eleven shillings. To bury the
dead and mark the grave with a post had cost six shillings.[61] Including
the trial, the witch-hunt set the town back in excess of £40. This was
one-seventh of the corporation's entire budget for the year, and could
not be met out of normal revenue from taxation and the rent of
market stalls. A special levy was therefore authorized and two partial

payments were received from Thomas Johnson in the spring, one of which came directly from former bailiff Richard Browne, like Johnson one of the richest men in the town.[62] But most people were poor. Like the inhabitants of Ipswich, Aldeburgh was now to learn the true price of witchfinding, and to realize that, for a decayed port with paupers and plague victims to care for and seaborne enemies to repel, it was not a sustainable campaign.[63]

The intense cold held throughout January. The Thames froze over, and when the witches were being hanged at Aldeburgh, Londoners were able to walk from one side to the other of their river. In provincial towns the streets were heaped up with soiled snow, and the price of wheat escalated in the markets. The rivers that carried food to the towns were impassable, and stores of rye became a staple for many, especially the poorest.[64] Conditions had been ideal for the growth of the toxic ergot fungus, and ergot poisoning may explain some symptoms of bewitchment, if by no means all; but it is not a more convincing explanation for witch-hysteria than the power of belief and fear.[65]

Ten months into his work, Matthew Hopkins had dealt with dozens of cases of bewitchment, all of them demonstrating just that: belief in the devil, and fear of those who tapped his strength for malevolent ends. To stop the spread of evil involved ruinous costs, of a magnitude that was beginning to make the godliest communities think twice about prosecution, and Hopkins had cut legal corners in a way that raised eyebrows in Westminster. Whether news of the east-coast trials reached London is unknown. The recorder of Yarmouth, Miles Corbett, resumed his inquisitorial work at the Committee of Examinations, and Parliament redoubled its efforts to make peace, thereby 'putting an end to the bleeding calamities of these nations'.[66] The witchfinder, meanwhile, had almost finished his work in Suffolk and by the middle of the month was riding inland, wending his way through the rutted lanes, all narrow passes and blind corners, hemmed in by thicket. On the 13th a poor labourer, William Payne, was tried for witchcraft at Beccles quarter sessions; but the north-easterly location suggests that Hopkins' influence must have been indirect.[67]

Thirty miles west of Aldeburgh lay the town of Stowmarket, one of the largest in Suffolk and a model of the Reformation. The church of St Peter and St Mary had been cleared of images in the 1540s, and its sister foundation demolished because of its associations with the abbey at St Osyth. As in most godly towns, pockets of Catholicism invigorated the reformers; puritanism by its very nature thrived on opposition. William Manning, churchwarden, and Thomas Young, vicar (and sometime tutor to John Milton), had welcomed William Dowsing in 1644 and were pleased to erase an inscription from the monument recently erected by the recusant Tyrell family.[68] John Stearne visited a year later and testified in person at the assizes that two men accused by their neighbours were witches, but the grand jury rejected the charges; Elizabeth Hubbard, who had confessed to *maleficium* within her own family, was probably hanged. William Manning and another parish officer, John Heywood, had been active in the interrogations, and reported having heard Widow Hubbard tell of her pact with the devil and a promise of money that came to nothing. According to Stearne, her three hungry imps arrived in the guise of children – a perverted remembrance of babies lost; the raw marks where they suckled were visible to the good women of Stowmarket who searched her.[69]

Matthew Hopkins had been there too, and probably returned in the early spring of 1646. Accusations were levelled against Goodwife Low and Goodwife Mills, but many more must have been examined because Hopkins was paid more than £23 for his work; it would have taken even a well-paid craftsman, toiling six days a week, a year to earn as much. The witchfinder's expenses were covered in addition, including nine shillings and sixpence paid to an innkeeper for bed and board.[70] By comparison, the cost of repairing the church after Dowsing's visit had been trivial. Nor could such charges be defrayed by petitioning for a share of a witch's property; as the Ipswich gaoler had pointed out, usually they owned nothing. So the burden fell on those who could pay. Within a month of the trial at Yarmouth, the corporation ruled that in future no more than four women were to be employed as searchers; similar economies were implemented else-where.[71] The authorities at Stowmarket, as in Ipswich, might hide behind the ruling from the Bury assizes, but rulings did not calm discontent. Though calculated according to means, the levy still averaged around three or four shillings per head. Twelve defaulters listed in the parish accounts owed almost £2 between them despite the best efforts of the constables, among whom were the ubiquitous William Manning and John Heywood.[72]

Resistance to the charges was not without precedent. The inhabitants of Copdock had already challenged the quarter sessions order that parishes had to pay gaol fees for their own witches, a dispute which had led to two magistrates arbitrating between them and Rigges the Ipswich gaoler. The principle had been upheld, and presumably the defaulters gave in. At Stowmarket the authorities were forced to initiate legal proceedings to recover money owed to the public chest, and Halesworth was threatened with legal action if it did not set a rate at once. Every parish was reminded 'that all discharges disbursed in discov[er]inge of Witches should be paid by a rate p[ro]porc[i]onable to the rate for the poore'. Protests also came from the neighbouring villages of Athelington and Horham, twelve miles from Framlingham. Most extraordinary were the complaints of parishioners at Brandeston – not that their minister John Lowes had been set up on a charge of witchcraft and hanged like a dog, but that now they were expected to pay for it. In the spring of 1646 the controversies at Athelington, Horham and Brandeston were communicated to the magistrates, who ordered them and all other rated parishes to conform, stipulating that defaulters were to be referred to the court. On 10 April 1646 the order was reiterated at Ipswich quarter sessions and the people of Stowmarket were told to pay their rates to Manning, Heywood and the other constables, or find themselves hauled before an assize judge.[73]

It was around April 1646 that John Stearne returned home to Lawshall to spend time with his wife Agnes and their family. Their first child Anne had turned two in February, and the witchfinder can have seen little of her.[74] This would also have been the time that Stearne revisited the village of Rattlesden, scene of so many horrific discoveries the previous year and still a place cursed by misfortune. Locals directed him towards a suspected boy of perhaps eight or nine whom Stearne had questioned before at Rougham, near Bury St Edmunds, as he quickly realized. The boy had then told him a pitiful tale of poverty, ostracism, and the desire for revenge, for instance against a farmer who had blamed him for spoiling some grease, when the boy had seen chickens peck at it. An imp had offered its services and the boy had accepted. Stearne had been sympathetic, and satisfied when a jury at Bury discharged him because he was of an age 'when all know he could not be of much capacity'. The boy had returned home to Rougham, an outcast even before he reached adolescence. Within a few weeks his mother had been arrested for witchcraft and taken to Bury, where she was executed in the autumn. No mention was made of his father. The boy seems to have left Rougham for nearby Rattlesden, to stay with relatives, or to live rough. But he had carried his damnable reputation with him, and suspicions of him festered over the winter and into 1646.[75]

That spring, Stearne's hopes for his amendment were dashed. The boy admitted that after his mother was hanged he had felt more malicious than ever, and had renewed his 'league and Covenant with the Devill', this time sealing it with blood. Now the devil came to him 'in the likenesse of a black browne Mare, and would carrie him wither hee desired' – presumably far from his miserable existence in Rougham and Rattlesden. The pact had also restored his destructive power, which he exercised freely in the neighbourhood, with catastrophic results. Stearne had done what he could for the boy; now it was time for the law to decide, and it was not long before he was back in the prison at Bury St Edmunds where his mother had spent her final desperate hours, and where he himself had once sat waiting to be called before a jury.[76]

No record of the boy's fate survives, but he was in still in gaol in the summer of 1646. Stearne heard from the gaoler that even behind bars he continued to deal with the devil. The story went that an especially notorious offender, put in with the boy and chained hand and foot, mysteriously vanished one night. On discovering the escape, the gaoler threatened the boy with violence until he confessed that his mare-like demon had carried the prisoner over the walls so that he could go home to his wife twelve miles away. A search-party sent out

by the gaoler followed the boy's precise directions and found the fugi-
tive, shackles still in place, enjoying some final hours with his wife.
Perhaps the boy prayed for the day the mare would return to free him
from gaol; or perhaps by this stage in his young life he had already
lost hope.

8

Contagion

———•———

AFTER CROSSING NEWMARKET Heath and the Devil's Dyke, travellers riding west from Bury St Edmunds passed through a vale
of corn-fields, then the road descended until the brow of a hill was
reached: beyond this, the city of Cambridge opened up before them.
The cluster of spires and finialled rooftops promised unsullied wisdom
and worship, the only blemish a cloud of brown smoke hanging like
a judgement. Once the city-gates had been reached, the illusion dis-
sipated. The sweet air of the heights was replaced by the stench of
urban life: heaps of dung and straw in the narrow streets, the fug of
greasy steam from college kitchens, and the bodies of the unwashed
hawkers and beggars and the rows of cloth-wrapped corpses awaiting
disposal. By the 1640s attacks of smallpox had become common. It
was an affliction made worse by poverty and overcrowding, and the
town and University authorities averted catastrophe by controlling the
sub-division of houses (also insisting on brick-and-tile buildings, to
inhibit fire). The civil war brought more woe, and had fighting not
disrupted the regular assizes, the plague would have seen to it. By 1643
disputations and sermons had been suspended, and many doctors and
scholars had fled. Those who stayed behind had watched as their
college chapels were desecrated, their plate sequestered, and their gra-
cious staircases and parlours turned into lousy billets.[1]

Cromwell had studied at Cambridge, but had little time for nostalgia. Like other leaders of the Eastern Association he was interested
only in suppressing opposition, and improving fortifications to stop a
royalist army advancing from the north-west. By 1646 those college
fellows who had refused the Solemn League and Covenant had been
turfed out, and the masters protecting them gaoled. Stone earmarked

for new buildings had been commandeered to build parapets on Castle Hill, orchards cut down for firewood. This humbling of the university was not unwelcome to the townsmen, especially the godly. With a few exceptions – notably Emmanuel and Sidney Sussex – the colleges had favoured Laudian innovations in the 1630s, and so deserved puritan punishment.[2] Threats to academic life were financial as well as spiritual. Fen drainage had endangered the navigable rivers that sustained academic life with food, fuel and other necessities; meanwhile, colleges were under pressure to contribute more towards relieving the poor: not only did their courts and gardens occupy a third of the town's land, but their demand for servants attracted many to the city who subsequently became a burden on the parish rates. The town authorities were strained to breaking point by the cost of their obligations, which since 1642 had included maintaining the destitute and sick on Jesus Green, disposing of diseased corpses, and hiring constables to press soldiers into service.[3]

A purged University exemplified wider achievements in ecclesiastical renewal. Arminian opposition to the puritans of Cambridgeshire had entailed indifference to such reformist ambitions as keeping the Sabbath and punishing witches. The visitation articles drawn up in 1638 by the new Bishop of Ely, Matthew Wren, had omitted injunctions against soothsayers and sorcerers, but made special provision for the restraint of puritans and sectaries. By 1640 the tide was turning. In that year the gentry of Cambridgeshire successfully petitioned Parliament to impeach Wren for encouraging the 'advancement of Romish superstition' and endangering the commonwealth by his 'tyrannicall courses and administrations'.[4] Freed from the strictures of diocesan authority, finally the county was able to start ridding itself of its scandalous ministers and offensive church decorations, its Sabbath-breakers and idolators, magicians and witches.

There is no way of knowing how many witches had been tried at the assizes after the passing of the Witchcraft Act in 1563; only anecdotes survive. At an execution of mother and daughter in Elizabethan Cambridge, it was said, the mother had protested that the devil had been faithful to her for sixty years; the daughter repented, and the devil shook the gallows with a furious wind. Many cases (mostly to do with sorcery and cunning magic) came before the ecclesiastical courts, although popular hysteria about witches (almost exclusively accused of inflicting harm) caused the Church more concern than did witchcraft itself.[5] In the later sixteenth century godly ministers like Richard Greenham at Dry Drayton and his admirer Henry Holland at Orwell were constantly frustrated by crack-brained witchmongering among their parishioners. As discerning theologians they detected the devil at work as much in witch-hunting as in witchcraft – a paradox never successfully communicated to the people Holland derided as 'our blockish Christians'.[6]

The University had a restricted legal jurisdiction over the people of Cambridge, and from time to time its courts too heard cases involving witchcraft. In the reign of James I a decade-long dispute between Margaret Cotton and Dorcas Swettson of Great St Mary's, a parish at the heart of the University, resulted in at least two witchcraft trials at the assizes and one at Star Chamber.[7] In 1605 another witchcraft case demanded the University's attention. During a round-up of witches and prophets in the county, it transpired that two adolescent girls were claiming to be bewitched. The king ordered them to be secretly detained and examined by the learned doctors of the University, away from prying undergraduate eyes; in the end the girls' illness was pronounced to be natural in origin, 'though somewhat strange and extraordinarie'.[8] The fascination of University divines, physicians and philosophers with such matters was remarkable. William Perkins, a plain-speaking Calvinist preacher at Christ's College, had a special interest in witchcraft and its threat to Christianity. After his death in 1602 a Fellow of Emmanuel named Thomas Pickering edited his papers into what soon became a demonological classic. Perkins argued that witchcraft was a sin of pride, in which the individual exchanged a covenant with Christ for one with the devil, with a view to emulating God's power.[9] It was an idea that in the 1640s had a profound influence upon Matthew Hopkins and John Stearne.

Then there was Henry More. William Perkins had been dead and buried for almost thirty years by the time More entered Christ's in 1631, but his spirit lived on in the college's courts and cloisters. It may be that More, a passionate believer in ghosts and witches, believed this to be true in a literal sense. Unlike Perkins he did not adhere to strict Calvinist tenets, and with the coming of the civil war remained an unrepentant royalist. Addicted to contemplation and conversation, More was an open-minded mystic, an occultist who believed in a universe full of metaphysical phenomena; at the same time, he was a committed Anglican Christian and, significantly, an empiricist belonging to a burgeoning tradition of science and experimentation, rather than to Perkins' generation of beetle-browed disciplinarians. His way of thinking was mirrored in courtrooms across the country in the mid 1640s. It had long seemed *possible* to prove the reality of witchcraft by precept and example; now it had become very *necessary* to do so, when sound proof of a demonic pact was required. More believed that collecting true stories (especially of confessions, sabbats and physical marks) performed a valuable service to religion because it helped demonstrate the existence of evil spirits – and, by implication, of good ones too. Witchcraft was a helpful providential sign in an era plagued by atheism, schism and disorder.[10]

Although many of Henry More's anecdotes were derived from foreign authors, by 1645 the profusion of confessed witches was supplying him with home-grown examples. Like other counties, Cambridgeshire had probably seen few trials in the preceding decade. Stories which had achieved popular currency – such as that of the king sending his physician William Harvey to Newmarket in 1630, in order to study a witch's familiar – were told for entertainment, not moral edification.[11] But a seed of change had been sown. While Harvey was, allegedly, dissecting Alice Bird's pet frog, a London printer was preparing a new edition of Michael Dalton's *Countrey Justice*, the magistrate's handbook. Having recently read an authoritative guide to identifying witches by Richard Bernard (another Christ's graduate), Dalton, a Cambridgeshire magistrate, incorporated Bernard's observations about animal imps, physical covenants, bodily marks and the supremacy of confessions as revisions to his own work. In turn, his rampant plagiarism suggests that John Stearne must have read either Bernard or Dalton, or both. Directly and indirectly, the ideas contained in these works and in those of William Perkins and of Continental authorities like Jean Bodin entered the heads of the witchfinders, prompting them to demand – and to go to great lengths to satisfy – fixed criteria of proof.[12] Without the guidelines laid down by this intellectual and administrative framework, the tragedy of the East Anglian witch-hunt might never have happened.

Like Hopkins and Stearne, Henry More had the benefit of the very best evidence of all: that gathered by his own eyes and ears. It was probably in the spring of 1646, when he was in his early thirties, that More learned two witches were being held in Cambridge Castle. He had examined witches there the previous year and, having heard confessions from four or five, now considered himself an expert.

Accompanied by his friend Ralph Cudworth, Henry More made his way down the long street from Christ's, which across the river continued up the hill leading to the castle. Cudworth, appointed Master of Clare Hall after the parliamentarian purge, was another moderate Anglican Platonist and shared More's commitment to defending religion by challenging scepticism about witches and spirits.[13] The castle keep was a contrast between decay and progress with its dilapidated medieval structures adapted, dismantled and rebuilt into tenements and, under Cromwell's orders, walls, casemates and barracks. The ruinous gatehouse had long served as a gaol. There was a town prison, the Tolbooth, which contained a separate chamber for witches, but the castle was more convenient for the Shire House where the assizes were held. The gaoler, who occupied an upstairs chamber of the gatehouse, permitted More and Cudworth to speak with the two accused women, one of whom was married and at least middle-aged, the other somewhat younger. The interview was conducted in the castle hall, with the black-suited gentlemen seated some distance from the prisoners as slight protection from foul smells and contagious disease.[14]

More's experience of witches meant that he did not immediately dismiss what he heard as 'mere idle fancy or sick mans dream'. The younger of the two women accused the other, Goodwife Kendall, of having seduced her into witchcraft by promising her a husband.[15] She had found one, sure enough, 'a good proper Yeomanlike Man' – a real catch – but the courtship was ruined when, unexpectedly, he turned into a puppy. She had seen Kendall at a sabbat, she said, where at the head of a table laden with roast meat sat the devil, speaking a strange language. A male witch known as 'Old Stranguidge' had also been present. More had heard of his exploits before, noting later that 'there hath been reported ever since I came to the Universitie that he was carried over Shelford Steeple upon a black Hogge and tore his breeches upon the weather-cock'. Goodwife Kendall strenuously denied these charges, and in desperation offered to say the Lord's Prayer and the Creed to clear her name. More and Cudworth agreed to the experiment. Kendall started well but stumbled on the Creed, which to More was a proof neither of guilt nor innocence. That was for a court to decide. In the end, a judge – possibly the Earl of Warwick – sentenced her to death, and she was hanged on Jesus Green before a seething crowd of townsfolk, scholars and dons.[16]

John Stearne was certainly aware of Goodwife Kendall's execution, but whether he had a hand in her identification is unknown. She may have been the 'honest woman' that one sceptical writer said had been executed at Cambridge 'for keeping a tame Frogge in a Box for sport and Phantasie'.[17] Taking all the evidence into consideration, Henry More was undecided about her guilt. He recognized that insane people 'have confidently affirmed that they have met with the Devil, or conversed with Angels, when it has been nothing but an encounter with their own fancie', yet the idea of a demonic conspiracy, and 'the frequent discoveries of this very Age' made by the witchfinders, continued to captivate him. In a metaphysical poem composed within a year of the encounter at Cambridge Castle More fantasized about malevolent hags dancing round a goat-like devil, whose backside they kissed to 'taste his deadly chear' – the *osculum infame* of demonological lore.[18] His interest may even have infected his students. Thomas Plume, an undergraduate at Christ's in the later 1640s, wrote about witchcraft in his notebook, including a tasteless joke where a witch about to be burnt asked for a drink of water, and an earthy story of how King James and the Duke of Buckingham exposed the fraudulence of 'a yong wench th[a]t confest she had made a contract w[i]th ye devill, & c[ou]ld doe strang things'.[19]

Nor was the meeting at the castle necessarily More's last experience of witches. Great St Mary's, parish of the warring Cottons and Swettsons, was in crisis by 1646. People had started to complain that the subsidy demanded for assisting more needy parishes was excessive when they had eighty families of their own to support. An influx of migrants from Ireland had not helped, and the cost of reglazing the church after Dowsing's visit had been considerable. Rate defaulters had their goods distrained and were reduced to penury themselves. In 1644 the vestrymen had petitioned to have the rates reduced, but had not neglected the cause of their suffering: heaven's judgement for sin. The following year their minister had been replaced by an orthodox divine from St John's College, and a remaining glass image of St Mary had been removed. Then they had a witch-hunt. Forty years after Dorcas Swettson first went to law there were still people in her parish paranoid about witches; Swettson herself, now an old woman, was one of them.[20]

A witch feeds a chestful of hungry imps with a spoon.

William Cropley, a vestryman in his thirties (whose baby son died suddenly in 1646), led the campaign at Great St Mary's, and as one of the wealthier ratepayers put up the money for it himself. How many witches they discovered and whether they summoned Hopkins or Stearne is unknown; they certainly employed search-women, and a jury of matrons seems to have been hired in the outlying village of

Chesterton. In a list of special disbursements for 1647–8, after a number of entries for looking after the sick, buying clothes for the poor and burying the dead, comes a record of two shillings and six-pence 'payd to willyam Cropley in part of the money he layd out by order for searching the witches'; another shilling and threepence fol-lowed in due course.[21]

This was one of many stories about witches current in Cambridge. A scholar of St John's, said to have compacted with the devil to become a doctor of divinity, vanished leaving his gown floating in the river; a suspected witch was found dead with a broken back after a man struck a strange cat with a fire-fork; a woman rumoured to be '*incantata et perturbata*' was treated by the astrologer William Lilly using a 'purge with Jollop' (a purgative derived from bindweed).[22] But whereas Henry More believed that such reports suggested the reality of the spirit world, the witchfinders offered more than mere suggestion: they illuminated the dark arts, uncovered the occult, and fixed the furtive and fleeting to the spot. Academic logic-chopping could be left to the gentlemen of the universities so far as Hopkins and Stearne were concerned; their business was to supply prima facie evidence for the courts.

In 1646 the witchfinders operated together at the neighbouring vil-lages of Over and Fen Drayton on the road to Huntingdon. Over was a small river port of 200 souls, among them puritans and radical sec-taries, many of whom had lost pasture to drainage schemes in the 1630s. The mid 1640s were also testing times, times of retribution. Epidemic disease carried off a fifth of the population, including the minister and his wife; and the birth-rate plummeted. According to John Stearne he and Hopkins were invited there, causing panic to at least one suspect who 'heard of our coming to town, and plucked her marks off the night before, because she would not have been found, as she confessed before a Justice of Peace of the same town at large, both of the Covenant and her Imps, and the harms she did both to him and others by her Imps'.[23] Fen Drayton was also struggling. Parishioners fought with the tenant farmer of their absentee lord, and were resent-ful that their parsonage was in the gift of Christ's College, which appointed ministers 'of scandalous lives and unsound doctryne'. In

1644 their minister had been replaced by 'a learned, orthodox, and pious Divine', but without provision from sequestration funds to pay him. Several poor women were examined here, and made 'very large Confessions'. Stearne records that the devil had warned them of the witchfinders' arrival, 'but withal told them they should be searched, but should not be found; wherein they said they found him a lyar'. The devil was also shown to have lied about providing for the women in return for their souls.[24] This was the lesson of the witch-hunt: that in the end truth would vanquish falsehood.

A year after they left Manningtree, the hunt was going on all around the witchfinders: at places they had been, and places where news of their work had reached; by rivers and ponds where villagers were swimming suspects; in the magistrates' parlours and quarter sessions courts where accusations were still taking shape; and in the gaols where suspects waited on remand, and the acquitted languished unable to pay their fees. On 10 March 1646 pardons for the nine reprieved Essex witches were finally granted by Parliament; criticism of the evidence upon which they had been convicted was implicit in the judgment. For Dorothy Waters reprieve came too late: she had died of plague, aged about forty, in the last week of February. Nor were the others released, presumably because they were unable to pay the bill for their eight months of imprisonment. If the complaints of Stephen Hoy the gaoler can be believed, there were eighty prisoners in Colchester Castle at this time, 'committed for Murder, horse stealeing, witchcraft & other hainous offences'. Servants and guards were stretched to the limit, and every day brought fear of an uprising.[25]

Elsewhere in Essex, early in 1646 the people of Asheldham, led by their minister, were emboldened to report 'a woman of turbulent and unquiet Spirit' who terrorized them with a strange power; she had sold a sow and piglets to a farmer, but made the animals die when her husband found a counterfeit coin in the remittance. A few days later, on the other side of the county at Elsenham, a woman was presented for having bewitched her neighbours, and within a year another two suspects had been arrested: a woman from Ridgewell near the Suffolk border, and Nicholas Leech from Manningtree, probably a relative of the hanged Anne Leech of Mistley.[26] At Little Laver, Eleanor Aylett, a gentlewoman of Magdalen Hall, believed herself, her family, house and cows to be cursed by a cabal of male and female witches; her fears dated back more than thirteen years, but like others too scared to confront their tormentors she had avoided legal action.[27] Meanwhile, in Ipswich, two women acquitted the previous September were tried again on new indictments, and in the autumn a third woman was convicted and hanged.[28]

Doubtless oblivious to much of this, Hopkins and Stearne continued to solicit and nurture accusations across the eastern counties. Preliminaries leading to arrests in Northamptonshire, a county of dense forests and rural radicalism, closely resembled the witchfinders' interrogations to date but also echoed an earlier case.[29] In 1612, a month before the Lancashire witch-trials reached their conclusion, at least twelve witches had been tried at Northampton, among them a widow and her daughter and daughter-in-law from Guilsborough. They had been meticulously searched on the orders of a godly minister, and suspicious teats had been found in their mouths; he had also made them recite the Creed, which – like Goodwife Kendall in the presence of Henry More – they had failed to do to his satisfaction. Thirty miles away at Raunds, the puritan magistrate Sir Gilbert Pickering had ordered that Arthur Bill and his impoverished parents should be subjected to the water ordeal. All three had floated and were gaoled; here, the father turned evidence against his wife and son and the woman slit her own throat. Protesting his innocence to the end, Arthur Bill was hanged in July 1612, as were two of the Guilsborough women and two others from Stanwick and Thrapston near the Huntingdonshire border. Matthew Hopkins had probably heard of these cases.[30]

By the mid 1640s the experience of Northamptonshire was a familiar one. Conflict between landowners, clergymen and tenants over tithes was widespread; householders endured plague, rising prices and excessive taxes; and the godly wreaked havoc upon royalists, malignants, and scandalous ministers. Like the iconoclasts and witchfinders, men were paid to roam the countryside 'gathering up delinquents', just as Laudian bishops had paid people to harass puritans in the 1630s;

some of these men, shameless profiteers, even changed sides and in 1642 went after Catholics instead. Another problem shared with other parts of East Anglia was that in Northamptonshire, for all its malefactors against God and the state, too little justice was being dispensed. Commissions of gaol delivery were only infrequently carried out, and the judges who would normally have ridden out on circuit stayed at Westminster, far from the fighting. One remedy, by now a regular occurrence in London, was simply to let prisoners go. In November 1644 Parliament issued pardons for inmates of Northampton gaol at the request of magistrates who had been executing the assize commission for themselves; judging was one thing but, they admitted, 'wee finde it very prejudiciall in theis tymes to have our Gaole full of Prisoners'. Four men awaiting sentence agreed to fight for Parliament and were set free, even though two of them had been convicted of a capital crime: 'the Murther of a Woman by Ducking her in the Water for Witchcraft'.[31]

For the witch-hunt to have spread to Northamptonshire in 1646 was not in itself surprising. What was distinctive, especially compared to events in 1612, was that at least some of the suspects confessed. This can be attributed to the fact that John Stearne was working in an area to the north-east of Northampton in late spring or early summer. At Denford a farmer named Cox had accused a young man of the parish who had recently asked for work tending his cattle. Cox had refused, and soon after 'the Cattell ranne so violently away foming, that the owner had much adoe to catch them with a horse, and more to get them home into his yeard againe'. After undergoing Stearne's devious and degrading procedures the deranged suspect confessed to having sent an imp to torment the cattle, and to various heinous crimes besides.[32] Bleary-eyed and beyond caring, Anne Goodfellow of Woodford related

that soone after her Aunts decease, about three yeares before she was questioned, the Devill in the shape of a white Cat appeared to her, and spoke to her with a low voyce, and bad her not be afraid of it, for he was her Aunts spirit, and asked her to deny God, Christ and her Baptisme, which she said she did, for he promised her that she should be saved, and would doe for her what she desired, and then asked for

her bloud to seale the Covenant, and further she confessed that he bit
her on the second finger, and got bloud into his mouth . . .

What happened after that Widow Goodfellow was unable to say, but
she now was of the opinion that the devil was a filthy liar, for she
remained as poor as ever. A few miles to the south lay the town of
Rushden where another widowed woman, Elizabeth Currey, confessed that some years earlier she had made love to the devil, and so
denied God 'through her wilfulnesse, and poverty, with desire of
revenge'.[33] At Old and Burton Latimer, accused witches confessed to
membership of diabolic sects to whose meetings they were transported through the air.[34] John Browne, a tailor from Raunds (home
of the luckless Bill family in 1612), said he had pretended to John
Clarke, a suspect from Keyston in Huntingdonshire, that he had been
searched for a witch's mark, only to be told: 'I doe not beleeve you
are a Witch, for I never saw you at our meetings.'[35]

Confessions wove the desires of the impotent into the fabric of
ideas about witches. And these were not just simple tales of rejection
and resentment, as events at Thrapston were to demonstrate. This was
the stone-built town on the river Nene, surrounded by fields and
woodland, where one of the women hanged in 1612 had been
accused of bewitching a child and of manifesting images of toads and
snakes on the linen of the midwife who searched her. It was a tale
retold many times over the next thirty years, and doubtless known to
Sir John Washington, lord of the manor. Washington's ancestral home
was Sulgrave Manor, half a day's ride to the south-west, but he and
his family lived in Thrapston, a stone's throw from the church. A
pious, wise and generous man, he was used to an elderly farmhand
named Cherry asking for alms, and was 'loving to him in affording
him relief constantly'.[36] But Washington had problems of his own.
He had married in 1621, but was left with four young boys when his
wife died in 1624; remarrying, he was blessed with a daughter and a
son, but by 1639 both were dead, and by the start of the civil war
three of the sons from his first marriage had also died. In 1646
Washington was fifty-four, and had lost a wife and five children; now
his cattle were dying as well. To distress was added shame: his brother

was a scandalous royalist, ejected from his Essex rectory and currently drinking himself to death.[37] Perhaps, like Abraham, Washington felt he was being tested by God; his life certainly seemed uncannily blighted.

Many townsmen could have given him a more sinister explanation. A local farmer had died from a diseased tongue, which by the end had hung from his mouth by its roots. Before losing his speech the man had related how he had exchanged cross words with old Cherry over a dog that had scared his cattle from the path. Cherry had 'wished that his tongue might rot out of his head', and so it came to pass. When John Stearne arrived in Thrapston, he was informed of this – 'a fearful thing to be thought of' – and took charge of the interrogation. Cherry confessed to having made a pact with Satan, and to having suckled imps 'for revenge, with promise of freedom from hell-torments'. He had sent an imp to kill the farmer with whom he had quarrelled, and was responsible for at least two more strange deaths, and other tragedies. For Sir John Washington there was chilling news: Cherry had been picking off his patron's cattle with his 'wicked cursing'; whether he owned up to Washington's family deaths, Stearne did not record. Cherry's animus against Washington grew not in spite of the kindness he had received, but precisely because of it. 'The more he gave him,' Cherry explained, 'the more power he had over him to do mischief.'[38]

The suspected witches were despatched to Northampton, where the grand jury returned true bills against several, including the young man from Denford and old Cherry. The former was arraigned and condemned, but Cherry had already died, probably at his own hand. Like John Lowes, another old man bullied into submission, his inner turmoil had settled into puzzlement, dissociation, then mental dissolution. One night shortly before the assizes began the gaoler noticed that Cherry's coat was ripped down the back, and that his mouth had been plugged. After the blockage was cleared, in a barely coherent gasp Cherry claimed to have just returned from a bridge at Thrapston. Not long after this he was found dead with a ligature round his neck, possibly twisted from strips of fabric. He had avoided the gallows, but death had caught him all the same – 'a just judgement of God', Stearne noted with satisfaction.[39] All the evidence had pointed to his guilt.

A Northampton physician named Dr John Cotta would have been very interested in old Cherry: a poor man sick in mind and spirit, to be pitied and understood, but none the less deserving of punishment. A staunch believer in witchcraft, Cotta had advocated in an influential book that inability to explain a phenomenon did not make it a miracle, and that real diabolic effects should not be confused with effects of the imagination.[40] Neither credulous nor sceptical, this was exactly the kind of empirical thinking that spurred on John Stearne to obtain compelling evidence of his suspects' wickedness.

By the summer of 1646 plague was crowding the war from the newspapers. In London, where there were two hundred new cases a week, Parliament ordered that the sick were to be incarcerated, infected alehouses closed and corpses burned, at first by night but soon round the clock. Reports of serious contagion arrived from counties as far apart as Yorkshire and Devon. At Chelmsford gaol another two of the reprieved and now pardoned witches died, Susan Wente in April and Susan Cocke six months later.[41] Signs of natural corruption were everywhere, from the centre of the state to its ragged margins.

Political dissension, increasingly prevalent in parliamentarian ranks, was viewed as an abuse of power deserving of further punishment. At Barnstaple, moderate Presbyterians who met twice a week to pray for the plague to abate believed that sects and Independent congregations were to blame. Across England ministers and magistrates – mostly Presbyterians – developed a greater sensitivity to challenges to their authority, and sought tighter controls over rebels who took religion and the law into their own hands.[42] On top of political turmoil, economic conditions were making it harder to keep a grip on order. Communities were levied to pay for the implementation of plague directives; and in a county like Huntingdonshire, heart of the Eastern Association, the burden of taxation and appropriation was already crushing, with the assessment of just one division of one hundred in the shire running to nearly £1,000. The yearning for peace was intense.[43]

Home of Oliver Cromwell, Huntingdonshire became the symbolic centre of the puritan revolution. As in Essex and Suffolk, godly traditions had grown out of tensions with Catholics, but many of these roots of conflict had been torn up by 1646. The county still had its witches, of course, and witch-hunting was inseparable from the wider campaign for reform. Cromwell showed little interest in it, however, though he was presumably aware of stories of witchcraft in his own family's past: in 1593 three witches had been executed at Huntingdon for the murder of his grandfather's second wife. Sir Henry Cromwell had lived at Ramsey, north of Warboys where his friend Robert Throckmorton was manorial lord. Throckmorton's neighbours, the elderly Samuels, had been welcomed many times at the manor house, but the relationship ended when his five daughters and seven maid-servants began to suffer strange fits. The Samuels had no motive, but as in the case of Cherry of Thrapston their poverty and proximity alone were enough to make them suspect, and soon their daughter Agnes was implicated. Eminent physicians and clergymen from Cambridge confirmed witchcraft. After visiting her children Lady Cromwell fell mortally sick herself, and was troubled by dreams in which a cat scratched her. In the end, Alice Samuel confessed that she was to blame. At the gallows she mumbled the Lord's Prayer (failing to include the words 'but deliver us from evil'), then was strung up beside her husband and daughter. When the gaoler stripped her corpse he found between her legs a milky teat, which he showed to curious spectators.[44]

The legacy of this story was widespread and enduring. After the trial Sir Henry Cromwell had received the Samuels' property, worth £40, which he donated to the corporation of Huntingdon to endow an annual sermon warning against witchcraft. A best-selling tract about the witches of Warboys was also published.[45] Thus witch-craft remained a live issue in Huntingdon in the first half of the seventeenth century. At Huntingdon School, generations of boys were taught by the didactic puritan Dr Thomas Beard, author of a popular compendium of God's judgements (including some upon witches) which ran to several editions. Beard's most famous pupil, Oliver Cromwell, respected him more than he did the learned doctors at Cambridge.[46] Beard died in 1632 but his influence lasted into the next decade, by which time a judgement upon the whole nation was evident. Providentialism mixed potently with local superstitions – the belief that snow came from the stars, that a child conceived in darkness would have black hair, and that luminous sprites haunted the waterways. Farmers burned bewitched livestock, and had little more compassion for those they held responsible.[47] By 1646 the readiness to blame witches for misfortune was a vexation to orthodox ministers, who were offended by the impiety and lack of regard for their teaching that it implied.

It was inevitable that rumours about a witchfinder should have stirred things up in the spring of 1646. These days, Hopkins and Stearne had become more reluctant to give evidence in person, but sustained their initial enthusiasm for pre-trial investigations, joining the dots between sites of suspicion to form conspiracies and covens. Most of the accused in Huntingdonshire came from villages within a confined area to the south of Thrapston, and between late March and early May were examined by magistrates at Hartford, just outside Huntingdon. Tensions had been running high in these parts, the Huntingdonshire gentry having been keen enclosers of common land and their tenants equally keen to resist them.[48] Unlike Stearne, Matthew Hopkins did not play a significant role in this part of the campaign, and may have been detained elsewhere.

It all started at Great Catworth when two women were arrested, and probably searched and watched under Stearne's supervision.[49] Frances Moore was not as well-off as yeoman farmers like the Searles in neighbouring Little Catworth, but neither was she among the poorest. Married with children, she grew corn, kept pigs – and nursed grudges. William Searle was present when Moore admitted her crimes, and noticed how she forced the words from her mouth as though she was being unnaturally restrained. Goodwife Moore also seemed uncomfortable on her stool, as if something beneath her skirts were causing her pain. Searle waited patiently. Some years earlier his servants had set a dog on a pig of Moore's that had wandered into his yard; he had also refused to let her bake at his house. Subsequently one of Searle's own pigs had died, and his capons 'did fall a fluttering, and would never eate after'. Moore now admitted that she had been responsible for these misfortunes, or rather that her black puppy-like imp 'Pretty' was the cause. News travelled quickly in every direction. When Searle's neighbour, a shepherd named Peter Slater, heard that witches had been detected and caught, memories from twenty years before resurfaced, compelling him to speak to them – Frances Moore specifically – as soon as he could.[50]

Before Slater could get to Great Catworth, however, Moore and the other suspect, Elizabeth Weed, had been taken the twelve miles to Huntingdon and placed in the custody of the gaoler. On 31 March Widow Weed was examined by magistrates Robert Bernard and Nicholas Pedley, upon which she opened her heart with a candid and cathartic confession. Twenty-one years earlier, Weed said, she had sealed a covenant with three demons resembling a boy and two puppies, one of which, 'Lilly', had tried unsuccessfully to murder Henry Bedell, a gentleman who had angered her. Bedell's child had been easier to overpower, however, as had the horses of another immune enemy, Edward Musgrave, and likewise livestock belonging to his kinsmen. Widow Weed now longed to be rid of her 'unhappy burthen', especially as the contract was nearing expiry, when the devil would claim her soul. Panic about this had lately converted her into an avid attender at the sermons and catechisms of the minister Mr Poole, as if the key to her redemption might lie there.[51]

That was the Tuesday. On Friday 3 April the shepherd Peter Slater visited Frances Moore, who had not yet been examined. In the late 1620s his wife had died in childbirth following a row with Moore in which Moore had wished that 'shee should never be untwin'd' – chilling words that Slater had found it impossible to forget. Now, all these years later, with the suspect in the clutches of the law, he needed to know whether this witch had killed his wife. Indeed she had, came Moore's reply – 'by cursing her'.[52]

Over the weekend of 4–5 April Peter Slater brooded, and on Tuesday testified before Robert Bernard, as did his neighbour William Searle. Later that day Bernard and his fellow magistrate Nicholas Pedley also took informations against a suspect from Keyston, four miles west of Catworth. In the autumn of 1644 Mary Darnwell, wife of a well-respected blacksmith in the village, had reported Elizabeth Chandler as a common scold, for which Chandler had been put in the ducking-stool. Theoretically the humiliation of this punishment made disorderly women repent, but Widow Chandler's ordeal merely deepened her hatred of Mary Darnwell.[53] Chandler was a lonely woman, reliant on a meagre income from minding the children of more prosperous neighbours. During 1645 she had spent her days at

A woman accused of scolding is lowered into a river on a ducking-stool.
Legend has tended to confuse the ducking (or 'cucking') of scolds with the
swimming of witches

the house of William Browning, her nights fantasizing about vengeance on Mary Darnwell for her 'hard usage'. Defences built up by prayer were undermined by such thoughts until they collapsed like the walls of Jericho; then, undefended, the citadel of the heart was stormed by Satan. What Widow Chandler called 'roaring things' started visiting her in bed, creatures she neither saw nor felt but which slithered beneath the covers 'in a puffing and roaring manner'. After they left, 'she found her body sore about the bottome of her belly' and prayed they would never return.[54]

One day in the spring Mary Darnwell had invited women from the neighbourhood to her house for furmety, a spiced wheat porridge. Elizabeth Chandler was not among the guests, and the party did not go well: the pot had boiled over, and would not stop even when Goodwife Darnwell lifted it from the fire. For over an hour, she said, she had filled plates and dishes with furmety, which just kept rising out of the pot in the most unnerving manner. For this alone she might not have accused Elizabeth Chandler of witchcraft, but what came next was a step too far. Her nine-year-old daughter Katherine had been playing with William Browning's child when a fight developed; Chandler the nurse had separated and chastised them. Arriving home later Katherine Darnwell told her mother that Widow Chandler had boxed her ear; the child then fell sick, and as her condition deteriorated, so she cried out that the old woman 'did come to her and would kill her'. So it seemed: within three weeks, her life had been snuffed out like a candle.

In custody at Huntingdon, Elizabeth Chandler confessed that her animosity towards Mary Darnwell might have attracted the attention of diabolical imps, but she denied that she had ever consciously tried to hurt anyone. Unfortunately she had already made a much more damning statement at Keyston, in the presence of John Stearne, though now she could barely remember what she had said. Mary Darnwell had been present, and now deposed that Chandler had admitted bewitching the furmety, using her imp 'Beelzebub'. When the confused woman was brought before the magistrates Bernard and Pedley she was asked directly whether or not she had ever entertained two spirits named 'Beelzebub' and 'Trullibub'. Evidently perplexed by the question, after a pause Widow Chandler replied that she had never done such a thing, and could say only that 'she did call a logg of wood Beelzebub, and a sticke Trullibub' – no more than a lonely woman's wooden pets.

Joseph Coysh graduated from Cambridge in 1638 and was ordained the same year; this makes him about thirty when he took charge of the life-and-death situation at Bythorn.[55] Elizabeth Chandler had effectively confessed to witchcraft at Huntingdon, and it was clear that the discovery of witches was not yet over. Behind Coysh stood a party of parish notables, farmers ready to crush anyone jeopardizing their livelihood – anyone like Anne Desborough. A poor widow, she had lived in Bythorn most of her life, although born at Titchmarsh in Northamptonshire. Titchmarsh was home to the Pickerings, godly gentry whose past services to witch-hunting had included testifying at the Warboys trial, publishing William Perkins' papers, and ordering the swimming of Arthur Bill and his parents.[56] Widow Desborough was arrested in April 1646, and at John Stearne's instigation she was watched. By the time she was taken before Coysh she was ready to talk. Asked how long she had been a witch and how she came to be one, she replied that thirty years before at Titchmarsh she had dreamt that a small creature nipped her breast; she prayed to God and it vanished. Days later the imp returned accompanied by another mouse-like beast, saying 'We must sucke of your body.' This they had continued to do every day, right up to her apprehension. When she had finished her story Joseph Coysh drew up a signed statement which he entrusted to yeoman Thomas Becke, a witness to the confession.[57]

Women like Anne Desborough were harangued from the pulpit about sin and self-discipline, and chastised by their peers. Silent acceptance was the usual response, carrying with it feelings of guilt which surfaced through sleep and hardened, like the crust on a vat of ale. Only the elect would be saved, they were told, and only the pure of heart could possibly be the elect – a terrifying prospect for those who had given in to the frustrations of a deprived life. At Hartford Eleanor Shepherd, a labourer's wife from Molesworth, confessed to the magistrates that in about 1641 she had sworn at her misbehaving children – a terrible loss of control – and had been propositioned by a grey rat-like spirit. She had shouted the preacher's familiar maxim, 'Avoid Satan', but the corruption of her soul had left her helpless:

> Within a short time after, going into the field, cursing, and fretting, and blaspheming, there appeared three Spirits more with the former in the fashion of Rats, of an iron-grey, and said, you must forsake God and Christ, and goe with me, and take those spirits for your Gods, and

you shall have all happinesse, whereunto she consented: And moreover they said unto her, that when she dyed, they must have her body and soule, and said, they must have blood from her.

She agreed, and they suckled her 'upon and about her hippes'. Questioned about happiness and harm, she said the imps had brought neither, although they had tormented her that afternoon in the gaol. She vowed to stop swearing, the sin that had been her undoing.[58]

The next day, Thursday 9 April, Thomas Becke and others from Bythorn took Anne Desborough to Hartford and delivered Coysh's statement. Later the magistrates heard the confession of Frances Moore of Great Catworth, which this time she made without discomfort. She blamed Widow Weed and another neighbour for supplying her with familiars, and admitted having murdered a man to avenge his threat to hang her children 'for offering to take a piece of bread'. One of her familiars, which looked like a puppy, had killed two cows that had strayed into her corn-field. In a bid to escape the cycle of sin she had killed her imps in 1645, but they had returned to haunt her. This accounted for her odd behaviour when she was first interrogated: the ghosts of her imps had 'crept under her cloathes, and tortured her so that she could not speake, to confesse freely'.[59]

On the Saturday justice of the peace Robert Bernard was presented with another suspect from Molesworth, John Winnick. An illiterate labourer probably in his late fifties, he had been searched by John Stearne, who discovered three teats; Winnick affirmed that these were used to feed familiar spirits.[60] Winnick now repeated a confession made earlier at Molesworth, that thirty years before he had lived at Thrapston, the town where old Cherry had bewitched Sir John Washington's cows. He had been a servant-in-husbandry on a farm there, and one day discovered that his savings of seven shillings – amounting to a fortnight's wages – had been stolen, he presumed by someone in his master's family.

In the days that followed Winnick's fury had become all-consuming. He had been tying bales of hay in the barn, 'swearing, cursing, raging, and wishing to himselfe that some wise body (or Wizzard) would helpe him to his purse and money again' when 'there appeared unto him a Spirit, blacke and shaggy, and having pawes like a Beare, but in bulk not fully so big as a Coney'. The beast had promised to return his purse if he would forsake God, upon which he fell to his knees, hands raised in praise. The next day Winnick had returned to the barn, where he was reunited with his money – and the bear-like spirit. According to John Stearne, who heard his confession, the creature

> told him, hee must fall downe and worship him againe, and then he fell downe, and said, Oh my Lord, my God, I thanke thee, and then hee asked him to deny God, and Christ, and to serve him as Lord, and then he should never want, which he confessed he consented to, then he demanded bloud, and he bade him take it, so he skipped on his shoulder, and fetched bloud with his claw, on the side of his head . . .[61]

Winnick received two imps (a cat to kill people and a rabbit for cattle), to which he had devoted himself body and soul. He said he never used them for ill, but did receive food from a maidservant he knew at Molesworth. The bear-spirit had her in its thrall, and incited her to steal from her master – an act of domestic rebellion to match Winnick's own rebellion against God.

At Keyston, Joan Wallis, a 'very ignorant, sottish woman' according to Stearne, confessed to the lord of the manor, Sir Edward Wingfield. Wingfield had been born at Kimbolton, studied at Cromwell's college of Sidney Sussex, and married a daughter of another prominent Titchmarsh family. In 1641 he had signed the Protestation Oath, and the following year went to fight Catholic rebels in Ireland. In May 1644 his son and heir had died in infancy, and in 1646 he and his wife were still waiting for another child. In bereavement, puritans focused their thoughts on God's purpose; but sometimes it was hard, even for an educated man like Wingfield, to keep suspicions of witchcraft at bay.[62] Goodwife Wallis was searched, and when incriminating nipples were discovered two people were appointed to watch her. Stearne was informed that no imps had appeared, but that something strange did occur: despite the fact that she never left her chair, Wallis had been seen in the yard outside the house. Questioned about this, she admitted that the devil had assumed her likeness so that she could go and feed her imps.

On the evening of Tuesday 14 April Joan Wallis was taken before Sir Edward Wingfield and another prominent man, John Guylatte. About a year earlier, Wallis said, she had been visited by a spirit 'like a man something ancient, in blackish cloathes, but he had ugly feet uncovered'. 'Blackman', as she called him, had given her two familiars in the shape of bristle-backed dogs. She had asked them to feed at her breasts, but they always went for the secret place found by the searchers. When Wingfield asked for more details of her sexual depravity, she made him promise to keep a secret; as he later testified, 'shee said, if I would not tell, shee would confesse, but she hoped that I would love her never the worse'. Privately holding that there was no honour between a gentleman and a witch, Wingfield agreed. Although her imps only ever suckled her, she said, she had intercourse with Blackman two or three times a week. He was a 'filthy rough', but did send the spirits to steal money for her. Wingfield and Guylatte retired to discuss the case over dinner, while Wallis was allowed to rest. Then they interviewed her again, and agreed that this confession was almost identical to the first. Wingfield summarized the proceedings on paper, which he and Guylatte then signed.[63]

There had however been one difference between the two versions. Initially Joan Wallis had called her familiars 'Grissel' and 'Greedigut', but by the time Wingfield and Guylatte had finished eating she had forgotten these names. Wingfield pressed her, but she could only remember the name 'Blackman'. Stearne had heard her mention these names, and also fancied they were feeding even as she stood before him. This she denied, but did confess to having had a cloven-hoofed lover, 'uglier then man and not as her husband, which speaks to her like a man'.[64]

Two days after her confession to Sir Edward Wingfield Wallis was taken before another magistrate, Sir Robert Osborn. This time she managed to remember her imps' names, and said they brought her food when she prayed to them. Asked about 'Blackman', she admitted having been 'very fearefull of him for that he would seem sometimes to be tall, and sometimes to [be] lesse, and suddenly vanished away'. She denied having had sex with him, perhaps believing that Wingfield would keep her secret. But Goodwife Wallis was soon to learn that there were no secrets from heaven: Wingfield was ready to fight Satan in Huntingdonshire with the determination he had brought to fighting Catholic rebels in Ireland. She was not the last to be examined. According to John Browne – the tailor from Raunds in Northamptonshire – the Clarkes of Keyston had been searched, but their son John had escaped detection by cutting off his suspicious marks three days before the witchfinders came. This much the youth admitted on being taken to Hartford on 2 May, but he claimed ignorance of witchcraft and devil-worship. Stearne thought otherwise. Later he recalled how John Clarke's mother had escaped through a tiny hole in a stone wall, and conceded that the cunning nature of witches made their guilt hard to detect. 'Yet I say,' he added confidently, 'if those which looke to them be carefull, it is to be discerned.'[65]

May 1646 was a hot month, filled with strange events. Abandoning hope the king headed north, and on the 5th surrended to the Scots at Newark. Except for the defiance of his Court at Oxford, the war was over. Divisions among the victors muted their triumphant celebrations, however decisively providence had sided with Parliament. No one knew what might happen next, and anxiety among the people was reflected in a rash of supernatural phenomena in East Anglia. On the 21st, at Swaffham in Cambridgeshire, a meteorite was reported to have left an acre of corn in a sulphurous blaze. Hailstones the size of pigeons' eggs fell from the sky – some with holes in them, which people wore like rings. One hysterical woman foretold Judgement Day and managed to persuade the minister of Swaffham, 'a pious Man, with a disorder'd Head'. The same day a vision of three men fighting in the sky was seen at Newmarket, suggesting conflict between England, Scotland and Ireland. Just outside Cambridge, a squad of militiamen saw a steeple flanked by edged weapons, a spectacle which also appeared at Thetford and at Brandon in Norfolk. Thunder imitating a drum-roll was heard here, and near King's Lynn and in Suffolk too.[66]

The times became more unsettled as the end of the war drew nearer, the call for moral reformation louder than ever. 'The Lord grant that all the people of this Kingdome may take heed to every warning Trumpet of his,' implored one godly sage, 'that we may speedily awaken out of our sins, and truly turne to the Lord.' Victory against Satan seemed almost as distant as it had in 1642, and there was no room for complacency. To satisfy God, pious folk believed, England must continue to 'fight his battles against our spirituall Enemies, and get those inward riches of which we cannot be Plundered of, and so seek an inward Kingdome of Righteousness and Peace'.[67]

9

Sticklers

———◆———

A WORLD TURNED upside-down was not to be set right by military victory. English life continued to be turbulent throughout 1646 as the constitutional and religious questions over which the civil war had been fought remained unanswered, and new ones came to the fore. Puritan preachers, grateful for God's deliverance, could not ignore the wickedness of cavaliers, malignants, papists and atheists that still contaminated every corner of the land; the devil, it was said, made them hate peace as much as they had hated Parliament. Godly reformation,

A woodcut from 1647 depicting the world turned upside-down. A dismembered man, an inverted church, and a rabbit chasing a fox here symbolize political and religious chaos

declared one minister, drove them to a frenzy: 'this to them is as salt to live Eeles, it frets them to the heart to have their besmearing slime purged from them'. Four years earlier it had been reasonable to suppose that order would return once the enemy had been defeated; but parliamentarians now had one another to contend with, as moderate Presbyterians crossed swords with radical Independents.[1] The political and spiritual future of the nation became more precarious than at any time during the hostilities.

Religious sects proliferated, offering freedom from hierarchy and Calvinist theology. But one man's libertarian was another's libertine: like Jews, Turks, heathens, papists and witches, it was said, sectaries 'trod underfoot the bloud wherewith they were sanctified'. Their apostasy was outrageous. A man at Rochester called Christ 'a bastard', and said he would be ashamed of him if ever he returned to earth. An apprentice-turned-preacher at Yarmouth said the Bible was just a pile of paper. God's punishment of such people was equally remarkable, like the woman in Colchester delivered of a headless child – a judgement on its Anabaptist father. Among the sects, the devil masqueraded as a heavenly saviour encouraging sins of the flesh – 'adultery, fornication, idolatry, witchcraft, murther, drunkennesse, &c.' – that by the winter of 1646 were being perceived as epidemic.[2] The fact that some independent preachers happened to be women encouraged rumours of sexual deviance. Like a coven of witches, 'this affronted, brazen-faced, strange, new feminine Brood' was believed to lead Christians into error.[3]

In this poisonous atmosphere the eastern counties remained a fertile breeding ground for witch-hunting, yet at the same time a determination 'to bring things to the old course and way of government' dictated that righteous ends could no longer justify unlawful means.[4] Perhaps sensing that time was short, Hopkins and Stearne became even more careful to test opinion at the places they visited, if possible by soliciting letters of invitation in advance. There were witches still to be processed at Huntingdon, but once a suspect was in the hands of a magistrate, the witchfinders were now inclined to feel that their work was done and it was best to move on.

They left few tracks in Bedfordshire, though its religious polarization, its many tales of witchery and the fact that jury charges specified witchcraft as an offence in the years 1644–5 seemed to mark the county as fertile territory for their work.[5] For thirty years a celebrated case from Milton Mills had lent empirical substance to the water ordeal popularized by James I, and the practice had become part of rural life. A woman was swum in 1637, alongside the maidservant she was supposed to have bewitched: the innocent girl sank, underlining the witch's guilt.[6] By the time of the civil war swimmings were common in Bedfordshire, but magistrates were less likely to approve of them after Serjeant Godbold's prohibition in the summer of 1645. Later, the witchfinders insisted that they had obeyed this ruling, eschewing all cruel and superstitious methods. Sleep deprivation, they said, was confined to 'the infancy of this discovery', and the swimming test was condemned as 'one way of distrusting Gods providence . . . [that] hath ever since been left, and not many before so used'. But these were weasel words, for Matthew Hopkins continued to believe that ordeals were well suited to his purposes. As he explained, witches would inevitably float, 'as the Froath on the Sea, which the water will not receive, but casts it up and downe, till it comes to the earthy element [of] the shore'.[7] More importantly, ordinary people believed in the efficacy of the ordeal, and Hopkins was unswerving in his mission to nurture suspicions, not let them wither away.

By this time folk wisdom was familiar with the notions that witches made blood pacts, belonged to covens, and congregated at sabbats. Fantastical tales of the Lancashire trials of 1612, which had owed much to a magistrate having read William Perkins and other daemonologists, helped disseminate these ideas.[8] Hopkins and Stearne naturally exploited and encouraged the fear thus generated, which tended to exceed parochial witch-panics focusing on the destruction of life and property. In the early summer of 1646 they were travelling along the border between Bedfordshire and Huntingdonshire when they heard that a coven had been identified at Tilbrook, a parish where the minister – once the scourge of local puritans – had been hounded from office. It is doubtful that they investigated, but the news was still useful intelligence.[9] Hopkins visited nearby Kimbolton, a town where accusations had been made in recent years but not followed by legal action. A resident of the old priory had been in conflict with 'a woman of a bad conversation in revileing, curseing, swearing & so noted by her neighbours for that divers of her neighbours have suspected her to be the only occasion of the losse of their severall goods as horse[s] Cowes Calfes, pigs & hens ducks'. The minister-cum-healer Richard Napier had once eased the afflicted woman's 'pangs of death', but in 1646 Hopkins perhaps offered a more lasting cure.[10]

Napier had also treated supposedly bewitched patients from St Neots, a town eight miles away. Like Kimbolton, St Neots was a former priory town haunted by Catholic ghosts and now economic-ally overstretched and emotionally overwrought. These days only the gatehouse of the priory was intact, but even this was an irksome reminder to godly folk that the town's founding saint was buried there. Nearby was the market-place leading to the bridge over the Great Ouse, meandering from its Northamptonshire source to the sea at King's Lynn. Many poor people shared their lives with nature along this valley, tending sheep and cattle, snaring rabbits and magpies, pol-larding and hedging. They were vulnerable and diffident, but by the time the witchfinders arrived in May 1646 the men and women who had gathered in the town centre were baying for blood.

Spokesmen for the town informed Hopkins and Stearne that they had recently decided to get rid of a detestable wretch believed to have caused them much harm. A team of experienced women had searched her twice, but on neither occasion were any incriminating teats or blemishes discovered. Stearne reassured them that the devil often sharpened a witch's cunning to enable her to conceal the place where she fed her imps, especially if she had received advance warning that she was to be searched.[11]

The townsmen went on to describe how the woman's flight from St Neots had intensified suspicions, though in the end she had nowhere to go except home; on her return a mob threw her off the bridge into the river, and an innocent man volunteered to follow her as a control. As might have been expected, a large crowd gathered on the bridge and river-banks, and watched the woman bob around until she was dragged out. She had not been immediately committed for trial; perhaps use of the ordeal caused the magistrates to reject the case.

So a party went to her house and carried out yet another search. Once again no teats were found, but they did see bite-marks on her neck and bruising elsewhere. Like a bloodhound with a scent, Stearne tracked down a local farmer who told him that an unfamiliar dog had wandered into his yard, and that he had set his mastiff on it. The mastiff had been oddly reticent, so the man's son had struck the trespassing dog across its back. Encouraged by this, their spayed bitch bit the dog on the neck before it managed to escape.[12] There the story ends, but the unhappy woman's prospects would seem to have been bleak in St Neots, whether at the hands of a lynch mob or committed to the mercy of the law.

If she escaped with her life, it was probably thanks to the increasing number of men prepared to stand up to disorderly witchfinding. As one writer put it later, 'they saw that unless they put a stop, it would bring all into blood and confusion'.[13] At Great Staughton, on the road between St Neots and Kimbolton, a minister named John Gaule had been exasperated for some time by his parishioners' readiness to blame witches for misfortunes caused by their own sins; an active witch-hunt was beyond the pale. Hearing about the confessions at Huntingdon, reports of which soon reached Cambridge and beyond, he visited the gaol and spoke to one of the women. Their conversation did nothing to change Gaule's mind or cool his temper about the madness engulfing Huntingdonshire. 'It is strange to tell what superstitious opinions, affections, relations, are generally risen amongst us', he remarked acidly, 'since the Witchfinders came into the Countrey.'[14]

As soon as Matthew Hopkins got wind of Gaule's intervention he took fright. He was still working in St Neots, but had been planning to leave for Kimbolton in a few days. In Great Staughton he found a contact – now known only as 'M. N.' – and wrote the following letter:

> My service to your Worship presented, I have this day received a Letter, &c. – to come to a Towne called Great Staughton to search for evill disposed persons called Witches (though I heare your Minister is farre against us through ignorance). I intend to come (God willing) the sooner to heare his singular Judgment on behalf of such parties; I have known a Minister in Suffolke preach as much against their discovery in a Pulpit, and forc'd to recant it (by the Committee) in the same

place. I much marvaile such evill Members should have any (much more any of the Clergy who should daily preach Terrour to convince such Offenders) stand up to take their parts against such as are Complainants for the King, and sufferers themselves with their Families and Estates.

Hopkins went on to say there was a ten-to-one chance he would visit Great Staughton before Kimbolton, and to enquire 'whether your Town affords many Sticklers for such Cattell, or willing to give and afford us good welcome and entertainement'. If the former, Hopkins added, then he would steer clear of Great Staughton, 'and betake me to such places where I doe and may persist without controle, but with thankes and recompence.'[15] No reply survives; perhaps none was ever composed or delivered. What is known is that Hopkins' coolly contemptuous letter was passed to John Gaule, who settled himself at his desk and began to compose a public retaliation.

It was mid May. As Hopkins waited for a reply to his letter, a messenger rode into St Neots requesting his presence in King's Lynn. He accepted the invitation, for his usual fee, but was unable to offer a date before the Huntingdon assizes, perhaps not before the end of August: sticklers notwithstanding, there was still much to occupy the witchfinders that summer. It is possible that they decided to ride south into Hertfordshire before venturing north again. As in Bedfordshire, at least one well-known Jacobean case had originated here, and in the early 1640s two suspects had been swum at Baldock with their toes and thumbs tied together. This was no isolated occurrence: a woman at St Albans refused to sink even when pushed under the water with long poles. She confessed afterwards that her imp had kept her afloat, and so was packed off to Hertford gaol. There she proudly showed off her swollen teats, as did a male prisoner who appeared to have an entire female breast hanging from his side.[16] Whether or not Hopkins and Stearne were involved, it was a case bearing all their hallmarks.

Even more compelling proof of the witchfinders' presence in Hertfordshire – and of the restraining effect of sticklers – is to be found in a London newspaper. Two condemned witches due to be executed at Hertford that summer were reprieved because of nagging doubts about the safeness of the evidence against them. 'Some feare the witch-takers seeke the prise of blood more then to discover witches,' read the report, 'which is a fearfull thing if true.' After the excesses at the Chelmsford assizes in 1645, it was desirable that men in authority should 'examine the businesse'. In Kent, meanwhile, popular witch-hunting seems to have spiralled out of control. 'The multitude without order take women (when it is said they are witches) and threw them into a River, to try if they will swim.'[17] Magistrates and ministers refused to wait for these witch-scares to burn themselves out, but determined that they should be stamped out by the forces of authority and law.

Magistrates and ministers often turned a blind eye when communities shamed wrongdoers in seeking to defend the moral order. But by 1646 witch-hunting had exceeded what could be regarded as a tolerable degree of self-policing, and at Great Staughton John Gaule was determined to nip the problem in the bud. His manorial lord and patron, Valentine Walton, was acquainted with the situation. Walton had obtained the manor of Great Staughton from Sir Edward Wingfield, the interrogator of witches at Keyston, having been an MP for Huntingdon, a commander at Edgehill, and an assistant to Cromwell in the confiscation of plate from the Cambridge colleges; he was also married to Cromwell's sister. Until his death in 1629 Gaule's patron had been Viscount Campden, whom he had served as chaplain; in 1632 Gaule was presented to the vicarage of Great Staughton, and took up the living five years later. By then he was already a published theologian, having tackled such diverse subjects as Christ's passion, the perils of avarice, and the meaning of death.[18] But no training could have fully prepared him for the practical challenges he was to face in the mid 1640s.

At Great Staughton, the greatest barrier to good neighbourliness was poverty. The overseers of the poor strived to match their receipts with their disbursements for everything from mending clothes to burials and, like other East Anglian parishes in the 1640s, had to cope with a stream of Irish migrants. The elderly widows who consumed half the relief budget in the years 1644–6 were no doubt a source of resentment for those villagers who refused to pay the rate.[19] When old women were the least productive members of a community, and so many witches seemed to be old women, it was easy for people to imagine that their parish's fortunes were under attack from witches.

John Gaule dismissed this as nonsense. It was not that he was sceptical about witchcraft, still less about the agency of spirits; rather, he objected to witch-hunting as a superstitious reflex that discounted the agency of providence and further destabilized an already chaotic world. However necessary the civil war might have been, Gaule believed it was time to get back to the *status quo ante bellum* before intemperance and violence destroyed the commonwealth. At heart he was a conservative. Privately he noted how episcopacy had slid into independency, oaths had become covenants, and churches were used as stables, stables as churches. Liberty had turned into licentiousness, government into tyranny, plenty into poverty, and peace into war. The revulsion Gaule felt for witchfinders was therefore concerned not merely with their impiety, but with their assumption of authority. Above all, he prayed for an end to the 'Coblers and Tinkers turn'd Preachers, Souldiers turn'd Lawgivers, Subjects turn'd Tyrants, and Servants turn'd Masters'.[20]

Gaule launched a campaign of preaching in Great Staughton intended to suppress the appetite for witch-hunting. In writing his sermons he drew on fieldwork as much as theology, interviewing parishioners about witchfinding and making notes on what he had gleaned at Huntingdon. In a state of intense agitation Frances Moore had told him how she killed the cat and dog she believed to be her familiars; but it was what she had said next that troubled him the most. After her arrest she had been forced to sit cross-legged on a stool, then tied up and watched for the space of twenty-four hours without food, water, or the chance to relieve herself. Gaule had checked the veracity of Moore's account by writing to one of the witchfinders, who had brazenly confirmed her story.[21]

In a defiant sermon larded with Scripture and spiced with wit Gaule invited his congregation to consider what it really meant for a woman like Frances Moore to believe her pet animals to be demons, and for her persecutors to think the same of insects in the watching chamber. Was it not troubling to their consciences, he demanded to know, 'that an invention or practise of so much folly & superstition should arise amidst so cleare a light of the Gospell?' Not only were such practices based on unlawful error: they actually seduced honest Christians from true religion, much as the radical sects – and witches themselves – were said to do. On this matter Gaule spoke plainly: 'The Country People talke already, and that more frequently, more affectedly, of the infallible and wonderfull power of the Witchfinders, then they doe of God, or Christ, or the Gospell preached.'[22] Witchfinding, it appeared to him, usurped the authority of heaven and earth alike.

Every Sunday for a month the parishioners of Great Staughton fidgeted in church as their minister harangued them. One of Gaule's key propositions was that the evidence used against witches – what he called 'Tokens of Tryall' – was invalid. If burying charms under the threshold, burning bewitched animals and ordeal by water were true signs to reveal a witch, he argued, then 'certainly it can be no other Witch but the user of them'. Even lawful proofs were to be handled with care. Confessions should be regarded circumspectly even if supported by visible marks, and completely discounted without them. The evaluation of evidence, moreover, was a matter for magistrates and ministers alone, and should never be an office 'taken upon them by any privat persons, as a Calling, Profession, occupation or Trade of Life'. Considering their base and mercenary ambitions, not to mention their reliance on error and ordinary senses, witchfinders were no better than Catholic inquisitors and exorcists, inflicting pain and nurturing superstition among simple folk. Witchcraft *was* a spiritual threat; but popular beliefs offered no solution, only distraction from the real danger. The worst distraction of all, concluded Gaule, remained the faith that scores of people were now investing in the witchfinders.[23]

A conviction of the need to dissuade witchmongers was nothing new among country ministers. In Elizabethan Cambridgeshire, Richard Greenham and Henry Holland had held forth on the subject; and in the winter of 1644 the Archdeacon of Colchester had preached 'that most of the witches that ever have beene discovered, have beene so by malice. So sometime it hath served as a bawd to covetousnesses to bring wealth.'[24] The following year an anonymous minister in

Suffolk had spoken out against the witchfinders and, according to Hopkins' letter to M. N., had been censured for it by the county committee. This may be a reference to Samuel Fairclough at the Bury St Edmunds assizes; his caveats could easily have been interpreted as criticism, which would explain why neither of the sermons he delivered there appears to have been published.[25] By this time lay and clerical observers alike were beginning to notice how often neighbours falsely accused each other, and to realize that witches might confess simply as a result of being 'bewitch'd with fear, or deluded with phancy'.[26] Opponents of the devil, it was decided, should not be given the benefit of the doubt just because their adversary was devious; indeed, accusers themselves might be diabolically led astray.

None of this amounted to a landslide of opinion. Doubtless John Gaule's audience grumbled about him in the alehouse, if not actually to his face. To them, the danger posed by witches made the risk of injustice seem worthwhile, and four years of war had hardened them to hazard. The idea that 'nowe theire is now king, noe Lawes, nor noe Justice', as one Norfolk woman put it, had been infectious, leading random assertions of self-will to displace sound judicial principles.[27] Even with the mob behind them Hopkins and Stearne fought shy of debate, recognizing that the strength of local power which had abetted their sweep from the Tendring Hundred into Suffolk and beyond could just as easily bring them down; the challenge at Colchester had taught them that. There does seem to have been at least one encounter between the witchfinders and the man destined to become their nemesis. Gaule went to hear one of the pair – probably Hopkins – address a crowd on the nefarious practices of witches, including how they married Satan using the Book of Common Prayer; but there is no record of a confrontation, or even that Gaule made himself known.[28] He preferred to snipe at the witchfinders from a distance, and they at him.

Huntingdon was an unremarkable clutter of buildings on the Great Ouse, surrounded by water-meadows where cattle and sheep grazed. This sunlit arcadia – a perfect image of a new Jerusalem – contrasted starkly with the picture of hell in the gaol. Prisons were 'the grave of

the living', places of sullen despair where 'men huddle up their life
. . . as a thing of no use'. Lice infested hair and clothes, rats came
through the bars, and thoughts of death and damnation gnawed at
inmates' brains like worms. Straw was burnt for relief from the stench,
and a pennyworth of bread might have to last a day, or a week.[29]
During the summer, thirst was a constant torment. At least eight of
the prisoners at Huntingdon were accused witches, among them
Frances Moore, the woman interviewed by John Gaule; Elizabeth
Chandler, the nurse who had bewitched the porridge-pot; and John
Winnick, the poor labourer who had bowed down to a bear-like devil
in order to recover his stolen purse.

They might have been entitled to expect a proper trial. In February
of that year a parliamentary resolution had ordered assize judges to
return to their peacetime circuits, and called for routine commissions
to be restored; this resolution did not come into force until June,
however, and the Huntingdon trials were at the end of May. The
acting judges, therefore, were county magistrates more concerned
with local interests than impartial justice.[30] These were the very men
John Gaule had come to resent: godly officers of the Eastern
Association, too far gone in blood to leave room for compassion.
More outspoken critics called Parliament men wolves in sheep's clothing, betraying the nation as Judas had Christ; the most tyrannical, it
was said, were soldiers in the guise of judges. 'That verie Sword which
is drawn to defend and maintain Law,' remarked one preacher, 'will in
some things, at some times breake Law, such are the evill effects of
War.' Justice was trodden underfoot, order cast out, and confusion
engendered. Gaule himself saw how war and disorder had 'turned
Courts of known Law, into a High Court of unknown Justice', with
disastrous consequences. 'God forbid they should be punished for
Witches that indeed are no Witches,' he enjoined his parishioners, for
innocent blood polluted the land and cried to heaven for vengeance.[31]

John Davenport, a servant to the justices, was present at the
Huntingdon trials and recorded much of the testimony against the
alleged witches. Like his masters, Davenport believed that 'more full
and cleare confessions, more satisfactory Evidence, and a clearer
Conviction, could not be in a case of this nature'. John Stearne also

attended, and probably Hopkins as well, although neither seems to have testified. If they were afraid, on this occasion at least they had no need to be. Stearne heard again the confession he had extracted from John Winnick, and the court was shown the scar on the arraigned man's head where the devil was supposed to have drawn blood for their pact. At least five witches were convicted, demonstrating that jurors were willing to accept forced confessions; yet one woman was acquitted, despite a weight of evidence.[32] Perhaps she was saved by a patron or a faction in her neighbourhood; or perhaps the jury, however mistaken their conclusions in other cases, in this instance paid attention to the quality of the proofs as well as their quantity.

As the witches of Northampton were being tipped into their graves, so the proceedings at Huntingdon drew to a close. The convicted prisoners were brought out of the gaol for the last time, and positioned before the gallows. Standing high on the ladder, surveying the crowd, one of the women from Great Catworth repeated her confession. John Winnick did likewise, and even took the opportunity to enlarge upon his earlier disclosures – 'the last words he spoke', recalled Stearne, before his soul was claimed by Satan according to the sordid deal struck in the barn at Molesworth.[33]

Whatever satisfaction it gave accusers, witnesses and witchfinders to watch these wretches launched into eternity, one man at least was appalled. As John Gaule finished editing and annotating his sermons, news of the executions crystallized everything he feared and loathed about the witch-hunt. He dedicated his work, entitled *Select Cases of Conscience Touching Witches and Witchcrafts*, to his patron Valentine Walton, and added a preface in which he explained that he had been moved to publication by personal criticism, including hostile remarks about his preaching 'from one I never saw before'. Presumably this was Matthew Hopkins, for a complete transcript of his provocative letter to 'M. N.' occupied the next two pages. Gaule sent the manuscript to London, where on 29 May a puritan press licenser pronounced it 'learned & judicious . . . solide and seasonable'. A month later the printer delivered the completed 200-page book to Richard Clutterbuck's shop near St Paul's Cathedral.[34]

It was midsummer, a time for revels and bonfires to ward off evil

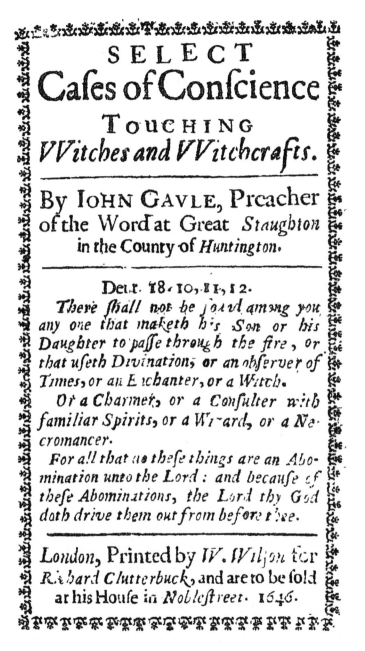

SELECT
Cases of Conscience
Touching
Witches and Witchcrafts.

By Iohn Gavle, Preacher
of the Word at Great *Staughton*
in the County of *Huntington.*

Deut. 18. 10, 11, 12.

*There shall not be found among you,
any one that maketh his Son or his
Daughter to passe through the fire, or
that useth Divination, or an observer of
Times, or an Enchanter, or a Witch.*

*Or a Charmer, or a Consulter with
familiar Spirits, or a Wizard, or a Ne-
cromancer.*

*For all that as these things are an Abo-
mination unto the Lord : and because of
these Abominations, the Lord thy God
doth drive them out from before thee.*

London, Printed by *W. Wilson* for
Richard Clutterbuck, and are to be sold
at his House in *Noblestreet.* 1646.

Title-page to John Gaule's influential critique of Hopkins' witchfinding
campaign

spirits. This year there was extra cause for celebration, for on 24 June Oxford surrendered, formally ending the war. A sermon of thanksgiving to the House of Commons predicted that 'all sorceries, witchcrafts and stratagems, contrived and carried on by the wit and malice and power of hell against the Church of God, shall prove vaine and succeslesse'.[35] But a restitution of order was some way off, and John Gaule's critique of arbitrary government, private office and popular excess seemed especially relevant as England faced the future. In the first week of July John Davenport published *The Witches of Huntingdon* through the bookseller handling Gaule's work. Davenport's intention was to demonstrate 'how craftily and dangerously the Devill tempteth and seizeth on poore soules', and to warn how anger, malice and lust dragged them to perdition. As a postscript, Clutterbuck the publisher added an advertisement for 'that learned discourse of Mr John Gaules', hopeful that curious readers would venture further into the debate. Many did, and in due course the seeds sown by Gaule's book became Hopkins' undoing.[36] For the moment, however, the witchfinder was off again, to keep his appointment in the Norfolk port of King's Lynn.

Situated where the Great Ouse flows into the Wash, King's Lynn had long exported everything from Lincolnshire salt to Derbyshire lead, and distributed imports as diverse as Scandanavian coal and Siberian furs. Independent and proud, the merchants ran the corporation like a city-state. From the time of Elizabeth the town had been gradually rebuilt in brick, with sewers laid to drain away floods and discourage the spread of disease.[37] In 1642 the walls had been fortified against royalist gentry in Norfolk, a coup had been defeated the following year, and now it was the most important garrison in the Eastern Association. But the costs were staggering, and by 1646 the mayor of King's Lynn was looking to his counterpart in Norwich to relieve the city's 'miserable Condic[i]on'.[38]

The eradication of sin and crime was a constant preoccupation for the town. Pillories and whipping posts stood in both market-places – the Tuesday market being the principal site of execution – and at nearby Purfleet Quay could be found a ducking-stool for scolds and a gibbet for exhibiting the corpses of heinous offenders. Lynn had its share of tales about executed witches, including Mother Gabley who had boiled eggs in a pail of water to sink a ship returning from Spain and a woman whose beating heart was said to have leapt from her body at the moment of her death. The most famous story was that of struggling cheesemonger Mary Smith, hanged in 1617 for having forsaken God for the devil, who came to her in the shape of a black man. She had used her power to get ahead in trade and to wither away the body of a sailor who had struck her son. A godly minister had immortalized the story in a book, graciously dedicated to the mayor and aldermen.[39]

Thirty years later the civic authorities were expressing their fear of witches once more. On 11 May 1646 Mayor Edward Robinson had instructed an alderman named Captain Revett to send for Matthew Hopkins, 'his Charges and Recompence to be borne by the Towne'. Hopkins was known to be working in St Neots at that time, so Revett had sent a trooper there to deliver the invitation. The witchfinder probably did not arrive in Lynn until August, by which time the excitement was such that two of Revett's men were ordered to the city gate, one on horseback to act as an escort, the other to drum Hopkins through the streets like a liberating hero. After this formal reception, he wasted little time. The cramped undercroft of the town hall, converted from a wine cellar into a gaol, now contained nine suspects, eight women and a man. All had been committed for trial after a panel of midwives and honest matrons had found suspicious marks on them.[40]

On 2 September the corporation awarded Matthew Hopkins £15 for his services 'in discovering of witches' – about what the drummer who had heralded his arrival earned in sixteen months.[41] The money was paid to the witchfinder in person by Mayor Robinson, who also asked him to appear as a witness at the next sessions of gaol delivery in three weeks' time. Robinson promised 'further satisffaccion' upon his return. Another £3 was disbursed to Captain Revett for his troubles.[42]

It was harvest time, when women from King's Lynn migrated into the fields to look for work. This year, however, the summer had turned exceptionally wet, leading to disease in both livestock and crops. Wheat was 'exceedingly smited and dwindled and lanke', rye was 'spurred' with the black rot of ergot, and the cost of beef, mutton, butter and cheese escalated sharply. Grain prices, which had risen by a third during the war, rose by another fifth in the first year of peace. Desperate farmers were forced to sell or eat their seed-corn, risking penury the following year.[43] The poor added wild plants like nettles and docks to their pottage, and ground-up roots to the flour for their bread. When ergot found its way into that flour the medical consequences were paralysis, fits, hallucination, gangrene, and the sensation that the skin was being pricked and torn. Mothers stopped lactating, and the flesh of weaker victims mortified until they died.[44]

As soldiers drifted home from war, spreading infestation and infection, plague became rampant in town and country, adding to the pressures on every community in Norfolk.[45] Dearth and disease combined with religious tension and political uncertainty made for an autumn of rumours. From London came reports of people who had slept an extraordinary length of time; at Rochester one woman was accidentally buried alive.[46] The rural population of Norfolk – a county with strong Catholic traditions and, until recently, many Arminian clergy – was steeped in superstition. A bird tapping at the window presaged death, sprites were said to pull men from their horses, and it was common for bewitched boats and animals to be burned.[47] County folklore was rich in stories about witchcraft, of which there had been several remarkable cases earlier in the century.[48] A number of executions had taken place in 1645, but details of them are sketchy. According to Matthew Hopkins, a baker called Meggs was hanged at Norwich after volunteering to be searched.[49]

To the west Norfolk's pasture and ploughland, its skyline broken by flint towers and clumps of beech and oak, led into the vast brooding wetlands of the East Anglian fen. Travellers, including the drainers and fen adventurers, considered it a barren and unwholesome place – a wilderness forgotten by God after the Flood. Its inhabitants knew a different world. There were fertile grasslands for the breeding of horses, sheep and cattle, and huge quantities of butter went from here to feed the navy. Manure and the natural soil made this one of the best arable regions in England, and corn, wheat, barley and rye were shipped north through King's Lynn and south to London. The rivers were teeming with eel and pike, the banks rich in sedge and reed for thatching and weaving. In the wet season, when the land was flooded, farmers moved through the low-lying mists on causeways, punts and stilts, and dug drains and ditches to allow the worst to soak away.

Schemes for drainage and the introduction of cash crops threatened this way of life, and in the 1630s had led to rioting and sabotage. A satirical ballad spread by word of mouth had invoked 'the ffrogges and Mierye Bogges' like a malevolent spell, to thwart the ambitions of the projectors. The cottagers who worked this gnat-infested, malarial land were widely reputed to be of bleak and stoical temperament, strong-willed, defiant, and especially prone to belief in witches; 'from their blacke & sooty blood', it was said, 'gloomie fuliginous spirits do fume into their braines'.[50] Further south, where the Fens reach the Isle of Ely and Cambridgeshire, people worried that drainage would antag-onize vengeful water-spirits. Rumours also circulated that the ambi-tious and secretive drainers were planning to use witchcraft to impose themselves upon nature.[51]

Matthew Hopkins passed through here after leaving King's Lynn and stopped off in at least two places: Upwell, straddling the border with the Isle of Ely, and Littleport, his ancestral home, where his father had been born. Villagers from both places visited magistrates between 14 and 19 September 1646, indicating that the witchfinder must have been there around that time, possibly accompanied by John Stearne.

At Upwell, Ellen Garrison had been suspected as a witch for more than two decades, and her mother before her. In March Robert Parsons, a butcher, had agreed to sell her a pig, subject to his wife's approval. But Katherine Parsons did not approve, so when Goodwife Garrison returned with her daughter, Parsons had bad news for them. He invited them into the house and offered to return her deposit, but Garrison flew into a rage, banging the table and swearing that he would regret his decision. From that moment, dread suffused the Parsons household – a sense that evil was incubating within their walls. Within a couple of hours Katherine Parsons felt a pricking and tearing at her skin, and soon was 'tormented all over as if some were pulling her into peeces'. She staggered from the house and banged on Goodwife Garrison's door, apologizing and offering her the pig. The witch came straight over and took it, but the Parsons' ordeal was not at an end. Within a few weeks four of their bullocks had died – a devastating loss, but worse was to follow: their two children, a seven-year-old and a baby, fell quiet and weak, their skin as pale as tallow. Helplessly the parents watched as the lives of their offspring ebbed away and hope faded that the tide would ever turn. The children died.

Grief, paralysing at first, soon grew into a fury in which the Parsonses indulged without regard for their own safety. Perhaps the arrival of the witchfinders boosted their confidence with a sense that providence was with them, and that a conviction at law would destroy Ellen Garrison. Hopkins called for volunteers, and sent a constable to make the arrest. Avis Savory and Anne Morrice, married women of good reputation, came forward to act as searchers. They stripped Garrison and examined first the surface of her body, then its creases and crevices, and reported the finding of 'twoe very smale teates neare to her fundament'; Hopkins thereupon ordered that the watchers, among them Goodwife Savory, should begin their vigil.

Avis Savory was the type of woman to stand up and be counted: a decade earlier her husband had been arrested for having 'made insurrection & mutinously disturbed the drayning of the fennes' and had only escaped punishment because, like most of the other rioters, he was so poor. One among them, however, described as 'the first mover of this mutinie', had been committed to Wisbech prison, and may well have been Ellen Garrison herself. She was 'by her neighbors esteemed a witch', and the messengers sent by the Privy Council to apprehend the rioters had certainly agreed that she was one, 'for they takeinge [a] boate neere her house were bitterlie accursed by her & soone after a strong man the waterman was striken w[i]th such a lamentable Crick in his backe that he was constrayned to get helpe'.[52]

Hopkins told the watchers to expect to see Ellen Garrison's imps, so they focused their attention as best they could by candlelight and the glow of the hearth. But when a creature finally appeared it took everyone by surprise. Avis Savory saw 'a thinge in likenesse of a beetle come into the Roome', and reported 'that one of the watchers killed it, and that about an hower after a Crickett came from herward but she beleives it came from the Chimney'. Hopkins ordered a second body-search, this time led by Anne Clarke, a midwife from the parish of Outwell. Ann Morrice and Avis Savory were amazed to see that there were now three teats between Garrison's legs, and that they were swollen. Anne Clarke pronounced them 'such as she never sawe before and that (by her experience being a Midwife) shee veryly beleives then not to be naturall'. They looked to Matthew Hopkins for confirmation. As Goodwife Savory later recalled, 'some that were there whoe p[re]tended to have skill in the discovery of witches sayd that some of the divles Impes had sucked her'.

The witchfinder left Upwell soon afterwards, but the witch-hunt continued. That night, having slept for some of the day, Avis Savory steeled herself for another session of watching. She was joined by Richard Denton, a blacksmith, who three years earlier had been part of a press-gang that had knocked at Ellen Garrison's door looking for her son. Garrison had warned them 'they had better be[e]n at home in their beddes', and within a fortnight each of them had lost a cow. Now, spurred on by the witchfinder's visit, Denton was ready to get justice for the neighbourhood. After several hours the watchers 'sawe a thinge in [the] likenesse of a Beetle Runneing in the roome (where they watcht) Rownde about the Chayer where shee satt and under her Feete'. From where he was sitting, it seemed to Richard Denton that 'it went much faster then ever he sawe any thinge before'.

The following Friday, 18 September, Avis Savory, Anne Morrice, Robert Denton and the Outwell midwife Anne Clarke went to the magistrate. Also present were the Parsonses, who undertook to prosecute Ellen Garrison. Katherine Parsons declared that 'shee dare take her Oathe shee bewitched her Children to death and that shee hath bin accompted a witch at least Twenty yeares'. The watchers and searchers then gave their evidence, Denton the blacksmith pointing out that Garrison had been 'searcht by the direction of Mathewe Hopkins'. Years of tolerating this witch were at an end, thanks to him. Garrison was sent to the gaol at Ely, the administrative heart of the diocese.

The next day, search-women at Littleport deposed to another magistrate, Lieutenant Colonel Thomas Castell, that on the body of a suspected woman, Ann Green, they had found three long teats the like of which they had never seen before. They also alleged that Widow Green had said that if she were a witch, she knew nothing about it.[53] This followed events of 14 September, when two Littleport inhabitants had approached Castell to report that Green had killed livestock, whereupon the magistrate had ordered a search and the constable had appointed four women from respectable yeoman families in the parish.[54] Like Upwell, Littleport had suffered at the hands of drainers and witches in the previous decade. Ann Green had been prosecuted in 1634 for 'chiding and giving evill language about the sittings in the church' when newcomers forced her from her pew, and again in 1639, when this bone of contention had become an accusation of witchcraft.[55]

Matthew Hopkins was back in King's Lynn by 24 September, when the sessions of the peace and gaol delivery were held. As he passed through the grand porch of the Trinity Guildhall, nine accused witches were waiting anxiously in the vaults beneath his feet. The recorder of the city was Miles Corbett, scourge of the witches at Yarmouth the previous year. The mayor, Edward Robinson, was also in attendance, as were the aldermen and justices of the town and the keepers of the gaol. Grace Wright, Cecily Taylor, Katherine Banks, Emma Godfrey and Lydia Browne, all widows, were charged with 'felonious witchcraft and feloniously consulting and covenanting with an evil spirit', as were three other women – Dorothy Griffin, Thomasine Parker and Dorothy Lee – and the male suspect, a labourer called Thomas Dempster. All the arraigned prisoners pleaded not guilty, and so put themselves on the country. Hopkins gave evidence in person against Dempster, in whose body-search he had participated, and against Cecily Taylor and Lydia Browne. Most of the other witnesses were searchers or watchers. Once the evidence against the witches had been heard, two labourers accused of robbery were brought forward, followed by a thief on the run from London.[56] At this point the main body of the proceedings was over, and the jurors retired to consider their verdicts.

The outcome was not what Hopkins or his fellow accusers had intended; in fact, it was almost the reverse of what had occurred at Huntingdon. Of the nine witches, six were acquitted and one, Lydia Browne, was judged to be *non compos mentis* and so not fit to be tried. Only Grace Wright and Dorothy Lee were convicted; they were sentenced to be hanged in the Tuesday market-place, which sentence was carried out just as news started to spread that the plague had returned to the town. Hopkins was paid another £2 for giving testimony and departed promptly, possibly in some embarrassment.[57]

It is hard to say what had happened. Evidently in the summer of 1646 the corporation of King's Lynn had felt passionately that, despite its financial commitments to maintain the garrison, control plague and relieve the poor, it should employ a witchfinder to stop diabolists bringing the city to its knees; yet when those people were brought to trial, the well-to-do citizens on the jury doubted the evidence before them. Hopkins had not been invited to identify specific witches – that was the responsibility of the townsfolk – but to gather and record effective proof against those already presumed to be guilty. He had been paid a lot, but produced little. His days as a witchfinder were numbered, if not thanks to the sceptics and the sticklers then because hiring him no longer made commercial sense. It is tempting to think that the borough of Yarmouth had reached the latter conclusion. All six of the arraigned witches had been convicted there in December 1645 (with one reprieve), but there had since been a spate of fresh accusations of entertaining evil spirits, five of which had come to trial in April 1646; this time all had been acquitted. It is quite possible that because of the acquittals Hopkins never received his promised payment; the chamberlain of Yarmouth certainly did not record it in his otherwise meticulously-kept account book.[58]

Two days after the sessions at King's Lynn, three witches were tried at the Ely court of assize and gaol delivery. The judge was the chief justice of the Isle of Ely, none other than the venerable John Godbold, special commissioner at Bury St Edmunds the previous summer. Ann Green was indicted for employing evil spirits to cause harm, but pleaded not guilty and was acquitted by the jury, possibly under Godbold's direction. Another woman, Ann Disborough, was also acquitted. Of the two bills of indictment against Ellen Garrison, that for the murder of the Parsons children was thrown out on a technicality, and on the other she was acquitted.[59] After the disaster at King's Lynn, Hopkins had failed here too. Assuming that Robert Garrison was able to scrape together a few pence to pay his wife's gaol fees,

Robert and Katherine Parsons now had no choice but to return to Upwell and, as best they could, get on with living opposite a woman they had denounced as a murderous witch.

Apocalyptic prophecies seemed borne out by events in the last quarter of 1646. Just as when God grew tired of mankind once before, so now the heavens opened and the waters prevailed upon the earth. In October crops rotted, pasture was trodden into mud, and little wheat or rye could be sown. Work was hard, and prices continued to rise. A new moon in November brought starlight and frost, and with them hope of better days; but it remained 'the extremist wet time for soe long together as hath beene knowne in the memory of man'. Preachers saw God's punishment in this, and a sign that the king should return to the throne. But peace brought recrimination, not reconciliation. Returning Catholic gentry punished tenants for having supported Parliament and sued those who had seized their property; banished ministers found new parishes in which to espouse royalism. With December came dryer days but snowy nights. Smallpox swept through overcrowded communities like a scythe, as did tuberculosis of the lungs with its fevers, sweats and hacking coughs.[60] Mysterious deaths at Heptonstall in Yorkshire led to the beating of a suspected witch until she confessed – as she told magistrates, 'in hopes to be freed from further blows'. All was confusion. At Westminster Abbey the Earl of Essex's hearse was defaced by a frantic visionary who claimed that without repentence London would go the way of Sodom and Gomorrah.[61]

Second only to London in size, industry and iniquity, Norwich was a provincial capital of thirty parishes and 20,000 souls. In November the river Wensum broke its banks and people rowed through the streets; in December, a poor harvest, a food excise, a trade slump and plague led to riots which made the aldermen fear for their lives. Political rebellion was also imminent as parliamentarian and royalist factions vied for power, widening divisions left over from the 1630s. In 1642 Norwich, gateway to the Eastern Association, had first been fortified, then fought over. The bishop, Joseph Hall, had been deposed, his palace turned into tenements, the cathedral pillaged.

Godly townsmen had enjoyed a bonfire of devotional paintings in 1644. During this time the authorities had done their best to govern the city – maintaining the hospital, licensing apothecaries, whipping vagrants, and so on; but by late 1646 discontent and want were widespread, and the massed ranks of the poor had to be restrained from begging on the streets. The city remained politically polarized too. Royalism had been given a new lease of life in 1646, though Presbyterianism remained the dominant faction.[62]

Earlier that year a Norwich doctor named Thomas Browne had published an enquiry into 'Vulgar and Common Errors', satirizing the ignorance of the age. But like Henry More at Cambridge, Browne was not averse to mixing his empiricism with ethereal mysticism, and had been roundly criticized for it by the royalist courtier Sir Kenelm Digby. Preoccupied as he was with the mysteries of death, and convinced that Satan caused all suffering, Browne's attitude to the black art had been hardened by the recent trials: 'for my part I have ever beleeved, and doe now know, that there are Witches; they that doubt of these do not onely deny them, but Spirits; and are obliquely, not consequently, a sort not of infidels but Atheists.' This, then, was Matthew Hopkins' contribution to the philosophy of witchcraft. But Browne's dogma was not uncontroversial: in 1645 Alexander Ross, a chaplain to the king, had questioned the relationship between spirits and witches asserted by him, arguing that it was possible for one to exist without the other. Browne did concede that the content of witches' confessions was probably a consequence of melancholic delusion, and was perplexed by the idea of their sexual congress with demons. Pregnancy from such a union he thought no more likely than if a man and a woman were to share bath-water.[63] The reality of intimacy with Satan could be ruled out; yet the concept seemed untestable and so, like the power of witchcraft in general, it was doomed as a scientific principle. That, too, was part of Hopkins' legacy.

In the end, reasoning at law proved a more powerful weapon against witchfinding than the musings of philosophers and physicians. After a winter of death and deprivation, by the spring of 1647 the weather had improved, the floods had receded, and the plague had moved on. The Norfolk assizes, which the previous year had been suspended (or possibly moved to Thetford), again resumed in the Norwich Shire House at the castle keep. The judges, Baron Thomas Trevor and Justice of Common Pleas Peter Phesant, travelled up from Westminster as they had before the war, and were entertained at the Guildhall and at the church of St Peter Mancroft, where a sermon was read.[64] Weavers left their looms to watch the procession, taken to be a sign that the days of disorder were numbered. There is good reason to think Matthew Hopkins was present, perhaps as a witness in a trial he had helped to bring about. If so, he was in for a shock. Some gentlemen of the county, sticklers influenced by John Gaule's *Select Cases of Conscience*, had drawn up a list of questions for the witchfinder, which they handed to the judges for their consideration. Whether Hopkins was examined on that occasion or whether the gauntlet was thrown down in person or in writing, it is certain that he was pulled up short by the intervention.

The first question took literally Gaule's suggestion that superstitious methods of investigation made witches of the witchfinders. Did Hopkins' success not indicate that he himself had a diabolical secret? And was the rumour not true that he had stolen the devil's book containing the names of all the witches in England? Playful mockery gave way to excoriating interrogation. If his knowledge did not originate in study, why was *he* specially blessed with expertise? Why should the devil, an ethereal spirit, need to suck blood for sustenance, and could signs of this be trusted as such when so many were 'troubled with naturall wretts on severall parts of their bodies, and other naturall excressencies, as Hemerodes, Piles, Childbearing, &c.'? Furthermore, did Hopkins use 'unlawfull courses of torture to make them say any thing for ease and quiet'? Were they deprived of sleep, as one might tame a colt or a hawk, then walked up and down until their feet were blistered? Had he not staged 'an abominable, inhumane, and unmercifull tryall of these poore creatures, by tying them, and heaving them into the water; a tryall not allowable by Law or conscience'? Did he not put words in suspects' mouths and cajole them with threats and blandishments?[65]

Finally, the gentlemen of Norfolk asked whether Hopkins could deny that all witchfinders really did was 'fleece the country of their money'?[66] Nowhere in this or in any of the other questions was the reality of witchcraft at stake, nor were statutory or biblical justifications for witch-trials disputed. Instead, this particular rebuke recalled John Gaule's insistence that the discovery of witches was not for the layman to take upon himself – an idea that Gaule had inherited from William Perkins, and Perkins from Elizabethan authorities before him. Witches should be detected by the God-given sense of magistrates and ministers, then convicted by juries guided by a learned judge. Better than any other reason this explains why witchfinders had never troubled England before: until the upheavals of the civil war, the state – a network of social and legal power joining centre and regions – had been too effective to permit their existence. When episcopal authority and the Court of Star Chamber had so effectively exposed false accusations of witchcraft and possession in the reign of James I, the abolition of these institutions in 1641 may well have removed a powerful brake on systematic witch-hunting.[67]

Hopkins wasted little time preparing his answers and arranging for them to be published so that all the world could learn the truth of his godly integrity and purpose. By then it is probable that he was ailing, however, despite his youth and recent vitality. Perhaps, like many sickly East Anglians, he blamed the 'base unwholesome air' of the Fens for his dizziness and fatigue, his lack of appetite, and the rasping cough that no medicine or recipe would cure.[68] It is less likely that he attributed his malady to prolonged confinement with the poor in infected gaols and airless watching chambers. And he cannot have imagined that his great self-vindication in print, about to go on sale in bookshops in Norwich and London, would also prove to be his valediction.

IO

The Biter Bit

———•◦•———

PREDICTIONS FOR 1647 were as bleak as they had been for the previous year. January brought snow and shortages, and communities struggled to feed both paupers and soldiers home from the war. In the spring, tempests and floods were fewer than feared, but 'great storms from womens tongues, reproaches, and backbitings' were more apparent – to men, at least. A sense that patriarchy had become anarchy caused alarm, from the House of Commons to the remotest cottage. When a nation dared to rebel against its prince, even poor men expected that their own households would turn against them; the hoary old notion of wives out to 'vex, perplex, and any way torment their husbands' had never been more believable.[1] Generations of balladeers had raised laughter by imagining gender in reverse – the man at the spinning wheel, dandling the baby, the woman shouldering a musket as she marched off to war. But these days the joke seemed less funny: in life, comedy had turned to tragedy.

The civil war did make women more prominent. Many were active in radical congregations, though fewer than was popularly supposed.[2] Most women came to the fore because, with their husbands serving, killed, missing or maimed, they needed to work harder to maintain their households. The wives clamouring at the gates of Westminster Hall at this time were seeking not their masters' power, but bread for their children.[3] At home it is likely that they had received the unwelcome attentions of male neighbours, and had been abused by both armies – lawless and drunk, many soldiers acted impulsively against opposition real or imagined, their brains overheated by an urge to fight diabolism in all its forms. Such men were addicted to rumour, and rumour spoke of female soldiers on both sides. In fact there were even fewer women in the ranks than there were female preachers, but the paranoid horror they excited was greater, encouraging violence against women in general and witches in particular. Witches were living symbols of rebellion against God and man, and to punish them was to strive for civil order.[4]

By the time this woodcut was published in 1646, the fantasy of a parliament run by women was an image of inverted social values as much frightening as comic

Winning the peace – the quest for political stability – dominated affairs of state, and while the king had been arrested, a moderate majority in Parliament had yet to confront the Independents, and an army that refused to disband. Godly millenarians were pessimistic and foresaw further slaughter, after which nations would bow before the sceptre of Christ. Meanwhile a tailor was tried at the Old Bailey for proclaiming that he *was* Christ, and in May reports of the Second Coming at Sandwich led to public debate about diabolical delusion. The devil himself was sighted in London: 'a great tall blacke man . . .

at least six yards in height'. People dubbed 1647 'the Yeare of Miracles'. When a cloud of flies engulfed Cornwall, it was feared that locusts, worms, frogs and pestilence would follow if English men and women did not repent, and once again learn to love their king.[5]

Love for the king had been scarce among fen-folk: for many he was lord of the manor as well as monarch, and land reclamation a means for him to make money. Much of the fen was taken up by the Isle of Ely, where an archipelago of small communities was linked by deep roads and rickety causeways, and sober-minded labourers and husbandmen eked out a living digging peat, cutting reeds, and catching eels and wildfowl. Rare visitors considered them 'rude, uncivil and envious to others'. At the heart of this diluvian world, with its low mists and curved horizons, stood the diocesan city of Ely, virtually cut off during the winter or when spring tides were high. Waters lapped at the edges of the hilly streets, and travellers alighting from boats would gaze up at the weathered cathedral tower, its lantern poking out of the mist as if wrapped in blankets.[6]

Cromwell, who had lived in Ely in the 1630s, wanted to uproot the sinful wretches of the Isle and colonize it with godly families. Before the war, the bishop – the detested Matthew Wren – had enjoyed supreme authority in matters ecclesiastical and temporal. Like Joseph Hall at Norwich, Wren had been turfed out, and his property donated to the Cambridge colleges. The office of chief justice of the Isle of Ely had survived, and continued to be held by John Godbold, who in May 1647 was appointed a judge of the Court of Common Pleas.[7] Out in the countryside, many ministers had been ejected: the rector of Newton for jeering at Cromwell, Mr Mapletoft of Downham for calling parliamentarians 'worse than the Devils their government in Hell' in a rabble-rousing sermon. At Soham the minister had paid the price for failing to offer customary thanks to God for delivering Parliament from destruction in the Gunpowder Plot of 1605.[8]

In these dispersed and insular parishes formal religion did not dominate lives to the extent it did in Cambridgeshire. A basic understanding of God acquired in church was fed from below by homespun radicalism and hand-me-down beliefs, resulting in a spectrum of nonconformity from orthodox Presbyterianism to pared-down Independence. Not for nothing was the Isle of Ely deprecated at this time as 'that Island of Errors and Sectaries'.[9] In gatherings at the hearthstead or around the alehouse table, the exchange of news and folktales often concerned witches: in these parts, more than in the towns or larger villages, the balance of fortune and misfortune was seen to be harnessed to magical power.[10] The right to worship according to conscience, like rights of common in the fen, were mainstays of indigenous culture. In the 1630s the arrival of Bishop Wren from the diocese of Norwich at the same time as drainers from the Low Countries had imperilled this way of life, fomenting dissent and disorder of the sort seen at Upwell and Littleport.[11] By 1645 a wave of reform was already in motion, set against a backdrop of advancing militarization and the looming threat of invasion by Antichristian royalist forces.

It was perhaps inevitable that bottled-up fear and frustration in these parts should be manifested as accusations of witchcraft, with or without the influence of witchfinders.[12] Matthew Hopkins may have visited Ely briefly in 1647, but it is more likely that he had already returned home to Manningtree on the orders of a physician. While witches from his neighbourhood were still being brought to trial he retreated to bed, where his consumption tortured him with coughing fits, enervating sweats, and intense nightmares.[13]

The final phase of the witch-hunt was left to John Stearne. Compared to what had gone before, the venture was neither intensive or extensive – a seventy-five-mile circuit running north to south from Ely, with just a few stops along the way. Yet there was a unique quality to this journey: unlike Essex and Suffolk with their enclosed highways and lanes, here in the fenland a solitary horseman might contemplate the vastness of God's creation – its majesty and corruption, its beauty and cruelty – beneath the dome of a rose-tinted sunset. In this sparse, silent territory, the witchfinder was one with the kestrel hovering over stubble-fields and the roving fox sniffing the breeze for prey. To begin with, Stearne's investigations centred on three villages south-west of Ely – Haddenham, Stretham and Sutton – in which Anabaptists and other sects thrived, mostly led by humble

243

artisans and women, and where every day the devil lured the weak in spirit into darkness.[14]

After the king, one of the most aggressive landlords in the Isle of Ely was Sir Miles Sandys, who in the 1620s had acquired large estates in order to profit from drainage and enclosure. At Sutton 4,000 acres of common land were taken away, robbing the poor of food and fuel; thirty families who had built cottages there lost the right to live in them. A petition to the Court of Chancery was endorsed by almost a hundred signatories; but Sandys was experienced in challenging rights of common, and had besides bought off the Bishop of Ely with some of the richest land. When petitioning failed the inhabitants of Sutton resorted to rioting and wrecking, and by 1638 Sandys was talking of 'general rebellion' in the region; there was also resistance to authority in church. By 1645 people at Sutton were declaring the truth of the proverb 'Wealth maketh many freinds, but the poore is sep[a]rate from his neighbour'; and in that year Sir Miles Sandys junior, sitting on the governing committee at Ely, responded to a petition to Parliament by imprisoning seven of its authors, all parliamentarian soldiers. They in turn protested that he was a royalist who kept taxes for himself, and that he had tried to stop them fighting the king. By September Sandys had several writs of outlawry filed against him, and at least one of his estates had been sequestered.[15] Meanwhile, the village remained over-crowded and underfed.

The manor of Sutton was dominated by the younger Sir Miles Sandys. The Pedleys, Guntons, Jetherells and Wynes – lesser gentry – owned estates of between thirty and sixty acres, and there were many more parcels of less than five acres in the hands of yeoman farmers and their tenants. As in Manningtree and at Bacton in Suffolk, these men regarded the presence of witches on their land as an affront to Christian decency and a danger to their livelihood. Farmers in the neighbouring parish of Witchford felt the same, and bore sufficient animosity to certain individuals at Sutton to think that they might try to bewitch them and their animals. At Sutton a gentleman named Benjamin Wyne led the counter-attack, and doubtless had a hand in inviting John Stearne to the village.[16]

At Ely on Wednesday 26 May 1647 Lieutenant Colonel Thomas Castell, the magistrate who had examined Ann Green at Littleport the previous year, heard evidence against four suspected witches variously accused of consorting with evil spirits and destroying livestock. William Watson, an old man of low estate and base reputation, was one of those Sutton folk who had protested against the elder Sir Miles Sandys in the 1620s. He had been a poor man even then, scraping a living from the fen to feed his wife and five children, two of whom perished within two years of birth; in fact, allegations against him dated back to that time.[17] Three witnesses – Benjamin Wyne, John Sisson and the constable, John Lynwood – testified that Watson had confessed to witchcraft, probably following Stearne's sleep deprivation and intimidation. Watson had told them that thirty years earlier he was feeding cattle when the devil appeared to him as a large mouse, demanding his soul. Hesitantly Watson had agreed a contract '& seald it w[i]th his blood upon Condition that the divell should be obedient to his Command in bewitching any mans Cattell that he had a minde unto'. Two cows in Sutton had died soon afterwards, as had a pair of red heifers belonging to Richard Gunton of Witchford. Next William Watson himself was taken before Lieutenant Colonel Castell, and repeated almost every detail of his earlier confession. He also admitted having killed seven sheep and a goose, for which he was very sorry and 'desier[ed] god to forgive'.[18] The forgiveness of his neighbours was too much to expect.

Among other suspects examined that day were a married couple, the Bonhams. Bridget Bonham, who had been imprisoned at Ely five days earlier, was taken from the gaol to be questioned alongside her husband. John Bonham was sixty-nine years old, and like William Watson had once resisted the enclosure of the west fen. According to another Sutton constable, Charles Lamb, after being taken into custody Bonham had confessed that he and his wife suckled diabolical imps. Bridget Bonham had then been arrested and temporarily locked up at the house of her neighbour, Thomas Day.[19]

Women came and searched her, reporting to Benjamin Wyne and others outside that she bore suspicious marks. John Stearne may also have been present. Confronted by the accusation that she fed evil spirits, Goodwife Bonham asked to be left alone with Lamb the constable.

According to him, Bridget Bonham admitted the charge, then asked him to leave her but not to divulge her secret. When Lieutenant Colonel Castell challenged the old woman, asking if she would now confess herself a witch, she replied with dangerous ambiguity 'that if she be a witch it is more than this ex[amina]te knoweth'; in her opinion her husband, however, was definitely a witch. John Bonham admitted as much. He had already told Benjamin Wyne about a spiritual alter ego called 'John', a mole-like creature which he fed drops of blood in exchange for the power to kill livestock. Standing before Castell now Bonham elaborated on this, recalling how he had been hedging in a neighbour's cherry orchard when the creature first came to him. Like Eleanor Shepherd, one of the accused at Huntingdon, he had refused to surrender his soul and, squaring up to the beast, 'bad hime a voyd Satan'. But to no avail. In the end Bonham cut a finger on the blade of his hatchet, and the pact was made. The spirit then set about picking off the cows and horses of local farmers against whom Bonham bore a grudge.

The Bonhams had never been respected in Sutton in all the twenty-seven years they had been married. Bridget was John Bonham's second wife – he had married her a mere seven weeks after his first wife's death – and together they had raised a son from his first marriage and had four children of their own. Bridget Bonham was especially cruel to her stepson. One day in 1627 he disappeared, but his father refused to try to find him in Ely or Cambridge, saying it would be like looking for a needle in a haystack. Then, in the autumn of 1636, the Bonhams' neighbour Thomas Day was digging behind his house when he came across an earthenware pot full of bones. The constable, John Lynwood, was informed, as was the elder Sir Miles Sandys, the magistrate at that time. After a woman came forward to say she had once seen the pot at the Bonhams' house, John Bonham's sister smashed it, heightening suspicion. Women going out to milk in the fen left an accusatory thigh-bone at the Bonhams' door; the suspects' attempt to seize the rest of the skeleton only made matters worse. Sir Miles Sandys bound twelve witnesses to appear against John Bonham – whom he may have remembered as an opponent – and ordered an investigation. The thigh-bone was found to match that of an eleven-year-old in size, and Lynwood the constable confirmed from the parish register that the missing boy had been born in 1616, which would have made him eleven when he disappeared. Despite the momentum of the case, in court later that year the jury was not convinced, and John Bonham had returned home to face down his neighbours.[20]

It is too crude to suggest that the arrival of a witchfinder offered a chance to have the Bonhams hanged for an unproven murder; but the low social esteem in which they were held made it seem plausible that they might use witchcraft against their neighbours. The same was true of the last of the four Sutton suspects to be examined on 26 May 1647, Margaret Moore.[21] Her case was one of the most intriguing of the entire East Anglian witch-hunt, and the one among all the Ely discoveries that appears to have interested John Stearne most.

Little is known about Margaret Moore's life. She came from Stretham, seven miles away, and was almost certainly the Margaret Holland who had married Robert Moore at Sutton in May 1641. This Robert Moore was never again mentioned in parish records; like many men, he may have left to fight for Parliament and never returned. The Moores of Sutton were landowning yeoman stock, but this prosperity did not rub off on Margaret. She had four children, three of whom died in infancy.[22] She had also fallen out with three farmers in Witchford; as in the case of the Bonhams, the conflict leading to her arrest had begun at least a decade earlier. In 1636, before her marriage, Margaret Holland had bought a pig from Thomas Nix of Witchford, a husbandman with a fondness for drink and litigation. They had agreed a price, two shillings to seal the bargain and sixpence to follow, but the balance was never paid, and Nix was forced to ask Holland for it. This, he soon realized, was a mistake: he fell ill, was confined to bed, and stayed there all winter. 'In his sicknesse', Stearne heard from witnesses, '[he] cryed out of her, saying he could not depart this life, untill hee had spoken with her, so she was sent for, but she refused, whereupon (he lying in such extremity) she was by some of his friends . . . forced to goe to him.' In the spring of 1637 Nix had died; but no action was taken against Holland.[23]

Ten years later Benjamin Wyne and Perry Jetherell, fellow gentleman and landowners at Sutton, at last heard Margaret Moore confirm what locals had known for years: that she had bewitched Thomas Nix to death. And that was not all. She had commanded an imp she called 'Annys' to bewitch three bullocks belonging to Thomas Maynes, another adversary at Witchford; and her other spirit 'Margaret' had killed John Foster's cow there. Taken before Lieutenant Colonel Thomas Castell, she again admitted all these acts of witchcraft, adding that she 'hath done many more which now she is very sorrie for'.[24]

In her malice, apostasy and remorse Margaret Moore resembled many who had confessed to John Stearne and Matthew Hopkins over the preceding two years, yet her story also illustrates how, duress and delusion aside, certain desperate people either aspired to witchcraft or came to believe that such powers had been bestowed upon them.[25] The Earl of Warwick's steward Arthur Wilson explained that when some spiteful but innocent women were accused of witchcraft, 'they themselves by the strength of Fancie may thinke they bring such things to pass w[hi]ch many times unhapelie they wish for, and rejoice in, when done, out of the Malevolent humor that is in them, w[hi]ch passes w[i]th them as if they reallie Acted it.' By causing fear, more-over, a witch really could make people ill: 'the horrid truculent look of a malicious deformed Hag', opined one experienced physician, 'affrights children and tender natures; upon which proceeds an agita-tion and sudden commotion of the spirits and humours, whence ensueth diseases.'[26]

One aspect of Margaret Moore's confession marked her out as unusual, even to a seasoned witchfinder: in the first instance, her dia-bolical pact had been inspired not by bitter hatred but by tender feel-ings of love. After three of her children died, Goodwife Moore was left with just one, for which she thanked God – until the child fell sick. The story she told to the gentlemen Wyne and Jetherell, and then repeated to the magistrate Thomas Castell, was this. She had been asleep one night with her child beside her, when she was woken by the sound of someone calling to her from outside:

> she hard ye voyce of hir Children whoe had formerly died Calling unto hir in these words mother mother good sweet mother lett me In. This ex[amina]te hearing the voyce of hir Children she answered my Children Ile arise & lett you In & Immeadiatly this ex[amina]te went

to the dore to lett them Inn & when this ex[amina]te had opened the dore she saw nothing but hard a voyce saying good mother give me some drincke. This ex[amina]te answered that she had noe drincke but water whereupon this ex[amina]te shut to hir dore & went to bed agayne & was noe soner layd, but the voyce Came agayne as if it weare neare unto hir bed sid[e] & said mother mother Give me yor soule & I will save the life of yor 4[th] Child w[hi]ch is now livinge w[i]th yow. Upon these words this ex[amina]te Answered that she would give hir Consent that he should have hir soule.

One of the spirits then materialized in the shape of a naked child, and lay down at her side; this was 'Annys'. It suckled upon her – blood, not milk – and the pact was complete. Thereafter, whatever animus she had against the farmers of Witchford she indulged to her heart's desire. Fantasies of success and revenge were two sides of the same coin; the rich had to suffer for the poor to get ahead. The greater cost, of course, was to Margaret Moore herself. She had saved her child's life – or so she believed – but the price was death in this life, followed by damnation of her immortal soul. Disaster had been deferred, not averted, and now she would be made to face the consequences.

Confessions, however artfully directed by a witchfinder, revealed the secret agonies of people at the bottom of the pile, the inner torment of those fighting for advantage in this world or the next. Only a tiny minority ever owned up to witchcraft, yet the misery and anxiety they described were facts of life for the majority. Pre-Reformation Catholicism had revealed hell's torments to ordinary parishioners, but had at least offered hope of escape in good works, absolution and the other rites. By contrast, Calvinist predestination, which held that only the elect were saved, encouraged individuals to examine their lives for signs of God's secret plan. To the godly, a healthy family and food on the table hinted at paradise to come, whereas an ailing widow living on handouts was more likely to draw the opposite conclusion. The devil-worship that featured in confessions might not have been real, but the desperation was. Even the illusion of a diabolical saviour might be preferable to the certainty of God's damnation. The gloomy prospects offered by Calvinism explain the appeal of religious sects

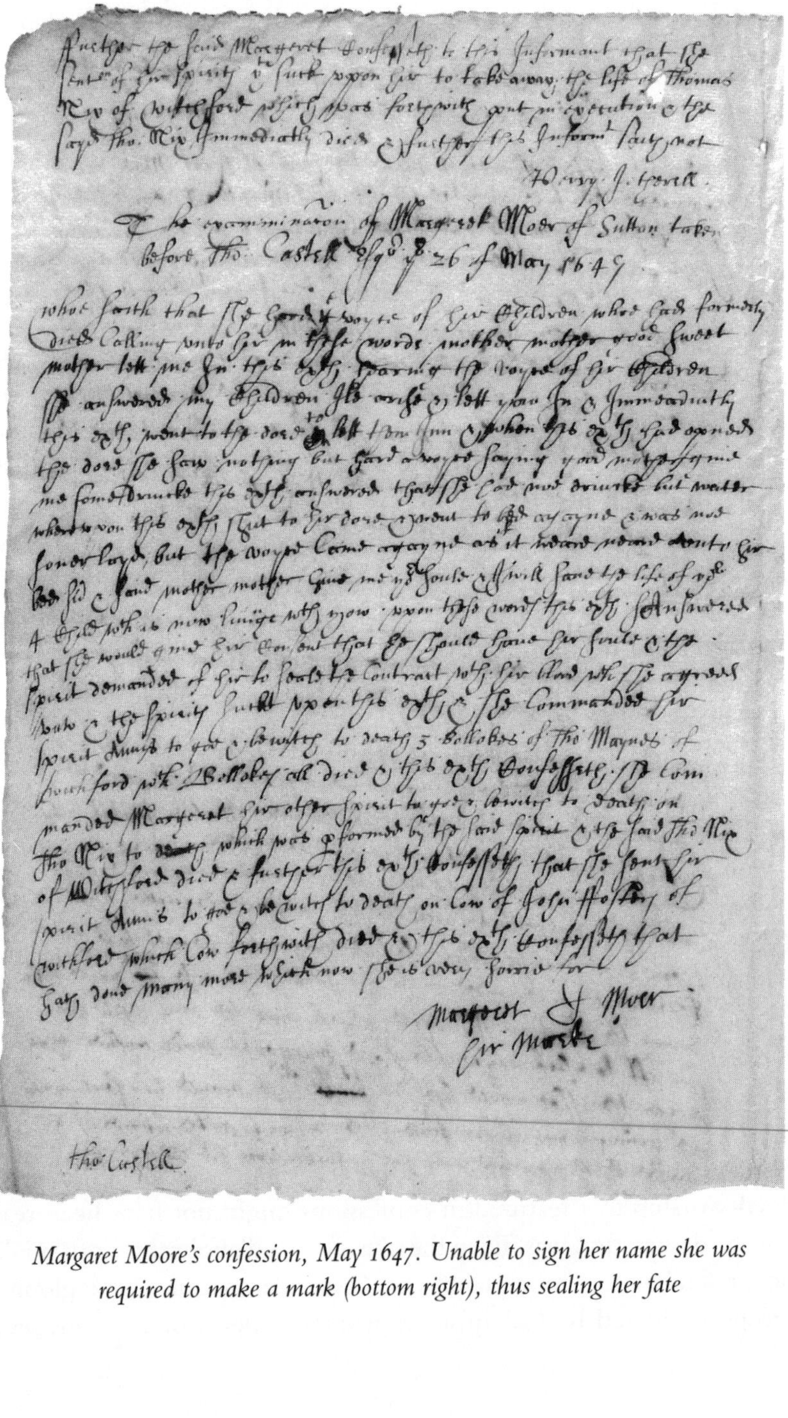

ffurther the said Margeret Confesseth to this Informant that she sent one of her spirits to sucke upon her to take away the life of Thomas Nix of Witchford which was forthwith put in execution & the sayd Tho: Nix Immediatly died & further this Informant saith not

Henry J. [illegible]

The examinacon of Margaret Moor of Sutton taken before Tho: Castell Esqr ye 26 of May 1647

who saith that she heard ye voyce of her Children which had formerly died Calling unto her in these words mother mother good sweet mother lett me in this exth hearing the voyce of her children she answered my Children I'le arise & lett you in & Immediatly this exth went to the door to lett them in & when this exth had opened the door she saw nothing but heard a voyce saying your mother give me some drinke this exth answered that she had noe drinke but water whereupon this exth shut the door & went to bed agayne & was not sooner layd, but the voyce Came agayne as it were round unto her bed side & said mother mother give me thy soule & I will save the life of ye 4 child which is now livinge wth you upon these words this exth answered that she would give her Consent that she should have her soule & the spirit demanded of her to seale the Contract with her blood which she agreed unto & the spirit suckt upon this exth & she Commanded her spirit thus to goe & bewitch to death 3 bullocks of Tho: Maynds of Southford which bullocks all died & this exth Confesseth she Commanded Margaret her other spirit to goe & bewitch to death one Tho: Nix to dy which was performed by the said spirit & the said Tho: Nix of Witchford died & further this exth Confesseth that she sent her spirit thus to goe & bewitch to death one Cow of John Foster of Witchford which Cow forthwith died & this exth Confesseth that she hath done many more which now she is very sorrie for

Margaret J Moor
her marke

Tho: Castell

Margaret Moore's confession, May 1647. Unable to sign her name she was required to make a mark (bottom right), thus sealing her fate

which taught that God's grace was freely given. Their search for signs was no less energetic, but focused on the Apocalypse, taking the Book of Revelation as a definitive guide: a sun as black as sackcloth, the blood-red moon, the falling stars, and angels crying: 'woe, woe, woe to the inhabiters of the earth!'[27]

It was a sea of turmoil – of communities, households and consciences – into which John Stearne rode in the last days of May 1647. After Sutton he moved on to Haddenham, where three suspected witches awaited his attention. Twice a widower and no longer a young man, Adam Sabie was too intimately involved in parish life either to move away or to live at peace. The previous September he had hired an attorney to defend him in a slander suit brought by his neighbour, Francis Coker. It was alleged that Sabie had called Coker 'a p[er]jured knave', swearing that Coker 'hath foresworne himselfe & is uppon recorde for itt'; in court Sabie had described himself optimistically as a gentleman. He was also at war with John Kirby, who accused him of having used the threatening words 'Kirbe Kirbe Ile utterly undoe the[e] for thy basnes towardes me.' But here the consequences of Sabie's malediction were more than just a damaged reputation: Kirby's bullocks died 'suddanly & most strangly', and both he and his child fell sick.[28]

Sabie was arrested, and subjected by John Stearne to a meticulous body-search. As the witchfinder later deposed, he

> being desired by the Inhabetance of Haddenham to search the body of Adam Sabie upon the search this Informant att the entrance of his fundement did ffynde on[e] Teate of the greatest leng[th] that he ever sawe upon the body of any man that hath by there owne Confession been witches or wizardes & this Informant saith by the expear[i]ence that he hath fownd by searching he veryly beleaveth the forsaid Teates are drawn by evell spirits w[hi]ch suck upon his body . . .

After the usual preliminaries Sabie confessed, explaining that at a time when he was troubled in his life he had been visited by a spirit in the shape of a child. They had fed each other, and 'the said spirit speake unto hime & said Sabie thou shalt never want'.[29] This admission of guilt was damning enough, and John Kirby was relieved to hear it; but

Sabie had more to reveal when he was examined by Lieutenant Colonel Castell on 1 June.

The principal farmsteads in Haddenham were situated along Hill Row, a rising approach road overlooking arable fenland stretching south towards Cottenham. To people like Thomasine Read, stuck in one-roomed cottages on the swampy north side of the village, Hill Row families embodied a new kind of social power, a self-interest not bothered by old-style paternalism. They were parvenus who feared God, worked hard, paid their taxes and ran the parish; a century of political, religious and economic change had set them apart. Thomasine Read had been born in Cottenham where, she now confessed, dissatisfaction with her lot and anger at people all around had invited the devil into her heart in the early 1630s; the death of her husband in 1632 had deepened her despair. Desiring to exploit her misery, Satan had appeared in the shape of a mouse, and pricked her thigh to seal their covenant. Some time later, after she moved to Haddenham,

> the divell appeared the second tyme & demanded of hir hir Child or els hir blood & presently the divell gave the said Tomison a prick or nip upon the breast & the spirit mus suckt hir blood & she comanded hir spirit mus to goe and bewitch & tutch the Child of John Miller which was spedily p[er]formed & the s[ai]d Child handled in a most greavus & tormenting Manner . . .

Robert Miller, the boy bewitched, came from Hill Row. He described how he had been lured to Thomasine Read's cottage by her adolescent son John, a plough-boy, and there had been given a white root to eat; this, he claimed, had been the start of his 'great payne & miserie'. The war against the Hill Row farmers intensified in April 1647 after John Read was laid off by Robert Gray, who had found a stronger lad to push his plough. 'Hath this Roug Gray taken another boy?' Thomasine Read was heard to ask on receiving the news. 'If I live Ile be even w[i]th him for so doing.' She was true to her word: within the hour, two of Gray's sheep were dead. No sooner had Thomas Woodbridge, a neighbouring farmer, told his shepherd that Read was to blame than he became the next Hill Row victim, also for refusing to employ her son. He lost twelve sheep.[30]

On 26 May Thomasine Read was arrested and searched, and teats were found. She confessed that her imps – a cat and a mouse – came to suckle at night 'in a great wynd'. She had ordered the mouse to enter Robert Miller's body; the cat had attacked the sheep of Gray and Woodbridge, and was also told to 'destroy the Corne that Groeth in Hillrow feild'. Three days later, Saturday 29 May, Read was taken to the house of the magistrate, Thomas Castell; John Stearne and the witnesses went too. Robert Miller was so disturbed that he had to be held down in a chair, but when Thomasine Read entered he wriggled free, and scratched her face with his nails. Read stood quite still, a symptom of shock perhaps but interpreted by Stearne to mean that the devil had deserted her. Earlier she had informed the magistrate that only the cunning man at Aldreth could undo her spell; in Stearne's opinion at least, Miller's recovery had proved her wrong.[31]

Perhaps Read really did believe that her power had been broken; perhaps her anger had helped persuade her of her own guilt. Not everyone was so suggestible. Although Joan Briggs, last of the Haddenham suspects, did not get on with her son-in-law, she steadfastly denied having killed his horses and bewitched her own grandchild. 'For the Teates that are fownd about hir body', she said, 'thay be nothing but wartes, & for any Contract or Conversation she made or hath with the divell she never had neither.'[32] Stearne knew that the devil was stronger in some witches than in others, something he must more than once have explained to disappointed villagers as they handed him his fee. When there was nothing more he could do, the witchfinder remounted his horse and bade them good day.

Beyond Haddenham lay Stretham, a small market town on the old Roman road north of Cambridge and a place peculiarly unsettled in its spiritual life. In 1644 a faction had successfully petitioned the Earl of Manchester to have their minister removed. Nicholas Felton, they said, was a brawler, bear-baiter and barrator, and 'a strict observer of late illegal innovations in worship'. But the parish was divided, even families were divided; Felton allowed a man named Robert Salter to preach the king's cause, and tried to persuade his parliamentarian brother not to fight. Matthew Clarke was appointed as Felton's replacement, but by the end of 1646 he too had fallen foul of the parish. Abiding by the Directory for Public Worship, Clarke refused to observe Christmas Day, whereupon a soldier preached instead; later on, Clarke was harried into the pulpit anyway. The next day the people sang as a woman's body was brought for burial, a superstitious custom in which Clarke refused to take part. An alehouse-keeper who had helped to get rid of Nicholas Felton dragged Clarke to the grave and threatened to throw him in. Clarke complained to Parliament, alleging that he had been called 'a parliamentary Preist, and none of theire Minister'; another man had 'hoped to live to see all the Roundheades hang'd'. The ringleaders of the affray were arrested and taken before the House of Lords, where they were ordered to pay Matthew Clarke's costs. By this time accusations of witchcraft were already flying around, and one of the miscreants, Rowland Taylor, a husbandman, was home in time to take part in the investigation.[33]

People at Stretham knew John Stearne was on his way. The night before he arrived Elizabeth Foot was panicking about her bodily excrescences, probably vaginal polyps resulting from childbirth a year earlier. Foot was worried that they might actually be the marks of a witch, for her mother had had that reputation. She confided in a neighbour, Ellen Barron, but Widow Barron would have nothing to do with her, so fraught with suspicion was the atmosphere. In despair Foot wept at the impurity of her blood, crying out 'Woe woe was the tyme that ever I was borne of such [an] accursed mother'. In the morning the midwife Mary Salmon chose four honest women to be her assistants, and together at Elizabeth Foot's house they 'did fynd that shee had two Teates upon hir body whereof on[e] was of a great bignes the other a small on[e]'. Salmon had never seen anything like it.[34]

Genital teats were also found on Joan Salter, whose royalist stepson had been cited in the expulsion of Nicholas Felton. Robert Salter now testified against her – his near relation – accusing her of making wheat boil over in a pot, even though there was no fire beneath it. In this crime he implicated Ellen Barron, which probably explains why she had distanced herself from Elizabeth Foot. Salter also alleged that his stepmother had visited a sick woman, and that 'going from hur house att the laines end, a black horse came to hur & crept betwixt hir leggs & carried hir over the Green to hir own howse'.

This sinister beast, he believed, had been 'the divell in the liknes of a horse'.[35]

At least fifteen witnesses went to Ely on Sunday 30 May to make statements against the Stretham witches. A woman accused Elizabeth Foot of bewitching her cows and chickens after a quarrel, to which Foot replied, as had Bridget Bonham, that if she was a witch, she was not conscious of it. Despite rumours that Joan Salter had boasted about her mysterious black mount – and had been laughed at for it – she now delivered a robust denial, protesting that 'The markes that she hath about hir are not the marks of a witch but cam[e] as it pleaseth god & as she beleaveth by Child Bearing.'[36]

Also examined that day were Robert and Dorothy Ellis, a poor couple long suspected in Stretham of being witches. A youth who had thrown stones at Goodwife Ellis, calling her an 'old witch', had been lamed by her imp; a baby she touched had suffered a swollen eye, and another child had died. Men of opposing religious views, Thomas Hitch (a critic of Nicholas Felton) and Rowland Taylor (a critic of Matthew Clarke), volunteered to help John Stearne search Robert Ellis's body. Affecting the cool detachment of a physician, Stearne reported finding '4 Teates upon the entrance of his fundament', of a size that surprised even a man of his experience. The Ellises had been detained separately and watched until Dorothy Ellis had confessed that thirty years earlier, 'shee being much troubled in hir minde there appeared unto hir the divell in the liknes of a great Catt'. She had admitted all the charges against her, including that of bewitching cows belonging to Thomas Hitch. Her husband had withstood the torture. Standing before the magistrate Thomas Castell, Robert Ellis explained that his 'teats' were due to 'a great labor' he had performed in his youth. With a snarl of defiance he concluded by assuring Castell 'that he would not confess hime selfe to be a witch though thay puld hime a peeces w[i]th wild horses'.[37]

By that time there were at least nine accused witches in the gaol at Ely, and others were to join them in the weeks ahead. John Stearne's work there was finished but for one last appearance before Lieutenant Colonel Castell. On Monday 31 May that contentious 'gentleman' Adam Sabie was taken from Haddenham to the gaol, and left there overnight. The next day Stearne was summoned to make a deposition, as was Sabie's adversary John Kirby. The prisoner had little to say about teats and familiar spirits, but he did want to talk about his spiritual transformation. He gave an account which surpassed even what Stearne and the other witnesses had heard him say at Haddenham, a clear indication of how in a confused mind biblical images could be conflated with a mundane fenland existence.

Adam Sabie explained that the child-like spirit of which he had spoken earlier had first come to him around 1612, behaving then like a gentle, merciful angel. The radiant creature informed Sabie that it was God's will that he should dwell in Haddenham, and so vanished, having asked nothing in return. In 1636 Sabie had experienced another epiphany:

> the said spirit came unto this ex[amina]te in a flame of fyer he being then in Sommersham wood [and] said unto him feare not Sabie for I am thy God & Immediatly there appeared a suddan darknes about the place where this ex[amina]te weare it then being about none day & the spirit said unto hime goe unto the howse of the lady Sandyes & she shall give the[e] xx*l* w[hi]ch she did.

It is unlikely that Lady Sandys did give him £20, but the story could not be checked since she was a recusant who had fled to Holland at the start of the war. The very implausibility of this story provided the essential substance of the fantasy, however. As if describing the Holy Spirit, Sabie related how the apparition had entered his body and had stayed there as both guide and guard, reassuring him with the words 'Adam I am thy god & feare not what man Can doe ag[ains]t the[e] for all thy wronges shalbe righted.' John Stearne, naturally enough, saw less of goodness in this communion. He knew from the Book of Revelation that when the righteous entered the kingdom of heaven at the last call, outside in the lake of fire and brimstone would be left the 'dogs and sorcerers, and whoremongers, and murderers, and idolators, and whosoever loveth and maketh a lie'.[38] It was plain to Stearne on which side of the wall Sabie was going to find himself.

News of the witch-hunt had spread extensively by the summer of 1647, and to many seemed yet another foreboding of Judgement Day.

Earlier in the year Endymion Porter, a Stuart courtier exiled in France, had received a letter from his friend James Howell, a royalist writer imprisoned in London for spying, in which Howell bemoaned the fact that the devil was so conspicuous and industrious in England; no wonder, he sighed, when all the crosses had been removed from the churches. Viewed from his gaol cell, the world seemed to be tipping off its axis in an age awash with monstrous and dismal occurrences. 'We have likewise multitudes of Witches among us,' he informed Porter,

> for in Essex and Suffolk there were above two hundred indicted within these two years, and above the half of them executed: More, I may well say, than ever this Island bred since the Creation, I speak it with horror. God guard us from the Devil, for I think he was never so busy upon any part of the Earth that was enlightened with the beams of Christianity.

Like the physician Thomas Browne, Howell accepted the possibility of witchcraft as a truth founded in custom, law and Scripture; but since the start of the civil war his belief had been bolstered by 'a cloud of Witnesses produc'd for the proof of this black Tenet'.[39] In Worcestershire, two hundred miles from East Anglia, puritan minister Richard Baxter shared this conviction. 'If any should doubt whether there be any such Witches,' he wrote,

> he hath as good opportunity now to be easily resolved as hath been known in most Ages. Let him go but into Suffolk or Essex, or Lancashire, &c. and he may quickly be informed. Sure it were strange, if in an age of so much knowledg and conscience, there should so many score poor creatures be put to death as Witches, if it were not clearly manifest that they were such. We have too many examples lately among us, to leave any doubt of the truth of this.

Baxter, like Howell, shuddered to think that abstract theory had become reality, but these were dangerous times, and he too recognized the folly of ignoring plain facts.[40]

Around this time Joseph Hall, the ousted Bishop of Norwich, was also reflecting on the devil's successes in promoting war, schism and heresy, seen 'most clearly in the marvellous multitude of Witches abounding in all parts'. Once, he observed, if a county came across a single witch she was 'hooted at as a strange Monster'; but now 'hundreds are discovered in one shire'. England had come to resemble the icy wastes of Lapland in its profusion of witches: 'the civillest, and most religious parts are frequently pestered with them, and not just old women any more but all sorts of people of both sexes.' It seemed to Hall that Satan knew his time was short, so was unleashing his fury while he could.[41] This awareness – in everyone from writers like Howell to churchmen like Baxter and Hall and right down to the unlettered labourers of Ely – owed a great deal to the labours of Matthew Hopkins and John Stearne. And the witchfinders had not finished.

Before he was incapacitated by a consumption Hopkins had begun his response to the questions asked at Norwich. The finished tract, just a few pages long, was weighed down with blithe evasion, hamfisted wit, and mealy-mouthed qualification. He displayed a self-important disregard for the questions, which he swatted one by one like annoying insects. In reply to the suggestion that it took a witch to catch a witch, he answered 'If Satans kingdome be divided against itselfe, how shall it stand?'; and he wished he *had* managed to get the devil's book of witches, for it would have made his job easier. He did not use any learned authority but relied on experience, 'which though it be meanly esteemed of, yet the surest and safest way to judge by'. He went on to tell the story of 'that horrible sect of Witches' at Manningtree and their familiars with names 'no mortall could invent'. Hopkins showed off his knowledge of witches' marks with the same hauteur affected by Stearne. When witches heard that he was coming, he said, they sent their imps away, leaving 'dry skinnes and filmes only' on their teats. He protested that sleep deprivation had been discontinued, but that watching remained an essential means of detection. If some witches stayed awake during it, he insisted, it was because 'their owne stubborn wills did not let them sleep, though tendered and offered to them'.[42] He failed to mention that they were bound, seated on a hard stool with their feet tucked beneath them.

In the remainder of his account Hopkins deferred to divines who condemned the water ordeal, but still managed to defend it on the

THE
Diſcovery of VVitches:

IN

Anſwer to ſeverall Q U E R I E S,

LATELY

*Delivered to the Judges of Aſſize for the
County of* N O R F O L K.

And now publiſhed

By M A T T H E VV H O P K I N S, Witch-finder.

F O R

The Benefit of the whole K I N G D O M E.

E X O D. 22. 18.
Thou ſhalt not ſuffer a witch to live.

L O N D O N,
Printed for *R. Royſton*, at the Angell in Ivie Lane.
M. DC. XLVII.

*Matthew Hopkins defends himself in print. The display of Exodus 22:18
was redundant because the justification for witch-hunting was not disputed.
Objections were directed solely against the witchfinder's pretended authority
and his vicious techniques*

grounds that James I had made it 'a certaine rule', and that apostates
who denied their baptism were exposed by this means. He protested
too much in discounting confessions extracted by walking, watching,
swimming or false promises – 'viz. if you confess you shall go home,
you shall not go to the Goale [sic], nor be hanged'. Equally hollow

were assurances that he never asked leading questions, and that he had ignored witches who 'confesseth any improbability', such as flying on broomsticks. Hopkins' description of diabolical agency was more orthodox. Satan, he said, was an impostor who persuaded witches that they had caused harm when 'neither he nor they had any hand in it', and nurtured discord between neighbours. Witches facing detection made anguished appeals to him, but discovered his indifference once they reached the gallows. Even in their last hours the devil would hold out false hope, teasing his supplicants as they squirmed in desperation. Here the witchfinder took a vicarious pleasure in acting out the part of his arch-adversary: 'What will you have me doe for you, my deare and nearest children, covenanted and compacted with me in my hellish league, and sealed with your blood, my delicate firebrand-darlings?'[43] That may or may not have been the true voice of the devil; it was the definitely the voice of Matthew Hopkins.

To the final, most trenchant question – was his motivation not money? – Hopkins replied sarcastically, 'judge how he fleeceth the Country, and inriches himselfe, by considering the vast summe he takes of every towne'. In this he lied – as he had lied about sleep deprivation, swimming, and forced confessions. He never took more than twenty shillings from a town, he averred, riding many miles there and back, supporting a company of three horses, sometimes staying a week, and all without additional expenses.[44] It is easy to imagine the outrage this self-pitying statement would have caused at Aldeburgh or King's Lynn, where his swingeing costs had run into pounds rather than mere shillings.

Though ailing, Hopkins may himself have taken his manuscript to London, where he arranged for it to be published by Richard Royston, a disreputable bookseller imprisoned in 1645 for producing scandalous works against Parliament. It was to be sold simultaneously at Royston's shop in Ivy Lane and at Edward Martin's shop in Norwich, where the sticklers' charges had been broadcast at the assizes. Hopkins called his pamphlet *The Discovery of Witches*, and set out a title-page informing readers that this was a personal reply to his critics, but intended 'For The Benefit of the whole Kingdome'. He styled himself simply as 'Witch-finder'. Either he or Royston also commissioned a finely detailed carved wooden print-block – an expensive undertaking – portraying Hopkins in his hat, cape and spurs, standing between Elizabeth Clarke and Rebecca West; the witches were shown naming their familiars as they gambolled merrily in the foreground. The heading was 'Matthew Hopkins Witch Finder Generall' – the first recorded use of this distinctive title, the sobriquet by which Hopkins has been remembered ever since.[45]

The Discovery of Witches went on sale in the last two weeks of May 1647, while John Stearne was busy discovering witches in the Fens. After testifying against Adam Sabie on 1 June Stearne disappears from the record for almost two months; most probably he returned to Lawshall to spend time with his family. In January the forecast for July had been hot and dry, a time when 'Prisons will grow full and Jaylors rich', and so it proved for the city of Ely.[46] Stearne returned to investigate fresh allegations, principally against Thomas Pye, a poor labourer and widower. Pye was accused of having driven a neighbour insane as revenge following an argument. On 24 July the witchfinder appeared before Dr Richard Stane – magistrate, physician and one-time county treasurer – and testified that he was able to identify marks on Pye's body as having been 'sucked or drawne by evill spirites called Imps by the experience he hath found in searching of others who have confessed them selves to be guilty'. Asked whether there was a chance the marks were natural, Stearne reiterated his opinion politely but emphatically. Thomas Pye denied the charge, protesting that he did not even know what an evil spirit was. Dr Stane was satisfied, and asked Stearne and the alleged victim to sign their depositions; Pye drew a little circle with a cross through it as his mark.[47] The prisoner was then locked up with the other accused witches, and Stearne went home.

In the summer of 1647 England was closer than at any time in living memory to political anarchy, an infirmity of the state that had correspondence throughout the natural realm. August may have been harvest month, but it was also 'the mother and nurse of most diseases and sicknesses'. People were advised to eat moderately to avoid indigestion, and to avoid sudden changes of temperature or risk piles, headaches, sciatica – and consumption. Plague spread through London, and in

John Stearne's deposition to Dr Richard Stane at Ely, in which he gives his diagnosis of marks found on Thomas Pye's body. There is a hesitant flourish to Stearne's signature

Cambridge the colleges were closed. On 12 August an Essex clergyman reflected upon 'a time of great sickness and disease across [the] nation', when agues and fevers were worse than ever, fruit rotted on the trees, and cattle succumbed to murrain. 'This portends something,' he said. On that same Thursday, Members of Parliament attended a sermon calling for peace between brethren, causing one to observe with shame that 'Civil war is most wretched among Gods people.'[48]

This was also Matthew Hopkins' last day on earth. He languished in bed at Manningtree, ashen and emaciated, his fatigue and dry cough having developed into a relentless fever punctuated by violent fits of expectoration. The familiar smell of pleural tuberculosis – the tang of onions – permeated the room. With each contraction of his lungs his stertorous breaths grew fainter, as the essence of his life was sucked away. Country people believed that the dying heard church bells calling their souls to paradise, but Hopkins would have tried to ignore such superstition; instead he would have focused on the image of Christ's passion, preparing to render himself unto heaven, confident that the reckoning of his life would prove him worthy of election to the sainthood. With dignity and determination, courage and conviction, he had acted upon his conscience and, like Saul, had driven the witches and wizards from the land. Scenes of damnation – too horrible either to contemplate or to ignore – must have flashed before him in those desperate hours, a fate officially defined that year as 'everlasting separation from the comfortable presence of God, and most grievous torments, without intermission, in hell-fire for ever'.[49]

Whether Hopkins died alone, no one can say. It is unlikely that in puritan Manningtree much ritual attended his passing – no solemn bells, no psalms, no sprigs of rosemary in the coffin – though it is tempting to imagine the women who laid out his corpse speaking to the souls of the dead through one of his ears or rubbing their warts on his skin. After all, this was the body of a famous witchfinder, feared and revered in life and imbued with a strange power in death. Hopkins was buried within a few hours of his last breath. His body was taken directly from the place where it was laid out to the church of St Mary at Mistley Heath and interred in the graveyard with no more ceremony than the simple ministrations of the newly arrived rector, John Witham, and the pious meditations of any who happened to be present. These days, the Westminster Assembly reminded mourners that prayers did not help the deceased, but only hurt the living by the offence they caused to God.[50] As the gravedigger piled in the earth the churchwarden returned to the vestry, where he scribbled this laconic record in the parish register: 'Mathew Hopkins sone of Mr James Hopkins Minister of Wenha[m] was buryed at Mistley, August 12th 1647.'[51] It was a very ordinary way to end a short but extraordinary life.

How John Stearne heard that Matthew Hopkins had died is not known, nor whether he visited him in his last hours or stood in contemplative silence at the graveside. He was almost certainly in Ely at the time, overseeing the interrogation of Ann Disborough, a middle-aged housewife. In June 1645, it was said, she had sunk a river boat on its way from Ely to King's Lynn, and a year later had caused a boy to fall from a dung-cart and break his leg. Later in the summer of 1646 she had threatened Francis Caule for insulting her daughter, whereafter he suffered violent fits. She went to his bedside, but he sent her away, saying 'The divell in hell take yow and if I was strong enough I would cudgell yow out of my howse for I shall never be well as long as yow are so neare me.' She had been tried at the 1646 Michaelmas assizes, but acquitted. Now Caule had another chance for redress. He was questioned by the physician Richard Stane, who asked specifically whether he thought Ann Disborough kept familiar spirits. Caule answered that a pair of imps had crawled into his mouth to torment him from the inside – something he had failed to mention to Thomas Castell the previous summer. The statement was all ready for Caule to sign when Stane thought to ask him to describe these imps, to which he replied 'in the likenes & shape of two dun mice'. As the scribe carefully inserted this extra detail, Stane bound Caule and two other witnesses to appear at the assizes, and committed Ann Disborough to gaol.[52]

The witchfinder, still at large in the Isle of Ely in September 1647, visited Wisbech, former seat of the Bishop of Ely. This was an anxious, divided town – just the sort of place to harbour witches – where during the war a parliamentarian majority had been on guard against a royalist minority, constantly braced for attack from over the border in Norfolk.[53] On the road to Ely Stearne also stopped at the small towns of Chatteris and March, where he heard 'large confessions', and at Wimblington to the south, where a single witch was exposed. Wisbech was notorious for its 'unlawfull meetinges & Conventicles', and all four places were prime recruiting-grounds for the Baptists in particular.[54]

In Wisbech lived a widow named Joan Pigg, 'a woman of evill fame and suspected for witchcraft'. In 1643 her daughter had died in an alehouse brawl, but the prosecution of the killer had collapsed on a technicality; she had lost her husband of twenty years soon afterwards. In the summer of 1647 a farmer named John Cuthbert summoned a farrier to examine his sick mare, but no sign of natural disease was found. A crowd gathered to see the animal everyone now said was bewitched, while Cuthbert's servant went looking for Widow Pigg. Upon her arrival, the crowd parted to reveal the prostrate mare and Goodwife Cuthbert, who lunged furiously at Pigg, scratching her face. Others joined in and hurled the suspect onto the horse, whereupon it miraculously recovered. It was said that Widow Pigg threatened revenge as she left, and within two months both the mare and a gelding had died. The farrier flayed them to examine the skins, but could find no natural cause of death. On 18 September a magistrate at Wisbech heard this evidence, and examined Joan Pigg. She denied having threatened the Cuthberts, protesting that she had walked from the scene of her violent humiliation without uttering a sound.[55]

That warm Saturday afternoon Joan Pigg was transported the twenty miles through the fen to Ely, where she joined sixteen other felons on remand. She learnt that eleven of them – mostly from Sutton, Haddenham and Stretham – also stood accused of witchcraft, and had been waiting in the gaol almost four months; it seems that Robert Ellis's wife Dorothy had died by this time. Two days later, on the Monday, Joan Briggs of Haddenham, who had denied charges against her at the end of May, was added to their dismal number, among them her neighbours Thomasine Read and Adam Sabie.[56]

On Thursday 23 September the assizes began at Ely. The chief justice, John Godbold, arrived from London and attended a sermon in the cathedral, while outside in the sunshine joiners were assembling the gallows. Perhaps hoping to catch this sessions, three men from the parish of St Mary's reported Peter Burbush, a blacksmith, to Richard Stane. A miller named William Shelley said Burbush had told him how to become a witch, a spell he had learnt from a labourer in the parish. It went like this:

> w[he]n a man came to the sacram[en]t, let him take the Bread and keepe it in his Hand & after y[a]t he hath drinke the wine to goe out w[i]th the bread in his Hand & pisse ag[ains]t the church wall at which time he shall finde somthing like a toade or ffrogge gapeinge to receive the s[ai]d Bread and after y[a]t ye Party should come to the knowledge how to be a witch.

Henry Freeman, another miller, deposed that Burbush had caused his windmill to collapse with a woman and child inside, and had killed horses belonging to him worth £18. His livelihood had been ruined, and now he feared for his life. Asked by the magistrate whether he thought an evil spirit was at work, Freeman said that he did.[57]

Peter Burbush, his wife Agnes and their daughters of seven and four were still relatively new to St Mary's.[58] Like all migrants, Burbush struggled to be accepted as a tradesman, a struggle lost when rumours that he was a witch started to spread. In the spring of 1647 Burbush had traced this whispering back to John Abraham, a weaver who had fallen into 'a verye strange Condic[ion]' in 1644 after his wife refused Burbush some odds and ends from beneath their loom. Summoned before Richard Stane even as proceedings were under way at the Shire House, Peter Burbush denied all charges and was sent to gaol. The calendar of prisoners had already been drawn up, so Burbush would have six months to wait before his trial. Accused witches from March, Chatteris and Wimblington also arrived too late to be tried at these assizes.[59]

As the judge, chief bailiff and other legal officers processed from the cathedral to the market-place where the sessions house stood, so the accused felons – filthy and trembling – were brought out in chains from the nearby Bishop's Gaol.[60] Once the ritual of arraignment had begun it was clear that this was no ordinary assizes. Normally the gaol held half the number of prisoners, and witches were comparatively rare. Now there were seventeen men and women to be tried: two thieves, one receiver of stolen grain, an infanticidal mother, and thirteen witches; of the witches, no fewer than five were men.[61] Veterans

Judge Godbold and John Stearne may have been the only ones in the courtroom not to be amazed by all this. The devil was at work in Ely, that much was evident; even the woman who had cut her baby's throat confessed that Satan had 'stirred upp & downe w[i]thin her' as the incessant crying drove her to distraction.[62]

Little is known about the outcome of the trials. John and Bridget Bonham were acquitted, despite abundant proof – their poor reputations, previous suspicions against them, and most recently their confessions. This in itself suggests that the jury, probably on Godbold's instruction, was aware that self-incrimination might be the outcome of torture or madness.[63] Parish records from after 1647 show that others must also have been spared that summer: Thomas Pye, the labourer who denied knowing what an evil spirit was; Joan Briggs, who protested that her imps' marks were just warts; and poor deluded Adam Sabie, the Haddenham mystic who saw salvation in his fiery visions.[64] The case of Margaret Moore was different. Stearne related how she confessed a third time before the court, and wept tears of remorse for what she had done to Thomas Nix and his neighbours at Witchford. For this moving and damning performance she was found guilty and sentenced to death by the judge.[65]

John Stearne did not wait to see the execution of Goodwife Moore and the rest of the condemned felons, but had already set off on the thirty-five-mile ride back to Lawshall by the time they climbed the ladder. How they conducted themselves will never be known. Perhaps, as happened elsewhere, they fell into raptures of prayer, or swigged at bottles thrown from the crowd; or perhaps they kissed the wet faces of their relatives and wished a pox on the rest. Margaret Moore died for the truth that she and others saw in her dreams, and which according to the law of England put her beyond reason or mercy.

Whatever visions disturbed Judge Godbold's sleep in the dead of night, he could at least be reassured that he was a servant of God's law; like Stearne, he had no need to see the stark reality of a hanging – the brickbats and spitting, the pathetic struggles, the piteous pleading, the giddiness of spectators pressing against the cordon. The dreams of such men were not haunted by the struggling limbs and bulging eyes, the involuntary excretion and arousal *in extremis*, the tragic spectacle of children pulling on their parents' legs, the sooner to end their suffering. As for the hangman's dreams, it was said they could be of 'nothing but wry mouthes, blabbed tongues, knots under the eare, and poore tottred wretches stript and tumbled stark naked into a nasty pit one upon another'.[66]

Epilogue

IN DECEMBER 1647 the wind and rain of autumn turned to storms and snow. John Stearne was at home in Lawshall where his wife was expecting their second child. His witch-hunt was over. Matthew Hopkins, bellicose soul of the campaign, was dead, and the exactitude of judges and juries meant diminishing returns in the courts, especially when compared to the triumphs of 1645. In town and country – particularly in Stearne's own Suffolk – grievance at the cost of keeping and prosecuting witches was common discourse, as were debts the jaded witchfinder never called in. Worse, lawsuits had been filed against him to overturn wrongful accusations, and apparently also to recover fees.[1] Hopkins, now dubbed 'Witchfinder General', had tried to set the record straight in print, pouring derision on the objections of sticklers and atheists and pontificating on the wickedness of witches and the revelatory power of his experience. The world might yet regret its pettiness and ingratitude. To encourage a revision of opinion – and to make money – Stearne knew he had to enlarge on *The Discovery of Witches*, to pile on accumulated evidence until the platform of aspersion buckled. To signal his continuation of Master Hopkins' work, Stearne decided to call his own book *A Confirmation and Discovery of Witch Craft*.

For all his aspiration, Stearne was no scholar. Much of the winter of 1647–8 was devoted to fitting his notes around a framework based on Richard Bernard's *Guide to Grand-Jury Men*, a copy of which he had at his side. In the end he found himself copying out passages from the *Guide* and inserting his own sometimes unreliable stories, backed by examples from the Bible.[2] His style was godly, for sure, albeit with a Pharisaical air. On the first page alone he fired off nine scriptural texts, from Deuteronomy to Revelation, to establish that his quarrel was not with addle-headed old women but with the idolators, sorcerers and murderers flushed out by the angels of the Apocalypse. His aim was to lay bare 'the diabolicall art, or crying sin, of Witch-craft . . . the greatest Apostacie from the faith; for [witches] renounce God and Christ, and give themselves by a covenant to the Devil, the utter enemy to God and all mankind.' And he challenged sticklers like Gaule who, in spite of all the laws of God and man, denied the existence of witches and said falsely

> that there are many poore silly ignorant people hanged wrongfully, and that those who have gone or beene instruments in finding out or discovering those of late made knowne have done it for there owne private ends, for gaine and such like, favouring some where they thought good, and unjustly prosecuting others.

Neither he nor Hopkins ever did such a thing, he affirmed; rather, they had always served the commonwealth above their own interests. If he had gone too far then he begged indulgence, likewise for his writing – the work of 'a plaine countrey man, who intend[s] not to pen any thing but what I shall be able to make appeare plainely to bee truth'.[3]

The manuscript was probably ready by January 1648 – 25,000 words of plagiarism, anecdote and nostalgia laced with exegesis and elliptical arguments and peppered with snorts of derision and the occasional shudder. Stearne must have felt better for having transferred his besieged conscience to the page. The weather improved, with warm days like an early spring, and in the last week of January Agnes Stearne gave birth to a girl they christened Mary.[4] Stearne delivered his book to the same London printer who had handled the works of John Gaule and John Davenport in 1646. It was never read as widely as either, however, nor did it have the impact of Hopkins' brief survey.[5]

For all his swagger, Stearne had started his crusade in 1645 in an impatient mood only to end it three years later beset by disappointment. Once his enemies had been witches; now they were those who sought to 'promote them [the witches] forward to take the least advantage by suit of law'.[6] The identity of these patrons and their protégés

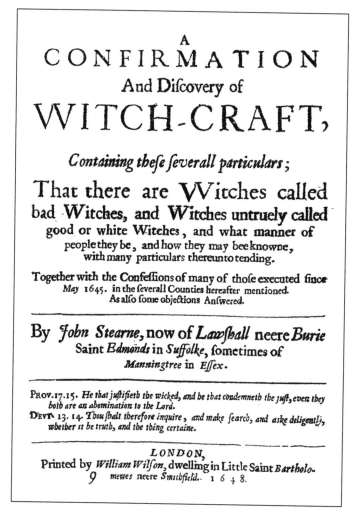

A

CONFIRMATION

And Diſcovery of

WITCH-CRAFT,

Containing theſe ſeverall particulars;

That there are VVitches called
bad Witches, and Witches untruely called
good or white Witches, and what manner of
peoplethey be, and how they may bee knowne,
with many particulars thereunto tending.

Together with the Confeſſions of many of thoſe executed ſince
May 1645. in the ſeverall Counties hereafter mentioned.
As alſo ſome objections Anſwered.

By *John Stearne*, now of *Lawſhall* neere *Burie*
Saint *Edmonds* in *Suffolke*, ſometimes of
Manningtree in *Eſſex*.

Prov.17.15. *He that juſtifieth the wicked, and he that condemneth the juſt, even they
both are an abomination to the Lord.*
Devt. 13. 14. *Thou ſhalt therefore inquire, and make ſearch, and aske diligently,
whether it be truth, and the thing certaine.*

LONDON,
Printed by *William Wilſon*, dwelling in Little Saint *Bartholo-
9 mewes* neere *Smithfield.* 1 6 4 8.

*John Stearne's memoir of the East Anglian witch-hunt, displaying both an
eagerness to hunt witches and an awareness that voices of protest had grown
louder since 1645*

remains a mystery; but the witchfinders had travelled too far and
delved too deep for there to be any shortage of candidates. Many of
the accused had died, but more had survived. Five of the women convicted at the 1645 Essex assizes and pardoned the following year were
still in Chelmsford gaol in March 1648.[7] For them, the witch-hunt

was not over. There is no record of Crown witness Rebecca West returning home after sending her mother to the gallows.[8] At Ely St Mary's, Agnes Burbush relied on charity to feed her daughters while her husband awaited trial, then probably fled never to return. Adam Sabie, the visionary of Haddenham, escaped with his life in September 1647 but died six months later, perhaps from strain.[9] At Brandeston in Suffolk Margaret Lowes, widow of the executed minister, died in 1648 without hearing the parish's final verdict that her husband 'was a contentious Man & made his Parishoners very uneasy, & they were glad to take ye Opportunity of those wicked times, & get him hanged rather than not get rid of him'.[10] In years to come, old cases flared up. An Essex woman tried in 1646 was searched in 1650 on the orders of a magistrate.[11] In 1662 John and Bridget Bonham (then in their eighties) were arrested by Sir Miles Sandys and tried at Ely for the murder of their son; again they were acquitted.[12]

England went though many changes. In the summer of 1648, the coldest and wettest in living memory, a second civil war broke out in East Anglia, Kent and the North, but was swiftly put down by star ascendant Oliver Cromwell. By December the army had imposed its will upon Parliament, and early in the New Year put Charles I on trial. What followed, on 30 January 1649, was more outlandish than any war or plague of witches: the king was displayed on a scaffold in Whitehall and beheaded before his subjects. At that moment, it was said, the sun broke through the clouds and a flight of ducks hovered overhead; at Dover, a monstrous whale was washed up on the beach, and a blind man on the Isle of Wight discovered he could see again.[13] The inverted world of wonders and omens would not right itself for many years to come, and for as long as God punished his people and the devil made sport of their lives, so witches would be sniffed out and scandalized. The splash made by Hopkins and Stearne even rippled across the Atlantic, for in 1648 a court in Massachusetts ordered 'the course w[hi]ch hath bene taken in England for discov[e]ry of witches, by watching them a certeine time' to be adopted for its suspects; this was, stated the order, 'the best & surest way'.[14]

Over the next decade more witches were tried in England and Scotland than a pair of witchfinders ever could have discovered. At St

Albans in 1649 a man and a woman were executed as members of 'the Conjuring conclave and the society of witches in England'. The same year women were tried in Leicestershire, Worcestershire, Gloucestershire; and in Edinburgh five witches were burned at the stake.[15] From Newcastle came news of a professional 'witch-trier' paid by the authorities to purge the city; and in Cumberland the sheriff wrote to the Council at Westminster to ask advice about 'the discovery of Witches'.[16] In the early 1650s, as the Commonwealth evolved into a republic under Cromwell, witch-trials continued to be held all over the country. In July 1652 at the Maidstone assizes in Kent eighteen people were tried, a third of whom were hanged – the first to die on the Home Circuit since 1645.[17] More were to follow. At Bury St Edmunds, Goodwife Boreham – possibly one of those acquitted in 1645 – was hanged alongside her daughter; and in London several witches were executed, including a healer with a squirrel for an imp, and a woman found to have 'three long Teats neer to her privie Parts, which she said was onely the Pyles'.[18] In 1655 even the famous astrologer William Lilly was indicted under the Witchcraft Act, but the case was thrown out.[19]

Without the events of 1645 to 1647, and the energy with which they were reported, it is hard to imagine that there would have been so much fuss about witches in the next decade. Ordinary people now 'knew' that witches fed blood to spirits, exchanged a Christian covenant for a satanic one, and worshipped covertly and lecherously at sabbats. Like idolaters, apostates and atheists, witches were confirmed as being both male and female, and might be persons eminent in piety and prosperity; in these last days, the devil was as devious as he was determined. These were the lessons of the witchfinders.

And yet Hopkins and Stearne were not commanders-in-chief of the witch-hunt: they were catalysts who gave accusers confidence by confirming their suspicions and beliefs. In their books they were emphatic that *they* had never accused anyone of anything: they went only to places where they were invited, and applied their expertise to suspects identified by the inhabitants.[20] There was truth in this. It was for the searchers and watchers appointed by their own parishes to decide whether there were grounds to prosecute, and for victims and their allies to choose whether to go to law. Thereafter the progress of a prosecution depended on the consideration of a godly magistrate (and sometimes a minister), and even then proceedings might still be thwarted by a grand jury, after that by a trial jury under the guidance of a judge. Even if a suspect were convicted and condemned, according to Scripture and the statute of King James I it was no more than he or she deserved. They were witchfinders and proud of it; but cunning folk, searchers, watchers and witnesses – likewise justices, jurors and judges – were witchfinders as well.

Few with a hand in the East Anglian witch-hunt ever doubted the wisdom or justice of their actions. Sir Harbottle Grimston remained MP for Harwich until his death in February 1648. His namesake son and heir was excluded from Parliament in the same year, and at the restoration of the monarchy in 1660 was appointed to the commission to try the regicides. The elder Grimston's fellow magistrate Sir Thomas Bowes continued to send witches for trial until 1670; on one occasion a Harwich woman confessed to him that she had suckled an imp in the shape of a bird.[21] Joseph Long, the witch-hunting vicar of Great Clacton, held on to his living until 1662, when he was ejected like those he had once persecuted.[22] In Suffolk, Samuel Fairclough, who had sat on the Special Commission in 1645, also lost his living, and died at Stowmarket in 1677. Edmund Calamy turned against the Commonwealth regime and became Charles II's chaplain; he died in 1666, heartbroken by the sight of London burning. The other commissioner, John Godbold, served the Western Circuit assizes after the Ely trials, but died a year later at his London home; a volume of his law reports was published in 1652.[23]

Miles Corbett, the 'Inquisitor General', who helped execute the king as well as the witches of Yarmouth, was himself hanged at Tyburn in 1662. If witches who had killed a few men could be hanged forty at a time, one minister reasoned, why should fanatics who had killed thousands receive mercy? In his gallows speech, Corbett protested that he had been motivated solely by public duty.[24] John Brinsley was ejected in 1660 and died without seeing Yarmouth become a new Jerusalem. At Dunwich Thomas Spatchet, a watcher in August 1645, suffered fits in the winter of 1665 and caused a beggar woman to be persecuted to death.[25] In Huntingdonshire John Gaule, whose book had wrecked Hopkins' reputation, remained vicar of Great Staughton until his death in 1687. He preached at the assizes, criticized fanatics, and denounced astrology. His parishioners remained as superstitious as ever. In 1660 Gaule distanced himself from his patron Sir Valentine Walton, who like Miles Corbett had signed Charles I's death warrant. Gaule was remembered by some as a bore and a turncoat, by others as 'Judicious Gaule'.[26] The manor of Great Staughton was confiscated by the Crown and Walton fled to Holland, where he ended his days as a gardener. Former manorial lord Sir Edward Wingfield, who had interrogated Joan Wallis at Keyston, died a debtor in the Fleet Prison in 1662.[27] Finally, Sir John Washington, whose family had seemed so accursed at Thrapston, lived to be almost a hundred; the great-grandson of his nephew who emigrated to Virginia in 1658 became the first President of the United States of America.[28]

The story of John Stearne's later life is fragmentary. Though resident at Lawshall he kept a house in Manningtree until the 1660s, and may have owned land at Clacton.[29] It is impossible to calculate how much he made from the witch-hunt. Like Hopkins he had the potential to earn more in a week than most earned in a year, but insisted he never received a penny above the set rate, adding that he would have been better off financially had he stayed at home. It was probably true that many parishes were unlikely to pay him unless he sued them – an unrealistic proposition when 'many rather fall upon me for what hath been received'. In 1648 he remained optimistic that 'such Suits will be disannulled, and that where I have been [with]out moneys for Towns in charges and otherwise . . . I may be satisfied and paid with reason.'[30]

Stearne was less sanguine later, by which time legal costs may have eroded his fortune and status. In 1651 he challenged a neighbour at Lawshall for working on the Sabbath, resulting in a counter-accusation that he was a thief. Stearne successfully petitioned for felony proceedings to be suspended, and pending a hearing declared himself worth less than £5; in the mean time, he was appointed free counsel. The dispute dragged on into 1654, by which point he had declassed himself from 'gentleman' to 'yeoman'. He was a perpetual thorn in his neighbours' sides, and in 1657 was bound over to keep the peace.[31] In that year he was bequeathed a much-needed £10 by a kinsman of his wife, and by this time he was employed – probably as a scribe – by a gentleman at Herringswell. The Stearnes had another five children between 1653 and 1660; the three sons named after Hebrew patriarchs flourished, but John's namesake died young. In 1670 Stearne received an inheritance from his mother-in-law, but had little time to spend it: he died early in the New Year and was buried at Lawshall on 20 January. Confident as he was of redemption, his epitaph might have been Revelation 22:14, which he had chosen as the coda to his book: 'Blessed are they that do his commandments, that they may have right to the tree of life.'[32]

Until the day he died Stearne attracted hostility for the witch-hunt, and for atrocities committed by others. He protested that he had never watched anyone so as 'to disturb them in their brains', and that all suspects were rested before evidence was taken.[33] This fell on deaf ears among writers who saw in witchfinding the barbarity of war and fanaticism spilling into the administration of justice – the safeguard of civil society. Attacking both religious enthusiasm and magic in 1650, the Cambridge occultist Henry More referred to Hopkins as 'that troublesome fellow' – a harsher judgement than it now sounds. To Thomas Ady, a physician and disciple of the sceptic Reginald Scot, the witch-hunt was 'The Grand Errour of these latter Ages'; even John Gaule was too credulous for him. In a book of 1655 Ady condemned 'blinde circumstances' like the water ordeal, asserting that women's 'spongiously hollow' bodies made them float. 'These delusions', he stressed, 'have been impiously acted here in England, of late in Essex, and Suffolk, by a wicked Inquisitor pretending authority for it, to the cutting off of fourteen innocent people at Chelmsford Assizes, and about an hundred at Berry Assizes, whereof one was a Minister neer Fremingham.' The tempest raised by John Lowes would have been a miracle even for Christ, and his marks were no more than piles; others had been convicted for having warts, verrucas, swollen tonsils, and 'fairy-nips' – bluish spots on the breasts of nursing mothers. A gaoler rumoured to have been paid to give evidence was

This frontispiece to Nathaniel Crouch's Kingdom of Darkness *assembles vignettes of witchcraft that had become standard images by the time it was published in 1688. Paradoxically, by then witchcraft had become virtually impossible to prove at law*

not fit to hold office in a Christian commonwealth. Hearing a Suffolk minister hold forth on the subject of witches having sent imps to assist both sides in the civil war, Ady challenged him on the scriptural basis of this belief, but found the churchman ignorant.[34]

For Hopkins to be remembered as a popish torturer was the ultimate irony and insult. The next generation even laughed at him, not just as an inquisitor but as a melodramatic exorcist – the type Samuel Harsnet had called 'holy Tragaedians'. The focus of a stage play of 1682 was a magistrate, Sir Jeffery Shacklehead, 'pretending to great skill in Witches, and a great persecutor of them'. To the suggestion that he is deluded, he splutters: 'My senses deceived! That's well. Is there a justice in Lancashire has so much skill in witches as I have? Nay, I'le speak a proud word; you shall turn me loose against any witch-finder in Europe; I'd make an ass of Hopkins if he were alive.' Shacklehead wants to search, watch, prick and swim a witch, but cannot remember more than the titles of the daemonological treatises he claims to have read. Teague O'Divelly, an Irish priest, serves to mirror and mock the witchfinder's superstition throughout the action.[35] Twenty-five years after Matthew Hopkins' death, his tragedy was being replayed as comedy.

After the Restoration polemicists lampooned 'The Distracted Puritane' – the stereotype of the tortured zealot from Emmanuel College, at war with Antichrist and images and obsessed with visions and prayer. The satirist Samuel Butler saw the fanatic as 'neither fit for Peace nor War, but Times of a Condition between both' – a saint on the outside, a reprobate on the inside.[36] These portraits were pleasing to Charles II, not least because enthusiasts had executed his father. The king even patronized Butler's most famous work, *Hudibras*, an epic poem which exposed the moral failings of puritanism: the absurd heroism, self-deception and rank hypocrisy. Naturally, Hopkins was mentioned:

> Has not this present Parliament
> A Ledger to the Devil sent,
> Fully impower'd to treat about
> Finding revolted Witches out?
> And has not he with in a year,

Hang'd threescore of 'em in one Shire?
Some only for not being drown'd,
And some for sitting above ground,
Whole days and nights, upon their breeches
And feeling pain, were hang'd for Witches.

In the end, Butler suggested, Hopkins had 'prov'd himself a Witch/And made a rod for his own breech'.[37] This picked up on a rumour that some gentleman had swum the witchfinder, and that he had floated. Some insisted he had fled; others that he was hanged. Now Butler's epic poem fixed the myth in folk tradition. According to a diarist in the 1680s, 'it is very satisfactory, to one's sense of poetical justice, to know that his favourite water ordeal was at length tried upon himself, by a party of indignant experimenters'.[38]

Charles II was encouraged to think of the Interregnum as a time when his loyal subjects had been under a spell, an argument that linked witchcraft with disobedience and disorder. 'And I observe', noted a loyal supporter, 'never more Witches in England since Monarchy and Hierarchy lay in the dust.'[39] Yet witches lingered on in literature, not just because they symbolized challenges to authority but because prosecutions persisted. In the 1660s a Worcestershire witch declared war on the king; witches allegedly sank an Ipswich ship; the case of a Yarmouth woman bitten by an imp was discussed at Cambridge; there was a 'strange discovery of witches' at Warwick; and in Somerset a real-life Sir Jeffery Shacklehead was at large.[40] A female witchfinder was operating in Northumberland in the 1670s, and a few years later a man taking confessions in Devon may have been one too.[41] The techniques perfected by Hopkins and Stearne remained in use, despite their prohibition. The difference now was that few cases resulted in convictions: grand jurors accepted their legal validity, but trial jurors were directed by judges to find the evidence lacking.[42]

In a strange way, the witchfinders had helped bring witch-trials to an end. For all its ferocity, the craze of the 1640s did not mark the height of witch-hunting: it was the final act. As in other parts of Europe, the craze first silenced demurrers by offering graphic evidence of witchcraft, but in time raised more doubts than it suppressed. Within five years of Matthew Hopkins' death the political theorist Sir

Robert Filmer was attacking the legacy of William Perkins and reliance at law on the diabolic pact. Filmer had attended the mass trial at Maidstone in 1652, and was horrified.[43] The witch-hunt first encouraged such trials, then made them impossible. By the 1670s Yorkshire doctor John Webster was ridiculing 'pitiful lying Witchmongers' and four of Hopkins' key points of proof – demonic pacts, the feeding of imps, copulation with Satan, and the manipulation of nature by shape-changing and raising storms; Webster was read by virtuosi such as Robert Hooke.[44] After 1680 it was a rare judge who condemned a witch just to avoid 'appearing to deny the very being of witches' and so giving 'occasion to set afoot the old trade of witch finding', as happened at Exeter in 1682. By the time that confessed witches were routinely discharged as lunatics, the witchfinders' operative principles had all but collapsed.[45]

This shift in opinion was driven by jurisprudential separation of 'matters of fact' from 'matters of law', but also mirrored a growing tendency among theologians to scrutinize occult phenomena more closely. As Henry More observed, this undermined the ability of the supernatural to explain the inexplicable. Like Francis Bacon in the 1620s, natural philosophers were 'putting nature to the question', a term meaning, literally, to interrogate nature under torture – ironically, the idea behind Matthew Hopkins' methods. More himself opposed experiments contrived to defend magic in nature, likening them to 'men on the rack or overwatched witches, that are forced many times over to confess that which they were never guilty of'.[46] The final outcome would be 'a declining sense of the miraculous' in the Western world, perhaps even 'the disenchantment of the world'.[47] There were also humanitarian undertones to these changes in thinking. New editions of Reginald Scot's *Discoverie of Witchcraft*, first published in 1584, moved the original theological arguments into the social sphere with the intention of exposing 'The Unchristian practices and Inhumane Dealings of Searchers and Witch-tryers' against people who would be better treated with food and medicine than torture and punishment. Henry More blamed mean-spirited neighbours for provoking revenge fantasies: 'it is the most probable', he said, 'that they that are the forwardest to hange Witches are the first that made them.'[48]

For the generation that remembered the 1640s, the last word belonged to a Suffolk clergyman named Francis Hutchinson. As a young man he had been the vicar of Hoxne, where he had met eyewitnesses to the witch-hunt and immediately conceived an abhorrence of the 'wandring scandalous people, that took up a Trade to get their Bread amongst the Rabble, by finding out Witches'. To his mind, the special commissioners at Bury St Edmunds were credulous witchmongers just like Hopkins and Stearne; Samuel Fairclough's sermons, for all their circumspection, had none the less 'recommended these Prosecutions as a Piece of Piety and Reformation, that shewed the Zeal of their Time'.[49]

In 1704, while working as a curate at Bury, Hutchinson became especially interested in the fate of John Lowes of Brandeston, and wrote to William Wilson, the current vicar, asking for information. Wilson passed his letter to Thomas Revett of Brandeston Hall, who obliged Hutchinson by copying out his father's account from the 1660s. Revett himself had known the men who swam Lowes – men who had regaled many with their story over the years. Before he sent the reply on to Hutchinson, William Wilson added a note to the effect that Dr Smith of Mendlesham had known Lowes well, and considered him 'too cleanly and ingenious a man to be guilty of w[ha]t th[e]y charged him with'. A decade later, when Hutchinson came to write up his notes for publication, he borrowed a copy of Hopkins' *Discovery of Witches* from a senior judge in London to see for himself the rationale of the witchfinder. Seventy years on the voice of Matthew Hopkins, callous and credulous, rang out from the page, advancing a logic that Hutchinson reversed with cold precision. 'The Discovery of Witches', he concluded, 'doth follow Principles; for if men believe none, it is not likely they should find any.'[50]

The appearance of Hutchinson's book in 1718 drew a line between memory and myth. The original actors were almost all dead, and subsequent generations would have to make do with secondhand stories of what had happened. Already the time when judges 'condemn'd many Innocent Persons upon the Testimony of Pretended Witchfinders' seemed to belong to a grimly exotic dark age of English history, an attitude exemplified by Daniel Defoe in the 1720s when he scoffed at the burning of Mother Lakeland at Ipswich. The charges against her, he wrote, were 'so formidable and extravagant, that I care not to put any one's Faith to the stretch about them'.[51] As some details were laughed out of the picture, so the legend that Matthew Hopkins had been lynched acquired greater solidity as truth. Within a year of Hopkins' death John Stearne was busily scotching these rumours, stating that he had died 'peaceably at Manningtree, after a long sicknesse of a Consumption, as many of his generation had done before him'.[52]

Yet the colourful version proved more popular. Francis Hutchinson was in no doubt that local gentry had consigned Hopkins to ordeal by water. 'That clear'd the Country of him,' he wrote with obvious pleasure, 'and it was a great deal of Pity, that they did not think of the Experiment sooner.' By the end of the century it was an established fact that the witchfinder had been hoist by his own petard.[53] A romantic novel of 1824 about 'that most useful auxilliary of justice, the pious Master Mathew Hopkins' ends with the witchfinder reduced to a 'dejected wretch' as he fails the swimming test, with fatal consequences. Subsequent to this retelling of the story, Sir Walter Scott condemned Hopkins for having put 'infirm, terrified, overwhelmed persons in the next state to absolute madness', and repeated the tale that he had cheated the devil out of the witches' register. Fortunately he had been swum, concluded Scott, 'so the country was rid of him'.[54]

In the first half of the twentieth century, efforts to separate fact from fiction achieved varied success. Scholarly investigation of the East Anglian witch-hunt put the record straight on several scores, and for the first time provided a basic account of what had happened.[55] But it was as a fictional character that Matthew Hopkins was most graphically reanimated in the post-war era. In a novel published in 1966 he is a parliamentarian pikeman who goes on to become 'a black-winged Attila, leaving behind him a trail of gibbet-hung corpses and vermin-infested gaols filled with beaten, terrified women'. At the end he is swum in the river at Ely, then hanged.[56] The book was made into a film that treated the facts in an even more cavalier manner, albeit with the serious aim of demonstrating how, as one critic observed, 'the ordinary man was capable of absolute evil'. The film achieved cult status, and in its wake, with the help of a tie-in paperback of the novel, the rector of Manningtree was bombarded with enquiries, which he termed 'Hopkinsmania'.[57] In 1976 the first full history of the witch-hunt was published, purporting to draw heavily on a previously unknown manuscript, 'The Tendring Witchcraft Revelations'; now, among other things, it could be shown how intimately Hopkins had been connected to the astrologer William Lilly and to royalist spy-rings. Alas, no historian has ever seen this manuscript, and the consensus today is that it was a clever hoax.[58]

Matthew Hopkins, once a sentient man of flesh and blood, lives on as anti-hero and bogeyman – utterly ethereal, endlessly malleable. At Mistley, sightings of his ghost in and around the Thorn Inn date back to the nineteenth century, testifying to the power of memory and tradition. At night the anguished cries of Elizabeth Clarke echo over the Stour estuary, and throughout East Anglia other victims are said to lament their suffering at the witchfinder's hands.[59] The mythology consists entirely in the memory of his monstrosity. He has been called 'a vile impostor', 'a loathsome conman', 'a human monster', 'the Napoleon of witch-finding', 'the Hangman of Manningtree', 'the foulest of foul parasites, an obscene bird of prey of the tribe of Judas and Cain', and 'one of the nastiest men in the records of English history'.[60] According to one author, 'there can rarely have been a man as wicked and depraved', and that barely two years after the end of the Second World War.[61] In myths, the wicked tend to meet dramatic ends. The fanciful version of Hopkins' death still finds its way into respectable works of non-fiction, including one which states that, in the absence of any record of his trial for witchcraft, 'most historians agree that he was probably lynched on the spot'.[62] More reliable portraits of the witchfinder have also been produced, mainly by historians who have overcome the discovery that, as one indignant account describes it, 'to study his life in any detail is to feel contaminated'.[63]

No one knows exactly how many suffered in the witch-craze of 1645 to 1647: as many as three hundred women and men were interrogated, of whom more than a hundred were put to death.[64] It was a terrible tragedy; but it needs to be seen as part of something even more terrible, a civil war characterized by bigotry, brutality and

Matthew Hopkins
Witch finder General.

James Caulfield, the eighteenth-century engraver responsible for this portrait of Hopkins, specialized in criminal biographies and human curiosities. The intense image from 1647 has been transposed to an arcadian setting, with the witchfinder staring wistfully into space. By 1800 the witch-hunt had become romantic legend, and Hopkins a mythical bogeyman

bloodshed. The conflict killed 190,000 Englishmen out of a population of five million, amounting to 3.7 per cent – a greater proportion
than during the First World War.[65] If one discounts the sensational,
the particular and the judgemental, one is left with a different kind of
Matthew Hopkins: an intransigent and dangerous figure, for sure, but
a charismatic man of his time, no more ruthless than his contemporaries and, above all, driven by a 'messianic desire to purify'. In this the
witchfinders resembled most puritans, believers with little breadth of
mind but considerable depth of spirit, even if they did mistake their
own passions for the word of God.[66] To them might be extended the
same understanding offered by historians to the iconoclast William
Dowsing: no longer a freakish extremist, he has become 'an unex-
ceptional member of the winning side in the Civil War, who worked
within his society not against it'.[67]

Nor should the other witchfinders be forgotten, for without them
Hopkins would have remained the obscure younger son of a country
clergyman. Despite the repeal of the Witchcraft Act in 1736 – in a
way *because* of the repeal – until the twentieth century English villagers
continued to scratch, swim and even murder suspected witches.[68]
There was a lynching as late as 1945.[69] Nowadays education, com-
munications and medicine, combined with greater economic security,
have neutralized the tendency to suspect witchcraft in the face of
senseless loss, even though Western minds remain strongly influenced
by religion and superstition. Large parts of the world, however, have
the superstition without the material security, so that poor and fearful
people still associate misfortune with ill-will, and take remedial action.
This means witch-hunting. In sub-Saharan Africa the problem is
endemic. In South Africa's poverty-stricken Northern Province, more
than two hundred witch-lynchings were recorded for the period
1985–95, but the real figure is probably much higher. Witchfinders
sniff out suspects who are then banished, beheaded, or burnt alive.
Similar patterns are visible in many other parts of Africa, including
Angola, Ghana, Kenya, Nigeria, Uganda, Zambia and Zimbabwe;[70]
the Ministry of Home Affairs in Tanzania estimates that as many as
5,000 were murdered there between 1994 and 1998, and in Ituri, a
Congolese province, more than eight hundred perished during a

single witch-hunt in June 2001.[71] In India, too, perhaps two hundred women die every year. This is a particularly acute problem in Bihar, one of the most lawless states, where 'ojahs' identify witches on behalf of the community. Here in 2000 a female witchfinder confirmed the guilt of five suspects, who were then brutally killed.[72]

All of which prompts the question: how different are we in mentality from our seventeenth-century ancestors? – a question that becomes even more taxing if 'seventeenth-century ancestors' is replaced with 'fellow human beings in Africa and India'. The truth that many find unpalatable, even inconceivable, is that in our ideas, instincts and emotions we are not very different at all. Without peace and prosperity, liberty and welfare, and the political and economic stability on which those things depend, the thinking of the next generation in the West might swerve off in an altogether more mystical and malevolent direction. The bloodletting in the developing world is too startlingly similar to that which occurred in England during the civil war for this not to be so. Then, as now, witch-hunts involved not just savage persecutors tormenting innocent scapegoats, but ordinary neighbours with a close affinity to one another who also happened to believe in witchcraft powerfully enough to act out their most violent fantasies. This was as true of people who believed themselves to be witches as it was of those who pointed the finger. As a consequence, the seventeenth-century tragedy of the witchfinders is only partially that of Matthew Hopkins, the flawed protagonist, and of the harrowing deaths of his victims. It is at least as much a tale about feeling anxious and vulnerable in an indifferent world – a sensation of humanity.[73]

Notes

Abbreviations

BL	British Library, London
Bod.	Bodleian Library, Oxford
CRO	Cambridgeshire Record Office, Cambridge
CSPD	*Calendar of State Papers, Domestic*
CUL	Cambridge University Library
DNB	*Dictionary of National Biography*
EDR	Ely Diocesan Records (in CUL)
ERO	Essex Record Office, Chelmsford
EROC	Essex Record Office, Colchester
ESRO	East Suffolk Record Office, Ipswich
Essex 1645	H. F., *A true and exact Relation . . . of the late Witches* (1645)
Ewen I	C. L. Ewen, *Witch Hunting and Witch Trials* (1929)
Ewen II	C. L. Ewen, *Witchcraft and Demonianism* (1933)
HMC	Historical Manuscripts Commission
HRO	Cambridgeshire Record Office, Huntingdon
JHC	*Journals of the House of Commons*
JHL	*Journals of the House of Lords*
NRO	Norfolk Record Office, Norwich
PRO	Public Record Office, Kew ('The National Archives')
PSIA	*Proceedings of the Suffolk Institute of Archaeology*
Stearne	John Stearne, *A Confirmation And Discovery of Witch-Craft* (1648)
Suffolk 1645	*A True Relation of the Araignment of eighteene Witches* (1645)
VCH	*The Victoria History of the Counties of England*
WSRO	West Suffolk Record Office, Bury St Edmunds

For printed works, the place of publication is London unless otherwise stated.

Prologue

1. Firth and Rait (eds), *Acts and Ordinances*, i, 580. On the weather at this time, see Macfarlane (ed.), *Diary of Ralph Josselin*, 31.
2. Essex 1645, 1.
3. Edmund Staunton, *Rupes Israeliis* (1644), 10–11.
4. Essex 1645, 1. In the neighbouring parish of Bradfield, a woman of the same name was receiving charitable payments as early as 1610–11: EROC, D/Q 23/15/1, f. 147ᵛ.
5. Briggs, *Witches and Neighbours*, 8–9, 23, 68, 95; Alison Rowlands, 'Telling witchcraft stories: new perspectives on witchcraft and witches in the early modern period', in *Gender & History*, 10 (1998), 296–7.
6. See page 51. Cf. C. W. Cunnington and Phillis Cunnington, *Handbook of English Costume in the Seventeenth Century*, 2nd edn (1966), 11–12, 21–2, 29–30. For mention of Hopkins' dog, see Essex 1645, 3.
7. Hopkins, *Discovery*, 2–3.
8. The legend that Hopkins' first victim was a senile woman named Lacy, whom he tortured in a barn using a bradawl, appears to be fictitious: ERO, T/P 51/3.

1. Origins

1. Genesis 3:16; David Cressy, *Birth, Marriage, and Death: Ritual, Religion, and the Life-Cycle in Tudor and Stuart England* (Oxford, 1997), 55–73.
2. Durston and Eales (eds), *Culture of English Puritanism*, 1–31; Ronald Hutton, *The Rise and Fall of Merry England: the Ritual Year, 1400–1700* (Oxford, 1996), chs 4–6.
3. Thomas, *Religion*, 42–3, 68–9.
4. Ibid., 31, 222–3; Merry Wiesner, *Women and Gender in Early Modern Europe* (Cambridge, 1993), 64–7.
5. A likely date for Hopkins' birth is 1620. A bequest to the family in 1619 suggests that Hopkins had not yet been born, but by 1641 he was acting as a legal witness, indicating that he was at least 21: ESRO, IC/AA1/55/173; HD 10/1/9.
6. Linda Pollock, *Forgotten Children: Parent-Child Relations from 1500 to 1900* (Cambridge, 1984), 219–20, 222; Ralph Houlbrooke, *The English Family, 1450–1700* (1984), 129–34; Carew Hazlitt, *Popular Antiquities*, ii, 151, 155–6; iii, 243.

7. Pollock, *Forgotten Children*, 236, 250; Houlbrooke, *English Family*, 141, 149.

8. On the puritan mentality, see: Cliffe, *Puritan Gentry*, chs 1–3; Underdown, *Revel, Riot and Rebellion*, 41–2; F. D. Dow, *Radicalism in the English Revolution, 1640–1660* (Oxford, 1985), 60–2. For a telling illustration, see Tom Webster and Kenneth Shipps (eds), *The Diary of Samuel Rogers, 1634–1638* (Woodbridge, 2004).

9. W. H. Barrett, *Tales from the Fens* (1963), 131–2.

10. Venn and Venn (eds), *Alumni Cantabrigienses*, ii, 406; CRO, VC 17:298 (1583); P109/25/1. In 1549 a Mr Hopkins owned pasture in Littleport: VCH, *Cambs*, vol. 2, 72.

11. Thomas Alfred Walker (ed.), *A Biographical Register of Peterhouse Men*, 2 vols (Cambridge, 1927–30), ii, 184. Walker was mistaken to suggest that the witchfinder's father was a royal chaplain and the author of *A Sermon on Ezra* (1604).

12. CRO, VC 21:50 (1600).

13. H. R. Barker, *East Suffolk Illustrated* (Bury St Edmunds, 1909), 497–8; VCH, *Suffolk*, vol. 1, 686.

14. ESRO, IC/AA1/55/173.

15. CRO, P109/25/5; VCH, *Cambs*, vol. 4, 95–102. This had led to rioting by 1619, and caused a lingering legal dispute: Lindley, *Fenland Riots*, 39–40; CRO, P109/28/4, 17–19.

16. NRO, NCC 1634/233 (Playford).

17. Thomas, *Religion*, 200.

18. John Rylands Library, Manchester, English MS 524, ff. 9, 13, 15^v, 47, 63.

19. Webster, *Godly Clergy*; Holmes, *Eastern Association*, 28–9.

20. In 1635 Archbishop Laud reported to the king that the diocese of Norwich was 'much out of order': William Scott and James Bliss (eds), *The Works of the Most Reverend Father in God, William Laud*, 7 vols (Oxford, 1847–60), v, 334.

21. Venn and Venn (eds), *Alumni Cantabrigienses*, ii, 405. On godly education and Emmanuel College, see Cliffe, *Puritan Gentry*, ch. 5; Webster, *Godly Clergy*, 15–23.

22. Charles B. Jewson (ed.), *Transcript of Three Registers of Passengers from Great Yarmouth to Holland and New England, 1637–1639* (Norwich, 1954), 5, 10, 13.

23. James O. Halliwell (ed.), *The Autobiography and Correspondence of Sir*

Simonds D'Ewes, 2 vols (1845), ii, 116; Francis J. Bremer, 'The heritage of John Winthrop: religion along the Stour Valley, 1548–1630', in *New England Quarterly*, 70 (1997).

24. G. W. Robinson *et al.* (eds), *The Winthrop Papers*, 5 vols (Boston MA, 1929–47), iii, 105–7.

25. NRO, NCC 1634/233 (Playford). John Hopkins, a preacher in London and Essex in 1645, may have been Matthew's brother: Matthews (ed.), *Walker Revised*, 55, 166.

26. Lewis Hughes, *Grievances, or the Errours of the Service-Booke* (1641), 3, 8–10.

27. Katharine R. Firth, *The Apocalyptic Tradition in Reformation Britain, 1530–1645* (Oxford, 1979), ch. 7; John Morrill, *The Nature of the English Revolution* (Harlow, 1993), 118–47; Conrad Russell, *The Causes of the English Civil War* (Oxford, 1990), 222–4.

28. *A wonderfull And Strange Miracle* (1642); *A Relation of a Strange Apparition In an Ale-house* (1641), 2; [John Taylor], *The Liar* (1641), A2; *A Strange Wonder, Or, The Cities Amazement* (1642), A2–A4; *Five Strange and wonderfull Prophesies and Predictions* (1642); *Two strange Prophesies Predicting wonderfull events* (1642); *A Relation of a terrible Monster taken by a Fisherman neere Wollage* (1642), 2–3.

29. *A Strange And Lamentable accident . . . at Mears Ashby in Northamptonshire* (1642).

30. *Strange Newes from France* (1642); *The New Yeares Wonder* (1643), 3–7; John Vicars, *Prodigies & Apparitions, or Englands Warning Pieces* (1643), 2–4, 53. Some witnessed flocks of birds fighting in the sky: Carew Hazlitt, *Popular Antiquities*, iii, 188.

31. NRO, NCC 1634/233 (Playford). The approximate value of the legacy is calculated from Phelps Brown and Hopkins, 'Seven centuries of building wages', 168–78.

32. *Notes & Queries*, 2 (1850), 413–14; V. Heddon, 'The last of the witch-finders', in *National Review*, 96 (1931), 85; ESRO, HD 10/1/9. The Matthew Hopkins of Southwark pleading poverty in 1644 is not the witchfinder: M. A. E. Green (ed.), *Calendar of the Proceedings of the Committee for Advance of Money, 1642–1656*, 3 vols (1888), i, 457.

33. CUL, Palmer B62, A2–B3ᵛ; BL, Add. 5829, f. 9.

34. Ian Green, 'The persecution of scandalous and malignant parish clergy during the English Civil War', in *English Historical Review*, 94 (1979); James Sharpe, 'Scandalous and malignant priests in Essex: the impact of

grassroots Puritanism', in Colin Jones *et al.* (eds), *Politics and People in Revolutionary England* (Oxford, 1986).

35. George Salteren, *A Treatise against Images and Pictures in Churches* (1641), 7–8, 23–4, quotation at 7.

36. Everitt (ed.), *Suffolk and the Great Rebellion*, 11. See also: John Walter, 'Popular iconoclasm and the politics of the parish in eastern England, 1640–1642', in *Historical Journal*, 47 (2004); Manning, *English People and the English Revolution*, ch. 7.

37. PRO, SP 28/227 (unfol., 20 Mar. 1645).

38. Cooper (ed.), *Journal of William Dowsing*, 349–50; John Morrill, 'William Dowsing and the administration of iconoclasm in the Puritan revolution', ibid., 2–5.

39. Morrill, 'William Dowsing', 8, 12–13.

40. Deuteronomy 17:3, 18:10–12; II Chronicles 33:6–7; Revelation 21:8. See also Clark, *Thinking with Demons*, chs 23–5.

41. On the witch as arch-idolator, see John Hacket, *A Century of Sermons* (1675), 383. See also connections between idolatry, heresy and witchcraft in the 1640s: Benjamin Hubbard, *Sermo Secularis* (1648), 19; William Strong, *A Voice from Heaven* (1654), 4–5.

2. Strange Effects

1. Adam Fox, *Oral and Literate Culture in England, 1500–1700* (Oxford, 2000), ch. 5.

2. 33 Hen. VIII, c. 8 (1542); 1 Edw. VI, c. 12 (1547).

3. Sharpe, *Instruments of Darkness*, 88–90; Ewen II, 45–7.

4. Malcolm Gaskill, 'Witchcraft in early modern Kent: stereotypes and the background to accusations', in Barry *et al.* (eds), *Witchcraft in Early Modern Europe*, 263–4, 272–7; 5 Eliz. I, c. 16 (1563).

5. Ewen I, 117–18, 120–2, 124–31, 133–5, 137–43; *Examination . . . of certaine Wytches at Chensforde*; *A Detection of damnable driftes, practized by three Witches* (1579); G. R. Elton, *The Parliament of England, 1559–1581* (Cambridge, 1986), 190.

6. W. W., *A true and just Recorde, of the Information, Examination and Confession of all the Witches, taken at S. Oses* (1582); Ewen I, 143–6; Macfarlane, *Witchcraft*, 28; *The Apprehension and confession of three notorious Witches . . . at Chelmes-forde* (1589).

7. Thomas, *Religion*, 557.

8. I Jac. I, c. 12 (1604). In reaction to the Gunpowder Plot, the Act was revised in 1607 to cover treasonable cases: David Harris Wilson (ed.), *The Parliamentary Diary of Robert Bowyer, 1606–1607* (Minneapolis, 1931), 351–5.

9. James, *Daemonologie*; Notestein, *History of Witchcraft*, 101.

10. PRO, SP 38/10, Docquet, 2 July 1611; *CSPD 1611–18*, 53.

11. *CSPD 1611–18*, 398.

12. PRO, STAC 8/32/13.

13. Michael MacDonald, *Witchcraft and Hysteria in Elizabethan London* (1991), vii–lxiv.

14. BL, Add. 36674, ff. 134–7, quotation at f. 134^v.

15. Ewen I, 212–21.

16. It is important to see how far witchcraft was not just a belief but a self-evident reality: Briggs, *Witches and Neighbours*, 6–13, 164–6, ch. 10; David D. Hall, 'Witchcraft and the limits of interpretation', in *New England Quarterly*, 58 (1985), 259–61.

17. Edward Fairfax, *Daemonologia: a Discourse on Witchcraft*, ed. William Grainge (Harrogate, 1882); Notestein, *History of Witchcraft*, 144–5.

18. BL, Add. 32496, f. 5^v.

19. See, for example, the seriousness with which the alleged bewitchment of the Duchess of Buckingham was taken in September 1640: HMC, *Hastings*, iv, 89.

20. Bod., Ashm. 178, 184. See also Ashmole, *Lilly's History*, 46–8, 54–5.

21. Bod., Ashm. 186, f. 132.

22. Morant, *Essex*, i, 431–502; ERO, T/P 195/8, no. 13. Prince Hal calls Falstaff 'that roasted Manningtree ox': *Henry IV, Part One*, II: iv. For other literary references, see 'Notes & Queries: Manningtree', in *Essex Review*, 2 (1893), 261.

23. C. Fell-Smith, 'A note on Manningtree in 1611', in *Essex Review*, 15 (1906); Hollis Drake and Monica Drake, 'The Church of St Mary and St Michael, Mistley' (unpub. pamphlet, n.d.), 4, 7, 10–11; VCH, *Essex*, vol. 2, 268–9, 276–7, 351.

24. David Cressy, 'The Protestation protested, 1641 and 1642', in *Historical Journal*, 45 (2002); Edward Vallance, 'Protestation, vow, covenant and engagement: swearing allegiance in the English Civil War', in *Historical Research*, 75 (2002); Holmes (ed.), *Suffolk Committees*, 20–22; Walter, *Understanding Popular Violence*, 292–6, 304–5.

25. BL, Add. 5829, ff. 18–21; ERO, Q/SBa 2/56–8; Q/SR 324/118–19. For earlier witchcraft accusations at Stisted, see Macfarlane, *Witchcraft*, 258, 261–2, 265, 292.

26. Ewen I, 218–19; Macfarlane, *Witchcraft*, 143, 144; Bod., Tanner 180, f. 72.

27. *DNB*, s.v. 'Grimston, Harbottle' (Grimston's son); Venn and Venn (eds), *Alumni Cantabrigienses*, ii, 269; Cokayne (ed.), *Complete Baronetage*, i, 106.

28. Ewen I, 230; Essex 1645, 27. From here, Ewen I is used as a convenient source for indictments held at PRO, ASSI 35/86/1/1–2, 4–5, 7–13, 19, 41–6, 52–73, 78–91, 97–9.

29. Essex 1645, 21–9; Ewen I, 225, 230–1.

30. Macfarlane, *Witchcraft*, 138; Essex 1645, 8; Ewen I, 225. Details vary between Richard Edwards' deposition and the terms of the indictment.

31. Ewen I, 227–8; Ewen II, 262; Macfarlane, *Witchcraft*, 136; Essex 1645, 12.

32. Macfarlane, *Witchcraft*, 138; Ewen I, 218–19, 221, 225; Ewen II, 430; Essex 1645, 12–13, 22–3. On the fear of Catholics in these parts in 1645, see ERO, Q/SR 324/33.

33. Stearne, 39; Essex 1645, 12.

34. Ewen I, 220, 221, 224; Macfarlane, *Witchcraft*, 143, 144.

35. Bod., Rawl., B.393, f. 38ᵛ.

36. Stearne, 36; WSRO, IC 500/2/65/9. Stearne does not appear on the militia muster for 1638 at Long Melford or Lawshall, nor did he pay Ship Money in 1640; but there were men of that name at five other locations: Banks (ed.), *Able Men of Suffolk*, 117, 259, 271, 327, 360; Redstone (ed.), *Ship-Money*, 14, 168, 176, 202, 203.

37. WSRO, FL 600/4/1–2. There was a new minister at Lawshall in 1644: Francis Haslewood, 'Ministers of Suffolk ejected, 1643–4', in *PSIA*, 9 (1897), 309.

38. Bod., Ashm. 184, ff. 3, 36.

39. Ibid., ff. 37ᵛ, 39, 46ᵛ, 49. In March 1645 Lilly treated the wife of a Shoreditch weaver said to be bewitched: ibid., f. 82ᵛ.

40. Davies, *Four Centuries of Witch-Beliefs*, 179–80; *A True and Faithful Narrative of Oliver Cromwell's Compact with the Devil* (1720).

41. Bod., Ashm. 186, ff. 145–7ᵛ.

42. Essex 1645, 11–12.

43. Macfarlane, *Witchcraft*, 142; Webster, *Godly Clergy*, 46–7; Ewen I, 224–5.

44. Sharpe, *Instruments of Darkness*, 141.

45. Bowes was knighted in 1630, and sent his four sons to Cambridge between 1646 and 1663. So he was probably 35–45 in 1645: Venn and Venn (eds), *Alumni Cantabrigienses*, i, 191; W. A. Shaw (ed.), *The Knights of England*, 2 vols (1906), ii, 198.

46. Stearne, 14–15.

47. James, *Daemonologie*, 79–80. For a critique of royal opinion, see Perkins, *Discourse*, 206–8. Stearne said Clarke threatened him 'because I would have swome her': Stearne, 15.

48. The quotation comes from a book by Grimston's son, in which he passed on moral advice to his own son: Harbottle Grimston, *A Christian New-Years Gift* (1644), 80.

49. James Hart, *The Diet of the Diseased* (1633), 356.

50. Darren Oldridge, *The Devil in Early Modern England* (Stroud, 2000), ch. 4; Brian P. Levack, *The Witch-Craze in Early Modern Europe*, 2nd edn (Harlow, 1995), 29–38.

51. *Examination . . . of certaine Wytches at Chensforde*, A6ᵛ–7.

52. Clive Holmes, 'Popular culture? Witches, magistrates and divines in early modern England', in Steven L. Kaplan (ed.), *Understanding Popular Culture* (Berlin, 1984).

53. Thomas Potts, *The Wonderfull Discoverie of Witches in the Countie of Lancaster* (1613), ed. James Crossley (Manchester, 1845).

54. CUL, Palmer B62, A2. See also: Carlo Ginzburg, *Ecstasies: Deciphering the Witches' Sabbath* (1990), 1–6; Briggs, *Witches and Neighbours*, 31–59.

55. BL, Add. 36674, ff. 193–7, quotation at f. 196; Bod., Dodsw. 61, f. 47.

56. PRO, SP 16/268/22; Edward Hawkins (ed.), *Travels . . . (1634–1635) by Sir William Brereton*, Chetham Society, 1 (1844), 33. Cf. HMC, *Gawdy of Norfolk*, 147.

57. PRO, SP 16/271/15; Geoffrey Keynes, 'William Harvey and the witches', in John Carey (ed.), *Eyewitness to Science* (Cambridge MA, 1997). The Lancashire witches were also examined by the Bishop of Chester: HMC, *Cowper*, ii, 77, 80.

58. Barbara J. Shapiro, *Probability and Certainty in Seventeenth-Century England* (Princeton, 1983), chs 5–6; Unsworth, 'Witchcraft beliefs and criminal procedure', 90–8; Christina Larner, 'Crimen exceptum? The crime of witchcraft in Europe', in V.A.C. Gatrell *et al.* (eds), *Crime and*

the Law: the Social History of Crime in Western Europe since 1500 (1980). From a modern perspective, of course, standards of evidence fell: Ian Bostridge, *Witchcraft and its Transformations, c. 1650–c. 1750* (Oxford, 1997), 86.

59. CUL, Add. 6160, f. 141ᵛ.

60. Thomas, *Religion*, 532–3; Clive Holmes, 'Women: witnesses and witches', in *Past & Present*, 140 (1993); Jim Sharpe, 'Women, witchcraft and the legal process', in Kermode and Walker (eds), *Women, Crime and the Courts*.

61. Walter Stephens, *Demon Lovers: Witchcraft, Sex, and the Crisis of Belief* (Chicago, 2002).

62. E. Brooks Holifield, *The Covenant Sealed: the Development of Puritan Sacramental Theology in Old and New England* (New Haven, 1974); Thomas, *Religion*, 522–34. By the 1630s physical covenants had already been fully described in Thomas Cooper, *The Mystery of Witch-craft* (1617), chs 5–6; and Bernard, *Guide to Grand-Jury Men*, 105–117. In 1643 a man was prosecuted for making a written pact with the devil: J. C. Jeaffreson (ed.), *Middlesex County Records*, 4 vols (1886–92), iii, 88–9.

63. Cornelius Burges, *The First Sermon Preached to the Honourable House of Commons . . . at their Publique Fast* (1641), 27–9, 32–3, 64, quotation at 64.

64. Essex 1645, 10.

65. Thomas R. Forbes, 'The searchers', in Saul Jarcho (ed.), *Essays on the History of Medicine* (New York, 1976); Linda Pollock, 'Childbearing and female bonding in early modern England', in *Social History*, 22 (1997), 300–1; Laura Gowing, 'Ordering the body: illegitimacy and female authority in seventeenth-century England', in Michael J. Braddick and John Walter (eds), *Negotiating Power in Early Modern Society* (Cambridge, 2001). The first recorded official search of a witch was in 1579: Ewen II, 75.

66. J. A. Sharpe, 'Witchcraft and women in seventeenth-century England: some northern evidence', in *Continuity & Change*, 6 (1991); Diane Purkiss, 'Women's stories of witchcraft in early modern England: the house, the body, the child', in *Gender & History*, 7 (1995); Louise Jackson, 'Witches, wives and mothers: witchcraft persecution and women's confessions in 17th-century England', in *Women's History Review*, 4 (1995).

67. BL, Royal 17, C.XXIII, f. 7.

68. Elmer, 'Towards a politics of witchcraft', 110.

69. Breward (ed.), *Westminster Directory*, 23–4.
70. G[eorge] H[erbert], *Outlandish Proverbs* (1640), no. 297.
71. Clarke's interrogation is described in: Essex 1645, 2–6; Stearne, 14–16. 'Sack & Sugar' was not a toad, as Stearne recalled, but a rabbit.
72. Stearne, 16.

3. The Initiation

1. VCH, *Essex*, vol. 2, 67–132; Cockburn, *History of English Assizes*, 107; F. W. Austen, *Rectors of Two Essex Parishes and their Times* (Colchester, 1943), 49–50.
2. Allen H. Lanner (ed.), *Richard Brathwait's Whimzies* (New York, 1991), 178–82; Nickalls (ed.), *Journal of George Fox*, 432–3. On the terrible conditions in Colchester Castle, see James Parnell, *The Lambs Defence against Lyes* (1656), 3–4.
3. The means by which accusations spread outwards from Clarke to the other women is described in: Essex 1645, 6–10; Stearne, 39; Ewen I, 223, 227–8; Ewen II, 262. For details of Edwards and Tayler, see Macfarlane, *Witchcraft*, 143.
4. Ewen I, 218–19, 221; Essex 1645, 10.
5. Lonely women without male protection might become vulnerable if they sought company in pets: Alison Rowlands, 'Witchcraft and old women in early modern Germany', in *Past & Present*, 173 (2001), 64–9, 84–6; Erica Fudge, *Perceiving Animals: Humans and Beasts in Early Modern English Culture* (Basingstoke, 2000), 134. See above, page 208.
6. The witches' meeting is described in: Stearne, 16, 38; Essex 1645, 11–15; Ewen I, 224; Macfarlane, *Witchcraft*, 135–6. Regarding Rebecca West, compare the story in which a woman meets a dog that becomes her husband: Philip (ed.), *English Folktales*, 299.
7. The date for this given in the printed account is 'the 21. of March', which makes no sense – unless it was actually meant to read 'the 21. of April'.
8. Essex 1645, 12–13.
9. Ibid., 11–13.
10. Ernest Alan Wood, *A History of Thorpe-le-Soken* (Thorpe-le-Soken, 1975), 18, 50, 102–4, 108–16, 134–46; Matthews (ed.), *Walker Revised*, 149–50; Bowden (ed.), *Economic Change*, 140, 152.

11. The story of Margaret Moone is taken from: Essex 1645, 21–5; Ewen I, 225.

12. Essex 1645, 15–17.

13. Ibid., 15–18; Ewen I, 226; Nicholas Butler, *The Story of Wivenhoe* (Wivenhoe, 1989), ch. 2, esp. 15, 17, 28; VCH, *Essex*, vol. 10, 274–95.

14. Ewen I, 225; Essex 1645, 22–3. Earlier that year Edwards had been presented for supplying beer to an unlicensed alehouse in Manningtree, 'to the greivance of the minister and well affected [in] that parish': ERO, Q/SR 323/50.

15. Matthews (ed.), *Walker Revised*, 158; 'Notes & Queries: Great Clacton', in *Essex Review*, 29 (1920), 116–17; Macfarlane, *Witchcraft*, 143. Surnames of the accused appear on a list of Clacton's poor; Widow Wiles regularly received a shilling: EROC, D/P 179/8/1.

16. Essex 1645, 18–19, 34; Ewen I, 223, 228–9; Ewen II, 262. The pamphlet account said 'Mary Smith' but this should have read 'Mary Wiles'.

17. Ewen I, 223, 227; Ewen II, 262.

18. Essex 1645, 20–1; Ewen I, 226.

19. Harwich Borough Archives, HB 29/4; 29/10; 98/14, f. 42; 100/1, f. 64; 133/2; Leonard T. Weaver, *The Harwich Story* (Dovercourt, 1976), 34–6. In 1633 a beggar at the harbour was accused of keeping imps in a box and using them to sink a ship: HB 65/7.

20. Essex 1645, 28; Macfarlane, *Witchcraft*, 143; David A. Male, *From Serf to Citizen: a Thousand Years of Local Government in Harwich* (Harwich, 2004), 14.

21. Essex 1645, 26–7, 29; Ewen I, 230–1.

22. A. Rupert Hall and Marie Boas Hall (eds), *The Correspondence of Henry Oldenburg*, 12 vols (1965–86), v, 15. For an even more dubious story about the accused women of St Osyth, see *Full Tryals . . . Of Four Notorious Witches*.

23. VCH, *Essex*, vol. 2, 157–62.

24. Essex 1645, 29–32. Ewen I, 230. Cocke's age is given at PRO, KB 9/838, m. 376.

25. The sources for the spread of the St Osyth accusations are: Essex 1645, 33–5; Ewen I, 218–19, 224–6, 229–31; Ewen II, 262; Macfarlane, *Witchcraft*, 143.

26. Charles Kirkpatrick Sharpe (ed.), *Memorialls . . . by the Rev. Mr. Robert Law* (Edinburgh, 1818), lxv.

27. For illustration of these conditions, see BL, Add. 37491.

28. Ewen I, 223, 225, 231. Starling's crime was allegedly committed on 17 May 1645. For a petition from 1642 made by the desperate clothiers of Langham and Dedham, see ERO, T/A 364/1. See also Manning, *English People and the English Revolution*, 196–215.

29. Bod., Firth 7. Stearne said all cases originated in the Tendring Hundred: Stearne, 58.

30. Ewen I, 226–7; Ewen II, 262; Macfarlane, *Witchcraft*, 268.

31. Cliffe, *Puritans in Conflict*, 138.

32. BL, Stowe 842, ff. 1–17; Geoffrey Martin, *The Story of Colchester* (Colchester, 1959), 55–8.

33. EROC, D/B 5/Aa1/14; D/B 5/Ab1/17.

34. PRO, ASSI 35/86/1/1–2, 4–5; Kingston, *East Anglia*, 196–7.

35. EROC, D/B 5/Sb2/8, ff. 1–1ᵛ.

36. EROC, D/B 5/Ab1/17 (unfol.). Comparison of cost calculated according to wage-rates: Phelps Brown and Hopkins, 'Seven centuries of building wages', 168–78.

37. Stearne, 58, 60; Baker, *English Legal History*, 65. Stearne and Hopkins are not listed in the Court of Exchequer's outlawry books: PRO, E 172/22–3, 173/1.

4. Dark Horizons

1. Stearne refers to a period of witch-hunting from March or May 1645 to mid August 1645: Stearne, 18. Only one confession gives the date of apprehension – Lydia Taylor on 30 July – but this is no help for plotting progress as the location is unclear: Ewen I, 294.

2. Cooper (ed.), *Journal of William Dowsing*, 237. Dowsing did overlook some tiles in the sanctuary decorated with the 'IHS' monogram: Leslie Boreham, 'The Church of St John the Evangelist at Great Wenham' (unpub. pamphlet, 2002), 5.

3. Butler, *Hudibras*, ed. Wilders and de Quehen, 161; VCH, *Norfolk*, vol. 2, 294.

4. Carlton, *Going to the Wars*, 34–7, 263–4; HMC, *6th Report*, 39.

5. Walter, *Understanding Popular Violence*, 210; Everitt (ed.), *Suffolk and the Great Rebellion*, 13–14; Holmes, *Eastern Association*, 18–20; Elmer, 'Towards a politics of witchcraft', 108–10.

6. For the plausibility of this idea, see T. S. Willan, 'River navigation and

trade from Witham to the Yare, 1600–1750', in *Norfolk Archaeology*, 26 (1938).

7. Harold Whitaker (ed.), *A Descriptive List of the Printed Maps of Northamptonshire, AD 1576–1900* (Northampton, 1948), 27–34.

8. Hopkins, *Discovery*, 10; Bowden (ed.), *Economic Change*, 166; PRO, SP 28/219, 234; Nickalls (ed.), *Journal of George Fox*, 218.

9. Stearne, 22, 36; Ewen I, 300. Depositions relating to the Suffolk witch-hunt can be found at BL, Add. 27402, ff. 104–21. They are accurately transcribed in Ewen I, 291–313 and summarized in Ewen II, 281–302. References here are to Ewen's transcript.

10. Stearne, 27–8; Ewen II, 296, 296n.

11. Stearne, 32. At this time Sudbury had another witch, 'pretending she could do by her witch-craft whatever she pleased': Morton, 'Laurence Clarkson', 182.

12. It is unlikely that either Stearne or Hopkins 'knew his female anatomy', and even less likely that such knowledge could have been exploited: Anne Llewellyn Barstow, *Witchcraze: a New History of the European Witch Hunts* (1994), 129.

13. Ewen II, 298; Stearne, 36–7. Sussums was rated at two shillings in 1640, suggesting that he was neither rich nor poor: Redstone (ed.), *Ship-Money*, 187.

14. Walter, *Understanding Popular Violence*, 39–46, 53, 60, 191–7, 208–10, 215.

15. Stearne, 37, 41–2; Matthews (ed.), *Walker Revised*, 326.

16. Walter, *Understanding Popular Violence*, 45, 46–7.

17. Bryan G. Zacharias, *The Embattled Christian: William Gurnall and the Puritan View of Christian Warfare* (Edinburgh, 1995), 9–15; William Gurnall, *The Christian in Compleat Armour, Part I* (1655; 1656 edn), A4.

18. William Gurnall, *The Christian in Complete Armour*, 2 vols, ed. J. C. Ryle (Glasgow, 1864), i, 101, 183, 201, 228–9; ii, 73–4; Exodus 8:16–18.

19. Stearne, 22–3.

20. *DNB*, s.v. 'Grimston, Harbottle'. Grimston's mother also hailed from a gentry family at Lavenham, the Risbys: Cokayne (ed.), *Complete Baronetage*, i, 106.

21. Stearne, 22–3, 30.

22. Gurnall, *Christian*, ed. Ryle, ii, 201.

23. Stearne, 32.

24. Beryl Sims, 'The population of Bramford, 1553–1700', in *Suffolk Review*

(Jan. 2001), 4–9; Ewen I, 293–4. See also Briggs, *Witches and Neighbours*, 43–4.

25. Ewen I, 293; Stearne, 30–1.

26. Ewen I, 294; Stearne, 26–7, 30.

27. Stearne, 17, 30, 44.

28. Aleksandr Solzhenitsyn, quoted in Martin Amis, *Koba the Dread* (2002), 60.

29. Duncan Forrest, 'The methods of torture and its effects', in Duncan Forrest (ed.), *A Glimpse of Hell: Reports on Torture Worldwide* (1996), 106, 108–9, 117–18.

30. Stearne, 16. The historical search for 'what really happened' in such cases can be misguided and condescending: David Harley, 'Explaining Salem: Calvinist psychology and the diagnosis of possession', in *American Historical Review*, 101 (1996), 330.

31. Stearne, 31–2. Many East Anglians will have seen real black people at this time; see, for example, the vagrants whipped at Colchester in 1639: EROC, D/B 5/Sb1/4.

32. Stearne, 18. Stearne wrote 'Rochester' instead of 'Rossiter'. Forced recruitment caused considerable conflict in Suffolk that summer: *CSPD 1644–45*, 496.

33. The child, Thomas, was born in October 1645. See his tombstone in Rattlesden church.

34. Stearne, 26, 53; CUL, Add. 7515/2, f. 47; Bullen, 'Catalogue . . . of clergy', 296.

35. Stearne, 12, 33; WSRO, FL 500/4/1 (marriages 1621, 1632). John Scarfe appears on the county muster roll for 1638: Banks (ed.), *Able Men of Suffolk*, 280.

36. Stearne, 25; WSRO, FL 500/4/1. This Henry Carre was too old to be either of the undergraduates of that name at Cambridge in the 1630s: Venn and Venn (eds), *Matriculations and Degrees*, 131; Venn and Venn (eds), *Alumni Cantabrigienses*, i, 295. He was not rated in 1640, suggesting poverty: Redstone (ed.), *Ship-Money*, 175–6.

37. Stearne, 25.

38. Thomas, *Religion*, 114–20.

39. I am grateful to Diarmaid MacCulloch for this observation. See also: Nigel J. H. MacCulloch, 'Brief Notes on the History of Wetherden' (unpub. pamphlet, 1996); C. R. Scott-Murray, 'Pedigree of the family of Sulyard', in *The Genealogist*, 4 (1880).

40. Cooper (ed.), *Journal of William Dowsing*, 104.

41. Ewen II, 288–9; Ewen I, 292; Walter, *Understanding Popular Violence*, 209.

42. I am indebted to Ivan Bunn for information about Bacton from his unpublished study 'The Suffolk Victims of Matthew Hopkins and John Stearne, 1645–46' (1999).

43. Redstone (ed.), *Ship-Money*, 105–6; Stearne, 28; Nesta Evans, 'Farming and land-holding in wood-pasture of East Anglia, 1550–1650', in *PSIA*, 35 (1984), 303–8, 313.

44. Carew Hazlitt, *Popular Antiquities*, iii, 60.

45. BL, Add. 5829, f. 12. For examples, see: 'When this Old Cap was New' (*c.* 1640), in Christopher Marsh (ed.), *Songs of the Seventeenth Century* (Belfast, 1995); 'The World is Turned Upside Down' (1646), in Rollins (ed.), *Cavalier and Puritan*, 160–2.

46. These themes are brilliantly explored in Lyndal Roper, *Witch Craze: Terror and Fantasy in Baroque Germany* (New Haven, 2004).

47. Ewen II, 283; Ewen I, 302; Bunn, 'Suffolk Victims', 14.

48. Bunn, 'Suffolk Victims', 10–12, 17; Stearne, 29; Ewen II, 284; Ewen I, 301. Mary Hoggard married Richard Bush at Bacton, 12 October 1612; his parents were probably newcomers in the 1590s: Bunn, 'Suffolk Victims', 10–11.

49. Ewen II, 299; Ewen I, 302. Elizabeth Watcham's birth is not recorded in the parish register. The Watchams appear in 1608, suggesting they were migrants. Even if Elizabeth was a baby then, she was at least 37 in 1645: Bunn, 'Suffolk Victims', 16–17.

50. Bunn, 'Suffolk Victims', 18; Banks (ed.), *Able Men of Suffolk*, 94; Stearne, 28.

51. Stearne, 29; Ewen I, 301; Bunn, 'Suffolk Victims', 11–12, 17. Bush said the devil had come fifteen years earlier, which fits in with the parish record of her husband's death.

52. Stearne, 28; Ewen I, 301–2; Bunn, 'Suffolk Victims', 18.

53. Ewen I, 308. Ewen wrongly attributed her story to Mary Bacon: Ewen II, 282.

54. Ewen I, 307–8. The original says 'Mother Shipper'. Ewen attributes to her what belongs to Anne Alderman: Bunn, 'Suffolk Victims', 33. On Nathaniel Bacon, see the Bacon genealogical website, http://loricase.com/gedcom/fam04290.htm.

55. Ewen I, 308; Walter, *Understanding Popular Violence*, 208–11.

56. Ewen I, 297–8.
57. Ibid.
58. Ibid., 312–13.
59. Ibid., 308, 312–13; ESRO, B105/2/1, f. 81ᵛ.

5. First Blood

1. Bod., Bankes 58, ff. 15–16.
2. Holmes, *Eastern Association*, ch. 2; Everitt (ed.), *Suffolk and the Great Rebellion*, ch. 4; ESRO, C/2/9/1/1/8/7, pp. 412–13. The iconoclast Dowsing had connections with the godly hierarchy in Ipswich: Cooper (ed.), *Journal of William Dowsing*, 334–6.
3. ESRO, C/3/3/2/68, ff. 5, 5ᵛ. This dinner cost an enormous sum: £17 3s. 9d.
4. BL, Add. 25344, ff. 85–93.
5. Bod., E Musaeo 173, ff. 37–7ᵛ; CUL, Add. 7515/11; Eveline C. Gurdon (ed.), *County Folk-Lore . . . Suffolk* (1893), 170; BL, Royal 17, C.XXIII, ff. 1–6ᵛ. See also: Thomas, *Religion*, 648–50, 655–8, 776–7; Carew Hazlitt, *Popular Antiquities*, iii, 67–78.
6. Bod., Ashm. 182, ff. 167ᵛ–70; Ashm. 198, ff. 186ᵛ–7; BL, Add. 36674, f. 148.
7. Stearne, 18; *Witches Apprehended . . . and Executed*, B1ᵛ, C3; BL, Add. 36674, f. 148. On the water ordeal, see also: Kittredge, *Witchcraft*, ch. 15; Robert Bartlett, *Trial by Fire and Water: the Medieval Judicial Ordeal* (Oxford, 1986), 144–8.
8. Kittredge, *Witchcraft*, ch. 17; Michael Dalton, *The Countrey Justice* (1618), 251.
9. Ewen I, 294–5. Another Playford woman refused to confess: Ewen I, 298.
10. Dalton, *Countrey Justice*, 250–1. There is some truth in the statement that 'Hopkins was the first to reduce the practice of witchfinding to a science and to systematise the methods in vogue': J. O. Jones, 'Matthew Hopkins, Witchfinder', in Thomas Seccombe (ed.), *Lives of Twelve Bad Men* (1894), 58.
11. Bod., Don, c.95, ff. 7–7ᵛ; R. M. Phipson, 'Framlingham Castle', in *PSIA*, 3 (1863); John Ridgard (ed.), *Medieval Framlingham: Select Documents* (Woodbridge, 1985), 1, 5–7; R. Green, *The History . . . of Framlingham and Saxsted* (1834), 172–94.

12. NRO, NCC 1634/233 (Playford).

13. ESRO, JC 1/29/1, pt. 2, pp. 3, 34, 166; Muriel Kilvert, 'The Reverend Richard Golty and his tithe account book', in *Suffolk Review*, 17 (1991); Matthews (ed.), *Walker Revised*, 335–6; HMC, *7th Report*, 31–2; HLRO, Main Papers, 31 Oct. 1645, f. 128; PRO, SP 19/21; Walter, *Understanding Popular Violence*, 46, 208, 210.

14. ESRO, FC 101/E2/26; FC 101/G7/1–2; JC 1/29/1, pt.1, pp. 15–17, 25, 30; Ewen I, 304–5; Sharpe, *Instruments of Darkness*, 240n.

15. Ewen I, 304–5. In 1644, for example, Weeting went to court to have a pregnant unmarried woman removed from the parish: ESRO, FC 101/E2/26.

16. Ewen I, 305–7. It was believed that a supple corpse was an omen of another death in the same family: Opie and Tatem (eds), *Dictionary of Superstitions*, 98.

17. Ewen I, 303.

18. Ibid., 304, 306–7; ESRO, FC 101/E2/26.

19. Ewen I, 303–4; ESRO, FC 101/E2/26.

20. Ewen I, 304–6.

21. Ewen II, 286; Ewen I, 296.

22. Anne Driver (related to Ellen Driver): Ewen I, 312.

23. Ibid., 311–12; *DNB*, s.v. 'Bacon, Nathaniel'.

24. Ewen I, 291; ESRO, B105/2/1, f. 136; Suckling, *History . . . of Suffolk*, i, 287–90.

25. Ewen I, 296.

26. Michael Gooch and Sheila Gooch, *The People of a Suffolk Town: Halesworth, 1100–1900* (Halesworth, 1999); Suckling, *History . . . of Suffolk*, ii, 325–69.

27. On the Everards, see: Suffolk 1645, 3–4; Ewen I, 309–11.

28. Ewen I, 311.

29. Ibid., 309.

30. Ibid., 302–3. Willan also persecuted Quakers: Elmer, 'Saints or sorcerers', 176–7.

31. Hutchinson, *Historical Essay*, 63–4; *DNB*, s.v. 'Hutchinson, Francis'. Hoxne had been unusually active in ejecting its minister: Holmes (ed.), *Suffolk Committees*, 74–5.

32. Barbara Donegan, 'The clerical patronage of Robert Rich, 2nd Earl of Warwick, 1619–1642', in *Proceedings of the American Philosophical Society*, 120 (1976); *DNB*, s.v. 'Rich, Robert', 'Wilson, Arthur'; Walter,

Understanding Popular Violence, 42–3. Warwick attended a committee on 11 July, then was absent from Parliament for the week of the 12th–19th: *CSPD 1645–47*, 14, 18, 22–8; *JHL*, vii, 493, 503.

33. Ewen I, 46; Firth and Rait (eds), *Acts and Ordinances*, i, 191–2; Morrill, *Revolt in the Provinces*, 92–3, 107–8, 116–17.

34. Walter, *Understanding Popular Violence*, 129–32.

35. ERO, Q/SR 326/64, gaol delivery, 17 Jul. 1645; CUL, Add. 33, ff. 1, 22–23. On Wilson's reflections, see also Francis Peck, *Desiderata Curiosa* (1732), 26–7.

36. Gilbert Torry, *The Book of Chelmsford* (Buckingham, 1985), 11; Philip Lee Ralph, *Sir Humphrey Mildmay: Royalist Gentleman . . . 1653–1652* (New Brunswick, 1947), 152; Walter, *Understanding Popular Violence*, 24, 61, 125, 147, 221, 277, 295, 328.

37. Torry, *Book of Chelmsford*, 13, 81.

38. PRO, ASSI 35/86/1/99; Cockburn, *History of English Assizes*, 61–2.

39. Cockburn, *History of English Assizes*, 108; PRO, ASSI 35/86/1/1–2, 4–5.

40. Margery Grew and Joan Rowle: Ewen I, 222. Rebecca West was not listed.

41. PRO, ASSI 35/86/1.

42. David Laing (ed.), *Letters and Journals of Robert Baillie*, 3 vols (Edinburgh, 1841–2), i, 316. On courtroom procedure, see: Baker, *English Legal History*, 509–11; Cockburn, *History of English Assizes*, 66–8, 116–24; PRO, SP 16/520/33.

43. Delivered by proclamation and bound over to the next assizes: Ewen I, Appendix I. Rejected bills – marked '*ignoramus*' – may have been filed separately, and lost.

44. PRO, ASSI 35/86/1/14, 99.

45. Essex 1645, 32; Macfarlane, *Witchcraft*, 143; Ewen I, 224; Ewen II, 262.

46. Essex 1645, 7–8, 13.

47. Ewen II, 262; Ewen I, 223; Macfarlane, *Witchcraft*, 267.

48. Essex 1645, 35–6. A later commentator reprimanded Bowes for his credulity, assuming that the informant must have been drunk: Morant, *Essex*, i, 442n.

49. Essex 1645, 12; Macfarlane, *Witchcraft*, 135; Ewen I, 224.

50. Macfarlane, *Witchcraft*, 268; Ewen II, 262.

51. HLRO, Main Papers, 10 Mar. 1646, f. 136; Macfarlane, *Witchcraft*, 269. The clergyman was a Mr Gray, who had Mary Coppin of Kirby-le-

Soken spared: PRO, ASSI 35/86/1/97^v. On Conyers, see the note in Gaskill (ed.), *Hopkins Trials*, 465.

52. Macfarlane, *Witchcraft*, 269; Ewen I, 230–1; Essex 1645, 26–9.

53. Essex 1645, 10, 13, 18, 28.

54. Ewen I, 225; Essex 1645, 25; *Scotish Dove* (25 Jul.–1 Aug. 1645), 732; Macfarlane, *Witchcraft*, 269; PRO, KB 9/838, mm. 372, 382.

55. Warwick returned to the Lords on 21 July: *JHL*, vii, 503; *CSPD 1645–47*, 30.

56. CUL, Add. 33, ff. 22–3^v.

6. Malignants

1. Essex 1645, A2; Plomer, *Dictionary of Booksellers*, 142; Gaskill (ed.), *Hopkins Trials*, 1–2, 465–6. For another version, see R. B., *Kingdom of Darkness*, 148–62.

2. Peter Ackroyd, *London: the Biography* (2000), 469.

3. Bernard Capp, 'Popular culture and the English Civil War', in *History of European Ideas*, 10 (1989). On the supply of news, see: Joseph Frank, *The Beginnings of the English Newspaper, 1620–1660* (Cambridge MA, 1961), chs 2–3, 5–6; Joad Raymond, *The Invention of the Newspaper: English Newsbooks, 1641–1649* (Oxford, 1996).

4. Quoted in Douglas Bush (ed.), *English Literature in the Earlier Seventeenth Century, 1600–1660* (Oxford, 1962), 48.

5. The book-collector George Thomason obtained his copy on 19 August.

6. Bod., Ashm. 186, f. 165^v. For more astrological predictions at this time, see William Lilly, *A Collection of Ancient and Moderne Prophesies* (1645).

7. *A Diary, or an Exact Journall* (1–8 May 1645), 8; Joseph Glanvill, *A Blow at Modern Sadducism* (1668), 43. On the fear of child-abduction at this time, see also Anne Laurence, *Women in England, 1500–1760: a Social History* (1994), 84–5.

8. Whitelocke, *Memorials*, i, 431; *JHC*, iv, 90, 105, 113, 134–5, 171, 206, 246, 254; Firth and Rait (eds), *Acts and Ordinances*, i, 681.

9. See, for example, Joseph Caryl, *The Arraignment of Unbelief* (1645), 13–17.

10. *The City Alarum, Or The Weeke of our miscarriages* (1645), 2. For a similar analogy, see Christopher Love, *Englands Distemper* (1645), 16–17, 21.

11. [Edward Fleetwood], *A Declaration, Of a strange and Wonderfull Monster* (1645), 4; *A Strange and Wonderfull Example of Gods Judgements* (1645); *The most Strange and Wounderfull apperation of blood in a poole at Garraton* (1645), 2, 7.

12. Ephraim Pagitt, *Heresiography* (1645), C4ᵛ; *XXXVI Severall Religions, Held by the Cavaliers* (1645), A4ᵛ.

13. *JHL*, vii, 503.

14. [John Downame], *Annotations upon all the Books of the Old and New Testament*, 2nd edn, 2 vols (1651), i, see under Exodus 22:18.

15. Ewen, *Trials of John Lowes*, 1; Robert Warner, 'All Saints' Church, Brandeston, Suffolk' (unpub. pamphlet, 1994), 1–3, 5, 9.

16. BL, Add. 5829, f. 3 (1757). Cf. David Cressy, *Agnes Bowker's Cat: Travesties and Transgressions in Tudor and Stuart England* (Oxford, 2000), ch. 9, esp. 139–40.

17. PRO, STAC 8/200/27, m. 1–2; KB 27/1448, Pt. 1, m. 79; KB 9/747, Pt. 2, m. 97.

18. PRO, KB 27/1451, Pt. 1, m. 113.

19. PRO, STAC 8/200/27, m. 2; KB 27/1464, Pt. 1, mm. 337–337ᵛ; Ewen, *Witchcraft in the Star Chamber*, 50. A judgment in favour of Lowes made at King's Bench was overturned at Exchequer: William Sheppard, *Action upon the Case for Slander* (1662), 42.

20. BL, Add. 27402, f. 114ᵛ; *Magazine of Scandall*, esp. A4ᵛ–B3.

21. There were at least three other cases, 1617–19: Gaskill, *Crime and Mentalities*, 56–7.

22. Baxter, *Certainty of the World of Spirits*, 53; *Magazine of Scandall*, B3ᵛ.

23. Ewen, *Witchcraft in the Star Chamber*, 51.

24. *Magazine of Scandall*; Matthews (ed.), *Walker Revised*, 334; HMC, *6th Report*, 180.

25. Stearne, 39; Essex 1645, 8. It was rumoured that Mistress Waite was executed, and that she was an Independent: *Parliaments Post* (23–29 Jul. 1645), 1, 8; *Weekly Account* (23–29 Jul. 1645), 3; *A Diary, or an Exact Journall* (24–31 Jul. 1645), 5–6.

26. II Corinthians 11:13–15; *Magazine of Scandall*, A3ᵛ–A4; Suffolk 1645, 3. Some said that Laud was at least a broker for Antichrist, and that Arminianism had 'bewitched' the nation: Christopher Hill, *Antichrist in Seventeenth-Century England*, revised edn (1990), 37, 68, 70, 75–7, ch. 3; Robert Baillie, *Errours and Induration* (1645), A2ᵛ.

27. Ewen I, 300–1, 307.

28. Bod., Walker, c.1, f. 298; Hutchinson, *Historical Essay*, 68.

29. Rivett-Carnac, 'Witchcraft'; Ewen, *Trials of John Lowes*, 6.

30. ESRO, FC 105/D1/1; Ewen I, 300, 307.

31. VCH, *Suffolk*, vol. 1, 192; Stearne, 23–4; Baxter, *Certainty of the World of Spirits*, 53. Alternatively, the ship came from *Harwich* and 'with the extreame tempesteous Seas raised by blusterous windes the said Ship was cast away, wherein were many passengers, who were by this meanes swallowed up by the merciless waves': Suffolk 1645, 3.

32. R. W. Ketton-Cremer, *Norfolk in the Civil War* (1969), chs 13–14. By 1676, 2.2 per cent was Catholic compared to a national average of 10 per cent: T. B. Trappes-Lomax, 'Roman Catholicism in Norfolk, 1559–1780', in *Norfolk Archaeology*, 32 (1961), 41.

33. NRO, C/S3, box 36 (unfol., 1644–5), indictments of Margaret Frances, Anne Forde, Alice Cooke, Robert Carsey and Margaret Mego. Frances came from 'Knishall', which may be Knetteshall in Suffolk, but perhaps the indictment should have read 'Rushall'.

34. David Dymond, *The Norfolk Landscape* (1985), 205, 209–13; W. G. Hoskins, *The Making of the English Landscape* (1988), 121.

35. *A Perfect Diurnall of Some Passages in Parliament* (21–28 Jul. 1645), 830; Ketton-Cremer, *Norfolk in the Civil War*, 304–9. Bulstrode Whitelocke learned of the executions when he heard that Scarborough Castle had surrendered on 22 July: *Memorials*, i, 487.

36. *Signes and wonders*, 2, 4–5. The same publication carried reports of a witch disguised as a gentlewoman at Swaffham, a town west of Norwich: ibid., 3–4.

37. HMC, *6th Report*, 42; HLRO, Main Papers, 10 Jan. 1645, ff. 53–9.

38. BL, Add. 19398, f. 200.

39. *True Informer* (21–26 Jul. 1645), 108–9.

40. *Parliaments Post* (23–29 Jul. 1645), 8. It was said that a youth conjured the devil, then tricked him into leaving the book behind: *Weekly Account* (23–29 Jul. 1645), 3.

41. *Scotish Dove* (25 Jul.–1 Aug. 1645), 732; Stearne, 54; *True Informer* (21–26 Jul. 1645), 109; Baxter, *Certainty of the World of Spirits*, 53. Mary Fuller of Combs confessed in the gaol at Bury, having formerly resisted under interrogation: Ewen I, 308.

42. *A Diary, or an Exact Journall* (24–31 Jul. 1645), 5–6.

43. *A Most Certain, Strange, and true Discovery of a Witch* (1643); *Mercurius Civicus* (21–28 Sept. 1643), 140; Gaskill (ed.), *Hopkins Trials*, 401–2;

Diane Purkiss, 'Desire and its deformities: fantasies of witchcraft in the English Civil War', in *Journal of Medieval and Early Modern Studies*, 27 (1997); Clark, *Thinking with Demons*, ch. 36.

44. Ewen I, 309–11; *Parliaments Unspotted-Bitch*, A2; *A Dialogue, Or Rather a Parley between Prince Ruperts Dogge . . . and Tobies Dog* (1643), A1^v; *Observations upon Prince Ruperts White Dog* (1643), A2, A4^v. According to one popular ballad, the dog was brought into the world by a witch, but soon 'Excell'd his Mother in her Witcherie': quoted in Tristram Hunt, *The English Civil War* (2002), 111–12.

45. *A Dog's Elegy, Or Ruperts Tears* (1644). For another account of the dog's death, see *Diutinus Britanicus* (25 Nov.–2 Dec. 1646), 2.

46. *A Diary, or an Exact Journall* (24–31 Jul. 1645), 6.

47. *Scotish Dove* (25 Jul.–1 Aug. 1645), 733; Joad Raymond (ed.), *Making the News: an Anthology of the Newsbooks of Revolutionary England* (Moreton-in-Marsh, 1993), 153; *Mercurius Aulicus* (10–17 Aug. 1645), 1697–8; I Samuel 15:23.

48. *Mercurius Britanicus* (25 Aug.–1 Sept. 1645). Cf. Francis Woodcock, *Christ's Warning-piece* (1644), 15–16, 18. On demonology as a form of political satire and as a means of explaining military victories, see: Elmer, 'Saints or sorcerers', 165–6; K. M. Briggs, *Pale Hecate's Team* (1962), 27–30.

49. PRO, C 181/5, f. 256^v; PRO, C 231/6, 13. Godbold had been commissioned as a judge in June 1640: PRO, C 181/5, f. 175^v; *DNB*, s.v. 'Godbold, John'.

50. Clark, *Lives of Sundry Eminent Persons*, 172.

51. Baker, *English Legal History*, 24. Records of special commissions issued at King's Bench are missing for 1632–61, as are Great Seal warrants for 1645–6. To accelerate justice, in August 1645 Commissioners of the Great Seal were ordered to issue special commissions to anyone they chose: *JHC*, iv, 247; *JHL*, vi, 683, 687, 688–9.

52. BL, Add. 36076. Serjeants were normally only judges of civil law but, because of the war, from August 1644 were authorized to execute assize commissions in such counties as were held by Parliament at that time: *JHL*, vi, 686, 687, 688, 689.

53. *DNB*, s.v. 'Calamy, Edmund'; BL, Harl. 1753, f. 47^v; Edmund Calamy, *A just and necessary Apology Against An unjust Invective* (1646), 7; Edmund Calamy, *An Indictment against England* (1645), 1–3, 8–9, 29–32; Cliffe, *Puritans in Conflict*, 50–1; Webster, *Godly Clergy*, 231, 233, 245, 260, 327.

54. *DNB*, s.v. 'Fairclough, Samuel'; Clark, *Lives of Sundry Eminent Persons*, 153–92; T. W. Davids, *Annals of Evangelical Nonconformity in the County of Essex* (1863), 609–15; Alan H. Nelson (ed.), *Records of Early English Drama: Cambridge*, 2 vols (Toronto, 1989), i, 543–4; Webster, *Godly Clergy*, 20–1, 30–1, 36–7, 101.

55. Samuel Fairclough, *The Troublers Troubled* (1641), 38.

56. Stearne, 16–17, 54–5.

57. PRO, SP 28/243 (unfol., 22 Oct. 1645); Dr Williams's Lib., MS 38.3, Pt. I, f. 84^v; *DNB*, s.v. 'Fairclough, Samuel'. Godbold visited Sudbury in 1645, staying at The Crown at a cost of six shillings: WSRO, EE 501/2/7, accounts 1645 (unfol.).

58. John Godbold, *Reports of Certain Cases . . . at Westminster* (1652), 341.

59. BL, Harl. 1753.

60. Unsworth, 'Witchcraft beliefs and criminal procedure', 76–8; Keith Parry, 'Witchcraft trials in 17th-century East Anglia', unpub. MA thesis, University of East Anglia, 1998, 15, 18, 40.

61. Macfarlane, *Witchcraft*, 269.

62. BL, Add. 25465, ff. 38–8^v; Walter, *Understanding Popular Violence*, 60.

63. *CSPD 1645–47*, 83, 84, 85, 90; *The Royall Entertainment of the King by the Royalists of Huntington* (1645), 7–8; Nehemiah Wallington, *Historical Notices of Events Occurring Chiefly in the Reign of Charles I*, 2 vols (1869), ii, 269–70.

64. ESRO, HD 36/A/163; David Allen (ed.), *Ipswich Borough Archives, 1255–1835* (Woodbridge, 2000), 583–7; Kingston, *East Anglia*, 218–20; VCH, *Hunts*, vol. 2, 19–20.

65. *Royall Entertainment of the King*, 6.

66. Suffolk 1645, 5; *Scotish Dove* (29 Aug.–6 Sept. 1645), 773; VCH, *Suffolk*, vol. 1, 678. One diarist recorded that he went 'to hear the triall of the Witches' on 20 August, but this probably just indicates the delay in proceedings: James Crossley (ed.), *The Diary and Correspondence of Dr John Worthington*, Chetham Society, 13 (1848), 22.

67. Clark, *Lives of Sundry Eminent Persons*, 172.

68. Ibid.

69. Ewen II, 281.

70. Ewen I, 292, 294, 300, 307–8; Stearne, 55.

71. Stearne, 18, 36–7; Ewen I, 307–8; Ewen, *Witchcraft in the Star Chamber*, 7. It is very unlikely that Lowes cross-examined Hopkins: R. Freeman Bullen, 'Sequestrations in Suffolk: part II', in *PSIA*, 19 (1927), 143.

72. Clark, *Lives of Sundry Eminent Persons*, 172; Ewen I, 309–11.
73. Stearne, 25; Suffolk 1645, 5.
74. Stearne, 14.
75. Ibid.
76. James Bland, *The Common Hangman* (Hornchurch, 1984), 17.
77. Stearne, 24; Hutchinson, *Historical Essay*, 66–8.

7. Hellish Invention

1. Brian Bailey, *Hangmen of England* (1989), 7–8, 14. On execution crowds, see also: J. A. Sharpe, *Judicial Punishment in England* (1990), 31–5; V. A. C. Gatrell, *The Hanging Tree: Executions and the English People, 1770–1868* (Oxford, 1994), esp. chs 2–3.
2. 'Burials on the north sides of churchyards', in *Essex Review*, 1 (1892).
3. Stearne, 36–7.
4. 'Extracts from the sessions order book, 1639–1651', in *PSIA*, 15 (1915), 181; Ewen II, 299; ESRO, B105/2/1, f. 136; Stearne, 25.
5. ESRO, C/2/9/1/1/8/7, p. 417; B105/2/1, ff. 78–9. In France, in the years 1643–4 – a time of high taxation – witchfinders' fees left communities in debt, rapidly cooling their witch-hunting ardour: Briggs, *Witches and Neighbours*, 193–4, 196–9, 308–9.
6. CUL, Buxton Papers, Box 96/3 (Norfolk); EDR, E45, assizes: act books and calendars (Isle of Ely); EROC, D/B 5/Ab1/17 (Essex quarter sessions, 1645).
7. PRO, SP 28/243 (unfol., 22 October 1645); Everitt (ed.), *Suffolk and the Great Rebellion*, 25, 73; WSRO, EE 501/2/7, Sudbury accounts 1645.
8. ESRO, B105/2/1, ff. 93^v, 136.
9. Mitchell and Struthers (eds), *Minutes . . . of the Westminster Assembly*, 133; John Lightfoot, *A Sermon Preached before the . . . Commons* (1645), 1, 22.
10. BL, Add. 27402, ff. 104–21.
11. Plomer, *Dictionary of Booksellers*, 89; Suffolk 1645, 5.
12. P., *The Antidote Animadverted* (1645), 8; *Scotish Dove* (29 Aug.–6 Sept. 1645), 773; *Parliaments Post* (2–9 Sept. 1645), 7.
13. *Moderate Intelligencer* (4–11 Sept. 1645), 217; *Signes and wonders*, 2–3; *Scotish Dove* (29 Aug.–6 Sept. 1645), 773; *Strange and fearfull newes from Plaisto* (1645).
14. P., *Antidote Animadverted*, 8.

15. HMC, *Rye & Hereford*, 216; William Turner, *A Complete History Of the Most Remarkable Providences* (1697), 116–20.

16. Bod., Rawl., Poet 16. I am grateful to Heide Towers for bringing this manuscript to my attention. See also Jane Milling, 'Siege and cipher: the closet drama of the Cavendish sisters', in *Women's History Review*, 6 (1997).

17. *The Examination, Confession, Triall, and Execution of Joane Williford, Joan Cariden, and Jane Hott . . . At Feversham* (1645). In the previous year a woman had been hanged at Sandwich, another self-governing Kentish Cinque Port: William Boys, *Collections for an History of Sandwich*, 2 vols (Canterbury, 1792), ii, 714.

18. NRO, Y/C 19/7, f. 71^v; Harrod, 'Notes on . . . Great Yarmouth', 249.

19. ESRO, EE 1/12/2, ff. 248, 249^v. Approximate value of Phillips's fee calculated according to Phelps Brown and Hopkins, 'Seven centuries of building wages', 168–78.

20. John Patten, 'Patterns of migration and movement of labour to three pre-industrial East Anglian towns', in *Journal of Historical Geography*, 2 (1976).

21. BL, Add. 19398, f. 165.

22. *CSPD 1645–47*, ix–x; *Scotish Dove* (29 Aug.–6 Sept. 1645), 770, 772; H. G. Tibbutt (ed.), *The Letter Books of Sir Samuel Luke, 1644–45* (1963), 119; Thomas More, *A Discovery of Seducers* (1646), 12–13. The biblical text was Matthew 7:15: 'Beware of false prophets, which come to you in sheep's clothing.'

23. *DNB*, s.v. 'Corbett, Miles'; *Lucifers Lifeguard* (1660); Walker, *History of Independency*, 63. I am grateful to Ivan Bunn, from whose research these references came.

24. John Brinsley, *The Saints Solemne Covenant with their God* (1644), 36; *DNB*, s.v. 'Brinsley, John'; Matthews (ed.), *Calamy Revised*, 75; Webster, *Godly Clergy*, 65. This may have been Thomas Whitfield, author of *The Extent of Divine Providence* (1651).

25. *Parliaments Unspotted-Bitch*, A2^v.

26. This case is based on: Ewen II, 280; Hale, *Collection of Modern Relations*, 46–8; Stearne, 53–4. Unlike the accused, most accusers came from respectable families: *A Calendar of the Freemen of Great Yarmouth, 1429–1800* (Norwich, 1910), 60–82.

27. Hale, *Collection of Modern Relations*, 47–8.

28. NRO, Y/C 19/7, f. 76^v; HMC, *9th Report*, 320.

29. Henry Manship, *The History of Great Yarmouth* (1854), 256–7. The

account of the trial is based on the borough court sessions book, 1630–51: NRO, Y/S 1/2, ff. 195–200.

30. On the Fassetts, see Paul Rutledge (ed.), *A Calendar of Great Yarmouth Enrolled Apprenticeship Indentures, 1563–1665*, in *Norfolk Genealogy*, 11 (1980), 75.

31. NRO, Y/S 1/2, ff. 195–200; Manship, *History of Great Yarmouth*, 272–4.

32. ESRO, C/2/9/1/1/8/7, pp. 412–18; Vincent B. Redstone, *Memorials of Old Suffolk* (1908), 267–8. Women reputedly burned at Norwich in 1648 were in fact hanged: Philip Browne, *The History of Norwich* (Norwich, 1814), 49: NRO, NCR Case 20a/11, f. 110.

33. Thomas, *Religion*, 160; Ruth Campbell, 'Sentence of death by burning for women', in *Journal of Legal History*, 5 (1984).

34. *Lawes against Witches*, 7; Morton, 'Laurence Clarkson', 165–6. For a list of witnesses and charges against Mary Lakeland, see Redstone, *Memorials*, 268.

35. *A Lying Wonder discovered, and the Strange and Terrible Newes from Cambridge proved false* (1659); Elmer, 'Saints or sorcerers'; 145–79; Underdown, *Revel, Riot and Rebellion*, 252–4; J. F. McGregor, 'The Baptists: fount of all heresy', in J. F. McGregor and B. Reay (eds), *Radical Religion in the English Revolution* (Oxford, 1984), 4.

36. E. S. de Beer (ed.), *The Diary of John Evelyn*, 6 vols (Oxford, 2000), iii, 179. Evelyn's visit to Ipswich took place on 9 July 1656.

37. Stuart Clark, 'Inversion, misrule and the meaning of witchcraft', in *Past & Present*, 87 (1980).

38. *Lawes against Witches*, 7–8; ESRO, C/2/9/1/1/8/7, pp. 412–13, 415–16.

39. Peter Bishop, *The History of Ipswich* (1995), 64–5. A burning is described in *The Witch of Wapping* (1652), 7–8. On superstitions and souvenir-hunting at executions, see: John Aubrey, *Miscellanies* (1696), 97–8; Carew Hazlitt, *Popular Antiquities*, ii, 241–3.

40. *Lawes against Witches*, 8.

41. Gaskill (ed.), *Hopkins Trials*, 57; *Lawes against Witches*, 7.

42. ESRO, C/3/3/2/68, f. 5ᵛ. In 1646 it cost £1 to hang a witch: C/3/3/2/70, f. 4ᵛ.

43. ESRO, C/2/9/1/1/8/7, p. 417.

44. Based on costs accounted at Huntingdon in 1644: PRO, SP 28/234 (unfol.).

45. ESRO, B105/2/1, f. 79.

46. Quotation from *A New Bloody Almanac* (1645), A2–A3; *A Prognosticall*

Prediction Of Admirable Events (1644), 4; Symonds, 'Diary of John Greene
. . . part II', 603–4; Robert Bell (ed.), *Memorials of the Civil War
Comprising the Correspondence of the Fairfax Family*, 2 vols (1849), i, 273–4.

47. Thomas Carte (ed.), *A Collection of Original Letters and Papers Concerning
the Affairs of England, From the Year 1641 to 1660*, 2 vols (1739), i, 85.

48. Ernest Read Cooper, *Memories of Bygone Dunwich* (Southwold, 1948),
4–8, 17–20; Thomas Gardner, *An Historical Account of Dunwich* (1754),
40–1, 92–4; Suckling, *History . . . of Suffolk*, ii, 229–306. Between 1603
and 1670 the population of Dunwich fell from around 850 to 300:
Patten, 'Population distribution in Norfolk and Suffolk', 49.

49. Ewen I, 308–9. Churchwardens' accounts indicate that, like many places,
in 1645 Westleton was having to find extra money to care for Irish
refugees: ESRO, FC 63/E1/1.

50. Ewen I, 298–9.

51. John Brinsley, *A Looking-Glasse for Good Women* (1645), 4, 31–3, 40.

52. Walker, *History of Independency*, 63.

53. Hale, *Collection of Modern Relations*, 48; Ewen II, 279–80; Harrod, 'Notes
on . . . Great Yarmouth', 249–51; Stearne, 53–4. It is possible that as
many as sixteen women were hanged at Yarmouth: Hutchinson,
Historical Essay, 37.

54. For the bitterness of this winter, see Macfarlane (ed.), *Diary of Ralph
Josselin*, 53.

55. BL, Add. 41605, ff. 129–31; Nicholas Fenwick Hele, *Notes or Jottings
about Aldeburgh* (Ipswich, 1890), 30–42, 45; Arthur T. Winn (ed.),
Aldeburgh Poll Tax, 1641 (Colchester, 1926), 3; Vincent B. Redstone,
'Aldeburgh', in *PSIA*, 12 (1906), 203–6; ESRO, EE 1/12/2, ff. 248–50.
Between 1603 and 1670 the population of Aldeburgh almost halved:
Patten, 'Population distribution in Norfolk and Suffolk', 49.

56. Redstone, 'Aldeburgh', 214; *A Syne from heaven* (1642); Arthur T. Winn,
(ed.), *Records . . . of Aldeburgh: the Church* (Aldeburgh, 1926), 5–6, 13–19;
Cooper (ed.), *Journal of William Dowsing*, 56; BL, Add. 41605, ff. 126–7;
Vincent B. Redstone, 'Presbyterian church government in Suffolk,
1643–1647', in *PSIA*, 13 (1909), 135–8.

57. On weather conditions, see Symonds, 'Diary of John Greene . . . part
III', 106–7.

58. Hele, *Notes . . . about Aldeburgh*, 43–4; Winn (ed.), *Records . . . of
Aldeburgh*, 14; ESRO, EE 1/12/2, f. 249.

59. PRO, C 181/5, f. 265ᵛ; Hele, *Notes . . . about Aldeburgh*, 44.

60. Winn (ed.), *Aldeburgh Poll Tax*, 9; Hele, *Notes . . . about Aldeburgh*, 42–4.

61. ESRO, EE 1/12/2, ff. 248–50, 258^v, 273^v.

62. Hele, *Notes . . . about Aldeburgh*, 44; Winn (ed.), *Aldeburgh Poll Tax*, 4, 10.

63. There was also a criminal trial along the coast at Southwold, where Miles Corbett was town steward. It seems likely that witches were accused here in 1645; one certainly was in January 1646: PRO, C 181/5, ff. 257^v–258; C 231/6, 14; KB 9/838, mm. 90–1.

64. Symonds, 'Diary of John Greene . . . part III', 106–7. Between 1645 and 1646 the price of wheat rose by almost 27 per cent: Bowden (ed.), *Economic Change*, 157. For the connection between agrarian crisis and witch-hunting, see: Wolfgang Behringer, 'Weather, hunger and fear: origins of the European witch hunts in climate, society and mentality', in *German History*, 13 (1995); Emily Oster, 'Witchcraft, weather and economic growth in Renaissance Europe', in *Journal of Economic Perspectives*, 18 (2004), 216–18.

65. For the link between ergotism and witchcraft, see: L. R. Caporael, 'Ergotism: the Satan loosed in Salem', in *Science*, 192 (1976); Matossian, *Poisons of the Past*, chs 5, 9.

66. *CSPD 1645–47*, 306–7, 328, quotation at 307.

67. ESRO, B105/2/1, f. 80.

68. Cooper (ed.), *Journal of William Dowsing*, 103; Bullen, 'Catalogue of . . . clergy', 320. Young became head of a Cambridge college in 1644, so may not have met Hopkins: Herbert W. Tompkins, *Companion into Suffolk* (1949), 86; *DNB*, s.v. 'Young, Thomas'.

69. Stearne, 26; Ewen I, 292. This was possibly the same Elizabeth Hubbard accused at Halesworth: Ewen I, 310. John Heywood was also one of the witch-rate collectors.

70. A. G. H. Hollingsworth, *The History of Stowmarket* (Ipswich, 1844), 169–71. On average a skilled craftsman earned eighteen pence a day at this time: Phelps Brown and Hopkins, 'Seven centuries of building wages', 168–78.

71. NRO, Y/C 19/7, f. 76^v. For a case where the keeper of Norwich gaol was ordered to surrender a witch's property so that it could be sold for the benefit of the city, see Francis Blomefield, *A Topographical History of the County of Norfolk*, 10 vols (1804), iii, 401.

72. Hollingsworth, *History of Stowmarket*, 169–171. The population nearly doubled in the period 1603–70: Patten, 'Population distribution in Norfolk and Suffolk', 49.

73. ESRO, B105/2/1, ff. 80ᵛ–81ᵛ, 84. In 1640 the constable found it hard to exact rates from Brandeston's householders: Redstone (ed.) *Ship-Money*, 12.

74. WSRO, FL 600/4/1–2. Presumably Stearne was at home then, as his wife gave birth nine months later. I am grateful to Jonathan Hacker for this observation.

75. Stearne, 19–20. James I had argued that because children were incapable of reason, they were incapable of witchcraft: *Daemonologie*, 76–7.

76. Stearne, 20.

8. Contagion

1. CUL, Palmer A16, ff. 6–7; UA, T.X.1 (a); UA, Collect.Admin.8, 504–5; CRO, CCCA Box X/18; Cooper, *Annals of Cambridge*, iii, 373–419; Arthur Gray, *The Town of Cambridge: a History* (Cambridge, 1925), 122–3.

2. VCH, *Cambs*, vol. 2, 405–10; vol. 3, 199–210; John Twigg, *The University of Cambridge and the English Revolution, 1625–1688* (Woodbridge, 1990), chs 4–6; Arthur Gray, *Cambridge University: an Episodical History* (Cambridge, 1926), 187–9. In the summer of 1645 rumours of traitors abounded in Cambridge: *CSPD 1644–45*, 564.

3. BL, Add. 5813, ff. 92–3; Gray, *Town of Cambridge*, 118; CUL, UA, T.X.1 (b); PRO, SP 28/222, Pt. II, f. 154; Cooper, *Annals of Cambridge*, iii, 400–1, 415.

4. CUL, Palmer B62, C3; Palmer A12, 11–55, quotations at 11, 18.

5. More, *Antidote Against Atheisme*, 111; *Calendar of the Patent Rolls, Elizabeth I*, 8 vols (1939–86), iv, 69, 214.

6. Henry Holland, *A Treatise Against Witchcraft* (Cambridge, 1590), quotation at B1; Stuart Clark, 'Protestant demonology: sin, superstition and society (*c.* 1520–*c.* 1630)', in Ankarloo and Henningsen (eds), *Early Modern European Witchcraft*, 55–8, 60–3.

7. CUL, UA, Comm.Cts: II.10, ff. 68–72ᵛ; II.11, ff. 7–20, 25–7, 47, 53; II.12, ff. 11ᵛ, 14–17ᵛ, 20v–21ᵛ, 25–33, 59ᵛ–60; III.13, ff. 3, 5, 8–12. V.C. Cts: II.8, ff. 109Aᵛ–B; III.2, f. 312; III.12, ff. 164–6ᵛ. See also: *CSPD 1603–10*, 465; PRO, SP 14/37/89; STAC 8/95/4. I am grateful to Alex Shepard for advice about the University courts.

8. BL, Add. 6177, ff. 199–200; PRO, SP 38/8, Docquet, 21 May 1605; CUL, Mm.1.40, ff. 384–5; HMC, *Salisbury*, xvii, 19–20, 22, 31, 33, 36,

65, 121, 222–3; *CSPD 1603–10*, 218; CUL, UA, Lett.II.A (C). 9a–b, quotation at 9b.

9. Perkins, *Discourse*, 43–4, 51; Ady, *Candle in the Dark*, 162–3; John L. Teall, 'Witchcraft and Calvinism in Elizabethan England: divine power and human agency', in *Journal of the History of Ideas*, 23 (1962); Clark, 'Protestant demonology', 55, 65.

10. A. Rupert Hall, *Henry More: Magic, Religion and Experiment* (Oxford, 1990), ch. 7; Coudert, 'Henry More and witchcraft'; *DNB*, s.v. 'More, Henry'. On the question of demonology and proof, see: Richard Weisman, *Witchcraft, Magic and Religion in 17th-Century Massachusetts* (Amherst, 1984), 98–105; Clark, *Thinking with Demons*, 174.

11. PRO, SP 14/161/89; Ewen I, 134–5; Peter May, *The Changing Face of Newmarket: a History, 1600–1760* (Newmarket, 1984), 13–14.

12. Davies, *Four Centuries of Witch-Beliefs*, 104–8; *DNB*, s.v. 'Dalton, Michael'; Bernard, *Guide to Grand-Jury Men*, esp. 102–17; Ewen I, 267–9; Clark, 'Protestant demonology', 70; Kittredge, *Witchcraft*, 273, 564; Gaskill (ed.), *Hopkins Trials*, 488–95. On Bodin's influential ideas, see Clark, *Thinking with Demons*, ch. 44.

13. Ralph Cudworth, *The True Intellectual System of the Universe* (1678), 702.

14. CUL, Palmer B35 (unfol.); T. D. Atkinson, *Cambridge Described and Illustrated* (1897), 92–3; Porter, *Cambridgeshire Customs*, 158; VCH, *Cambs*, vol. 2, 107–8.

15. Stearne and More call her 'Lendall', but no Lendalls are recorded in any Cambridge parish registers for this period, whereas there were Kendalls in St Clement's in 1644–6.

16. More, *Antidote Against Atheisme*, 128–30; Glanvill, *Saducismus Triumphatus*, 208; John Bowtell, cited in Porter, *Cambridgeshire Customs*, 158. The Earl of Warwick was entertained in Cambridge on 2 Sept. 1645: PRO, SP 28/222, Pt. II. f. 151.

17. Stearne, 39; Ady, *Candle in the Dark*, 135; Cooper, *Annals of Cambridge*, iii, 398 .

18. More, *Enthusiasmus Triumphatus*, 5; Henry More, *Philosophicall Poems* (Cambridge, 1647), B1ᵛ.

19. Thomas Plume's Library, Plume MS. no. 30, pp. 17, 34–5. When the king ordered Buckingham to grab the entranced woman 'by ye Quuent', her blushes gave her away.

20. CRO, P30/4/2; CUL, UA, Comm. Ct. III.20.

21. CRO, P30/4/2; P30/1/1; P30/11/1.

22. *A strange and true Relation of a Young Woman possest with the Devil* (1646), 5–6; Glanvill, *Saducismus Triumphatus*, 205; Bod., Ashm. 178, f. 116; Ashm.185, f. 58ᵛ.

23. Stearne, 45. VCH, *Cambs*, vol. 4, 339–55; CUL, Palmer B25, B59; Margaret Spufford, *Contrasting Communities: English Villagers in the Sixteenth and Seventeenth Centuries* (Cambridge, 1974), 18, 282–4, 295; CRO, P129/1/1–2. The people of Over had lost common land due to drainage and enclosure: Lindley, *Fenland Riots*, 12, 93.

24. Stearne, 45–6; VCH, *Cambs*, vol. 4, 289–303; Bod., Gough, Camb.69, ff. 23–37; *JHC*, iii, 655; iv, 147; HLRO, Main Papers, 17 May 1645, f. 14; CUL, Palmer B40.

25. HLRO, Main Papers, 10 Mar. 1646, f. 136; PRO, KB 9/838, m. 380; ERO, Q/SBa 2/61, petition of Steven Hoy, gaoler, midsummer 1646.

26. ERO, Q/SBa 2/59–60; Q/SR 328/94, 106; Macfarlane, *Witchcraft*, 269, 275–6.

27. Bod., Ashm. 412, ff. 13ᵛ, 16, 19ᵛ, 117, 125, 141ᵛ, 145ᵛ, 146, 153ᵛ, 157, 175ᵛ, 279, 282ᵛ, 292ᵛ; Ashm. 178, f. 31; Ashm. 185, f. 270ᵛ.

28. ESRO, C/2/9/1/1/8/7, pp. 418, 423, 425.

29. R. L. Greenall, *A History of Northamptonshire* (1979), chs 10–11; W. J. Sheils, *Puritans in the Diocese of Peterborough, 1558–1610* (Northampton, 1979), chs 6–8. Most of the parishes in Northamptonshire and Huntingdonshire where witchcraft accusations occurred in 1646 had had their ministers purged in the previous three years: Matthews (ed.), *Walker Revised*, 206–7, 209, 251–2, 276, 279, 280–1, 283–4, 286.

30. *The Witches of Northamptonshire* (1612); BL, Sloane 972, ff. 7–7ᵛ; Ewen II, 206–12; Gaskill (ed.), *Hopkins Trials*, 478.

31. PRO, SP 28/238, Pt. II, f. 250; HMC, *6th Report*, 36, 41, 120; Robin Clifton, 'The popular fear of Catholics during the English Revolution', in *Past & Present*, 52 (1971), 53; HLRO, Main Papers, 30 Nov. 1644, f. 262; *JHL*, vii, 78.

32. Stearne, 23. Stearne calls him 'Cocke', but the parish register suggests that his name would have been 'Cox', probably Thomas Cox: Northants RO, 101P/1.

33. Stearne, 31. Stearne says 'Risden, in Bedfordshire', but no such place exists; Rushden is close to the border between Northamptonshire and Bedfordshire. Stearne also calls her 'Gurrey', but see the parish register: Northants RO, 258P/205.

34. Stearne, 53. Both were blighted by poverty in the 1640s, and probably

by epidemic disease too: Northants RO, 55P/508; 55P/3; 55P/58; 246P/1. Formerly the rector of Burton Latimer had insisted upon extreme obedience to the king: VCH, *Northants*, vol. 3, 180.

35. Davenport, *Witches of Huntingdon*, 14–15. Browne had been embroiled in a legal dispute in 1630: Joan Wake (ed.), *Quarter Sessions Records . . . of Northampton* (Hereford, 1924), 37. He was buried at Raunds in 1650: Northants RO, 278P/1–2.

36. VCH, *Northants*, vol. 3, 139–42; *Witches of Northamptonshire*, D1ᵛ; Stearne, 35.

37. Northants RO, 325P/1–2; SOX/340/5, ff. 44–7ᵛ, 114–15; Walter, *Understanding Popular Violence*, 136.

38. Stearne, 34–5. The man's death cannot be confirmed as there is a gap in the Thrapston parish register between 1642 and 1655: Northants RO, 325P/1–2.

39. Stearne, 23, 35.

40. John Cotta, *The infallible, true, and assured witch* (1625); Notestein, *History of Witchcraft*, 229–31. See also Elmer, 'Towards a politics of witchcraft', 107.

41. *JHC*, iv, 649; *Mercurius Civicus* (3–10 Sept. 1646), 2372–3; Symonds, 'Diary of John Greene . . . part III', 107; Josten (ed.), *Elias Ashmole*, ii, 389. On the deaths of Wente and Cocke: PRO, KB 9/838, m. 381; KB 29/296, m. 74.

42. *Five Wonders Seene in England* (1646), 1–2.

43. PRO, SP 28/234 (unfol.); Underdown, *Revel, Riot and Rebellion*, 149–52; Ian Gentles, 'The impact of the New Model Army', in John Morrill (ed.), *The Impact of the English Civil War* (1991), 90–1. Many exhausted communities gave up taking sides in the civil war, wishing only to be left alone: Morrill, *Revolt in the Provinces*, 56–7, 119–23.

44. *The most strange and admirable discoverie of the three Witches of Warboys* (1593); Moira Tatem, *The Witches of Warboys* (March, 1993). In 1559 Frances Throckmorton had been accused of bewitching her husband: BL, Add. 32091, ff. 176–7.

45. M. J. Naylor, *The Inantity* [sic] *and Mischief of Vulgar Superstitions* (Cambridge, 1795), vi–vii. The 1593 pamphlet account inspired a case of fraudulent demonic possession in 1604: James Sharpe, *The Bewitching of Anne Gunter* (1999), 164.

46. Thomas Beard, *The Theatre of Gods Judgments* (1597); Thomas, *Religion*, 109–10; Davies, *Four Centuries of Witch-Beliefs*, 102–3.

47. C. F. Tebbutt, 'Huntingdonshire folk and their folklore II', in *Transactions of the Cambs. and Hunts. Archaeological Society*, 7 (1950), 54, 60–3; More, *Enthusiasmus Triumphatus*, 43–4; H. S. Scott (ed.), *The Journal of Sir Roger Wilbraham* (1902), 69.

48. VCH, *Hunts*, vol. 2, 124; Peter Bigmore, *The Bedfordshire and Huntingdonshire Landscape* (1979), 154–60; Wickes, *History of Huntingdonshire*, 76–7.

49. Stearne was definitely at neighbouring Molesworth before 11 April: Stearne, 21.

50. Davenport, *Witches of Huntingdon*, 7. Searle and Slater signed the Protestation in 1641: HRO, transcript of signatories to the Protestation Oath, 1641–2.

51. Davenport, *Witches of Huntingdon*, 1–2. Men of the Bedell, Musgrave and Thorpe families signed the Protestation: HRO, transcript of signatories to the Protestation Oath, 1641–2. Weed may be the Catworth woman who made a large confession: Stearne, 39.

52. Davenport, *Witches of Huntingdon*, 5–6. Slater's wife gave birth in 1627, and was not buried after 1631; she must have died *c.* 1628–30: HRO, AH28/84/1.

53. Davenport calls her 'Darnell', but from the parish register she is 'Darnwell', wife of William Darnwell, blacksmith, who died in 1656: HRO, HP51/1/1/1. On ducking-stools, see: John W. Spargo, *Juridical Folklore in England Illustrated by the Cucking-Stool* (Durham NC, 1944), chs 1, 4; Carew Hazlitt, *Popular Antiquities*, ii, 362–4.

54. Chandler's story comes from Davenport, *Witches of Huntingdon*, 7–9.

55. Venn and Venn (eds), *Matriculations and Degrees*, 181; Venn and Venn (eds), *Alumni Cantabrigienses*, i, 409.

56. Davies, *Four Centuries of Witch-Beliefs*, 37–9, 132–3; C. Smith, 'Northamptonshire in the history of witchcraft', in *Northants. Past and Present*, 4:6 (1971–2), 343–5.

57. Davenport, *Witches of Huntingdon*, 11–12.

58. Ibid., 9–10. Davenport calls her 'Ellen' but she was Eleanor Milward who married William Shepherd in 1634: HRO, HP54/1/1/1.

59. Davenport, *Witches of Huntingdon*, 5–6, 10–11.

60. Stearne, 21. We know this happened at Molesworth, because Stearne says that Winnick confessed again before the JPs, and then a third time at his trial.

61. Stearne, 20–1; Davenport, *Witches of Huntingdon*, 3–4.

62. Stearne, 13; Davenport, *Witches of Huntingdon*, 12–14; HRO, transcript of signatories to the Protestation Oath, 1641–2. For Wingfield's biography, see HRO, HP51/1/1/1, and the genealogical website http://wingfield.org/charts.

63. Davenport, *Witches of Huntingdon*, 12–14.

64. Stearne, 13.

65. Ibid., 17; Davenport, *Witches of Huntingdon*, 12–15.

66. CUL, Palmer A16, ff. 275–6; Edmund Calamy, *An Abridgement of Mr. Baxter's History of his Life and Times*, 2 vols (1713), ii, 114, 117; *Sad Newes From the Eastern Parts* (1646); *Severall Apparitions Seene in the Ayre* (1646), 4–5.

67. *Signes from Heaven . . . in the Counties of Cambridge and Norfolke* (1646), 5.

9. Sticklers

1. John Benbrigge, *Gods Fury, Englands Fire* (1646), 40–1; *Distracted Englands Lamentation* (1646); David Cressy, 'Revolutionary England 1640–1642', in *Past & Present*, 181 (2003), 57; Hill, *World Turned Upside Down*, 342–3, 355.

2. John Eachard, *The Axe Against Sin and Error* (1646), 16, 25–7; Thomas Edwards, *Gangraena*, 2 vols (1646), i, 161; ii, 4–5, 161–3; Theophilus Philalethes Toxander, *Vox Coeli to England* (1646), 2.

3. *A Spirit Moving in The Women Preachers* (1646), 1.

4. Morrill, *Revolt in the Provinces*, 166.

5. W. M. Wigfield, 'Recusancy and nonconformity in Bedfordshire', in *Publications of the Bedfordshire Historical Society*, 20 (1938); Ross Lee, *Law and Local Society in the Time of Charles I: Bedfordshire and the Civil War* (Bedford, 1986), 61, 66–7, 85, 95. For mention of two women hanged as witches in the 1590s, see Joyce Godber, *A History of Bedfordshire, 1066–1888* (Luton, 1969), 200, 223.

6. *Witches Apprehended . . . and Executed*; [Drage], *Daimonomageia*, 41.

7. Stearne, 18, 61; Hopkins, *Discovery*, 5, 6–7. Stearne's literary mentor rejected the water ordeal as unreliable and ungodly: Bernard, *Guide to Grand-Jury Men*, chs 19, 22.

8. Jonathan Lumby, ' "Those to whom evil is done": family dynamics in the Pendle witch trials', in Robert Poole (ed.), *The Lancashire Witches:*

Histories and Stories (Manchester, 2002), 64, 67–8; Kittredge, *Witchcraft*, ch. 16.

9. Wickes, *History of Huntingdonshire*, 73–4; Stearne, 53.

10. Bod., Ashm. 412, ff. 201ᵛ, 209ᵛ; Ashm. 1447, Pt. IX, 14.

11. Stearne, 19; PRO, SP 28/219; VCH, *Hunts*, vol. 2, 337–46.

12. Cf. the story of the 'witch-hare': Philip (ed.), *English Folktales*, 302–3.

13. John Hale, quoted in Gregory Durston, *Witchcraft and Witch Trials: a History of English Witchcraft and its Legal Perspectives* (Chichester, 2000), 18–19.

14. Gaule, *Select Cases of Conscience*, 77–8, 150; VCH, *Hunts*, vol. 2, 354–69. Henry More heard about events at Huntingdon: *Antidote Against Atheisme*, 125–6. See also the account provided in R. B., *Kingdom of Darkness*, 159–62.

15. Gaule, *Select Cases of Conscience*, A3–A3ᵛ. 'M. N.' may have been Michael Nicholls, an established householder. In the parish register 32 surnames begin with the letter 'N', of which only 15 were present before 1650: HRO, HP82/1/1/1/1–2.

16. Lewis Evans, 'Witchcraft in Hertfordshire', in William Andrews (ed.), *Bygone Hertfordshire* (1898); *The most cruell and Bloody Murther . . . With the severall Witch-crafts . . . of one Johane Harrison and her Daughter* (1606); [Drage], *Daimonomageia*, 40. Another witch had been indicted at Hertford in 1641: Ewen I, 220–1.

17. *Perfect Occurrences Of Both Houses of Parliament* (14–21 Aug. 1646), Ii3.

18. *DNB*, s.v. 'Walton, Valentine', 'Gaule, John'; H. G. Watson, *A History of the Parish of Great Staughton* (St Neots, 1916), 9–10, 19, 33–6. Gaule had also written: *Practique Theories* (1629); *Distractions* (1629); and *A Defiance to Death* (1630).

19. HRO, HP82/12/1; HP82/5/1, ff. 33–6.

20. Notestein, *History of Witchcraft*, 237n; Gaule, *Admonition*, 55–6, 60–1, 75, 97–8.

21. Gaule, *Select Cases of Conscience*, 77–80; Davenport, *Witches of Huntingdon*, 5–6.

22. Gaule, *Select Cases of Conscience*, 79, 93.

23. Ibid., 5–6, 74–83, 88–98, 108–21, 192–7; Notestein, *History of Witchcraft*, 165–6, 236–7; Perkins, *Discourse*, 200–1, 218–19; George Gifford, *A Dialogue concerning Witches and Witchcraftes* (1593), H4.

24. Josias Shute, *Judgement and Mercy* (1645), 119.

25. Gaule, *Select Cases of Conscience*, A3; Hutchinson, *Historical Essay*, 61.

26. Zephaniah Smyth, *The Conspiracie of the Wicked against the Just* (1648), 6, 8, 14–15; Thomas Fuller, *The Profane State* (1647), 351.

27. NRO, C/S3, box 34, bundle 3 (1642–5), information of William Stanton, 1643; 'A Godly Exhortation to this Distressed Nation' (1642), in Rollins (ed.), *Cavalier and Puritan*, 144–9, esp. 146. See also Underdown, *Revel, Riot and Rebellion*, 218–19.

28. Gaule, *Select Cases of Conscience*, A2–A2ᵛ, 63–4.

29. [John Earle], *Micro-cosmographie* (1629), no. 12; James (ed.), *Norfolk Quarter Sessions Order Book*, 15; Nickalls (ed.), *Journal of George Fox*, 492.

30. *JHL*, viii, 163, 372. Local courts tended to be harsher on witches than central ones: Brian P. Levack, 'State-building and witch hunting in early modern Europe', in Barry *et al.* (eds), *Witchcraft in Early Modern Europe*; Briggs, *Witches and Neighbours*, 331–7.

31. George Smith, *Englands Pressures, or the Peoples Complaint* (1645), 11, 14–15; Gaule, *Admonition*, 61; Gaule, *Select Cases of Conscience*, 88–9, 175–82, quote at 177.

32. Davenport, *Witches of Huntingdon*, A2ᵛ; Stearne, 21. If Joan Wallis was in fact *Joyce* Wallis, then she died a widow at Keyston in 1657: HRO, HP51/1/1/1.

33. Stearne, 11, 21, 39.

34. Gaule, *Select Cases of Conscience*, A1–A3ᵛ. Thomason's copy is dated 30 June.

35. C. F. Tebbutt, 'Extracts from Assize Rolls of Huntingdonshire in the Seventeenth Century', copy at CUL, Add. 7515/4; Henry Wilkinson, *Miranda Stupenda* (1646), 2.

36. Davenport, *Witches of Huntingdon*, A1–A2ᵛ, 15. Thomason's copy is dated 7 July.

37. Paul Richards, *King's Lynn* (Chichester, 1990), 1, 9–10, 67, 75–6, 78–80; Henry Harrod, *Report on the Deeds & Records of . . . King's Lynn* (King's Lynn, 1874).

38. Richards, *King's Lynn*, 122, 126–7; *JHC*, iv (1644–46), 102; BL, Add. 15903, f. 63; Mackerell, *History . . . of King's Lynn*, 236.

39. Henry J. Hillen, *History of the Borough of King's Lynn*, 2 vols (Norwich, 1907), ii, 851–9; James Bulwer, 'Notices of the church at Wells', in *Norfolk Archaeology*, 5 (1859), 87; Alison Gifford, *Ghosts and Legends of Lynn* (n.p, n.d.), 25–7; Alexander Roberts, *A Treatise of Witchcraft* (1616), 45–80.

40. Borough Archives, King's Lynn, KL/C7/10, f. 187; KL/C39/102, f. 41;

KL/C21/2, ff. 47–48ᵛ; Vanessa Parker, *The Making of King's Lynn* (1971), 143, 145; Richards, *King's Lynn*, 122.

41. Like labourers, soldiers received eightpence a day: Austin Woolrych, *Britain in Revolution, 1625–1660* (Oxford, 2002), 306.
42. Borough Archives, King's Lynn, KL/C7/10, f. 193ᵛ; KL/C39/102, f. 41.
43. CUL, Add. 7515/8; Macfarlane (ed.), *Diary of Ralph Josselin*, 69; Symonds, 'Diary of John Greene . . . part III', 107–8. Grain prices rose by 45 per cent between 1644 and 1647: Bowden (ed.), *Economic Change*, 140, 152, 157.
44. John Giorgi, 'Diet in late medieval and early modern London: the archaeobotanical evidence', in David Gaimster and Paul Stamper (eds), *The Age of Transition . . . 1400–1600* (Oxford, 1997), 202–3, 207; Matossian, *Poisons of the Past*, 70, 75–9.
45. George Alfred Carthew, 'Extracts from a town book of the parish of Stockton in Norfolk', in *Norfolk Archaeology*, 1 (1847), 186–7.
46. *A strange and wonderfull Relation of The burying alive of Joan Bridges* (1646); *The True Relation of two wonderfull Sleepers* (1646), 3–6, 8.
47. Bod., Rawl., B.924, ff. 208–12; John Glyde (ed.), *Folklore and Customs of Norfolk* (Wakefield, 1973), 21–2, 31–2, 50, 54–5; 'Proverbs, adages and popular superstitions . . . of Irstead', in *Norfolk Archaeology*, 2 (1849), 300, 306–7.
48. See, for example: BL, Add. 5487, f. 173ᵛ; Add. 28223, f. 15; Egerton 2714, f. 104; Egerton 2884, f. 14; HMC, *10th Report*, Pt. II, 71; HMC, *Salisbury*, xxix, Addenda, 109–11; Bod., Tanner 168, f. 104; PRO, STAC 8/140/23, m. 13; STAC 8/276/25, m. 14; PRO, SP 38/7, Docquet, 16 Apr. 1604; *CSPD 1603–10*, 96, 598.
49. Hopkins, *Discovery*, 6. See also above, page 144.
50. *Anti-Projector*, 1, 2, 7–8; BL, Harl. 837, ff. 75ᵛ–77ᵛ; Harsnet, *Declaration*, 131–3; Enid Porter, 'Some folk beliefs of the Fens', in *Folklore*, 69 (1958), 112–22.
51. PRO, SP 14/128/149–54; *CSPD 1619–22*, 370; Andrewes Burrell, *Exceptions Against Sir Cornelius Virmudens Discourse For the Draining of the great Fennes* (1642), A2; Darby, *Changing Fenland*, 55–7, 60–2, 70–2.
52. The case of Ellen Garrison comes from EDR, E44/3; E12 1647/1–2. On the witch and the drainage riot, see: PRO, SP16/357/107, 158; Lindley, *Fenland Riots*, 92–3.
53. EDR, E12 1647/4–5.
54. CRO, P109/25/7–8. The 1639 trustees of the 'Guild Hall' house and

lands came from their families. However, all four made marks not signatures: EDR, 1647/4. A Crabbe and a Gotobed had been witnesses to
Hopkins' grandfather's will. Elizabeth Crabbe, wife of Thomas Crabbe,
yeoman, fought a civil action in 1646 as executor of her husband's will:
EDR, E2/3/7, plea roll 1646; EDR E12 assizes 21 Car. I (26 Sept.
1646).

55. VCH, *Cambs*, vol. 4, 97; Michael Cross, 'The church and local society
in the diocese of Ely, *c.* 1630–*c.* 1730', unpub. PhD thesis, Cambridge
University, 1991, 55; EDR, E12 depositions 1639. In 1642 the Littleport
sluice was sabotaged: EDR E12 1641–2, gaol delivery, f. 29. See also the
protracted lawsuit of 1665–74: CRO, P109/28/4, 17–19.

56. Borough Archives, King's Lynn, KL/C21/2, ff. 47–8ᵛ.

57. Mackerell, *History . . . of King's Lynn*, 236; Borough Archives, King's
Lynn, KL/C21/2, ff. 47–8ᵛ. A note dated 2 Sept. recorded that Hopkins
was to be paid £15 and to receive 'further satisffaccion' – a sum of forty
shillings – after the next sessions.

58. NRO, Y/S 1/2, ff. 203–5; Y/C 27/2.

59. EDR, E12 1647/6; E2/3/7; E11 (ii); E12 indictments 1646.

60. Genesis 6:13, 7: 10–11, 24; Macfarlane (ed.), *Diary of Ralph Josselin*, 72–6,
81–5; Symonds, 'Diary of John Greene . . . part II', 108; John Bryan, *A
Discovery of the Probable Sin Causing this great Judgement of Rain and Waters*
(1647). For complaints against royalist gentry and ejected ministers, see
Bod., Tanner 59B, f. 792.

61. PRO, ASSI 45/1/5/38–9; Ewen II, 394–5; HMC, *6th Report*, 152; *JHL*,
viii, 653–4.

62. William L. Sachse (ed.), *Minutes of the Norwich Court of Mayoralty,
1630–1631* (Norfolk Record Society, 1942), 18, 25–8, 30–48; David
Galloway (ed.), *Records of Early English Drama: Norwich* (Toronto, 1984),
xv, xix–xxv; John Pound, *Tudor and Stuart Norwich* (Chichester, 1988),
85–93, 116–17; Goddard Johnson, 'Chronological memoranda touching
the city of Norwich', in *Norfolk Archaeology*, 1 (1847), 156–7; NRO,
NCR Case 20/12, f. 157; John T. Evans, *Seventeenth-Century Norwich:
Politics, Religion and Government, 1620–1690* (Oxford, 1979), chs 4–5.

63. Thomas Browne, *Pseudodoxia Epidemica*, ed. Robin Robbins, 2 vols
(Oxford, 1981), i, 65, 572, 586–7; Thomas Browne, *Religio Medici*
(1642), 56–7 (quotation); Kenelm Digby, *Observations upon Religio Medici*
(1643); Alexander Ross, *Medicus Medicatus* (1645), 41; R. T. Petersson,
Sir Kenelm Digby (1956), 166–7, 171.

64. James (ed.), *Norfolk Quarter Sessions Order Book*, 8–9, 15; Cockburn, *History of English Assizes*, 272, 290, 292.
65. Hopkins, *Discovery*, quotations at 3, 5–6.
66. Ibid., 9.
67. Brian P. Levack, 'Possession, witchcraft and the law in Jacobean England, in *Washington & Lee Law Review*, 52 (1996), 1637–8. In decentralized Scotland, witchfinders were more plentiful until government intervention in 1662: W. N. Neill, 'The professional pricker and his test for witchcraft', in *Scottish Historical Review*, 19 (1922); Ewen I, 63; *Mercurius Politicus* (28 Oct.–4 Nov. 1652), 1982–3.
68. Quotation from Daniel Defoe, *A Tour Through the Whole Island of Great Britain*, ed. P. N. Furbank and W. R. Owens (New Haven, 1991), 31.

10. The Biter Bit

1. Leonard de Bolingbroke, 'The hundred of Clackclose and the Civil War', in *Norfolk Archaeology*, 14 (1901); *Bloody Almanack*, A1ᵛ; William Jenkyn, *A Sleeping Sicknes* (1647), A3. On 'gender crisis', see: David Underdown, 'The taming of the scold: the enforcement of patriarchal authority in early modern England', in Anthony Fletcher and John Stevenson (eds), *Order and Disorder in Early Modern England* (Cambridge, 1985); Martin Ingram, ' "Scolding women cucked or washed": a crisis in gender relations in early modern England?', in Kermode and Walker (eds), *Women, Crime and the Courts*.
2. Thomas, 'Women and the Civil War sects'. For an example, see the satirical pamphlet *A Parliament of Ladies: With their Lawes Nearly Enacted* (1647).
3. Bruno Ryves, *Micro-Chronicon* (1647), G2.
4. Carlton, *Going to the Wars*, 256–63, 296–9, 307–9; Garthine Walker, *Crime, Gender and the Social Order in Early Modern England* (Cambridge, 2003), 93–5; Jerome Friedman, *Miracles and the Pulp Press during the English Revolution* (1993), ch. 9.
5. *Strange Newes from New-gate* (1647); *The Divell in Kent, or His strange Delusions at Sandwitch* (1647); *Fearefull Apparitions or the Strangest Visions* (1647); *Strange and true Newes of an Ocean of Flies* (1647). For apocalyptic imagery at this time, see a letter written to Lady Vere: BL, Add. 4275, f. 173 (13 Sept. 1647).

6. Darby, *Changing Fenland*, 52; Symonds, 'Diary of John Greene . . . part II', 600–1; Christopher Morris (ed.), *The Illustrated Journeys of Celia Fiennes* (Exeter, 1982), 141–3.

7. Everitt (ed.), *Suffolk and the Great Rebellion*, 32; VCH, *Cambs*, vol. 4, 16–19; CUL, Palmer A45; PRO, C 231/6, p. 90; HMC, *6th Report*, 173; *JHL*, ix, 163, 171.

8. BL, Add. 19038, f. 5; CUL, Palmer B58/29–34, 45, 52–5.

9. Thomas Edwards, quoted in Hill, *World Turned Upside Down*, 47. The city of Ely was a centre for the Seekers in the mid 1640s: Morton, 'Laurence Clarkson', 175, 177n.

10. W. H. Barrett *More Tales from the Fens* (1964), 99–150; Christopher Marlowe, *Legends of the Fenlands* (1926), 149–240; Porter, *Cambridgeshire Customs*, chs 5–6.

11. Bod., Tanner 62, f. 181; *CSPD 1644–45*, 488, 498, 526–7, 540–1; Firth and Rait (eds), *Acts and Ordinances*, i, 744; Manning, *English People and the English Revolution*, 183–96; Underdown, *Revel, Riot and Rebellion*, 160.

12. Many cases of witchcraft can be found in the records of the diocese of Ely, 1560–1640: EDR, B2/5–40, D2/2–32, E6–E12, E44, E1/9, E2/1–3, E42/6, K1–17. For some examples, see Gaskill, *Crime and Mentalities*, 48–9, 55, 58, 61–5, 73, 75–7.

13. Macfarlane, *Witchcraft*, 269. Evidence that Hopkins was plying his trade in Worcester in this year is flawed: *Full Tryals . . . Of Four Notorious Witches*, 3.

14. CUL, Palmer B25; Laurence Clarkson, *The Lost Sheep Found* (1660), 19; Nickalls (ed.), *Journal of George Fox*, 218; Thomas, 'Women and the Civil War sects', 47.

15. VCH, *Cambs*, vol. 4, 159–64; *Anti-Projector*, 2; Bod., Tanner 60, f. 136; HLRO, Main Papers, 1649, f. 112; HMC, *7th Report*, Pt. 1, 75; CUL, Palmer B70; EDR, B2/35, ff. 207–219^v; PRO, E 172/1; PRO, SP 19/21, f. 11^v; Lindley, *Fenland Riots*, 37–40, 60, 64, 86, 96–102, 142–3. See also Proverbs 19:4.

16. CUL, Palmer B70. Benjamin Wyne and the other principal accusers at Sutton were landowners and ratepayers: Palmer, *Cambridgeshire Subsidy Rolls*, 66–7.

17. CRO, P148/1/1–2; CUL, Palmer B70.

18. EDR E12 1647/16–16^v.

19. The Bonhams' case comes from: EDR, E12 1647/9, 22–3; CUL, Palmer B70.

20. CRO, P148/1/1–2; EDR, E9/6/4–7A^v; E9/1/20–7, 29–31; CUL, Palmer A45.
21. See Malcolm Gaskill, 'Witchcraft and power in early modern England: the case of Margaret Moore', in Kermode and Walker (eds), *Women, Crime and the Courts.*
22. CRO, P148/1/1–2; C32, ff. 219–20 (will of Thomas More, 1672). A Margaret Holland was born in Stretham in 1586, but this is too early to be the same woman: CRO, P147/1/1. Moore's children were not registered at Sutton, either because they died before baptism, or because of under-registration during the civil war: CRO, P148/1/2.
23. Stearne, 21–2; CRO, Ely CC will, Thomas Nix, 1637. Evidently Nix was a contentious man – see his dispute with a neighbour in 1628: EDR, E7/6/18.
24. For evidence against Moore, including her confession, see EDR E12 1647/14–14^v.
25. Robert Rowland, '"Fantasticall and devilishe persons": European witch-beliefs in comparative perspective', in Ankarloo and Henningsen (eds), *Early Modern European Witchcraft,* 163–4; Briggs, *Witches and Neighbours,* 104–5; Gaskill, 'Witchcraft and power', 129–30, 135–7.
26. CUL, Add. 33, ff. 22–3^v; Alexander Ross, *Arcana Microcosmi* (1651), 165. On the psychology of bewitchment, see also Edward Bever, 'Witchcraft fears and psychosocial factors in disease', in *Journal of Interdisciplinary History,* 30 (2000).
27. Hill, *World Turned Upside Down,* 154–5, 160, 171–3; Revelation 6:12–17; 8:13. One rumour predicted that Judgement Day would fall on 3 April 1647: *Perfect Occurrences Of Both Houses of Parliament* (26 Mar.–2 Apr. 1647), 104. For examples of men terrified by their apocalyptic dreams, see: BL, Sloane 979, ff. 8–11; HMC, *Portland,* i, 677.
28. EDR, E2/3/7, plea roll 1646; EDR E12 assizes 21 Car. I (29 Sept. 1646); EDR E12 1647/17. Sabie's wives died in 1624 and 1633: CRO, P82/1/1. The people of Haddenham had experienced a major witch-trial thirty years earlier, in 1615: EDR E7/1/33–4.
29. EDR E12 1647/17.
30. VCH, *Cambs,* vol. 4, 140–9; CRO, P82/1/1 (John Read the elder, buried 29 August 1632); EDR, E12 1647/11–11^v. The principal accusers were all landowners and ratepayers; the accused were not: Palmer, *Cambridgeshire Subsidy Rolls,* 66.
31. EDR, E12 1647/11–11^v, 11A; Stearne, 37–8.

32. EDR, E12 1647/10.
33. VCH, *Cambs*, vol. 4, 151–9; BL, Add. 15672; CUL, Palmer B58/1–9; HLRO, Main Papers, 7 Jan. 1647, ff. 68–70; HMC, *6th Report*, 152; *JHL*, viii, 651, 693; Matthews (ed.), *Walker Revised*, 70–80.
34. EDR, E12 1647/7.
35. EDR, E12 1647/20. Joan Webb married Thomas Salter in 1626: CRO, P147/1/1.
36. EDR, E12 1647/7, 20.
37. EDR, E12 1647/15, 18, 23. Robert and Dorothy Ellis had married in 1618, and apparently had been suspected even then: CRO, P147/1/1.
38. EDR E12 1647/17–17^v, 23; Revelation 22:14–15; Catherine E. Parsons, 'Notes on Cambridgeshire witchcraft', in *Proceedings of the Cambridge Antiquarian Society*, 18 (1913–14), 32–3. In 1640 Lady Sandys' husband, Sir John Holland, defended MPs with recusant wives: Bertram Schofield (ed.), *The Knyvett Letters, 1620–1644* (1949), 99n.
39. Joseph Jacobs (ed.), *Epistolae Ho-Elianae: the Familiar Letters of James Howell*, 2 vols (1890–2), i, 506, 513, 514–15, 538, 539, 547–51.
40. Richard Baxter, *The Saints Everlasting Rest* (1650), 244–5.
41. Joseph Hall, *Soliloquies*, 3rd edn (1659), 49–52.
42. Hopkins, *Discovery*, 1–5. Cf. Bernard, *Guide*, 102–117. Hopkins attributed to the Manningtree witches the names 'Grizzel' and 'Greedigut', but according to the records these were first mentioned by a Huntingdonshire witch in 1646: Davenport, *Witches of Huntingdon*, 12–14; Stearne, 13; Gaskill (ed.), *Hopkins Trials*, 477, 486.
43. Hopkins, *Discovery*, 6–8.
44. Ibid., 9–10. Cf. Perkins, *Discourse*, 22–3, 30–1, 43–4.
45. Donald Wing (ed.), *Short-Title Catalogue of Books . . . 1641–1700*, 3 vols (New York, 1945–51), ii, 206; Plomer, *Dictionary of Booksellers*, 158–9; Gaskill (ed.), *Hopkins Trials*, 317–18, 485; Hutchinson, *Historical Essay*, 69.
46. Gaskill (ed.), *Hopkins Trials*, 317; *Bloody Almanack*, A2.
47. EDR, E12 1647/21. Thomas Pye had married in 1620, and his wife died ten years later. They had one son together, born in 1626: CRO, P67/1/1.
48. Morrill, *Revolt in the Provinces*, 169–70; William Dade, *A New Almanack and Prognostication* (1647), B3^v; HMC, *6th Report*, 191; Josten (ed.), *Elias Ashmole*, ii, 457–8; Macfarlane (ed.), *Diary of Ralph Josselin*, 101; *Moderne Intelligencer* (12–19 Aug. 1647), 1; Margaret Stieg (ed.), *The Diary of John Harington MP, 1646–53*, Somerset Record Society, 74 (1977), 57.

49. CUL, Add. 7515/12; Ralph Houlbrooke, 'The puritan death-bed, *c.* 1560–1660', in Durston and Eales (eds), *Culture of English Puritanism*; I Samuel 28:9; Mitchell and Struthers (eds), *Westminster Assembly*, 359, 398–400, quotation at 398. As the son of a godly minister, Hopkins was 'without doubt within the Covenant': Stearne, 61.

50. CUL, Add. 7515/2, 14; Opie and Tatem (eds), *Dictionary of Superstitions*, 97–101; John Brand, *Observations on Popular Antiquities*, 2 vols (1813), ii, 144; Ralph Houlbrooke, *Death, Religion and the Family in England, 1480–1750* (Oxford, 2000), chs 9, 11; Breward (ed.), *Westminster Directory*, 28–9; Matthews (ed.), *Walker Revised*, 170. John Witham was almost certainly the son of the former rector, Thomas Witham, who died in 1644: Venn and Venn (eds), *Alumni Cantabrigienses*, iv, 443.

51. EROC, D/P 343/1/1; *Notes & Queries*, 10 (1854), 285.

52. EDR, E12 1647/19–19A, 44–4^v; EDR, E12 indictments 1646; EDR, E12 1647/23. Ann Smith married Philip Disborough in 1619: CRO, P67/1/1.

53. Bod., Tanner 62, f. 181.

54. Stearne, 17–18; EDR B2/52, f. 138^v; VCH, *Cambs*, vol. 4, 109, 119, 121.

55. EDR, E12, gaol delivery 1641–2, ff. 18–19; E12 indictments 1642–3; E12 1647/8, 13. She married Henry Pigg in 1624: CRO, marriage transcript, Wisbech St Peter.

56. EDR, E12 1647/23.

57. EDR, E2/3/8; EDR E12 1647/12–12^v. On the unusually warm weather in September 1647, see Symonds, 'Diary of John Greene . . . part III', 107.

58. CRO, P68/1/1 (21 June 1640, 20 November 1642). Peter and Agnes's marriage is not recorded, nor are there any other Burbushes in the parish register. In 1647 the parish was supporting a considerable number of poor people: CRO, P68/5/1, f. 22.

59. EDR E12 1647/12, 23.

60. VCH, *Cambs*, vol. 2, 108; vol. 4, 19–20; Pamela Blakeman, *The Book of Ely* (Buckingham, 1990), 39, 47, 69, 87.

61. EDR, E12 1647/23. At the 1642 assizes, there had been nine prisoners (none of them witches), and in 1646 eight (three of them witches): EDR, E12 inquisitions 1644–5 (wrapper of bundle); E12 assizes 1647/5.

62. EDR, E12 1647 (unfol.), information of Jane Hall, Newton.

63. EDR, quarter sessions, gaol calendar, E45 1662 (unfol.). This tendency is visible elsewhere at this time: the trial of three women for witchcraft

at Hertford on 16 August 1647 resulted in one bill being thrown out, one acquittal and one reprieve: Ewen I, 234.

64. CRO, P67/1/1 (Pye buried 1657); P82/1/1 (Briggs buried 1649, Sabie 1648).

65. Stearne, 17, 22.

66. *The Wandering-Jew, Telling Fortunes to English-men* (1640), 64. For an evocative and moving description of an execution at this time, see *A Wonder of Wonders. Being a faithful Narrative and true Relation, of one Anne Green* (1651), 3–4.

Epilogue

1. Stearne, A3–A3ᵛ, 60. On the weather, see H. J. Morehouse (ed.), 'Adam Eyre', in *Yorkshire Diaries and Autobiographies*, Surtees Society, 65 (1875), 73–4, 78, 81.

2. Kittredge, *Witchcraft*, 273, 564; Gaskill (ed.), *Hopkins Trials*, 331–2, 488–95; John Beaumont, *An Historical, Physiological and Theological Treatise of Spirits* (1705), 71.

3. Stearne, A2–A3ᵛ; Revelation 9:20–1.

4. Macfarlane (ed.), *Diary of Ralph Josselin*, 110; WSRO, FL 600/4/1–2.

5. Stearne may have distributed it personally as no bookseller is mentioned. Even the avid collector George Thomason overlooked it: Gaskill (ed.), *Hopkins Trials*, 332.

6. Stearne, A3.

7. They were Mary Coppin, Mary Johnson, Mary Starling, Anne Thurston and Bridget Mayers, see: Macfarlane, *Witchcraft*, 268; Ewen I, 231. There is no trace of Starling, Thurston or Mayers in parish records after 1648: EROC, D/P 154/1/1; D/P 396/1/1.

8. EROC, D/P 347/1/1; D/P 107/1/1.

9. CRO, P68/1/1; P82/1/1 (Sabie was buried 11 February 1648).

10. ESRO, FC 105/D1/1, ff. 2, 62ᵛ; Rivett-Carnac, 'Witchcraft', 223.

11. Macfarlane, *Witchcraft*, 275–6; ERO, Q/SBa 2/74.

12. EDR, Q/S Files, gaol calendar, E45 1662 (unfol.); plea roll, E42 Fragments (unfoliated). In 1636 Bonham had stated that he was 58 years old: E9/6/4. Sandys was back on the commission of the peace by 1653, if not earlier: BL, Add. 5821, f. 204.

13. Josten (ed.), *Elias Ashmole*, ii, 485.

14. Nathaniel Shurtleff (ed.), *Records of the Governor and Company of Massachusetts Bay in New England* (1628–1686), 5 vols (Boston MA, 1853–4), ii, 242; iii, 126; Robert C. Winthrop (ed.), *Life and Letters of John Winthrop*, 2 vols (Boston, 1869), ii, 375–6; Burr (ed.), *Narratives of the Witchcraft Cases*, 363n. A colonial court ordered a suspect to be swum and searched as late as 1706: David F. Condon, 'Witchcraft trials in Virginia in the seventeenth century', in Watkin (ed.), *Legal Record and Historical Reality*, 105.

15. *The Divels Delusions, Or A faithfull relation of John Palmer and Elizabeth Knott* (1649), 2; Ewen II, 316; *The Moderate* (26 Jun.–3 Jul. 1649), 589; Helen Stocks and W. H. Stevenson (eds), *Records of the Borough of Leicester* (Cambridge, 1923), 398.

16. Ralph Gardiner, *Englands Grievance Discovered, In relation to the Coal-Trade* (1655), 107–10; Roger Howell, *Newcastle-upon-Tyne and the Puritan Revolution* (Oxford, 1967), 232–3; Ewen I, 62–3, 69; Whitelock, *Memorials*, iii, 221; PRO, SP 25/64/341.

17. *A Prodigious & Tragicall History of . . . six Witches at Maidstone in Kent* (1652); Ewen I, 239–43; Gaskill (ed.), *Hopkins Trials*, 455–6.

18. Hutchinson, *Historical Essay*, 38; Stearne, 32; *The Tryall and Examination of Mrs. Joan Peterson* (1652); *Grand Politique Post* (21–28 Feb. 1654), 1313.

19. *Lillyes Lamentations* (1652), 4–8; Ashmole, *Lilly's History*, 71–5, 115–16.

20. Hopkins, *Discovery*, 3, 7, 10; Stearne, A2^v–A3.

21. *DNB*, s.v. 'Grimston, Harbottle'; Cokayne (ed.), *Complete Baronetage*, i, 106–7; Ewen I, 238–9, 253, 257; Morant, *Essex*, i, 442.

22. Macfarlane, *Witchcraft*, 143.

23. *DNB*, s.v. 'Fairclough, Samuel', 'Calamy, Edmund', 'Godbold, John'; *JHL*, ix, 170; Cockburn, *History of English Assizes*, 273.

24. *DNB*, s.v. 'Corbett, Miles'; George Starkey, *Royal and Other Innocent Bloud Crying Aloud to Heaven* (1660), 41.

25. Matthews (ed.), *Calamy Revised*, 75; Samuel Petto, *A Faithful Narrative of the Wonderful and Extraordinary Fits . . . by Witchcraft* (1693); Ewen I, 299.

26. John Gaule, *A Sermon of the Saints judging the World* (1649); *Sapienta Justificata* (1657); *The Mag-Astro-Mancer* (1652), 177–8; *Admonition*, 55–6; HRO, HP82/1/1/1/2; *DNB*, s.v. 'Gaule, John'; Burr, *Narratives of the Witchcraft Cases*, 216.

27. *DNB*, s.v. 'Walton, Valentine'. On Wingfield, see http://wingfield.org/charts. Wingfield's co-interrogator, John Guylatte, died in 1652: HRO, HP51/1/1/1.

28. Northants RO, SOX/340/5, ff. 44–7ᵛ.

29. Ewen II, 261n; PRO, E 179/246/20; PRO, E 134/21Chas2/Mich5. A man named John Stern paid hearth tax at the Essex village of Gt Braxted in 1662: ERO, Q/RTh1/526.

30. Stearne, 60.

31. PRO, SP 24/10, ff. 102ᵛ–3; ESRO, B105/2/3, ff. 30ᵛ, 38ᵛ, 39, 45ᵛ, 89; B105/2/4, f. 29. I am very grateful to Peter Elmer for these references.

32. PRO, PROB 11/307; WSRO, FL 600/4/1–2; IC 500/2/65/9; Revelation 22:14.

33. Stearne, 61.

34. [More], *Anthroposophia Theomagica*, 2; Ady, *Candle in the Dark*, A3, 100–2, 106–14, 127–35, 165–6. Cf. Meric Casaubon, *A Treatise Concerning Enthusiasme* (1655).

35. Harsnet, *Declaration*, 18–24; James O. Halliwell (ed.), *The Poetry of Witchcraft Illustrated by Copies of the Plays on the Lancashire Witches* (1853), 11, 25–7.

36. J. A. W. Bennett and H. R. Trevor-Roper (eds), *The Poems of Richard Corbett* (Oxford, 1955), 56–9; BL, Add. 5829, f. 2; Charles W. Daves (ed.), *Samuel Butler 1612–1680: Characters* (Cleveland OH, 1970), 126–8. See also More, *Enthusiasmus Triumphatus*, A3ᵛ; Peter Heylyn, *Aerius Redivivus* (Oxford, 1670), 454.

37. Samuel Butler, *Hudibras*, ed. John Wilders (Oxford, 1967), xxxix, xl, 156; *DNB*, s.v. 'Butler, Samuel'; BL, Add. 32625–6. See also the biographical note added by Butler in 1673: *Hudibras Parts I and II*, ed. Wilders and de Quehen, 161.

38. Edward L. Cutts, 'Curious extracts from a MS. diary of the time of James II and William and Mary', in *Transactions of the Essex Archaeological Society*, I (1858), 126–7.

39. John Douch, *Englands Jubilee* (1660), A3ᵛ.

40. T. B. Howell (ed.), *A Complete Collection of State Trials*, 42 vols (1809–98), iv, 827n–828n; Marjorie Nicholson and Sarah Hutton (eds), *The Conway Letters, 1642–1684* (Oxford, 1992), 293–5; Josten (ed.), *Elias Ashmole*, ii, 457–8; *CSPD 1666–69*, 25; Glanvill, *Sadducismus Triumphatus*, 290–313.

41. PRO, ASSI 45/10/3/34–8, 42, 45–51; Peter Elmer (ed.), *The Later English Trial Pamphlets*, vol. 5 in Sharpe and Golden (eds), *English Witchcraft*, x.

42. Of forty accused witches at the Home Circuit assizes, 1660–1701, only one was found guilty, and she was reprieved: Ewen I, 252–264, esp. 254.

For an example of the tendency, see *An Account of the Tryal and Examination of Joan Buts* (1682), 2.

43. Robert Filmer, *An Advertisement to the Jury-Men of England* (1653); Sharpe, *Instruments of Darkness*, 220–22; Gary K. Waite, *Heresy, Magic and Witchcraft in Early Modern Europe* (Basingstoke, 2003), 216, 224–5.

44. John Webster, *The Displaying of Supposed Witchcraft* (1677), 11. Hooke's notes on the book concentrated on these points of evidence, see BL, Add. 4255, f. 39.

45. *CSPD 1682*, 347; Augustus Jessopp (ed.), *The Lives of the Norths*, 3 vols (1890), i, 166–9; iii, 130–3.

46. Barbara J. Shapiro, 'Religion and the law: evidence, proof and "matter of fact", 1660–1700', in Norma Landau (ed.), *Law, Crime and English Society, 1660–1830* (Cambridge, 2002), 204–6; Coudert, 'Henry More and witchcraft', 132–3; Lisa Jardine and Michael Silverthorne (eds), *Francis Bacon: the New Organon* (Cambridge, 2000); [More], *Anthroposophia Theomagica*, 37; Frederic B. Burnham, 'The More-Vaughan controversy: the revolt against philosophical enthusiasm', in *Journal of the History of Ideas*, 25 (1974). See also Frederick Valetta, *Witchcraft, Magic and Superstition in England, 1640–70* (Aldershot, 2000), 58–60.

47. W. E. H. Lecky, *History of . . . the Spirit of Rationalism*, 2 vols (1865), i, ch. 1; H. H. Gerth and C. Wright Mills (eds), *From Max Weber: Essays in Sociology* (1991), 155.

48. Reginald Scot, *The Discovery of Witchcraft* (editions of 1651 and 1665); More, *Antidote Against Atheisme*, 146.

49. Hutchinson, *Historical Essay*, 63–5, 67; *DNB*, s.v. 'Hutchinson, Francis'.

50. Bod., Walker, c.1, ff. 298–8ᵛ; Rivett-Carnac, 'Witchcraft', 223–4; Ewen, *Witchcraft in the Star Chamber*, 53; Matthews (ed.), *Walker Revised*, 339; ESRO, FC 105/D1/1; Hutchinson, *Historical Essay*, 50, 69.

51. *The Impossibility of Witchcraft* (1712), A3ᵛ; [Daniel Defoe], *The Political History of the Devil* (1726; 1739 edn), 313.

52. Stearne, 61.

53. Hutchinson, *Historical Essay*, 66; Richard Gough, *British Topography*, 2 vols (1780), ii, 254; Francis Grose, *A Provincial Glossary* (1787), 30; James Caulfield, *Portraits, Memoirs, and Characters* (1813), 122–7.

54. [Thomas Gaspey], *The Witch-Finder; Or, The Wisdom of Our Ancestors*, 3 vols (1824), i, 98, 287–90; iii, 46–9; Scott, *Letters on Demonology and Witchcraft*, 206–12. See also *Saturday Magazine* (1835), copy in ERO, I/Mb/230/1/5.

55. Notestein, *History of Witchcraft*, ch. 8; Montague Summers, *The Discovery of Witches: a Study of Master Matthew Hopkins* (1928).

56. Ronald Bassett, *Witch-finder General* (1966), 137. Recent novels in which Hopkins appears include: Rosemary Edghill, *Met by Moonlight* (New York, 1998); Barbara Erskine, *Hiding from the Light* (2002); and Julie Hearn, *The Merrybegot* (Oxford, 2005). Hopkins has also inspired the fictional witchfinders 'Ezekiel Oliphant', 'Newton Pulsifer' and 'Obediah Wilson': Nigel Williams, *Witchcraft* (1987); Terry Pratchett and Neil Gaiman, *Good Omens* (1990); Celia Rees, *Witch Child* (2000).

57. Iain Sinclair, *Lights Out for the Territory* (1997), 301–4; Peter Haining (ed.), *The Witchcraft Papers . . . Essex, 1560–1700* (1974), 11, 139, 177.

58. Richard Deacon, *Matthew Hopkins: Witch Finder General* (1976). Understandably, many authors have been taken in by Deacon's elaborate fantasies; see, for example, David Ryan (ed.), *The Discovery of Witches* (Leigh-on-Sea, 1988).

59. 'Stalking figure terrifies anglers', *East Anglian Daily Times* (16 Mar. 1994); Antony D. Hippisley Coxe, *Haunted Britain* (1973), 102, 104–7; Walton N. Dew, *A Dyshe of Norfolke Dumplings* (1898), 27–30, 31–5; Harry Price, *Poltergeist Over England* (1945), 301–2. In April 2004 Living TV's 'Most Haunted' programme broadcast a three-day ghost-hunt live from Manningtree, Mistley and Lawford.

60. Frederick Ross, 'Hopkins, the witchfinder', in William Andrews (ed.), *Bygone Essex* (Colchester, 1892), 217; Juliet Gardiner and Neil Wenborn (eds), *The Companion to British History* (1995), 389; ERO, T/Z 11/62, p. 37; Oliver Madox Hueffer, *The Book of Witches* (1908), 209; Haining (ed.), *Witchcraft Papers*, 11, 139, 177; Rossell Hope Robbins, *The Encyclopaedia of Witchcraft and Demonology* (1963), 249; Shirley Toulson, *East Anglia: Walking the Ley Lines and Ancient Tracks* (1979), 134. One historian concludes that Hopkins must have been 'half-mad': Diane Purkiss, *The Witch in History: Early Modern and Twentieth-Century Representations* (1996), 240.

61. Keith Irvine, 'Matthew Hopkins', in *East Anglian Magazine*, 7 (1947), 73.

62. Christopher Hibbert, *The English: A Social History, 1066–1945* (1981), 263; Gardiner and Wenborn (eds), *Companion to British History*, 390; Alan Palmer and Veronica Palmer, *Chronology of British History*, 2nd edn (1996), 182. The quotation comes from William Donaldson, *Rogues, Villains, Eccentrics* (2002), 345.

63. Tom Gardiner, *Broomstick over Essex and East Anglia* (Hornchurch, 1981),

43. Recent works include: Jim Sharpe, 'The devil in East Anglia: the Matthew Hopkins trials reconsidered', in Barry *et al.* (eds), *Witchcraft in Early Modern Europe*; Gaskill (ed.), *Hopkins Trials*, xi–xxix; Simon Peters, *The Witchfinder and the Devil's Darlings* (East Bergholt, 2003); Verena Perlhefter, *Die Gestalt des 'Hexenjägers' des 17. Jahrhunderts und sein gesellschaftliches und politisches Umfeld* (Frankfurt, 2003).

64. Sharpe, *Instruments of Darkness*, 129–30. In the mid eighteenth century Dr Zachary Grey estimated that some 4,000 witches had been executed in Britain between 1640 and 1645: John Glyde (ed.), *Folklore and Customs of Suffolk* (Wakefield, 1976), 191.

65. Carlton, *Going to the Wars*, 214.

66. Clark, *Thinking with Demons*, 377, 594; Briggs, *Witches and Neighbours*, 191; A. E. Green (ed.), *Witches and Witch-Hunters* (Wakefield, 1971), xvi; Samuel E. Morrison, *Builders of Bay Colony* (Oxford, 1930), 52–9. Even Sir Walter Scott, no apologist for witchmongers, admitted that Matthew Hopkins lived 'in those unsettled times, when men did what seemed good in their own eyes': *Letters on Demonology and Witchcraft*, 206.

67. Thomas Cocke, 'Foreword', in Cooper (ed.), *Journal of William Dowsing*, xviii.

68. William Gilbert, 'Witchcraft in Essex', in *Transactions of the Essex Archaeological Society*, 11 (1911); Davies, *Four Centuries of Witch-Beliefs*, 190; Isaac Nicholson, *A Sermon Against Witchcraft* (1808); L. F. Newman, 'Some notes on . . . witchcraft in the eastern counties', in *Folklore*, 57 (1946), 31; W. de S. Fowke, 'A case of witchcraft in the sixties', in *Essex Review*, 18 (1909); ERO, T/P 156/11; Miriam Akhtar and Steve Humphries, *Far Out: the Dawning of New Age Britain* (1999), 48–9.

69. Eric Maple, *The Dark World of Witches* (1962), 140.

70. Ronald Hutton, 'The global context of the Scottish witch-hunt', in Julian Goodare (ed.), *The Scottish Witch-Hunt in Context* (Manchester, 2002); R. G. Willis, 'Instant millennium: the sociology of African witch-cleansing cults', in Mary Douglas (ed.), *Witchcraft Confessions and Accusations* (1970); Audrey Richards, 'A modern movement of witch-finders', in Max Marwick (ed.), *Witchcraft and Sorcery* (1970); Isak A. Niehaus, 'Witch-hunting and political legitimacy', in *Africa*, 63 (1993); Susan Drucker-Brown, 'Mamprusi witchcraft, subversion, and changing gender relations', in *Africa*, 63 (1993); Blair Rutherford, 'To find an African witch', in *Critique of Anthropology*, 19 (1999).

71. Paul Harris, 'Hundreds burnt to death in Tanzanian witch-hunt', *Sunday*

Telegraph (22 Aug. 1999), 26; Adam Blomfield, 'Massacre by the jungle witch-hunters', *Daily Telegraph* (28 Jul. 2001), 15. See also: 'African witch hunts', *Fortean Times*, 156 (2002), 12; James Astill, 'Congo casts out its "child witches" ', *Observer* (11 May 2003), 23; 'DA warns against hiring karavinas', media release, *Times of Zambia* (11 Jul. 2004).

72. Richard Petraitis, 'Witch burning and human sacrifice in India', *REALL News*, 8 (2000), 1, 6; 'Indian villagers burn witches', *BBC News Online* (3 Aug. 2000); ' "Project Prahari" aims to end witch hunt', *Assam Tribune* (3 Oct. 2000). For a historical perspective on the problem, see Ajay Skaria, 'Women, witchcraft and gratuitous violence in colonial Western India', in *Past & Present*, 155 (1997).

73. Briggs, *Witches and Neighbours*, 410–11.

Select Bibliography

Most printed sources appear only in the endnotes; works listed here are those with multiple citations throughout the notes. Place of publication is London unless otherwise indicated.

1. Unpublished Manuscripts

Bodleian Library, University of Oxford

Manuscript collections: Ashmole 178, 182, 184, 185, 186, 198, 412, 1447; Bankes 58; Dodsworth 61; Don.c.95; E Musaeo 173; Firth 7; Gough, Camb.69; Rawlinson B.393, B.924; Rawlinson Poet 16; Tanner 59B, 60, 62, 168, 180; Walker, c.1

British Library, London

Additional Manuscripts: 4255, 4275, 5487, 5813, 5821, 5829, 6177, 15672, 15903, 19038, 19398, 25344, 25465, 27402, 28223, 32091, 32496, 32625, 32626, 36076, 36674, 37491, 41605

Other manuscript collections: Egerton 2714, 2884; Harleian 837, 1753; Royal 17, C.XXIII; Sloane 972, 979; Stowe 842

Cambridge University Library

Ely Diocesan Records: B2/5–52, D2/2–32, E1/9, E2/1–2, E2/3/7, E7/1/33–4, E7/6/18, E9/1/20–31, E9/6/4–7Aᵛ, E11 (ii), E42/6, E44/3, E45, K1–17

EDR E12: assize depositions, 1639; gaol delivery, 1641–2; inquisitions, 1644–5; indictments, 1642–3, 1646; depositions (witchcraft etc.), Michaelmas 1647

Palmer Papers, A2, A12, A16, A45, B25, B35, B40, B58, B59, B62, B70

University Archives: Collect.Admin.8, 504–5, Comm.Ct.II.10–13, Comm.Ct.III.20, Lett.II.A (C). 9a–b, T.X.1 (a–b), V.C.Ct.II.8, V.C.Ct.III.2, V.C.Ct.III.12

Miscellaneous manuscripts: Add. 33, 6160, 7515; Buxton Papers, Box 96/3; Mm.1.40

Cambridgeshire Record Office, Cambridge
Parish records: P30/1/1, 4/2, 11/1; P67/1/1; P68/1/1, 5/1; P82/1/1; P109/25/1, 5, 7–8; P109/28/4, 17–19; P129/1/1–2; P147/1/1; P148/1/1–2; Wisbech St Peter, marriages
Wills: VC 17:298 (1583); VC 21:50 (1600); Ely CC, Nix 1637; C32, More 1672
Cambridge City Corporation Archives, Box X/18

Cambridgeshire Record Office, Huntingdon Branch
Parish registers and other records: AH28/84/1, HP12/1/1/1–2, HP51/1/1/1, HP54/1/1/1, HP82/1/1/1/1–2, HP82/5/1, HP82/12/1
Transcripts of Protestation Oath signatories, 1641–2

Dr Williams's Library, London
Minutes of the Westminster Assembly: MS 38.3, Pt. I

East Suffolk Record Office, Ipswich
Quarter sessions books: B105/2/1, 3–4
Ipswich borough court records: C/2/9/1/1/8/7; C/3/3/2/68, 70
Aldeburgh borough accounts: EE 1/12/2
Parish records: FC 63/E1/1; FC 101/E2/26, G7/1–2; FC 105/D1/1
Miscellaneous manuscripts: HD 10/1/9; HD 36/A/163 (1645)
Will of Daniel Wyles, 1619: IC/AA1/55/173
Richard Golty's tithe accounts: JC 1/29/1

Essex Record Office, Chelmsford
Hearth tax, 1662: Q/RTh1/526
Quarter sessions informations: Q/SBa 2/56–8, 59–60, 61, 74
Quarter sessions rolls: Q/SR 323/50; 324/33, 118–19; 326/64; 328/94, 106
Clothiers' petition, 1642: T/A 364/1
Miscellaneous manuscripts: T/P 51/3, 156/11, 195/8; T/Z 11/62

Essex Record Office, Colchester Branch
Colchester borough records: D/B 5/Aa1/14, 5/Ab1/17, 5/Sb1/4, 5/Sb2/8
Parish records: D/P 107/1/1, 154/1/1, 179/8/1, 343/1/1, 347/1/1, 396/1/1
Dedham school register: D/Q 23/15/1

Harwich Borough Archives, Harwich
Borough court records: HB 29/4, 29/10, 65/7, 98/14, 100/1, 133/2

House of Lords Record Office
Main Papers: Nov. 1644, Jan. 1645, May 1645, Oct. 1645, Mar. 1646, Jan. 1647, 1649

John Rylands Library, Manchester
Arthur Hildersham's commonplace book: English Manuscript 524

King's Lynn Borough Archives
Borough accounts and minutes: KL/C7/10, KL/C21/2, KL/C39/102

Norfolk Record Office, Norwich
Quarter sessions rolls: C/S3, boxes 34, 36
Will of James Hopkins, 1635: NCC 1634/233 (Playford)
Norwich City quarter sessions: NCR Case 20/12, 20a/11
Great Yarmouth borough records: Y/C 19/7, 27/2; Y/S 1/2

Northamptonshire Record Office, Northampton
Burton Latimer parish records: 55P/3, 58, 508
Miscellaneous parish registers: 101P/1; 246P/1; 258P/205; 278P/1–2; 325P/1–2
T. C. Pinney, 'Washington Genealogy': SOX/340/5

Public Record Office, Kew (now 'The National Archives')
Home Circuit assizes: ASSI 35/86/1/1–2, 4–5, 7–13, 19, 41–6, 52–73, 78–91, 97–9
Northern Circuit assizes: ASSI 45/1/5/38–9; 45/10/3/34–8, 42, 45–51
Chancery books: C 181/5; C 231/6, 13, 14
Writs of outlawry: E 172/22–3, 173/1
Court of King's Bench: KB 9/747/2; 9/838; 27/1448/1, 1451/1; 27/1464/1; 29/296
Will of John Costine, 1662: PROB 11/307
State Papers, James I: SP 14/37/89, 128/149–54, 161/89
State Papers, Charles I: SP 16/268/22, 271/15, 357/107, 357/158, 520/33
Misc. State Papers: SP 19/21, 24/10, 25/64/341
County Committee orders: SP 28/219, 222, 227, 234, 238, 243
State Papers (Docquets): SP 38/7 (Apr. 1604), 38/8 (May 1605), 38/10 (July 1611)
Court of Star Chamber: STAC 8/32/13, 95/4, 140/23, 200/27, 276/25

Thomas Plume's Library, Maldon
Plume's commonplace book, *c.* 1648–9: Plume MS. no. 30

West Suffolk Record Office, Bury St Edmunds
Sudbury borough sessions of the peace: EE 501/2/7
Parish registers (Rattlesden and Lawshall): FL 500/4/1; FL 600/4/1–2
Will of Dorothy Causton, 1670: IC 500/2/65/9

2. Printed Primary Sources

Ady, Thomas, *A Candle in the Dark* (1655)
The Anti-Projector: or The History of the Fen Project (1646)
Ashmole, Elias, *Mr. William Lilly's History of His Life and Times* (1715)
B., R. [Nathaniel Crouch], *The Kingdom of Darkness* (1688)
Baxter, Richard, *The Certainty of the World of Spirits* (1691)
Bernard, Richard, *A Guide to Grand-Jury Men* (1627; 1629 edn)
A Bloody Almanack Foretelling many certaine predictions (1647)
Clark, Samuel, *The Lives of Sundry Eminent Persons in this Later Age* (1683)
Davenport, John, *The Witches of Huntingdon* (1646)
[Drage, William], *Daimonomageia. A Small Treatise of Sicknesses and Diseases From Witchcraft, and Supernatural Causes* (1665)
The Examination and confession of certaine Wytches at Chensforde (1566)
F., H., *A true and exact Relation Of the severall Informations, Examinations, and Confessions of the late Witches arraigned and executed in the County of Essex* (1645)
The Full Tryals, Examination, and Condemnation Of Four Notorious Witches (?1698)
Gaule, John, *Select Cases of Conscience Touching Witches and Witchcrafts* (1646)
—— *An Admonition Moving to Moderation* (1660)
Glanvill, Joseph, *Saducismus Triumphatus* (1681)
Hale, Matthew, *A Collection of Modern Relations of matter of Fact Concerning Witches* (London, 1693)
Harsnet, Samuel, *A Declaration of egregious Popish Impostures* (1603; 1605 edn)
Hopkins, Matthew, *The Discovery of Witches* (1647)
Hutchinson, Francis, *An Historical Essay Concerning Witchcraft* (1718)
James VI and I, *Daemonologie* (Edinburgh, 1597; English edn, 1603)
The Lawes against Witches and Conjuration and Some brief Notes and Observations for the Discovery of Witches (1645)
Mackerell, Benjamin, *History and Antiquities of King's Lynn* (1738)
A Magazine of Scandall. Or, A heape of wickednesse of two infamous Ministers (1642)

Morant, Philip, *The History and Antiquities of . . . Essex*, 2 vols (1768)

More, Henry, *Observations upon Anthroposophia Theomagica* (1650)

—— *An Antidote Against Atheisme* (1653)

—— *Enthusiasmus Triumphatus* (1656)

The Parliaments Unspotted-Bitch: In Answer to Prince Roberts Dog called Boy (1643)

Perkins, William, *A Discourse of the Damned Art of Witchcraft* (Cambridge, 1608)

Signes and wonders from Heaven. With a True Relation of a Monster (1645)

Stearne, John, *A Confirmation And Discovery of Witch-Craft* (1648)

A True Relation of the Araignment of eighteene Witches That were tried, convicted, and condemned at a Sessions holden at St. Edmunds-bury in Suffolke (1645)

Walker, Clement, *The History of Independency* (1660)

Witches Apprehended, Examined and Executed, for notable villanies (1613)

3. Contemporary Newspapers

A Diary, or an Exact Journall   *The Moderate Intelligencer*

Diutinus Britanicus   *The Moderne Intelligencer*

The Grand Politique Post   *The Parliaments Post*

Mercurius Aulicus   *A Perfect Diurnall of Some Passages in Parliament*

Mercurius Britanicus   *Perfect Occurrences Of Both Houses of Parliament*

Mercurius Civicus   *The Scotish Dove*

Mercurius Politicus   *The True Informer*

The Moderate   *The Weekly Account*

4. Modern Editions of Primary Sources

Banks, Charles E. (ed.), *Able Men of Suffolk, 1638* (Boston MA, 1931)

Breward, Ian (ed.), *The Westminster Directory* (Bramcote, 1980)

Butler, Samuel, *Hudibras Parts I and II, and Selected Other Writings*, ed. John Wilders and Hugh de Quehen (Oxford, 1973)

Cooper, Trevor (ed.), *The Journal of William Dowsing: Iconoclasm in East Anglia during the English Civil War* (Woodbridge, 2001)

Ewen, C. L'Estrange, *Witch Hunting and Witch Trials: the Indictments for Witchcraft from the Records of 1373 Assizes Held for the Home Court AD 1559–1736* (1929)

Firth, C. H., and Rait, R. S. (eds), *Acts and Ordinances of the Interregnum, 1642–1660*, 3 vols (1911)

Harrod, Henry, 'Notes on the records of the corporation of Great Yarmouth', in *Norfolk Archaeology*, 4 (1855)

James, D. E. Howell (ed.), *Norfolk Quarter Sessions Order Book, 1650–1657* (Norfolk Record Society, 1955)

Josten, C. H. (ed.), *Elias Ashmole (1617–1692)*, 5 vols (Oxford, 1966)

Lemon, R. *et al.* (eds), *Calendar of State Papers, Domestic*, 92 vols (1856–1924)

Macfarlane, Alan (ed.), *The Diary of Ralph Josselin, 1616–1683* (Oxford, 1976)

Mitchell, Alex F., and Struthers, John (eds), *Minutes of the Sessions of the Westminster Assembly* (Edinburgh, 1874)

Nickalls, John L. (ed.), *The Journal of George Fox* (Cambridge, 1952)

Palmer, W. M., *Cambridgeshire Subsidy Rolls, 1250–1695* (Norwich, 1912)

Redstone, Vincent B. (ed.), *The Ship-Money Returns for . . . Suffolk* (Ipswich, 1904)

Rollins, Hyder E. (ed.), *Cavalier and Puritan: Ballads and Broadsides . . . 1640–1660* (New York, 1923)

Symonds, E. M., 'The diary of John Greene (1635–57): part II', in *English Historical Review*, 43 (1928)

—— 'The diary of John Greene (1635–57): part III', in *English Historical Review*, 44 (1929)

Whitelocke, Bulstrode, *Memorials of the English Affairs*, 4 vols (Oxford, 1853)

5. Secondary Sources

Ankarloo, Bengt, and Henningsen, Gustav (eds), *Early Modern European Witchcraft: Centres and Peripheries* (Oxford, 1990)

Baker, J. H., *An Introduction to English Legal History*, 4th edn (2002)

Barry, Jonathan, Hester, Marianne, and Roberts, Gareth (eds), *Witchcraft in Early Modern Europe: Studies in Culture and Belief* (Cambridge, 1996)

Bowden, Peter J. (ed.), *Economic Change: Wages, Profits and Rents, 1500–1750* (Cambridge, 1990)

Briggs, Robin, *Witches and Neighbours: the Social and Cultural Context of European Witchcraft* (1996)

Bullen, R. Freeman, 'Catalogue of beneficed clergy of Suffolk, 1551–1631', in *Proceedings of the Suffolk Institute of Archaeology*, 22 (1936)

Burr, George L. (ed.), *Narratives of the Witchcraft Cases, 1648–1706* (New York, 1946)

Carew Hazlitt, W., *Popular Antiquities of Great Britain*, 3 vols (1870)

Carlton, Charles, *Going to the Wars: the Experience of the British Civil Wars, 1638–1651* (1992)

Clark, Stuart, *Thinking with Demons: the Idea of Witchcraft in Early Modern Europe* (Oxford, 1997)

Cliffe, J. T., *The Puritan Gentry* (1984)

—— *Puritans in Conflict* (1988)

Cockburn, J. S., *A History of English Assizes, 1558–1714* (Cambridge, 1972)

Cokayne, G. E. (ed.), *Complete Baronetage*, 5 vols (Exeter, 1900–6)

Cooper, Charles Henry, *Annals of Cambridge*, 4 vols (Cambridge, 1842–52)

Coudert, Allison, 'Henry More and witchcraft', in Sarah Hutton (ed.), *Henry More (1614–1687): Tercentenary Studies* (Dordrecht, 1990)

Darby, H. C., *The Changing Fenland* (Cambridge, 1983)

Davies, R. Trevor, *Four Centuries of Witch-Beliefs: with Special Reference to the Great Rebellion* (1947)

Doubleday, H. A., *et al.* (eds), *The Victoria History of the Counties of England* (1900–)

Durston, Christopher, and Eales, Jacqueline (eds), *The Culture of English Puritanism, 1560–1700* (Basingstoke, 1996)

Elmer, Peter, 'Saints or sorcerers: Quakerism, demonology and the decline of witchcraft in seventeenth-century England', in Barry *et al.* (eds), *Witchcraft in Early Modern Europe*

—— 'Towards a politics of witchcraft in early modern England', in Stuart Clark (ed.), *Languages of Witchcraft: Narrative, Ideology and Meaning in Early Modern Culture* (Basingstoke, 2001)

Everitt, Alan (ed.), *Suffolk and the Great Rebellion, 1640–1660* (Woodbridge, 1960)

Ewen, C. L'Estrange, *Witchcraft and Demonianism: a Concise Account Derived from Sworn Depositions and Confessions Obtained in the Courts of England and Wales* (1933)

—— *The Trials of John Lowes, Clerk* (n.p., 1937)

—— *Witchcraft in the Star Chamber* (n.p., 1938)

Gaskill, Malcolm, *Crime and Mentalities in Early Modern England* (Cambridge, 2000)

—— (ed.), *The Matthew Hopkins Trials*, vol. 3 in Sharpe and Golden (eds), *English Witchcraft*

Hill, Christopher, *The World Turned Upside Down* (1975)

Holmes, Clive (ed.), *The Suffolk Committees for Scandalous Ministers, 1644–1646* (Woodbridge, 1970)

—— *The Eastern Association in the English Civil War* (Cambridge, 1974)

Kermode, Jenny, and Walker, Garthine (eds), *Women, Crime and the Courts in Early Modern England* (1994)

Kingston, Alfred, *East Anglia and the Great Civil War* (1897)

Kittredge, George Lyman, *Witchcraft in Old and New England* (New York, 1929)

Lindley, Keith, *Fenland Riots and the English Revolution* (1982)

Macfarlane, Alan, *Witchcraft in Tudor and Stuart England: a Regional and Comparative Study*, 2nd edn, with an introduction by James Sharpe (1999)

Manning, Brian, *The English People and the English Revolution* (1976)

Matossian, Mary Kilbourne, *Poisons of the Past* (New Haven, 1989)

Matthews, A. G. (ed.), *Walker Revised* (Oxford, 1988)

—— (ed.), *Calamy Revised* (Oxford, 1988)

Morrill, John, *Revolt in the Provinces: the People of England and the Tragedies of War, 1630–1648* (1999)

Morton, A. L., 'Laurence Clarkson', in *Proceedings of the Suffolk Institute of Archaeology*, 26 (1955)

Notestein, Wallace, *A History of Witchcraft in England from 1558 to 1718* (Washington DC, 1911)

Opie, Iona, and Tatem, Moira (eds), *A Dictionary of Superstitions* (Oxford, 1989)

Patten, John, 'Population distribution in Norfolk and Suffolk during the sixteenth and seventeenth centuries', in *Transactions of the Institute of British Geographers*, 65 (1975)

Phelps Brown, E. H., and Hopkins, Sheila V., 'Seven centuries of building wages', in E. M. Carus-Wilson (ed.), *Essays in Economic History: Vol. 2* (1962)

Philip, Neil (ed.), *Penguin Book of English Folktales* (1992)

Plomer, Henry R., *A Dictionary of Booksellers and Printers . . . 1641–1667* (1907)

Porter, Enid, *Cambridgeshire Customs and Folklore* (1969)

Rivett-Carnac, J. H. 'Witchcraft: the Rev. John Lowes', in *Notes & Queries* (21 Mar. 1896)

Scott, Walter, *Letters on Demonology and Witchcraft*, ed. R. L. Brown (Wakefield, 1968)

Sharpe, James, *Instruments of Darkness: Witchcraft in England, 1550–1750* (1996)

—— and Golden, Richard (eds), *English Witchcraft, 1560–1736*, 6 vols (2003)

Suckling, Alfred, *The History and Antiquities of the County of Suffolk*, 2 vols (1846–8)

Thomas, Keith, 'Women and the Civil War sects', in *Past & Present*, 13 (1958)

———— *Religion and the Decline of Magic* (1971)

Underdown, David, *Revel, Riot and Rebellion: Popular Politics and Culture in England, 1603–1660* (Oxford, 1985)

Unsworth, C. R., 'Witchcraft beliefs and criminal procedure in early modern England', in Watkin (ed.), *Legal Record and Historical Reality*

Venn, John, and Venn, J. A., (eds), *The Book of Matriculations and Degrees . . . in the University of Cambridge, 1544–1659* (Cambridge, 1913)

———— (eds), *Alumni Cantabrigienses: Part I*, 4 vols (Cambridge, 1922–7)

Walter, John, *Understanding Popular Violence in the English Revolution: the Colchester Plunderers* (Cambridge, 1999)

Watkin (ed.), Thomas G., *Legal Record and Historical Reality: Proceedings of the Eighth British Legal History Conference, Cardiff, 1987* (1989)

Webster, Tom, *Godly Clergy in Early Stuart England: the Caroline Puritan Movement, c. 1620–1643* (Cambridge, 1997)

Wickes, Michael, *A History of Huntingdonshire* (Chichester, 1995)

Picture Acknowledgements

The author and publisher would like to thank the following for permission to reproduce the various copyright illustrations (place of publication is London unless otherwise stated) on the following pages:

Bodleian Library, University of Oxford: 4 (*The Miracle of Miracles*, 1613, 4° C16 Art Bs [4]), 148 (*A Most Certain, Strange, and true Discovery of a Witch*, 1643, Douce WW 98).

British Library, London: 14 (Edward Fairfax, *Daemonologia*, Add. MSS 32496), 19 (*A Prophecie of the Life, Reigne, and death of William Laud*, 1644, E.18 [8]), 35 and 79 (John Vicars, *A Sight of ye Transactions of these Latter Years*, 1646, E.365 [6]), 43 (*Newes from Avernus*, 1642, E.148 [9]), 146 (*Signes and wonders from Heaven*, London, 1645, E.295 [2]), 149 (*A Dog's Elegy, Or Rupert's Tears*, 1644, E.3 [17]), 165 (*A True Relation of the Araignment of eighteene Witches*, 1645, E.301 [3]), 176 (Thomas Kyd, *The trueth of the most wicked and secret murthering of John Brewen*, 1592, 2326.c.4), 196 (*A Rehearsall both straung and true, of . . . Fower notorious Witches*, 1579, C.27.a.11), 227 (John Gaule, *Select Cases of Conscience Touching Witches and Witchcrafts*, 1646, E.1192), 259 (Matthew Hopkins, *The Discovery of Witches*, 1647, E.388 [2]), 271 (John Stearne, *A Confirmation and Discovery of Witch-Craft*, 1648, C.54.e.6).

Syndics of Cambridge University Library: 45, 53, 127, 277 (R. B. [Nathaniel Crouch], *The Kingdom of Darkness*, 1688, Syn.8.68.68), 64 (J. W. Ebsworth, ed., *The Bagford Ballads*, 2 vols, Hertford, 1878, ii, 721.c.96.145), 92 (*The Witch of the Woodlands*, n.d., in John Ashton, *Chap-Books of the Eighteenth Century*, 1882, XIX.58.167), 120 (William Richardson, *Catalogue . . . of English Portraits*, 1816, Eb.22.39), 151 (Edmund Calamy, *The Nonconformist's Memorial*, 2nd edn, 3 vols, 1777, i, 9.27.15), 153 (Samuel Clarke, *Lives of Sundry Eminent Persons*, 1683, Oo.2.47), 184 (Ralph Gardiner, *Englands Grievance Discovered, In relation to the Coal-Trade*, 1655, Syn.7.65.77), 207 (George Fyler Townsend, *The Town and Borough of Leominster*, Leominster, 1863, Ll.52.7).

Keeper of Ely Diocesan Records, Cambridge University Library: 250 (Moore's confession, EDR E12 assizes, f. 14ᵛ), 262 (Stearne's deposition, EDR E12 assizes, f. 21).

Essex Record Office, Chelmsford: xiv (engraving published by Alexander Hogg, c. 1790, I/Pb 8/30/2); 284 (engraving by James Caulfield, in *The Wonderful Magazine*, c. 1803–8, I/Pb 8/30/4).

Ipswich Borough Council Museums and Galleries: 25 (portrait of William Dowsing, c. mid 17th century, oils, unsigned; currently on display at Christchurch Mansion).

Pepys Library, Magdalene College, Cambridge: 51 (frontispiece illustration to Matthew Hopkins, *The Discovery of Witches*, 1647, PL 2973/447a).

Suffolk Record Office, Ipswich: 23 (quitclaim, 1641, HD 10/1/9).

Wayland Picture Library: 29 (from *The Apprehension and confession of three notorious Witches*, 1589), 30 (from *Newes from Scotland*, 1591, which re-used a woodcut from *A brief treatise conteyning the most strange and horrible crueltye of Elizabeth Stile*, 1579), 106 (from *Witches Apprehended, Examined and Executed*, 1613), 215 (from *The World turn'd upside down*, 1647), 241 (from *The Parliament of Women*, 1646).

Index

Numerals in italics denote illustrations